SQUADRON HISTORIES

PETER LEWIS

Squadron Histories

R.F.C., R.N.A.S. AND R.A.F.
since 1912

WITH COLOUR PLATES
BY THE AUTHOR

PUTNAM & COMPANY
LONDON

To
ANN, DIANA
and
YVONNE

First published 1959
Second edition 1968

© *Peter Lewis 1959*
New edition © *Peter Lewis 1968*

S B N 370 00022 6

Printed and Bound in Great Britain for
Putnam and Company Limited
9 Bow Street, London, WC 2
by C. Tinling & Company Ltd, Prescot

Preface

The remarkably short space of forty-six years has seen British air power grow from a mere handful of flimsy flying machines, with little or no offensive qualities, to a force of a greater striking and deterrent strength than the Nation has ever possessed.

From the earliest days of the Royal Flying Corps and its companion-in-arms, the Royal Naval Air Service, and throughout the life of the present Royal Air Force, this new-found power has been expressed through the operational squadrons of aircraft and men, supported by a miscellany of training and other units. During the two great conflicts of the last half-century, the Royal Air Force has been built up to a massive peak strength, but allowed at other times to fall to a low level.

Over the years, a total of some 541 squadrons have been formed for varied purposes, including fighting, bombing, general purpose, reconnaissance, transport, special duties and many others. Often these units have long and exciting stories, each one worthy of a whole book to itself. With such a large number, it would have been impossible to include them all at length in one volume of reasonable size. The histories contained in this book are, therefore, necessarily of brief form. For the first time, however, the details given of all of the squadrons have been brought together for reference in a single book. In some cases, very little has survived to be recorded of the activities of a particular unit, owing either to its decimation at the hands of the enemy and the consequent loss of the Operational Records Books or the fact that the heat of battle and attendant mobility precluded such recording.

The information has been assembled over a period of some years, and I should like to record my great indebtedness to the Air Historical Branch of the Air Ministry and to its late Head, Mr. J. C. Nerney, I.S.O., for his interest and advice and his kindness in granting the necessary facilities for inspecting the squadron records up to 1946. My thanks are also due to members of his staff, Mr. M. B. Thornton and Mr. A. Hibbert, for their patience and assistance.

Others whom I should like to thank for helping are Mr. John H. Blake, Librarian of the Royal Aero Club; Mr. Leonard Bridgman; F/L R. A. Brown; Mr. J. M. Bruce; Mr. C. C. H. Cole of the Air Ministry Information Division; G/C C. P. Gabriel, O.B.E.; Mr. J. L. Golding of the Imperial War Museum Photographic Section; S/L T. N. Hayes, D.F.C.; Mr. John Tanner, Librarian of Cranwell College; Miss Constance Babington Smith; Mr. F. H. Smith, Librarian of the Royal

Aeronautical Society; Mr. Owen G. Thetford; the Royal Australian Air Force; the French and Greek Air Attachés in London.

In accordance with Security requirements, disbanding dates for R.A.F. and Commonwealth squadrons have been omitted, and the information included since 1946 is that made available in the Public Press and in Official Releases.

Benfleet, Essex.   P.M.H.L.
January, 1959.

PREFACE TO SECOND EDITION

The period of nine years since publication of the first edition of *Squadron Histories* has witnessed numerous changes in the equipment and status of many Royal Air Force squadrons. Various aircraft—popular with their crews and well-known to the public—have passed from the scene, their places being taken by new operational types of enhanced performance, culminating in the present late marks of Lightning, Victor and Vulcan accompanied by—among others—the Argosy, Andover, Belfast and VC-10, now well established in service. Where applicable, and in compliance with the claims of Security, the section covering the squadrons and the appendices have been revised to embody details released publicly.

Grateful acknowledgement is made of the kindness and interest shown by F/L R. A. Brown; F/L R. I. Campbell; Mr. R. E. Hall; Mr. A. Hepburn and W/C W. F. Knapper of Cranwell College in contributing useful additional material to this new edition.

Benfleet, Essex.   P.M.H.L.
April, 1968.

Contents

Squadron Histories

*In many cases the month and year shown against an aircraft
indicate the date of re-equipment with the type. Where this
cannot be established definitely, the year quoted is the earliest
during which the squadron is understood to have flown the
machine named, followed by the successive marks received later.*

No. 1 'Cawnpore' Squadron

Formed 1 April, 1911, as No. 1 (Airship) Company of the Air Battalion
at S. Farnborough with airships *Beta* and *Gamma*. C.O. Capt. E. M.
Maitland. Renamed No. 1 Airship and Kite Squadron on 19 May, 1912.
In Nov. 1912, received airships *Delta* and *Zeta*, and in Feb. 1913, the *Eta*.
At Farnborough until late 1913. Equipment transferred to Navy, 1 Jan.
1914. Renamed No. 1 Squadron, R.F.C., May, 1914, at Brooklands with
C.O. Maj. C. A. H. Longcroft. At Netheravon Aug. 1914, and reformed
as aeroplane unit with S7 Longhorn, S11 Shorthorn, Avro 504 (8),
B.E.8 (4) Blériot XI, Martinsyde Scout A. To St. Omer 7 March, 1915.
C.O. Maj. W. G. H. Salmond. Avro 504, Bristol Scout D, Caudron G3
and G4. Artillery observation at Bailleul 1916, with Morane Bullet and
Parasols (8 in Jan. 1916), Nieuport 2-seater (4) and Morane Biplane (6).
On general reconnaissance and contact patrols until Jan. 1917, when
became single-seater scout squadron with Nieuport 17C-1 (18), 23 and
27. Re-equipped Jan. 1918, with S.E.5 and S.E.5a. C.O. Maj. Phillip
B. Joubert de la Ferté. At Senlis, Oct. 1918, as fighter unit. Disbanded
20 Jan. 1920. Reformed 21 Jan. 1920, at Risalpur, India, with Snipes
and based at Bangalore and Hinaidi. Experimental trials with Night-
hawks. Disbanded Nov. 1926. under S/L J. B. Graham. Reformed
Feb. 1927, at Tangmere by S/L C. N. Lowe with Siskin 3a and Dual
Siskin. C.O. S/L E. O. Grenfell. Experimental trials with one Bulldog
in 1931. Received Fury 1 in 1932. C.O. S/L C. B. S. Spackman. 1938,
Gladiator. April, 1939, Hurricane F.1. (NA-). Sept. 1939, with A.A.S.F.
at Vassincourt and Berry-au-Bac. C.O. S/L Halahan. Aircraft coded
JX-. June, 1940, at Tangmere. Aug. 1940, at Northolt. Hurricane
F.2b, F.2c and F.10 (LK-, JX-) in 1941. Night-fighting from Wittering,
Kenley and Tangmere. C.O. S/L MacLachlan. Typhoon F.1b (JX-) in
1942 at Acklington and Lympne. Spitfire F.9 (JX-) at North Weald in
1943 and at Detling, Lympne and Manston in 1944. To France in 1944
with Spitfire F.9c and F.9e (JX-, LK-). Spitfire F.21 (JX-) in March,
1945, in Ayr and Cornwall, then to Tangmere in 1946, supplemented by
Harvard T.2b (JX-) for training. Operated as 11 Group's Instrument

Training Squadron using Oxford T.2 (JX–). Re-equipped with Meteor F.3 (JX–) in 1946. 1948, Meteor F.4 and T.7 (JX–). Sept., 1950, Meteor F.8 (JX–). C.O. S/L Ellacombe. 1953, C.O. S/L R. B. Morrison. 1955, Hunter F.4, F.5. Disbanded 23 June, 1958. Reformed 1958, from No. 263 Squadron at Stradishall with Hunter F.6. 1960, Hunter F.G.A.9.

No. 1 (Communication) Squadron

Formed Dec. 1918, as part of 86th Wing at Hendon with detachment at Paris. Used for transport of Government personnel to Peace Conference in Paris. Operated with D.H.4 and O/400. Service started in Jan. 1919. After March, 1919, the unit moved to Kenley. Disbanded in Sept. 1919.

No. 2 Squadron

Formed late May, 1912, at Farnborough. Feb. 1913, to Montrose with Cody Biplane, Bréguet Biplane, B.E.1. C.O. Maj. C. J. Burke. First aeroplane unit and the oldest one in the Service. B.E.2 in Feb. 1913. To Amiens on 13 Aug. 1914, B.E.2a No. 347, Lt. H. D. Harvey-Kelly, first R.F.C. aircraft in France. Used R.E.1, R.E.5, S7 Longhorn, S11 Shorthorn, B.E.2a, B.E.2b. In Aug. 1915, had B.E.2c, B.E.2d for corps reconnaissance. 1916, F.B.9, Bristol Scout D (1). June, 1917, B.E.2e, A.W.F.K.8. At Hesdigneul from June, 1915–April, 1917. Oct. 1918, Floringham. V.C.s won by Lt. A. A. McLeod and Lt. W. B. Rhodes-Moorhouse. Disbanded 20 Jan. 1920, at Weston-on-the-Green. Reformed in Ireland in Feb. 1920, with Bristol F2b. Based in 1922 at Digby and in Ireland. At Farnborough in 1923 on army co-operation. 1924, Andover and Manston. 1925, Hawkinge. April, 1927, to Shanghai on H.M.S. Hermes. Returned to England, Oct. 1928. At Manston in 1928. Received Atlas 1 in 1928 and Audax in 1933. C.O. S/L J. H. Green. 1938, Hector. 1938–39 at Hawkinge. Lysander 1, 2, 3 (KO–, XV–). To France in 1939. In 1940 at Hatfield, Sawbridge-worth, Cambridge. On army co-operation with Defiant (KO–). 1941, Tomahawk F.1, F.2a (XV–, KO–). 1942, Mustang F.1, F.2 (XV–) on photo-reconnaissance. Based Gravesend, Odiham, North Weald, Saw-bridgeworth, Gatwick. To France, July, 1944, with Spitfire F.R.14, P.R.11, P.R.19 (OI–) at Boisney, Fort Rouge, St. Denis Westrem. May, 1945, Celle, England, Germany. Aug. 1945, High-Level Photo-Recon-naissance Flight of Mosquito P.R.6 and P.R.16 added from No. 4 Squadron. 1951, Meteor F.8. In 1953, at Wahn in 2nd T.A.F., B.A.O.R., with Meteor F.R.9. C.O. S/L R. H. D. Weighill. 1956, Swift F.R.5 at Geilenkirchen. C.O. S/L R. S. Mortley. 1961, at Jever with Hunter F.R.10.

No. 2 (Communication) Squadron

Formed March, 1919, as part of 86th Wing for transport of Government personnel attending Peace Conference at Paris. Stationed at Buc and used D.H.4 and O/400. Disbanded in Sept. 1919.

No. 3 Squadron

Formed 1 April, 1911, as No. 2 (Aeroplane) Company of the Air Battalion at Larkhill. C.O. Capt. J. D. B. Fulton. 19 May, 1912, renamed No. 3 Squadron, R.F.C. C.O. Maj. H. R. M. Brooke-Popham. June, 1913, to Netheravon. Avro 504, Blériot XI (2), B.E.2a ('A' Flt.), H. Farman F20 ('B' Flt.), S7 Longhorn ('C' Flt.), Nieuport Monoplane (1), Deperdussin Monoplane (1), Bristol Monoplane (1), Bristol Boxkite (1), B.E.3, B.E.4, Avro 500. 1914, B.E.2c, B.E.8, Tabloid, S11 Shorthorn. Aug. 1914, C.O. Maj. J. M. Salmond. To Amiens, 13 Aug. 1914. Oct. 1914, received sole S.E.2a from No.5 Squadron, using it until March, 1915. 1915, scouting with Avro 504k, Bristol Bullet D. 1916, Morane Parasol and Bullet, also Morane Biplane. Role changed Oct. 1917, to fighter with Camel F.1. Oct. 1918, at Valheureux. Disbanded 27 Oct. 1919. Reformed Feb. 1920, at Ambala, India, with Snipes. Disbanded 1 Oct. 1921. Reformed 1 Oct. 1921, at Leuchars, Scotland, with West-land Walrus. At Gosport in 1922 with Avro Bison. Disbanded 1 April, 1923. Reformed 1 April, 1924, with Snipes. 1925, Woodcock for night-fighting (No. 17 Squadron only other Woodcock unit). C.O. S/L J. M. Robb. 1927, Gamecock 1. 1928, at Upavon. May, 1929, first to receive Bulldog 2 and 2a. 1934, at Kenley. 1935, C.O. S/L G. Martin. 1937, proving squadron for Gladiator 1 and 2 (OP-). 1938, Hurricane F.1 (OP-, QO-). Aug. 1940, at Wick. 1941, Hurricane F.2a, F.2b, F.2c (QO-). 1943, Typhoon F.1b (QO-). 1944, Tempest F.5, F.6 (QO-, J5-, JF-) at Volkel. 32 victories gained by Pierre Clostermann whose Tempest was named 'le Grand Charles'. Squadron destroyed 288 V.1 flying bombs. 1952, Vampire F.1, F.B.5 (J5-) in 2nd T.A.F., Germany. C.O. S/L W. J. S. Sutherland. May, 1953, first unit to operate Canadair-built Sabre F.4, also last to use it. 1954, at Geilenkirchen. C.O. S/L R. C. H. Simmons. 1956, Hunter F.4. C.O. S/L T. H. Hutchinson. Disbanded Sept. 1957. Reformed 1959, at Geilenkirchen with Javelin F.A.W.7 from No. 256 Squadron. 1960, Javelin F.A.W.4. Reformed 4 Jan. 1961, at Geilenkirchen with Canberra B.(I)8 from No. 59 Squadron.

No. 4 Squadron

Formed Sept. 1912, at Farnborough from part of No. 2 Squadron with Bréguet Biplane (5), Cody Biplane (1), B.E.2a, Avro 504. Moved to Netheravon using B.E.2, B.E.2b, S7 Longhorn, S11 Shorthorn, Martin-syde Scout A. First squadron to use air-to-ground radio. C.O. Maj. G. H. Raleigh. 'A' and 'B' Flts. to Amiens on 13 Aug. 1914, 'C' Flt. on 20 Sept. 1914. S11 Shorthorns of 'C' Flt. fitted with Lewis and Vickers guns. Sept. 1915, B.E.2c, B.E.2d, B.E.2e, F.B.5, on corps reconnaissance. Also used Bristol Bullet D, Tabloid, Caudron G3 and G4, Morane Bullet and Parasol, Voisin Biplane. May, 1917, R.E.8 on artillery observation. 1918, Bristol F3a at St. Marie Capel. Aug. 1919, at Northolt and Uxbridge. 1920, 'A' and 'B' Flts. at Farnborough, 'C' Flt. at Stonehenge, flying Bristol F2b. 'A' Flt. served with 11th Irish Wing, then complete squadron to Kilia Bay, Dardanelles, in Aug. 1922, returning to England in 1923. Until 1929, experimented with prototypes Vespa, Hyena, Bloodhound and Atlas. C.O. 1925–28, S/L J. Slessor at Farnborough. Oct. 1929, gave up its F2bs for Atlas. In Feb. 1932, was first squadron to use Audax for army co-operation. Feb. 1937, received first Hectors in service. Based at Odiham. 1938, Lysander 1, 2, 3 (TV-). 1940, in France and Belgium, using Tiger Moth, Magister, Moth Minor, Proctor, Dominie. June, 1942, Mustang F.1 (TV-) for reconnaissance, Master 3 and Battle 1. 1944 on photo-reconnaissance and fighter-reconnaissance with Spitfire P.R.11, P.R.13 and P.R.19. In same year used Mosquito P.R.16 and F.B.6, Typhoon F.1b. Stationed in France and Germany. Disbanded Aug. 1945, becoming High-Level Photo-Reconnaissance Flight of No. 2 Squadron. Reformed 31 Aug. 1945, from No. 605 Squadron with Mosquito F.B.6, P.R.16 (UP-). 1953 at Jever, Germany, with Vampire F.B.5 (UP-). C.O. S/L P. W. Gilpin. 1955, Sabre F.4. 1956, Hunter F.4. C.O. S/L J. R. Chapman. 1961, at Gütersloh with Hunter F.6, F.R.10.

No. 4a Squadron

Formed Jan. 1918, from 'A' Flt. of No. 4 Squadron with R.E.8. Unit on loan for corps reconnaissance with Portuguese Army in France until March, 1918.

No. 5 Squadron

Formed 26 July, 1913, at Farnborough from a flight of No. 3 Squadron. Received Sopwith 3-seater, Blériot XI, Avro 504, H. Farman F20, B.E.8, S7 Longhorn. At Gosport, July, 1914. C.O. Maj. J. F. A. Higgins. In Jan. 1914, had the sole S.E.2a which went to No. 3 Squadron in Oct. 1914. Crossed to Amiens 15 Aug. 1914. Engaged in scouting, and in 1915 used Voisin Biplane, Caudron G3 and G4, Avro 504j and 504k, Bristol Bullet D, F.B.5, Martinsyde Scout A. At Abeele in 1916, flying D.H.2, B.E.2e, F.B.9, F.E.8, B.E.2c, B.E.2d. May, 1917, on artillery observation with R.E.8. Oct. 1918, at Pronville. 8th Sept. 1919, to Bicester. Disbanded 20 Jan. 1920. Reformed 1 Feb. 1920, at Quetta, India, from No. 48 Squadron for army co-operation with F2b and Mk. 3 Fighter. Patrolled North-West Frontier. 1928, Risalpur. 1930, Quetta. 1931, Wapiti 2a. 1938, Audax at Chaklala. Also used Vincent 1 and Hart. Dec. 1939, first squadron to receive Mohawk F.B.4 at Calcutta. Bomber escort in Chindwin Valley. Lysander 2. Jan. 1942, at Assam with Hurricane F.1, F.2c and F.2d fighter-bombers. Sept. 1944, Thunderbolt F.1, F.B.2. March, 1946, at Poona, with Tempest F.2 (OQ-). Disbanded 1 Aug. 1947. Reformed 11 Feb. 1949, at Pembrey, Wales, as an anti-aircraft co-operation unit by renumbering No. 595 Squadron. Used Vampire F.1, Martinet T.T.1, Harvard T.2b, Oxford T.2, Spitfire T.T.9 and L.F.16e, Beaufighter T.T.10 (all coded OQ-). Disbanded 1 Aug. 1951. Reformed 1 March, 1952, in 2nd T.A.F. as a ground-attack fighter unit with Vampire F.B.5. At Wunstorf, C.O. S/L V. G. Daw. Dec. 1952, Venom F.B.1, Meteor T.7. July, 1954, Venom F.B.4. C.O. S/L P. V. Ayerst. Disbanded 1957. Reformed 1958 with Meteor N.F.11. 1959, renumbered in 2nd T.A.F. from No. 68 Squadron with Javelin F.A.W.6, F.A.W.4. 1967, Lightning F.6—first unit.

No. 6 Squadron

Formed 31 Jan. 1914, at Farnborough from parts of Nos. 1, 2, 3, and 4 Squadrons. C.O. Maj. J. H. W. Becke. Flew B.E.2 (2), B.E.2a, B.E.2b, S7 Longhorn (2), Blériot XI, H. Farman F20, B.E.8, R.E.5, Martinsyde Scout A, Bristol Scout D. Transferred to Belgium 7 Oct. 1914, with 13 aircraft. Carried out reconnaissance from Poperinghe and Abeele in 1915 with B.E.2c, B.E.2d, F.E.2a, F.E.2b, Voisin Biplane. 1916, B.E.2e. From May, 1917, used R.E.8, together with Nieuport 17C-1, for artillery observation. Oct. 1918, at Longavesnes. V.C. won by Maj. L. G. Hawker in 1915. Mid-1919, to Basra with R.E.8, changing to Bristol F3a, for army co-operation in 1921. 1924, Kingerban. 1928, Mosul. 1930, Ismailia. 1931, Gordon for day-bombing. C.O. S/L J. P. Coleman. 1935, Hart. 1936, Demon 1 and 2 (ZS-) at Ramleh and Ismailia. 1938, Hardy (ZD-, JV-). 1939, Gauntlet 2 (ZD-, JV-). Sept. 1939, Palestine, Transjordan. 1940, Lysander 2 (JV-). 1941, Gladiator 2 (JV-), Hurricane F.1, F.2b, F.2c (JV-). First 40 mm. cannon unit. Anti-tank operations. 1942, Blenheim 4 (JV-), Hurricane F.2d rocket-projectile, F.4 (JV-), Mustang F.2 (JV-). 1945, Spitfire F.9c (JV-). 1946, Tempest F.6 (JV-). 1950, Vampire F.B.5. Left Canal Zone in 1950 for Middle East. 1954, Venom F.B.1 1955, Venom F.B.4 (first unit). July, 1957, Canberra B.2. 1966, Canberra B.16.

No. 7 Squadron

Formed 1 May, 1914, at South Farnborough, later moving to Netheravon. B.E.2, Morane Biplane, Blériot XI, H. Farman F20, B.E.8, Tabloid. 1915, F.B.9, R.E.5 (2 flights), F.B.5 (1 flight), Voisin Biplane, B.E.2c, B.E.2d. To St. Omer, France, 8 April, 1915. Stationed also at Boulogne, Droglandt, Bailleul. V.C. won on 31 July, 1915, by Capt. J. A. Lidell in R.E.5. 1916, B.E.2e, Bristol Scout D. On artillery observation at Menin during 1917-18 with R.E.8. Disbanded 31 Dec. 1919, at Farnborough. Reformed at Bircham Newton on 1 June, 1923, for night-bombing with

Vimy. 1925, at Worthy Down flying Virginia X. 1935, at Finningley with Heyford 2, under W/C A. Gray. 'B' Flt. became No. 102 Squadron in 1935. 1937, Wellesley. 1938, Whitley B.3 (LT-). 1939, Hampden B.1 (MG-), Anson T.1 (MG-), Wellington B.1a (MG-). 1940, at Oakington, first squadron to equip with Stirling B.1, B.3 (MG-). Pathfinder Force. 11 May, 1943, received Lancaster B.1 (MG-, XU-), also B.3 and B.1 (F.E.) (MG-, XU-). At Mepal, Changi, Upwood. In 1950, was using Lincoln B.2 (MG-) at Upwood. 1953, C.O. S/L D. C. Saunders. 1954, in Malaya on anti-bandit operations. 1956, Valiant B.1. at Honington. 1960, C.O. W/C B. P. Mugford.

No. 8 Squadron

Formed on 1 Jan. 1915, at Brooklands with B.E.2, Bristol Scout D. To Abeele, France, on 15 April, 1915. First squadron completely equipped with B.E.2c, followed by B.E.2d and B.E.2e the following year for reconnaissance. Aug. 1917, F.K.8. V.C. won by Capt. F. M. F. West on 10 Aug. 1918. C.O. Nov. 1918-Dec. 1919, Maj. T. Leigh-Mallory. Oct. 1918, at Hervilly. After Nov. 1918, received Bristol F2b. Disbanded 20 Jan. 1920, at Duxford. Reformed 18 Oct. 1920, in Egypt as bomber squadron with D.H.9a. Experimental Trials with Nighthawk. 1921, Mesopotamia; 1924, Kingerban; 1928, Aden. 1928, Fairey 3f. 1935, Vincent 1 and Demon at Khormaksar. 1939, at Aden with Blenheim 1L and 4L (1 flight), Vincent (1 flight) for coastal reconnaissance and anti-submarine duties. Feb. 1943, partly re-equipped Hudson and Baltimore B.3 for anti-submarine. Dec. 1943, completely re-equipped Wellington G.R.13 and G.R.14 for same operations. Disbanded 1 May, 1945, to become No. 200 Squadron. Reformed 15 May, 1945, with Wellington G.R.13 for special duties against Japan. In Ceylon, using also Mosquito F.B.6 (RT-), Tempest F.6 (RT-), Harvard T.2B. Disbanded 15 Nov. 1945. Reformed from No. 114 squadron at Aden in Sept. 1946. Brigand B.1. (RT-), Buckmaster T.1 and T.11 (RT-). Stationed at Khormaksar with Vampire F.B.9. Four aircraft detached to Kenya in April, 1954, for anti-Mau Mau operations. 1954, Venom F.B.4. C.O. S/L A. J. Houston. 1958, using four Meteor F.R.9s late of No. 20 Squadron. March, 1960, first unit with Hunter F.G.A.9. At Aden.

No. 9 Squadron

Formed 8 Dec. 1914, at St. Omer as scouting unit from part of H.Q. Wireless Section. C.O. Maj. H. Musgrave. Received B.E.2, Blériot XI, S7 Longhorn, S11 Shorthorn. Disbanded in France 22 March, 1915. Reformed at Brooklands on 1 April, 1915, with Bristol Scout D, B.E.2c. June, 1915, at Dover. Rejoined B.E.F. in France 20 Dec. 1915. 1916, B.E.2e. Dec. 1916, C.O. Capt. I. A. E. Edwards. June, 1917, R.E.8 on artillery observation. Oct. 1918, at Montigny Farm. Feb. 1919, at Ludendorf with Bristol F2b. Disbanded 31 Dec. 1919, at Castle Bromwich. Reformed 1 April, 1924, at Upavon for bombing with Vimy. 1924, at Castle Bromwich. 1925, at Manston with Virginia. 1927, using Hyderabad. 1929, Virginia X. 1935, C.O. W/C G. H. Cock. 1936, at Boscombe Down and Stradishall with Heyford 2. Oct. 1938, first squadron with Wellington B.1c (KA–, WS–). C.O. W/C H. P. Lloyd. Attacked German warships in first raid of W.W.2. 1942, Wellington B.3 (WS–). Aug. 1942, Lancaster B.1 (WS–). Lancaster B.3, B.1 (F.E.), B.7 (F.E.) (WS–). At Bardney, Waddington, Binbrook, Yagodnik in Russia with No. 617 Squadron, then returned to Binbrook. In 1944 helped to sink the *Tirpitz*. In 1946, re-equipped with Lincoln B.2 (WS–). Used also Oxford T.2 (WS–). June, 1952, Canberra B.2. C.O. S/L J. C. M. Mountford. 1955, Canberra B.6. C.O. S/L L. G. Bastard. 1962, Vulcan B.2.

No. 10 Squadron

Formed 1 Jan. 1915, from part of No. 1 Reserve Squadron at Farnborough, for reconnaissance in France. Arrived there on 25 July, 1915, with Bristol Scout D. 1916, B.E.2c, B.E.2d, B.E.2e, B.E.12. July, 1917, F.K.8. Oct. 1918, at Abeele West. Disbanded 31 Dec. 1919. Reformed 3 Jan. 1928, at Upper Heyford as bomber unit with Hyderabad. 1931, using Hinaidi. 1934, Virginia X. 1935, Heyford 2. C.O. W/C M. B. Frew. 1937, at Dishforth, first squadron with Whitley B.1 (ZA–). At Finningley with Whitley B.2, B.3, B.5 (ZA–, PB–). C.O. W/C W. E. Staton. Took part in first leaflet raid on Berlin. Oct. 1941, Halifax B.2/1 Spec. (ZA–) at Melbourne. C.O. W/C D. C. T. Bennett. 1944, Halifax B.1a, B.3., B.6 (ZA–), Dakota C.3, C.4 (ZA–, OFA–, ODV–). 1953, Canberra B.2 and T.4. C.O. S/L D. R. Howard. Sept. 1955, at Honington. C.O. S/L Sproates. 1958, first to use Victor B.1. At Cottesmore. C.O. W/C C. B. Owen. 1967, VC-10 for transport.

No. 11 Squadron

Formed 14 Feb. 1915, at Netheravon from part of No. 7 Squadron with Bristol Scout D and Vickers Bullet. In July, 1915, received F.B.9 (12) and went to France as the first 2-seater fighter squadron on 25th of the same month. In 1916 on reconnaissance and photographic work with D.H.2, F.B.5, Nieuport 17C–1. V.C. won by Lt. G. S. M. Insall in Nov. 1915. Capt. A. Ball with squadron from May, 1916-Aug. 1916. 1917, F.E.2b. June, 1917, F2b at Bellevue. Oct. 1918, at Vert Galand as fighter-bomber unit. To Germany in 1919. Disbanded 31 Dec. 1919. Reformed 15 Jan. 1923, at Andover as bomber squadron with D.H.9a, later receiving Fawns. At Bircham Newton and Netheravon in 1924. 1926, Horsley at Netheravon until 29 Dec. 1928. Then to Risalpur, India, with Wapiti 2a. 1931, Hart. C.O. S/L O. Jones, 1936-38. 1939, Blenheim

1L (AD–, OY–). 1939, at Singapore; 1940, at Aden; 1940, Egypt and
Libya; Jan. 1941, Greece; July 1941, Syria; July 1942, Ceylon; Jan.
1943, Calcutta; March, 1944, Imphal. 1941, Blenheim 4L (AD–). 1943,
Hurricane F.2b. 1945, Spitfire L.F.8, F.R.14, F.R.18. Disbanded in
Japan in 1948. Reformed in 1949 by renumbering No. 107 Squadron.
Used Mosquito F.B.6. 1950, Vampire F.B.5 (EX–). 1953, first to receive
Venom F.B.1. At Wunstorf. 1955, Venom N.F.3. 1956, at Fassberg.
C.O. S/L E. Batchelar. Disbanded Nov. 1957. Reformed Jan. 1959, from
No. 256 Squadron with Meteor N.F.11. 1959, Javelin F.A.W.4. 1967,
Lightning F.6 at Leuchars.

No. 12 Squadron

Formed 14 Feb. 1915, at Netheravon with R.E.5, B.E.2c, B.E.2d. To
France 6 Sept. 1915. B.E.2e, R.E.7, Bristol Scout D (1), Martinsyde
Scout A. C.O. Maj. C. Newall. Aug. 1917, R.E.8. Oct. 1918, on artillery
observation at Mory. Dec. 1918, F2b. Nov. 1919, stationed on the Rhine.
Disbanded 27 July 1922, at Bickendorf. Reformed 1 April 1923, at
Northolt as a day-bomber unit with D.H.9a. March, 1924, Fawn. April,
1924, at Andover, staying there until 1930. Aug. 1926, became only
squadron to receive Fox, from which the unit earned its name of the
'Shiny Twelfth'. 1929, C.O. S/L S. Maynard. 1931, Hart. Stationed at
Aden. 1936, Hind. 1938, at Andover with Battle 1 (QE–, PH–). 1939,
A.A.S.F. in France at Amifontaine. 1940, first V.C.s of W.W.2 won by
F/O D. E. Garland and Sgt. T. Gray bombing Albert Canal bridges.
Nov. 1940, Wellington B.2 and B.3 (PH–). Sept. 1942, Lancaster B.1,
B.3 (PH–). At Wickenby. 1948, Lincoln B.2 (PH–). 1952, Canberra B.2
at Binbrook. C.O. S/L L. G. Press. June, 1954, Canberra B.6. C.O.
S/L F. C. D. Wright. 1955, Malaya. Disbanded July, 1961. Reformed
1962 with Vulcan B.2.

No. 13 Squadron

Formed 10 Jan. 1915, at Gosport with B.E.2c, B.E.2d, Bristol Scout D.
To France 19 Oct. 1915. 1916, B.E.2e. April, 1917, R.E.8. Oct. 1918,
artillery observation at Mory. Disbanded 31 Dec. 1919. Reformed
1 April, 1924, at Kenley for army co-operation with F2b. Stationed at
Andover, Netheravon, Old Sarum, Odiham. 1927, Atlas. 1930, at
Netheravon. 1932, Audax. 1937, Hector at Odiham. C.O. S/L S. H. C.
Gray. 1939, to France with B.E.F., using Lysander, 1, 2, 3, 3a (AN–,
OO–). 1940, Blenheim 1, 4L (OO–). 1942, to North Africa. Nov. 1942,
Blenheim 5d. Oct. 1943, converted temporarily to Ventura 5. 10 Dec.
1944, Boston B.3, B.4, B.5. C.O. S/L D. E. B. Wheeler. Oct. 1944,
Baltimore B.4, B.5, Marauder B.3. Disbanded 25 Sept. 1945, and re-
formed Aug. 1946. by renumbering No. 680 Squadron with Mosquito
P.R.16, P.R.34, T.3. Engaged on photo-reconnaissance. 1954, at Kabrit.

1955, at Abu Sueir with Meteor P.R.10. C.O. S/L P. P. Villa. 1956, Canberra P.R.7 at Akrotiri. C.O. S/L J. R. Field. Canberra P.R.9.

No. 14 Squadron

Formed 3 Feb. 1915, at Shoreham with B.E.2c. Nov. 1915, to Alexandria, then to Arabia. 1916, G–100 Elephant, Nieuport 17C–1, D.H.1A, Bristol Scout D. 1917, R.E.8. To Palestine in Jan. 1918. Carried out reconnaissance and escort duties from Junction Station until end of War. Disbanded 4 Feb. 1919. Reformed 1 Feb. 1920, in Palestine from No. 111 Squadron as fighter unit with Snipe. July, 1922, flights at Amman and Mafrak. 1927, using D.H.9a as day-bomber at Amman. 1930, flying 3f. 1932, Gordon. C.O. 1935-38, S/L T. C. Traill. 1938, Wellesley 1 and 2 (FB–). Aug. 1939, Ismailia. Dec. 1939, Amman. March, 1940, Port Sudan and East Africa. 1940, Blenheim 4. 1941, Blenheim 4L. March, 1942, first squadron to use Marauder B.1, B.2, B.3 torpedo-bomber. 1942, Tunisia. 1943, Sicily. 21 Sept. 1944, Chivenor. Boston B.3, Mustang F.1. Nov. 1944, operating over Atlantic from U.K. with Leigh-Light Wellington G.R.14 (CX–). Wellington C.16 (CX–). Disbanded 1 June, 1945, and became No. 143 Squadron. Reformed Dec. 1947, from No. 128 Squadron with Mosquito B.16, B.35 (CX–) as bomber unit. Aug. 1954, in 2nd T.A.F. at Fassberg, Germany, as fighter squadron with Sabre F.4. 1955, at Oldenburg. Aug. 1955, Hunter F.4, Vampire T.11. 1958, at Gütersloh with Hunter F.6. C.O. S/L K. E. Richardson. Reformed 12 Dec. 1967, at Wildenrath with Canberra B.(I)8, from No. 88 Squadron.

No. 15 Squadron

Formed 1 March, 1915, at Farnborough with Bristol Scout D, B.E.2c. April, 1915, at Hounslow. May, 1915, Dover. 23 Dec. 1915, to France. 1916, F.B.9, B.E.2d, B.E.2e. June, 1917, R.E.8. Oct. 1918, at Lechelle on artillery observation. Disbanded at Royston on 31 Dec. 1919. Reformed 20 March, 1924, at Martlesham Heath as day-bomber unit with D.H.9a. 1927, Horsley. From Feb. 1929, conducted trials with experimental types. 1 June, 1934, Hart. C.O. W/C T. W. Elmhirst. Dec. 1936, Hind. 1938, at Abingdon. Sept. 1939, to France with A.A.S.F. using Battle 1 (EF–). 1940, Blenheim 4L (LS–). Dec. 1940, Wellington B.1c, B.2 (LS–). 1941, Stirling B.1, B.3 (LS–). Dec. 1943, Lancaster B.1, B.3 (LS–) at Mildenhall. C.O. W/C D. T. Witt. 1945, Lancaster B.1 (Spec.) (LA–). 1946, Lincoln B.1 (LS–). 1950, Washington B.1 (LS–). May, 1954, Canberra B.2, T.4, at Honington. 1955, C.O. S/L Scott. Disbanded April, 1957. Reformed Sept. 1958, second squadron to fly to Victor B.1. At Cottesmore.

No. 16 Squadron

Formed 10 Feb. 1915, at St. Omer, France, from parts of Nos. 2 and 6

Squadrons and a flight of No. 5 Squadron. C.O. Capt. F. V. Holt. Received B.E.2, B.E.2c, Martinsyde Scout A, Blériot XI, Voisin Biplane, Bristol Scout D, S7 Longhorn. 1916, R.E.5, B.E.2e, F.B.9, F.E.2b, B.E.2d, D.H.2. Also had the B.E.9 for operational trials. May, 1917, R.E.8. Oct. 1918, on artillery observation from Camblain. Disbanded 31 Dec. 1919. Squadron pioneered use of wireless in co-operation with artillery. Reformed 1 April, 1924, at Old Sarum under S/L J. O. Atcher for army co-operation with F2b. 1927, Atlas. 1933, Audax. 1938. Hector. 1938, first to use Lysander 1, 2, 3 (KJ–, UG–). 1939, to France. 1940–41, air-sea rescue from Okehampton and Weston Zoyland. Gladiator 1 (UG–). 1942, Mustang F.1a. 1943, engaged on photo-reconnaissance and tactical-reconnaissance with Spitfire P.R.11, P.R.14, P.R.19. At Northolt, April, 1944. Tiger Moth 2, Proctor C.1. Disbanded 19 Oct. 1945, at Dunsfold. Reformed 20 Oct. 1945, at Celle, Germany, from No. 487 Squadron with Mosquito F.B.6 (EG–). Disbanded 30 March, 1946. Reformed 31 March, 1946, from No. 56 Squadron at Fassberg with Tempest F.5 and F.2 (EG–). 1 April, 1946, Tempest F.6 (EG–). Dec. 1948, at Gütersloh with Vampire F.1, F.3. 2 Nov. 1950, to Celle. 1951, Vampire F.B.5 (EG–). C.O. S/L L. H. Lambert. Feb. 1954, Venom F.B.1. C.O. S/L de Burgh. 1956, C.O. S/L G. Walkington. Disbanded Sept. 1957. Reformed 1 March, 1958, in Germany with Canberra B.(I)8. 1960, C.O. W/C J. R. Forsythe. At Laarbruch.

No. 17 Squadron

Formed 1 Feb. 1915, at Gosport. Operated in Middle East. 1916, B.E.12, F.K.8. July, 1916, B.E.2c (12), D.H.2 (2), Bristol Scout D (3). 'B' Flt. to Salonika, followed by 'A' and 'C' Flts. Later at Alexandria and Heliopolis. Bristol M.1c. 1917, Spad S–7 C.1, Nieuport 17C–1, Vickers Bullet. Stationed in Sudan. Feb. 1918, S.E.5a (4). 'C' Flt. to Serbia. Dec. 1918, D.H.9 (12) and Camel (6). Oct. 1918, operating as day-bomber unit from Stojakovo, Serbia. Disbanded 14 Nov. 1919, at Constantinople. Reformed 1 April, 1924, at Hawkinge with Snipe. C.O. S/L J. Leacroft. 1925, Woodcock for night-fighting at Upavon. 1928, Gamecock. 1929, Siskin 3a and Dual Siskin. 1929, Bulldog 2. 1935, at Kenley. C.O. S/L G. H. Broughall. 1936, Bulldog 2a. 1936, Gauntlet 2 (UV–). 1937, Gladiator. Aug. 1939, Blenheim 1f (YB–). 1940, Hurricane F.1 (UV–, YB–). June, 1940, in France with A.A.S.F. Aug. 1940, at Debden, then Martlesham and Kenley. Destroyed 81 E/A in Battle of Britain. 1942, to Burma with Hurricane F.2a, F.2b, F.2c (YB–). At Mingaladon and Calcutta. 1944, Spitfire F.8 (YB–). Shot down 31 Japanese aircraft. 1947, Spitfire F.R.14 (YB–). At Seletar. Disbanded, then reformed 11 Feb. 1949, from No. 691 Squadron for target-towing with Beaufighter T.T.10, Oxford T.2, Spitfire L.F.16e, Martinet T.T.1, Harvard T.2b (all coded UT–, 5S–). Disbanded 1951. Reformed 1956 with Canberra

P.R.3 in 2nd T.A.F. at Wahn. Canberra P.R.7. C.O. S/L B. R. M. Wade.

No. 18 'Burma' Squadron

Formed 11 May, 1915, at Northolt from No. 4 Reserve Squadron.C.O. Maj. G. I. Carmichael. Received Bristol Scout D, S7 Longhorn, Avro 504 (1), Martinsyde Scout A (1). Aug. 1915, to Mousehold Heath, Norwich. 6 Oct. 1915, F.B.9. 11 Nov. 1915, to le Havre, then to Rouen. 1916, F.E.2b, G–100 Elephant, D.H.2. Sept. 1916, at Lavieville. Dec. 1916, at St. Leger. 1917, C.O. Maj. R. M. Reid. June, 1917, D.H.4. March, 1918, D.H.9. 8 Sept. 1918, D.H.9a. Oct. 1918, operating as day-bomber from Maisoncelle. 1919, running mail service between Lympne and Cologne. Disbanded 31 Dec. 1919, at Keston-on-the-Green. Re-formed 20 Oct. 1931, at Upper Heyford for day-bombing with Hart. C.O. S/L T. C. Luke. 1935, C.O. S/L G. S. Shaw. May, 1936, Hind. 1939, with A.A.S.F. to France using Blenheim 1L, 4f, 4L (FV–, WV–), Battle 1 (FV–). 1942, Burma with Blenheim 5d (FV–). 1943, Boston B.3, B.4, B.5. Disbanded 29 March, 1946. Reformed 1 Sept. 1946, by re-numbering No. 621 Squadron with Lancaster G.R.3. Disbanded 15 Sept. 1946, in Palestine, becoming 'B' Flt. of No. 38 Squadron. Re-formed 8 Dec. 1947, with Dakota C.4 (MOFA–). Received eight and operated on Berlin airlift. C.O. S/L R. M. Burns. Disbanded 20 Feb. 1950, at Netheravon. Reformed 1 Aug. 1953, at Scampton under S/L R. A. Cooper with Canberra B.2. 1955, at Upwood. C.O. S/L A. H. Chamberlain. Disbanded 1957. Dec. 1958, renumbered from No. 199 Squadron at Honington with Valiant B.(K.)1. 1959, at Finningley. 1967, Wessex H.C.2.

No. 19 Squadron

Formed 1 Sept. 1915, at Castle Bromwich with B.E.2c, B.E.12. April, 1916, at Netheravon, then at Filton. 30 July, 1916, to France with B.E.12s fitted with Vickers interruptor gear. Also used R.E.7. Feb. 1917, first unit to have Spad S–7 C.1, later Spad S–13 C.1. Jan. 1918, first to receive Dolphin. Oct. 1918, at Savy as fighter unit. Destroyed 281 E/A. Disbanded 31 Dec. 1919. Reformed 1 April, 1923, at Duxford as a fighter unit with Snipe. 1924, Grebe semi-equipped. 1925, full three-flight strength of Grebes. 1927. Gamecock 1. 1928, Siskin 3a and Dual Siskin. 1931, Bulldog 2. C.O. S/L A. C. Sanderson. 13 May, 1935, first unit to receive Gauntlet 1, later Gauntlet 2. C.O. S/L J. R. Cassidy. 1938, Gladiator 1. Aug. 1938, first to fly Spitfire F.1. (WZ–, QV–). 1940, Spit-fire F.2a and F.5a (QV–). 1941, Spitfire L.F.5b, F.9b (QV–). 1943, Spitfire L.F.16e (QV–). 1944, Mustang F.3 and F.4 (QV–). To France, June, 1944. July, 1945, at Acklington. 1946, Spitfire F.22 (QV–). Oct. 1946, at Wittering with Hornet F.1 and F.3 (QV–). Moved to Church

Fenton. 1951, Meteor F.8, Mosquito T.3 (AV-) for training. C.O.
S/L B. L. Duckenfield. 1954, C.O. S/L B. Beard. 1956, C.O. S/L D. J.
Fowler. 1957, using Hunter F.6 at Church Fenton. C.O. Maj. R. G.
Newell, U.S.A.F. on exchange posting. 1967, Lightning F.2.

No. 20 Squadron

Formed 1 Sept. 1915, at Netheravon. Later at Filton, then to France
23 Jan. 1916, as first unit with F.E.2b. 1916, G-100 Elephant. Aug.
1916, R.E.7 (one 3-seater). 7 Jan. 1917, V.C. won by Sgt. T. Mottershead. 1917, F.E.2d. Sept. 1917, F2b. Oct. 1918, fighter-bomber unit at
Moislains. March, 1919, to India. 1928-30 at Peshawar and Kohat.
1931, Wapiti 2a. Dec. 1935, Audax 1 (HN-). 1941, Blenheim 1 and 4
(HN-). Dec. 1941, Lysander 2 (HN-). Feb. 1943, in Burma with
Hurricane F.2b and F.2d on anti-tank operations. At Arakan and Mani-
pur. Feb. 1945, Hurricane F.4. 1945, at Imphal with Spitfire L.F.8,
F.R.14 (HN-). 1946, Tempest F.5, F.2 (HN-), Spitfire L.F.16e (HN-),
Harvard T.2b (HN-), Tiger Moth T.2 (HN-). Disbanded 1947 in
India. Reformed in 2nd T.A.F. and stationed at Oldenburg, Germany,
with Vampire F.B.5. 1953, Venom F.B.1. 1954, Sabre F.4. C.O. S/L
I. Macdonald. 1955, Hunter F.4. 1959, at Gütersloh with Hunter F.6.
Disbanded 1960. 1961, reformed with Hunter F.G.A.9. At Tengah.

No. 21 'Norwich' Squadron

Formed 23 July, 1915, at Netheravon. Received B.E.2c, Bristol Scout
D. To France on 23 Jan. 1916, with R.E.7. July, 1916, at Fienvillers
with R.E.7 (14) B.E.2c (4), B.E.2e (1). 1916, G-100 Elephant. Aug.
1916, B.E.12. Feb. 1917, R.E.8. Oct. 1918, at Floringham on artillery
observation. Disbanded Jan. 1919. Reformed 3 Dec. 1934, as day-
bomber unit with Hart. 1937, at Lympne with Hind first to use. 1939,
Blenheim 1L (JP-). 1940, Blenheim 4L (YH-). Dec. 1941, in Malaya.
Oct. 1942, at Feltwell was first unit to fly Ventura B.1 (YH-). 1943, at
Sculthorpe with Mosquito B.4, F.B.6 (YH-), Oxford T.2 (YH-).
Reformed 1953. 1954, at Scampton with Canberra B.2. C.O. S/L N. B.
Freeman. Disbanded 15 Jan, 1959. Reformed 1 May, 1959, at Benson
with Twin Pioneer C.C.1. C.O. S/L W. J. Bishop. Sept. 1959, to East-
leigh, East Africa.

No. 22 Squadron

Formed 1 Sept. 1915, at Gosport from part of No. 13 Squadron. 1916,
F.E.2b. To France 1 April, 1916. July, 1917, F2b. March, 1918, at
Serny and Vert Galand. 1918, R.E.8. Oct. 1918, artillery observation at
Maisoncelle. Disbanded Dec. 1919. Reformed at Martlesham on 24 July,
1923, as torpedo-bomber unit for trials with experimental types. 1934,
Vildebeest 2 at Donibristle and Thorney Island. 1938, Vildebeest 3 and
4 (OA-). Dec. 1939, first to use Beaufort G.R.1 and G.R.2 (OA-). 1941,

V.C. won by F/O K. Campbell. On anti-shipping in Europe. 1944, Beaufighter T.F.10 in India and Burma. Disbanded 30 Sept. 1945. Reformed 1 May, 1946, from No. 89 Squadron with Mosquito F.B.6. Disbanded 15 Aug. 1946. Reformed 1 Feb. 1955, for coastal rescue with Whirlwind H.A.R.2 and Sycamore H.R.14. Main base at Thorney Island: detachments at Martlesham Heath and Valley. C.O. S/L P. C. Bowry. 1959, main base at St. Mawgan; detachments at Felixstowe, Thorney Island, Chivenor and Valley. 1967, Whirlwind H.A.R.10.

No. 23 Squadron

Formed 1 Sept. 1915, at Gosport from part of No. 14 Squadron. Received B.E.2c (1), S11 Shorthorn (5), Blériot XI (1), Caudron G3 (3), Avro 504. Jan. 1916, F.E.2b. To Matigny, France, 16 March, 1916. 1916, G-100 Elephant (2). Jan. 1917. Spad S-7 C.1. 1918, Spad S-13 C.1. April, 1918. Dolphin. Oct. 1918, fighter at Hancourt. Disbanded 31 Dec. 1919, at Waddington. Reformed 1 July, 1925, at Henlow as fighter squadron with Snipe under C.O. S/L R. Collishaw. Also used Dual Snipe. 1926, Gamecock 1—first squadron. At Northolt, C.O. S/L A. G. Jones-Williams in 1929. At Kenley, 1930, C.O. S/L A. P. Woollett. 1931, Bulldog (two flights), Demon (one flight added in 1932). 1932, at Biggin Hill. 1935, re-equipped fully with Demon, later using Turret-Demon (MS-). C.O. S/L G. H. Crowe. 21 Dec. 1937, to Northolt until 18 May, 1938. 1938, at Wittering, Sept. 1939, at Northolt. Blenheim 1f (MS-, YP-). C.O. S/L G. F. W. Heycock, Aug. 1940, at Colly Weston. 1940, Boston B.2, B.3 (YP-). April, 1941, Havoc N.F.1 (YP-) on intruder duties from Ford. July, 1942, Mosquito N.F.2 (YP-). 1945, Mosquito F.B.6 (YP-), N.F.30, N.F.36, T.3 (all YP-). Sept. 1945, disbanded. Reformed Wittering Sept. 1946. C.O. S/L P. G. K. Williamson. 10 Oct. 1946, became No. 23/151 Squadron when it combined with No. 151 Squadron. 1953, Vampire N.F.10. June, 1954, Venom N.F.2 at Coltishall. C.O. S/L P. S. Engelbach. 1955, Venom N.F.3. C.O. W/C A. N. Davies. March, 1957, Javelin FAW.4. At Coltishall. May, 1959, Javelin F.A.W.7. C.O. W/C G. I. Chapman. Javelin FAW.9. 1967, Lightning F.3 at Leuchars.

No. 24 'Commonwealth' Squadron

Formed 21 Sept. 1915, at Hounslow from part of No. 17 Squadron. Received F.B.5 (12). To France 7 Feb. 1916, with D.H.2 as first single-seater scout unit. C.O. Maj. L. G. Hawker, V.C. May, 1917, D.H.5. Jan. 1918, S.E.5, S.E.5a. Oct. 1918, as fighter squadron at Athies. Feb. 1919, to Northolt, then to London Colney and Uxbridge. Disbanded Jan. 1920. Reformed April, 1920, with F2b at Hendon. Jan. 1927, to Northolt for communication duties with Avro 504k, D.H.9a (7), Avro 504n, Tomtit, D.H.60 Moth, Fairey 3f. 1932, to Hendon. Hart, Wapiti.

1934, Osprey, Tutor. 1936, Tiger Moth, Dragon Rapide, Magister, Hart (C). 1938, Hind, Hart (T), Audax, D.H.86b, Nighthawk. 1939, Vega Gull. 1940, Hudson C.3, C.6 (ZK–), Boston C.3, Stirling C.5, Cygnet. 1943, Dakota C.3, C.4 (NQ–), Wellington C.1 (ZK–), Oxford, Hertfordshire, Wellington T.15, Lockheed 12a, Goose, Ensign, Anson, Skymaster C.1. 1946, Dakota C.3, C.4 (ODA–, MODA–, MODC–). 1948, York C.1 (OYD–, MOYD–, NQ–), Lancastrian C.2 (NQ–, MOKD–). Feb. 1946, to Bassingbourne. 1953, Hastings C.1 (NQ–), Valetta C.1, C.2 (NQ–). 1955, C.O. S/L R. B. Bolt. 1955, at Colerne. 1967, second squadron with Hercules C.1.

No. 25 Squadron

Formed 25 Sept. 1915, at Montrose, with S7 Longhorn, Caudron G.3, Curtiss J, Martinsyde Scout A, Bristol Scout D. Feb. 1916, F.E.2b. Squadron personnel went to France 20 Feb. 1916, aircraft following on 25 March, 1916. 1916, F.E.2c (1), F.E.2d. At St. Omer, Auchel, Bois-dinghem, Villers Brettoneux. Aug. 1917, D.H.4., D.H.9A. Oct. 1918, at Ruissenville for day-bombing. 1919, at Carlton. Disbanded 31 Jan. 1920, at Shotwick. Reformed April, 1920, at Hawkinge, C.O. W/C N. R. A. D. Leslie. Fighter unit with Snipe. 1922-23 at Constantinople. Oct. 1924, first squadron to receive Grebe. At Hawkinge. 1928, Siskin 3a and Dual Siskin. 1932, Fury 1. C.O. S/L W. E. G. Bryant. 1935, first to receive Fury 2. C.O. S/L W. F. Dickson. 1937, Demon, Gladiator. 1939, Blenheim 1f (RX–, ZK–). At Northolt, North Weald. 1939, Blenheim 1f (ZK–). 1940, one Whirlwind 1 for night-fighter trials. 1940, Beaufighter N.F.1 (ZK–). Aug. 1940, Martlesham, Debden. 1941, Beaufighter N.F.6f (ZK–) at Wittering, Church Fenton. 1943, Mosquito N.F.2 Intruder (ZK–), F.B.6 (ZK–), T.3 (ZK–). 1944, Mosquito N.F.13, N.F.17 (ZK–), Havoc N.F.1 (ZK–). Oct. 1944, Mosquito N.F. 30 (ZK–) at Boxted. 1948, Mosquito N.F.36 (ZK–) at West Malling. 1951, Vampire N.F.10. C.O. S/L D. G. Furse. 1954, Meteor N.F.12, N.F.14. C.O. S/L J. Cameron Cox. 1955, C.O. S/L P. W. Jamieson. Disbanded 23 June, 1958, at Tangmere. 1958, reformed at Waterbeach from No. 153 Squadron with Meteor N.F.12 and N.F.14. 1959, Javelin F.A.W.7. 1960, Javelin F.A.W.8. 1960, Javelin F.A.W.9, first unit. C.O. W/C J. H. Walton.

No. 26 'South African' Squadron

Formed Nov. 1914, at Netheravon from unit of the South African Aviation Corps. In Oct. 1915, became No. 26 'South African' Squadron of the R.F.C. 1915, B.E.2c, H. Farman F20 (steel version). To Mombasa 31 Jan. 1916. From Aug. 1917, used B.E.2c and B.E.2e only in East Africa. Returned to England in July, 1918, and disbanded at Blandford. Reformed 11 Oct. 1927, at Catterick with Atlas—first squadron.

1933, Audax. C.O. S/L C. H. Stillwell. 1938, Hector (HL–). 1940, in France with Air Component, B.E.F., using Lysander 1, 2, 3 (RM–), Battle 1 (RM–). 1941, Tomahawk F.1, F.2a (RM–). Feb. 1942, Mustang F.1, F.B.4 (RM–, XC–), Spitfire F.5, Spitfire P.R.11, F.R.14e (XC–). 1 April, 1946, renumbered from No. 41 Squadron with Tempest F.2, F.5 (XC–). 1953, in 2nd T.A.F. at Oldenburg, Germany, with Vampire F.B.5 (XC–). 1954, Sabre F.4. C.O. S/L K. Smith. 1955, Hunter F.4. C.O. S/L J. A. G. Jackson. Hunter F.6. 1959, at Gütersloh. 1960, C.O. S/L D. L. Edmonds. Disbanded 1961. Reformed 1961 with Belvedere H.C.1. At Khormaksar, Aden.

No. 27 Squadron
Formed 5 Nov. 1915, at Hounslow from part of No. 24 Squadron. Dec. 1915, at Dover. March, 1916, G–100 Elephant. 1 July, 1916, had seventeen Elephants and was only squadron fully equipped with them. Crossed to France 1 March, 1916, under Maj. A. E. Borton. Was the second unit to have single-seater aircraft for fighting. July, 1916, at Fienvillers. July, 1917, D.H.4. March, 1918, at Villers Brettoneux. July, 1918, D.H.9. Oct. 1918, day-bomber at Beauvois. Disbanded 22 Jan. 1920, at Shotwick. Reformed 1 April, 1920, from No. 99 Squadron in India with D.H.9a. 1923, at Risalpur, later Kohat. 1928, Wapiti 2a at Risalpur. 1936, C.O. S/L K. H. Riversdale-Elliott. 1939, Hurricane F.1. 1940, Blenheim N.F.1f (EG–). Dec. 1941, Malaya. Sept. 1942, Beaufighter F.1, T.F.10, Mosquito F.B.6, Vengeance. 1944, Madras. Disbanded Feb. 1946. Reformed in England in 1947 with Dakota C.4 (EG–, MODC–). Operated on Berlin airlift. Disbanded Nov. 1950. Reformed 15 June, 1953, at Scampton with Canberra B.2. C.O. S/L D. H. Chopping. 1955, C.O. S/L P. W. Helmore. Disbanded 31 Dec. 1957. Reformed 1 April, 1961, Vulcan B.2.

No. 28 Squadron
Formed 7 Nov. 1915, at Gosport from part of No. 22 Squadron. Received F.E.2b. July, 1917, at Yatesbury. Sept. 1917, Camel. 8 Oct. 1917, to France. 12 Nov. 1917, to Italy. 1918, F2b. Oct. 1918, fighter at Sarcedo. Oct. 1919, to Yatesbury, then Eastleigh. Disbanded 20 Jan. 1920. Reformed Feb. 1920, in India, with F2b. 1928, at Ambala. 1931, Wapiti 2a. 1936, Audax 1 (US–, BF–). 1941, Lysander 1, 2, 3 (BF–). 1942, Hurricane F.B.2b (BF–). Was only tactical-reconnaissance R.A.F. unit in Burma. 1945, Spitfire F.8, F.R.14, F.R.18. 1954, Vampire F.B.5 at Hong Kong. C.O. S/L J. Welch. Venom F.B.1. 1957, to Kai Tak from Sek Kong.

No. 29 Squadron
Formed 7 Nov. 1915, at Gosport from part of No. 23 Squadron. 25 March, 1916, to France to await aircraft. D.H.2, F.E.8. March, 1917,

Nieuport 17C-1 and 27. April, 1918, S.E.5a. Oct. 1918, fighter unit at Hoog Huys. Dec. 1918, at Bickendorf. Disbanded 31 Dec. 1919, at Spittlegate. Reformed 1 April, 1923, at Duxford with Snipe. 1925, Grebe. 1928, Siskin 3a and Dual Siskin. 1930, at North Weald. 1932, Bulldog 2a. 1934, Demon. C.O. S/L O. Chapman. In Egypt from 1935 until 1936. 1938, at Debden with Turret-Demon. C.O. S/L R. C. Jonas. 1939, Blenheim 1f at Digby. 1940, partly equipped with Hurricane F.1 (RE-, RO-, YB-). Sept. 1940, first unit to operate Beaufighter N.F.1f (RO-). 1942, Beaufighter 5 (RO-) with turret—one for trials. 1943, Mosquito N.F.12, T.3, F.B.26 (RO-). 1946, Mosquito N.F.30, N.F.36 (RO-) at Tangmere. 1952, Meteor F.8. C.O. S/L P. Horsley. 1953, first squadron to operate Meteor N.F.11. 1956, Javelin FAW.4 at Tangmere. C.O. W/C J. A. C. Aiken. Javelin FAW.6, FAW.9. 1967, Lightning F.3. At Wattisham.

No. 30 Squadron

Formed 24 March, 1915, at Suez with B.E.2c, B.E.2e, Bristol Scout D, S7 Longhorn, Voisin Biplane, Martinsyde Scout A. April, 1916, to Mesopotamia. 1916, flew supplies to besieged Kut-al-Imara. 1916, Spad S-7 C.1. Jan. 1917, at Arab Village. 17 Oct. 1917, R.E.8, G-100 Elephant. 1918, D.H.4. Oct. 1918, on reconnaissance from Kifrie, Persia. Nov. 1918–Feb. 1919, one flight to Kazvin. Disbanded*April, 1919. Reformed 1 Feb. 1920 with D.H.9a. 1921, in Mesopotamia. June, 1921, on airmail route from Cairo to Baghdad. 1924, at Kirkuk. 1928, Baghdad, Kirkuk. 1930, at Hinaidi, India. 1933, Wapiti 2a at Mosul. 1935, Hardy—first unit. In Iraq. 1938, Blenheim 1f, 1L, 4f (DP-, RS-). 1940, Crete. 1941, Hurricane N.F.2c in Egypt. Feb. 1942, in Ceylon, then India. 1944, Bengal. June, 1944, Thunderbolt F.B.2 (RS-). Stationed Arakan. 1946, Tempest F.2, F.5 (RS-). Aug. 1946, on North-West Frontier of India. Disbanded 1 Dec. 1946. Reformed 24 Nov. 1947, with Dakota C.4 (JN-, MODF-). 1953, Valetta C.2 (JN-, MORG-, MOSC-). 1954, at Dishforth for V.I.P. transport. 1957, Beverley C.1 at Dishforth. 1959, to Eastleigh, Nairobi.

No. 31 Squadron

'A' Flt. formed Aug. 1915, at Farnborough from part of No. 1 Reserve Squadron with B.E.2c (5). First R.F.C. squadron in India 26 Dec. 1915. At Nowshera, then Risalpur. 'B' Flt. formed Feb. 1916, from part of No. 22 Squadron with B.E.2c (6). 'C' Flt. formed 17 June, 1916, from 6th Brigade, Bombay. Oct. 1916, complete unit at Risalpur. C.O. Maj. C. R. S. Bradley. 1916, B.E.2e. 1917, F.E.2b. C.O. Capt. G. M. MacDonald. 1921, F2b, for army co-operation. 1928, at Quetta. 1931, at Karachi with Wapiti 2a. 1933, at Quetta. 1939, Valentia 1 (bomber-transport flight), Vincent. 1942, D.C.2, D.C.3, Atalanta, Dakota C.1,

C.3, C.4 (ODU–). At Agatarla operating over the Burma 'Hump', engaged on troop-carrying and supply-dropping. Disbanded 30 Sept. 1946, at Akyab. 1 Nov. 1946, renumbered from No. 77 Squadron. Reformed 13 Aug. 1948, at Hendon from No. 510 Communication Squadron with Proctor C.2, C.3, C.4 (VS–, CB–), Devon C.1 (CB–), Anson C.19/1, C.19/2, C.12/1, C.12/2 (CB–, MOAT–), Chipmunk T.10 (CB–). C.O. S/L N. Williamson. 1955, became Metropolitan Communication Squadron. Reformed as No. 31 Squadron, 1 March, 1955, with Canberra P.R.3 at Laarbruch in 2nd T.A.F. C.O. S/L J. C. Stead. 1956, first unit in 2nd T.A.F. with Canberra P.R.7.

No. 32 Squadron

Formed 12 Jan. 1916, at Netheravon from part of No. 21 Squadron. To France 28 May, 1916, with D.H.2. 1 July, 1916, V.C. won by C.O. Maj. L. W. B. Rees. 1917, Nieuport 17C–1. May, 1917, D.H.5. April, 1918, at Humiéres with S.E.5a. Oct. 1918, fighter at Bellevue. March, 1919, at Tangmere. Sept. 1919, at Croydon. Disbanded 29 Dec. 1919. Reformed 1 April, 1923, at Kenley with Snipe. Moved to Biggin Hill. 1926, Grebe. 1927, Gamecock 1. 1928, Siskin 3a and Dual Siskin at Kenley. 1932–34, C.O. S/L D. L. Blackford. 1935, Bulldog 2 at Biggin Hill. 1935, Gauntlet 2. C.O. S/L R. Pyne. 22 March, 1937, 'B' Flt. detached to become No. 79 Squadron. 1939, Hurricane F.1, F.2b, F.2c (KT–, GZ–). Aug. 1940, at Biggin Hill. 1942, North Africa with Spitfire F.5b, H.F.7, F.9c (KT–, GZ–). 1944, Italy with Spitfire F.R.18 (GZ–), later with Balkan Air Forces. 1945, Palestine. 1949, Vampire F.3. 1951, Vampire F.B.5, F.B.9. 1955, Venom F.B.1. At Shaibah. C.O. S/L A. H. W. Gilchrist. Jan. 1957, Canberra B.2, B.(I)8 in Cyprus. 1966, Canberra B.15.

No. 33 Squadron

Formed 12 Jan. 1916, at Filton from part of No. 20 Squadron. C.O. Maj. P. B. Joubert de la Ferté. Engaged on Home Defence and anti-Zeppelin patrols from Bramham Moor and Knavemuire with B.E.2c. Nov. 1916, F.E.2b, F.E.2d. Dec. 1916, H.Q. at Gainsborough; flights at Brattleby, Kirton-in-Lindsey and Elsham. 1917, F2b. 1918, Avro 504 single-seater. Oct. 1918, night-fighting from Kirton-in-Lindsey. Disbanded 13 June, 1919. Reformed 1 March, 1929, at Netheravon with Horsley. 1930, Eastchurch. April, 1930, first to receive Hart for day-bombing. Transferred to India. 1935, C.O. S/L J. W. Baker. 1 March, 1938, became fighter squadron with Gladiator 2 (SO–, NY–, NW–, TN–) at Ismailia. 1940, Hurricane F.1 (NW–). 1941, Hurricane F.B.2c (NW–) for long-range work. 1941, in Greece. 1943, Spitfire F.5c (NW–), Blenheim 4f. 1944, in England with Spitfire F.9c (5R–), Typhoon F.1b (5R–). Dec. 1944, Tempest F.5 (5R–). 1946, at Quakenbruck, Germany.

1948, Tempest F.2 (5R–) with rocket projectiles. 1953, in Malaya with Hornet F.3, F.4 (5R–). 1955, at Butterworth. C.O. S/L P. W. Hancock. 1955, amalgamated with No. 45 Squadron. Reformed Oct. 1955, as No. 33 Squadron. 1956, at Driffield with Venom N.F.2, N.F.3. Disbanded Jan. 1957. 1 Oct. 1957, reformed from No. 264 Squadron with Meteor N.F.12, N.F.14. C.O. W/C N. Poole. 1958, Javelin FAW.4. 1958, first unit with Javelin FAW.7. At Middleton St. George.

No. 34 Squadron

Formed 7 Jan. 1916, from part of No. 19 Squadron at Castle Bromwich. Received B.E.2c for Home Defence. May, 1916, became first unit to receive B.E.2e. June, 1916, at Severley and Lilbourne. 15 June, 1916, to Allonville, France, then to Dunkirk. Jan. 1917, received R.E.8 from No. 2 Squadron, moving on 13 Nov. 1917, to Italy, arriving in Milan 14 Nov. 1917. 1918, F2b for 'Z' Flt., which was detached in July, 1918, to form No. 139 Squadron. Oct. 1918, on reconnaissance from Santa Luca and Villaverla. Disbanded Sept. 1919, at Old Sarum. Reformed 3 Dec. 1935, at Bircham Newton with Hind as day-bomber unit. Oct. 1937, at Aldergrove. Dec. 1937, at Lympne. 1938, Blenheim 1 and 4L (LB–). 1938, at Lympne and Upper Heyford. 1939, E. Anglia. Sept. 1939, in Far East at Tengah, then to Alor Star and Palembang. June, 1942, at Allahabad. 1943, Hurricane F.2a, F.2b. 1945, Thunderbolt F.1, F.B.2 at Ondaw. July, 1945, at Meiktela. Disbanded 15 Oct. 1945. Reformed Aug. 1946, from No. 681 Squadron for photo-reconnaissance with Spitfire P.R.19. Disbanded Aug. 1947, to become part of No. 81 Squadron. Reformed March, 1949, from No. 695 Squadron for target-towing, anti-aircraft co-operation and radar calibration, using Beaufighter T.T.10 (4M–, 6J–), Martinet T.T.1 (6J–), Oxford T.2 (8Q–), Spitfire L.F. 16e (4M–, 8Q–). Disbanded Nov. 1952. Reformed June, 1954, at Tangmere as a fighter unit with Meteor F.8. Feb. 1956, Hunter F.5. 1958, renumbered No. 208 Squadron. Reformed with Beverley C.1.

No. 35 'Madras Presidency' Squadron

Formed 1 Feb. 1916, at Thetford with H. Farman F20, F.B.5, B.E.2c, F.E.2b. Jan. 1917, F.K.8, first unit. To France 26 Jan. 1917, for co-operation with Cavalry Corps. 1918, F2b. Oct. 1918, night-fighter at Longavesnes. Disbanded 26 June, 1919, at Netheravon. Reformed 1 March, 1929, at Bircham Newton for day-bombing with D.H.9a. 1930, Fairey 3f for general-purpose duties. 1932, Gordon at Worthy Down. C.O. S/L Buxton. 1938, Wellesley 1 at Cottesmore. Sept. 1939, Battle 1 (WT–), Anson 1 (WT–). Oct. 1939, Blenheim 4L (TL–), Wellington B.1c (TL–). Used Hereford with 5 Gp. Pool for training. Disbanded 3 April, 1940. Reformed 5 Nov. 1940, at Leeming and was first squadron to receive Halifax B.1 (TL–). C.O. W/C R. W. P. Collings. 5 Dec. 1940, to Linton-on-Ouse. 1942, Halifax B.2/1a, B.3 (TL–) with Pathfinder Force. Dec. 1943, Lancaster B.1, B.3, B.1(F.E.) (TL–) at Graveley. 1944, Liberator B.6, Anson 1. Raided *Scharnhorst* and *Tirpitz*. 1946, Lancaster B.7 (TL–). Goodwill tour of U.S.A., 8 July, 1946, until 29 Aug. 1946. 10 Sept. 1946, to Stradishall. 1949, re-equipped Lincoln B.2 (TL–). 1951, Washington B.1 (FB–). 1954, Canberra B.2 at Marham. 1959, at Upwood. Last Canberra Squadron in Bomber Command. 1966, Vulcan B.2.

No. 36 Squadron

Formed 1 Feb. 1916, at Cramlington for Home Defence, with Pup, B.E.2c, F.E.2b, B.E.2e, Avro 504, B.E.12. Engaged on anti-Zeppelin patrols. Dec. 1916, H.Q. at Newcastle with flights at Seaton Carew, Hylton and Ashington. 1917, F2b, F.E.2d, single-seater F.E.2b, F.K.8, Bristol Scout D. Oct. 1918, night-fighting at Usworth. 27 Nov. 1916, 2nd Lt. I. V. Pyott shot down L.34 over Hartlepool. Disbanded 13 June, 1919. Reformed 2 June, 1928, at Donibristle for torpedo-bombing with Horsley. At Leuchars from 30 Nov. 1930, until 30 Dec. 1930. Then to Seletar, Singapore. Also used Dart. July, 1935, Vildebeest 1, 2, 3, 4 (VU–). C.O. S/L G. B. Beardsworth. 1940, Albacore, Wellington B.2. 20 Oct. 1942, at Tanjore on anti-submarine and anti-shipping work. 1943, Wellington G.R.12, G.R.14 (RW–) in the Mediterranean. Also used Hudson G.R.3 (RW–). May, 1943, at Dhubalia. June, 1943, Blida. May, 1944, Reghaia. Then at Gibraltar, Sicily, Grottaglie, Monte Corvino. Oct. 1944, to Coastal Command. Nov. 1944, at Chivenor. March, 1945, at Benbecula. 1945, Dakota C.1 (RW–). Disbanded 4 June, 1945. Reformed Oct. 1946, from No. 248 Squadron, with Brigand T.F.1, Beaufighter T.F.10 (NE–), Mosquito F.B.6 (NE–, DM–). 1947, Brigand B.1. 1954, Neptune M.R.1 (T–) at Topcliffe. Fourth unit to receive Neptune. Disbanded, then reformed 1958 at Colerne from No. 511 Squadron with Hastings C.1. 1 Aug., 1967, first squadron with Hercules C.1.

No. 37 Squadron

Formed 15 April, 1916, at Orfordness as an experimental unit and disbanded during May, 1916. Reformed on 15 Sept. 1916, at Woodham Mortimer, Essex, under Maj. W. B. Hargrave for Home Defence. Used B.E.12. Dec. 1916, H.Q. at Woodham Mortimer, with flights at Rochford, Stow Maries and Goldhanger. 1917, One-and-a-half Strutter, S.E.5a. March, 1919, moved to Biggin Hill. Disbanded 1 July, 1919, and renumbered No. 39 Squadron. Reformed 26 April, 1937, at Feltwell from part of No. 214 Squadron with Harrow 1 and 2 (FJ–). Sept. 1939, flying Wellington B.1c. At Tengah. 1941, Wellington B.1c, B.3, B.10 (HS–) in Egypt. 1941, at Shaibah. Dec. 1943, Liberator G.R.5

(GR-) in Italy. Disbanded March, 1946. Reformed April, 1946, from No. 214 Squadron with Liberator B.8. Disbanded April, 1947. Reformed 14 Sept. 1947, at Ein Shemer, Palestine, with Lancaster M.R.3, A.S.R.3. April, 1948, to Malta. Dec. 1954, Shackleton M.R.1, M.R.2 at Luqa, C.O. S/L R. S. Smith. 1957, at Aden.

No. 38 Squadron

Formed 14 July, 1916, at Castle Bromwich from part of No. 54 Squadron for Home Defence and training. Sept. 1916, to Melton Mowbray. Used F.E.2b and Dual F.E.2b (18). Dec. 1916, H.Q. at Melton Mowbray, with flights at Stamford, Buckminster and Leadenham. 1918, F2b. 31 May, 1918, to Capelle, France. Oct. 1918, night-bomber at Harlebeke. Disbanded 4 July, 1919. Reformed 16 Sept. 1935, at Mildenhall with Heyford 2. 1936, only squadron to be fully equipped with Hendon 2. At Marham. 1938, Wellington B.1c (NH-). 1940, Wellington B.1a, B.1c (LF-). In Egypt and at Shaibah, Iraq. 1945, Wellington G.R.13, G.R.14, B.2 (NH-). At Foggia and Falconara. July, 1945, partly equipped with Warwick A.S.R.1 (RL-). Four received for A.S.R. from Malta. July, 1946, Lancaster G.R.3 (RL-). 1952, Lancaster M.R.3 for maritime reconnaissance from Malta. C.O. S/L E. D. T. Norman. Dec. 1954, Shackleton M.R.2. C.O. W/C D. E. Hawkins.

No. 39 Squadron

Formed 25 April, 1916, at Hounslow as first Home Defence squadron. H.Q. at Woodford Green, with flights of six aircraft each at Hainault, Sutton's Farm and North Weald Bassett. Received B.E.2c. V.C. won by Lt. W. Leefe-Robinson on 2nd Sept. 1916, for shooting down S.L.11. 23 Sept. 1916, L.32 shot down by 2nd Lt. F. Sowrey. 1 Oct. 1916, L.31 shot down by 2nd Lt. W. J. Tempest. 1918, F.E.2b for night-bombing. Oct. 1918, at Vavichove. Nov. 1918, F2b. Disbanded 16 Nov. 1918. Reformed 1 July, 1919, at Biggin Hill from No. 37 Squadron with eighteen D.H.9a. 1923, at Spittlegate. 1928, Wapiti. 1930, at Risalpur. 1931, Hart. 1939, Blenheim 1 and 4L (FJ-). In the Far East. 1940, in France. C.O. S/L C. M. M. Grece. 1941, Maryland B.1 on photo-reconnaissance until Jan. 1942. 1941, Beaufort 1 in Egypt. 1942, Boston B.3. June, 1943, Beaufighter T.F.10. Nov. 1944, Marauder B.3 in Balkans. Feb. 1946, Mosquito F.B.6, T.3, N.F.36, Tempest F.6. 1954, in Middle East with Meteor N.F.11, N.F.13. 1955, at Luqa, Malta. C.O. S/L J. M. O'Meara. 1 July, 1958, renumbered from No. 69 Squadron. 1959, Canberra P.R.3, at Luqa. C.O. W/C R. L. Wade. Canberra P.R.9.

No. 40 'Abingdon' Squadron

Formed 26 Feb. 1916, at Gosport. Aug. 1916, first unit to receive F.E.8. 2 Aug. 1916, 'A' Flt. to France. 25 Aug. 1916, 'B' and 'C' Flts. to France, with Nieuport 17C-1. 1917, Nieuport 23, 27. Oct. 1917, S.E.5,

S.E.5a. Oct. 1918, fighter unit at Bryas. Disbanded Feb. 1919. Reformed 1 April, 1931, at Upper Heyford and was first to receive Gordon. C.O. S/L Taylor. 1933, at Abingdon. C.O. F/L C. N. H. Bilney. 1936, Hind. 1938, Battle 1 (OX-). 1939, Blenheim 4L (OX-, BL-). Dec. 1940, Wellington B.1c, B.2, B.3 (BL-). 1944, Liberator B.6 (BL-). 1945, Lancaster B.7(F.E.) (BL-). 1946, York C.1 (LE-, MOWA-). Disbanded March, 1947. Reformed Jan. 1948, with York C.1. Disbanded 1950. 1953 reformed with Canberra B.2. 1955, C.O. S/L K. B. Rogers. At Wittering. 1957, at Upwood and combined with No. 50 Squadron as No. 40/50 Squadron. C.O. W/C E. P. London.

No. 41 Squadron

Formed 14 July, 1916, at Gosport, receiving F.E.8 for scouting. Proceeded to France 15 Oct. 1916, and re-equipped July, 1917, with D.H.5. Nov. 1917, S.E.5a. 4 July, 1918, Capt. W. G. Claxton shot down 6 E/A in one day. Oct. 1918, as fighter unit at Droglandt South. Destroyed 124 hostile aircraft and sent 112 down out of control. Later to Tangmere, disbanding Dec. 1919, at Croydon. Reformed 1 April, 1923, as a fighter squadron at Northolt with Snipes. 1923, Grebe. May, 1924, first unit to fly Siskin 3. 1928, Siskin 3a and Dual Siskin. C.O. S/L R.S. Atkin. Sept. 1931, Bulldog 2a. July, 1934, Demon 2 (PN-). C.O. S/L J. A. Boret. Oct. 1935, left Northolt for Catterick. Oct. 1937, Fury 2. Dec. 1939, Spitfire F.1, F.2 (EB-). Aug. 1940, at Hornchurch. 1941, Manston with Spitfire F.5a, F.5b (EB-). Later at Hornchurch. 1943, Spitfire F.2a, F.12, F.14, L.F.16e (EB-, PN-). Destroyed 53 V.1s. Stationed on Continent. Destroyed 200 enemy aircraft, together with 170 probables. 1946, Tempest F.5 (XC-). Disbanded 1 April, 1946, and renumbered No. 26 Squadron. Reformed 1947, with Spitfire F.21 (EB-). First fighter squadron to revive coloured markings after the war. 1947, at Church Fenton with Hornet F.1, F.3 (EB-). 1951, to Biggin Hill. Meteor F.8. Oxford T.2, Harvard T.2b used for training. C.O. S/L Miller. 1954, Meteor T.7. C.O. S/L M. Scannell. Vampire T.11. 1955, Hunter F.5. C.O. S/L J. Castagnola. Disbanded 16 Jan. 1958, and number taken over by No. 141 Squadron. Reformed 16 Jan. 1958, at Coltishall with Javelin FAW.4. Javelin FAW.5, FAW.8.

No. 42 Squadron

Formed 1 April, 1916, at Filton from part of No. 19 Squadron with B.E.2c, B.E.2d, B.E.2e. To France 8 Aug. 1916, artillery observation from Rely, Asoq. In Belgium, then to Italy on 17 Nov. 1917, with R.E.8s received May, 1917. 7 Dec. 1917, at Istrana. Returned to France, March, 1918, and in Oct. was at Crocques. Disbanded 26 June, 1919, at Netheravon. Reformed 14 Dec. 1936, at Donibristle as torpedo unit with Vildebeest 1 and 3. 1937, at Thorney Island with Vildebeest

4 (QD-, AW-). 1940, Beaufort G.R.1 (AW-), Anson 1 (AW-). At Bircham Newton and North Coates. 1942, Beaufort G.R.2 (AW-) at Leuchars. Jan. 1943, in Colombo with Blenheim 1L, 4L, 5d (AW-). Disbanded and reformed in Burma, Aug. 1943, with Hurricane F.B.2c (AW-). 1944, Thunderbolt F.B.2 (AW-). Disbanded Dec. 1945. Reformed Oct. 1946, at Thorney Island from No. 254 Squadron with Beaufighter T.F.10 (QM-). Oct. 1946, Brigand T.F.1. 1947, Brigand B.1. Disbanded and reformed June, 1952, with Shackleton M.R.1, M.R.2. C.O. S/L D. H. Sutton. 1967, Shackleton M.R.3.

No. 43 'China-British' Squadron

Formed 15 April, 1916, at Stirling with B.E.2c, Avro 504. June, 1916, Netheravon. Dec. 1916, at Northolt for Home Defence. Jan. 1917, One-and-a-half Strutter. 17 Jan. 1917, to France. Sept. 1917, Camel F.1. Sept. 1918, Snipe. Oct. 1918, fighter at Senlis. 24 March, 1918, Capt. J. W. Trollope shot down 6 E/A in one day; Capt. H. W. Woollett did the same on 12 April, 1918. Dec. 1918, to Bickendorf with Army of Occupation. Disbanded 31 Dec. 1919, at Spittlegate. Reformed 1 July, 1925, at Henlow with Snipe. 1926, Gamecock 1. 1928, Siskin 3a and Dual Siskin. C.O. S/L C. N. Lowe. May, 1931, first to fly Fury 1. 1935, at Tangmere. C.O. S/L A. M. Wray. 1940, Hurricane F.1, F.2 (NQ-, FT-). Feb. 1940, at Wick. Aug. 1940, at Tangmere. 1942, Havoc 1 Turbinlite (Hunter). 1942, Spitfire F.5b, F.8, F.9 (FT-). In North Africa and Italy. Disbanded 16 May, 1947. Reformed 11 Feb. 1949, from No. 266 Squadron. Vampire F.3. 1951, Meteor F.4, T.7. 1951, Meteor F.8. C.O. S/L H. R. Allen. 1952, at Tangmere. C.O. S/L E. M. Higson. July, 1954, at Leuchars. 31 July, 1954, first unit to fly Hunter F.1. C.O. S/L R. E. Lelong. 1956, Hunter F.4. 1959, Hunter F.G.A.9.

No. 44 'Rhodesia' Squadron

Formed 24 July, 1917, at Hainault Farm for Home Defence with One-and-a-half Strutter. Aug. 1917, first Home Defence unit to use Camel F.1. C.O. Maj. G. W. Murlis-Green. Disbanded 31 Dec. 1919. Reformed 8 Aug. 1937, with Hind at Wyton. Aug. 1937, at Waddington with Blenheim 1L (JW-). 1940, Hampden B.1 (KM-), Manchester B.1. Sept. 1941, Lancaster B.1 received for familiarization. Jan. 1942, became first squadron to receive Lancaster B.1, B.3 (KM-) at Waddington. First operation in March, 1942. V.C. won by S/L J. D. Nettleton on 17 April, 1942. 1943, at Dunholme Lodge. July, 1944, at Spilsby. Lancaster B.1 (F.E.). 1945, Lincoln B.2 (KM-). 1952, Washington B.1. 1954, Canberra B.2, T.4. 1955, at Honington. C.O. S/L Barling. Disbanded July, 1957. 1960, reformed from No. 83 Squadron with Vulcan B.1.

No. 45 Squadron

Formed 1 March, 1916, at Gosport, receiving six Avro 504 on 30 March, 1916. 1916, One-and-a-half Strutter. 12 Oct. 1916, to France. C.O. Capt. L. A. Strange. April, 1917, Nieuport 2-seater. 25 July, 1917, Camel F.1. Second R.F.C. unit to fly Camel. To Italy 17 Nov. 1917. Ceased to operate in Italy 12 Sept. 1918. To Independent Force on 22 Sept. 1918. Re-equipped with Snipe. Oct. 1918, fighter at Battoncourt. Disbanded 31 Dec. 1919. Reformed 1 April, 1921, at Suez with Vimy. In Mesopotamia. Nov. 1922, first to operate Vernon. 1924, at Kirkuk. C.O. S/L R. Hill. 1926, Victoria. 1927, operating Cairo-Baghdad airmail route. 1927, D.H.9a. 1928, at Helwan, Egypt. 1929, Fairey 3f. 1934, Gordon. 1935, Vincent. 1938, Wellesley 2 (DD–). 1938, Blenheim 1L (OB–). 1940, Blenheim 4L (OB–) in Egypt. 1942, Vengeance. 1944, using Mosquito F.B.6 (OB–) from No. 47 Squadron in Burma. 1945, Brigand B.1 (OB–). 1953, in Malaya with Hornet F.4 (OB–). 1955, absorbed No. 33 Squadron. 1955, at Tengah with Buckmaster T.1 (OB–), Beaufighter T.F.10, Brigand Met. 3. C.O. S/L V. K. Jacobs. Venom F.B.4. Disbanded 1957. Reformed 1 Nov. 1957, at Coningsby with Canberra B.2. 1958, to Tengah. 1967, Canberra B.15.

No. 46 'Uganda' Squadron

Formed 19 April, 1916, with Nieuport 2-seater. 26 Oct. 1916, to France. May, 1917, Pup. 10 July, 1917, to Sutton's Farm for Home Defence. Returned to France 30 Aug. 1917. Nov. 1917, Camel F.1. Oct. 1918, fighter at Athies. Disbanded 31 Dec. 1919. Reformed 3 Sept. 1936, at Kenley with Gauntlet 2. C.O. S/L Barwell. 16 Nov. 1937, to Digby. 1938, Gladiator 1, 2 (RJ–). 1939, Hurricane F.1 (RJ–, PO–). 26 May, 1940, until 7 June, 1940, operated from Bardufoss, Norway. Aug. 1940, at Digby, Hurricane F.2c (PO–). 1942, night-fighting with Beaufighter N.F.1c, N.F.6c (FH–). 1945, transport with Stirling C.5 (XK–), Dakota C.4 (XK–, OFG–, MOFG–). Disbanded then reformed as night-fighter unit. 1955, Meteor N.F.12, N.F.14. At Odiham. C.O. W/C F. E. W. Birchfield. Feb. 1956, Javelin FAW.1—first unit to receive Javelin. C.O. W/C H. E. White. 1957, Javelin FAW.2. 1959, Javelin T.3. C.O. W/C F. Sowrey. At Waterbeach. Javelin FAW.6. Disbanded 1961. Reformed 1967 at Abingdon as transport squadron with Andover C.1.—first unit.

No. 47 Squadron

Formed 1 March, 1916, at Beverley for Home Defence of Hull. Used F.K.8, F.K.3, Bristol Scout D (1 flight). 20 Sept. 1916, to Salonika. Bristol M.1c, Vickers Bullet, B.E.12, B.E. 12a, D.H.2, B.E.2e. At Mikra Bay, Yanesh, Snevche. Feb. 1918, received four S.E.5a. April, 1918, one flight of D.H.9. Oct. 1918, day-bomber at Hasdarli. July, 1919, reformed in England with one flight each of D.H.9, D.H.9a, Camel. The squadron sent a detachment to South Russia from May, 1919, until 1920, which operated from Novorossisk. 1 Feb. 1920, No. 206 Squadron renumbered No. 47 Squadron at Helwan, Egypt, with D.H.9a. June, 1921, flew the airmail route from Cairo to Baghdad. May, 1924, redesignated as a bomber squadron. 30 March, 1927, until May, 1927, four aircraft commanded by Air Comm. C. R. Samson flew Cairo-Cape-Cairo. Dec. 1927, Fairey 3f at Khartoum (first unit). 1934, Gordon (both landplane and on floats). 1937, Vincent. 3f also used on floats. Aug. 1939, Wellesley 2 (KH-, EW-), Vincent (one flight). 1940, at Erkoweit. Feb. 1941, at Buamed. April, 1941, at Agondat. 16 April, 1942, No. 47 Squadron Echelon Flight formed from one Wellesley flight and disbanded Feb. 1943. Sept. 1942, at Shandur with Beaufort G.R.1 for anti-submarine patrols. Blenheim 4 and 5d (KU-) also used. 1943, operating with one flight of Wellesley 2 (KU-), Maryland B.1 (KU-). June, 1943, Beaufighter T.F.1c, T.F.6c, T.F.10, T.F.11c anti-shipping strikes from Gambut. Sept. 1943, at Protville. C.O. W/C J. A. Lee-Evans. April, 1944, Madras. Oct. 1944, Mosquito F.B.6, Boston, Beaufighter. 1945, detachment to Java. Aug. 1945, completely re-equipped Mosquito F.B.6. Disbanded 21 March, 1946, in U.K. Reformed 1 Sept. 1946, as transport unit at Gastina from No. 644 Squadron with Halifax A.9 (MOHD-). C.O. W/C W. H. Ingle. Sept. 1946, to Fairford. 19 Sept. 1948, to Dishforth to become first unit with Hastings C.1, C.4. 1 Nov. 1948, on Berlin airlift. At Abingdon 1953. 12 March, 1956, first to receive Beverley C.1 (12). C.O. S/L D. P. Boulnois.

No. 48 Squadron

Formed 15 April, 1916. First unit to fly Bristol F2a. Received eighteen F2bs in March, 1917, proceeding to Flez, France, 8 March, 1917. Oct. 1918, at St. Marie Cappel as fighter squadron. 1919, to India. Disbanded 1 April, 1920, and renumbered as No. 5 Squadron at Quetta. Reformed 10 Feb. 1936, at Manston for general reconnaissance with Cloud. First unit to use Anson G.R.1 (ZW-, XZ-). C.O. S/L T. A. Langford Sainsbury. 1941, Hudson G.R.1, G.R.2, G.R.3, G.R.4, G.R.5 (ZS-, XZ-, OY-). 1942, Beaufort G.R.1 (XZ-, OY-). Engaged on anti-submarine patrols. Aug. 1945, flew to India for transport with Dakota. 15 Feb. 1946, renumbered from No. 215 Squadron at Singapore for transport with Dakota C.1, C.3, C.4 (I2-, ODR-), Stirling C.5 (I2-). 1953, Valetta C.1 at Kuala Lumpur. C.O. S/L B. V. Kerwin. Aug. 1957, Hastings C.1 at Changi.

No. 49 'Sheffield' Squadron

Formed 16 April, 1916, at Dover. R.E.7. 12 Nov. 1917, to la Bellevue, France, with D.H.4 for day-bombing. July, 1918, D.H.9. Oct. 1918, at

Beauvais. 18 July, 1919, disbanded. Reformed 10 Feb. 1936, at Bircham Newton from 'C' Flt. of No. 18 Squadron with Hinds. Later at Scampton. Sept. 1938, first to receive Hampden B.1 (XV-, EA-). April, 1942, Manchester B.1 (EA-) at Fulbeck. July, 1942, Lancaster B.1 (EA-). 1943, Fiskerton. 1944, Balderston. 1944, Lancaster B.3, B.1(F.E.) (EA-). March, 1945, at Fulbeck. July, 1945, at Mepal. 1953, Lincoln B.2 (EA-). C.O. S/L A. E. Newitt. Nov. 1953, to Kenya for anti-Mau Mau operations. Disbanded Aug. 1955. May, 1956, Valiant BK.1. At Marham.

No. 50 Squadron

Formed 15 May, 1916, at Dover for Home Defence with B.E.2c, B.E.2e, B.E.12, B.E.12a, Vickers Bullet. Dec. 1916, H.Q. at Harrietsham, with flights at Dover, Bekesbourne, Throwley. 1917, R.E.8, F.K.8, Pup, B.E. 12b, S.E.5. 1918, Camel. Oct. 1918, night-fighter from Canterbury. Disbanded 13 June, 1919. Reformed 3 May, 1937, at Waddington with Hind. 1940, Hampden B.1 (QX-, VN-). 1942, Manchester B.1a (VN-). July, 1942, Lancaster B.1, B.3 (VN-). At Skellingthorpe. 1947, Lincoln B.2 (VN-) at Waddington. Disbanded 31 Jan. 1951. Reformed Aug. 1952, Canberra B.2. 1957, combined with No. 40 Squadron as No. 40/50 Squadron at Upwood. C.O. W/C E. P. Landon. 1961, at Waddington with Vulcan B.1. 1966, Vulcan B.2.

No. 51 'York' Squadron

Formed 15 May, 1916, at Thetford for Home Defence. H.Q. at Hingham, with flights at Marham, Mattishall and Roudham. Later at Tydd St. Mary. Used, in 1916, B.E.2c, B.E.12, F.E.2b, B.E.2d, G-100 Elephant, B.E.12b. 1918, Avro 504, D.H.4, F2b, F.E.2d. Disbanded 13 June, 1919, at Sutton's Farm. Reformed 15 March, 1937, at Boscombe Down with Anson 1. 1937, Whitley B.1, B.4 (VT-) at Linton-on-Ouse. 1939, at Driffield. Whitley B.5 (MH-), B.3 (UT-). Carried out leaflet raids over Germany and first raid by Bomber Command in conjunction with No. 58 Squadron. C.O.W/C P. C. Pickard. 1941, Halifax B.1. At Dishforth. 1943, at Snaith with Halifax B.2/1a (MH-, LK-). 1944, Halifax B.3 (MH-, C6-), Stirling C.5 (TB-). 1946, transport at Waterbeach with York C.1 (TB-, OYA, MOYA-, MH-). 1959, renumbered from No. 192 Squadron at Watton with Canberra B.2. 1967, Comet C.2.

No. 52 Squadron

Formed 15 May, 1916, with B.E.2c. 21 Nov. 1916, to France from Hounslow with R.E.8, being first unit to use the type. Received eighteen B.E.2e on 9 May, 1917, after R.E.8s had been sent to No. 34 Squadron. Oct. 1918, artillery observation from Savy. Disbanded Oct. 1919. Re-

C

formed 18 Jan. 1937, with Hart. Later used Audax and Hind. 1937, Battle I (MB–) at Upwood. 1939, Anson. Disbanded 1940. Reformed July, 1941. Aug. 1942, Blenheim 1L, 4L (ZE–). Feb. 1943, Baltimore B.3, Audax 1. 1943, reformed from 'C' Flt. of No. 353 Squadron with Dakota C.3, C.4 (ODW–). 1953, at Changi with Valetta C.1 in Far East Transport Wing. Oct. 1960, at Butterworth. 1967, at Seletar for transport with Andover C.1.

No. 53 Squadron

Formed 15 May, 1916, with Avro 504, F.K.8. Dec. 1916, B.E.2e. 1 Jan. 1917, to France. Feb. 1917, R.E.8, B.E.2c. Oct. 1918, artillery observation from Abeele. Disbanded 25 Oct. 1919. Reformed 28 June, 1937, at Farnborough for army co-operation with Hector. 1939, Blenheim 4f (TE–, PZ–). Aug. 1941, Hudson G.R.3 (TE–), G.R.5 (PZ–). Feb. 1943, Whitley B.3 (TE–). 1944, Liberator G.R.5, G.R.6, C.6, C.8 (FH–) at St. Eval. Disbanded 15 June, 1946. Reformed 1946, with Dakota C.4 (PU–, ODT–, MODB–). 1953, Hastings C.1. C.O. S/L B. H. Worts. Feb. 1957, Beverley C.1—second squadron to equip. 20 Jan. 1966, received Belfast C.1 at Brize Norton.

No. 54 Squadron

Formed 15 May, 1916, at Castle Bromwich. 24 Dec. 1916, first squadron to proceed to France with Pup. Dec. 1917, Camel F.1. Oct. 1918, fighter at Avesnes. Disbanded 25 Oct. 1919, at Yatesbury. Reformed 15 Jan. 1930, at Hornchurch using Siskin 3a. 1930, Bulldog 2a. 1935, C.O. S/L G. D. Daly. 1937, Gauntlet 2. 1938, Gladiator. 1939, Spitfire F.1, F.2a (DL–, KL–). 1941, Spitfire F.5 (KL–). 1942, in Australia. 1944, Spitfire F.8, F.9. 1944, Typhoon F.1b (HF–). 1946, Tempest F.2 (HF–). Jan. 1947, renumbered from No. 130 Squadron with Vampire F.3. In 1948, made the first crossing of the Atlantic by jet aircraft. 1950, Vampire F.5. 1953, Meteor F.8 at Tangmere. May, 1955, at Odiham with Hunter F.1. Sept. 1955, Hunter F.4. 1957, Hunter F.6. 1960, at Stradishall. Hunter F.G.A.9.

No. 55 Squadron

Formed 27 April, 1916, as training squadron at Castle Bromwich. March, 1917, first to receive D.H.4. 6 March, 1917, to France. 11 Oct. 1917, attached to 41st Wing, Independent Air Force. 1918, D.H. 9, D.H.9a. Oct. 1918, day-bomber from Ajelot. July, 1919, to Constantinople. Then to Renfrew, disbanding 22 Jan. 1920, at Shotwick. Reformed 1 Feb. 1920, at Suez from No. 142 Squadron with D.H.9a. Stationed throughout 1920s Mesopotamia, Turkey, Basrah, Mosul, Hinaidi, Kirkuk, Baghdad. 1930, at Hinaidi with Wapiti 2a. 1938, Vincent at Dhibban and Habbaniya. July, 1940, in North Africa. 1941,

Blenheim 1L, 4L (GM–). 1942, Baltimore B.3, B.4, B.5. 1943, Boston
B.4, B.5. 1946, Baltimore B.3a. 1946, Mosquito F.B.26. Reformed Sept.
1960, Victor B.1, B.1a.

No. 56 'Punjab' Squadron

Formed 8 June, 1916, at Gosport from part of No. 28 Home Defence
Squadron. C.O. Maj. E. L. Gossage. 7 Aug. 1916, B.E.2c, B.E.2e,
B.E.12, Curtiss J, Bristol Scout D, One-and-a-half Strutter. 1917, at
London Colney. 13 March, 1917, received twelve S.E.5. 8 April, 1917,
to France under Maj. R. G. Blomfield, appointed C.O. 6 Feb. 1917.
Later used S.E.5a and one R.E.8. 20 April, 1917, returned to England
at Bekesbourne for Home Defence until 7 July, 1917. Crossed to
France again and destroyed a total of 395 E/A and 6 balloons. V.C.s
won by Capt. A. Ball on 8 June, 1917, and Maj. J. T. B. McCudden on
2 April, 1918. C.O. Maj. G. Maxwell. Oct. 1918, fighter at Valheureux.
March, 1919, at Bircham Newton. Disbanded 22 Jan. 1920. Reformed
1 Feb. 1920, from No. 80 Squadron in Egypt with Snipe. Disbanded
23 Sept. 1922, and one flight sent to Dardanelles in Oct. 1922. Reformed 1 Nov. 1922, at Hawkinge for Home Defence with Snipe. May,
1923, to Biggin Hill. Sept. 1924, Grebe. C.O. 1923-25, S/L C. J. Quin-
tin Brand. Also used 2-seater Grebe. 1928, Gamecock 1. Sept. 1927,
Siskin 3a and Dual Siskin. Dec. 1927, to North Weald. 1931, Bulldog 2a.
1935, C.O. F/L J. W. Colquhoun. May, 1936, Gauntlet 2. C.O. S/L
Lea-Cox. July, 1937, Gladiator. June, 1938, Hurricane F.1 (LR–).
1940, Hurricane F.2a (LR–, US–). Aug. 1940, at Rochford. Sept. 1941,
first to receive Typhoon F.1a, F.1b (US–) at Duxford. 1944, Spitfire
L.F.9b (US–) on weather-reconnaissance and air-sea rescue. 1944,
Tempest F.5, F.6 (US–). 1945, Tempest F.2. Destroyed 149 enemy aircraft. Disbanded 31 March, 1946, at Fassberg and became No. 16
Squadron. Reformed 1 April, 1946, by renumbering No. 124 Squadron
at Bentwaters with Meteor F.3 (US–, ON–), F.4 (US–). 10 May, 1950,
to Waterbeach. 1952, Meteor F.8, T.7. 20 Feb. 1954, only squadron to
receive Swift F.1, F.2. C.O. S/L C. J. Storey. May, 1955, Hunter F.5,
Vampire T.11. Dec. 1955. C.O. Maj. J. E. H. Kaisin on exchange posting from Belgian Air Force. 1958, Hunter F.6. 1960, Lightning F.1 at
Wattisham—second squadron. C.O. S/L J. R. Rogers. 1961, Lightning
F.1A, T.4. 1966, Lightning F.3.

No. 57 'Cheltenham' Squadron

Formed 8 June, 1916, at Copmanthorpe from a flight of No. 33 Squad-
ron for high-altitude reconnaissance. To France 16 Dec. 1916, with
F.E.2d for fighter-reconnaissance. May, 1917, D.H.4 for day-bombing.
Destroyed 166 E/A. Oct. 1918, at Vert Galand. Disbanded 31 Dec. 1919.
Reformed 20 Oct. 1931, at Netheravon with Hart. C.O. S/L H. G.

Bowen. 1933, at Upper Heyford. 1936, Hind. 1939, Blenheim 1L, 4 (EQ-, DX-). In France with Battle 1 (QT-). 1940, Wellington B.1c, B.3. (EQ-, DX-). 1941, Manchester 1a (QT-). 1942, Lancaster B.1, B.3, B.7 (DX-). Aug. 1943, at East Kirby. Engaged in bombing of Ruhr. 25 April, 1945, bombed Berchtesgaden. Sept. 1945, at Waddington with Lincoln B.1, B.2 (DX-). Disbanded 25 Nov. 1945. Reformed 26 Nov. 1945, from No. 103 Squadron with Lincoln. 1946, at Lindholm. May, 1951, Washington B.1. May, 1954, at Cottesmore with Canberra B.2, T.4. C.O. S/L I. G. Broom, Sept. 1955, at Honington. C.O. S/L Rothwell. 1960, Victor B.1. C.O. W/C Dudley. Victor B.1A.

No. 58 Squadron

Formed 10 Jan. 1916, at Cramlington from No. 36 Squadron for training. 1916, F.E.2b. 10 Jan. 1918, to St. Omer for night-bombing. Sept. 1918, O/400 at Alquines. 2 July, 1919, to Cairo. July, 1919, first to receive Vimy. Disbanded 1 Feb. 1920, and became No. 70 Squadron at Suez for communications. Reformed 1 April, 1924, at Worthy Down. Bugle 1 and 2 for service trials. Equipped with Virginia X. 1927, C.O. S/L O. R. Gayford. Oct. 1937, Anson G.R.1 at Boscombe Down. 1938, Whitley B.1, B.3 (BW-). 1939, first over Germany with No. 51 Squadron. Engaged in leaflet dropping. 1942, Whitley B.4, B.5, G.R.7 (GE-), Dec. 1942, Halifax B.2/1a, B.3a (BY-). 1944, Halifax G.R.5/1a, G.R.6, A.7 on meteorological-reconnaissance. Disbanded 25 May, 1945. Reformed 1946, for photo-reconnaissance with Mosquito P.R.19, P.R.34, T.3 (OT-). At Benson and engaged in mapping. Also used Anson C.19/1, C.19/2 (OT-). 1952, Mosquito P.R.35. 1955, at Wyton with Canberra P.R.7. Canberra P.R.9.

No. 59 Squadron

Formed 1 Aug. 1916, at Narborough, for artillery observation with R.E.8. 23 Feb. 1917, to Vert Galand, France. Oct. 1918, at Beugnatre. Disbanded 4 Aug. 1919. Reformed 28 June, 1937, at Old Sarum with Hector. 1938, Lysander 1 (PZ-) for army co-operation. 1939, Blenheim 4, 1f (TR-, PJ-). 1941, anti-shipping with Hudson G.R.3 (TR-). Aug. 1942, first unit with Fortress G.R.2. May, 1943, Liberator G.R.5, C.6 (TR-, WE-). 1943, Halifax G.R.2/1a, G.R.5/1a (BY-). 1945, Liberator C.8, G.R.3, G.R.7 (WE-, BY-). Later transport with York C.1 (OYR-, MOWB-, MOYD-, BY-). Disbanded and reformed with Hastings C.1. 20 Aug. 1956, at Gütersloh, Germany, renumbered from No. 102 Squadron with Canberra B.2. 1958, at Geilenkirchen with Canberra B.(I)8. 4 Jan. 1961, became No. 3 Squadron at Geilenkirchen with Canberra B.(I)8.

No. 60 Squadron

Formed 30 April, 1916, at Gosport and went to France 28 May, 1916.

In July, 1916, had two flights Morane Bullets (9), one flight Morane Biplanes (4). Also used Morane Parasol. Aug. 1916, Nieuport 17C-1. 1917, received one Spad S-7 C.1. At Izel-le-Hameau, Savy, Quievy. Col. W. A. Bishop, V.C., 72 victories, served with the squadron. July, 1917, S.E.5, S.E.5a. Oct. 1918, fighter at Baizieux. Squadron shot down 274 enemy aircraft. Disbanded 22 Jan. 1920, at Bircham Newton. Reformed 1 April, 1920, at Lahore from No. 97 Squadron. Used D.H.10 Amiens, D.H.9a. At Risalpur. 1924, at Kirkuk. 1928, Kohat. 1928, Wapiti 2a. 1936, at Kohat with Hart 2 (AD-). 1939, Blenheim 1f (MU-), at Mingaladon. 1941, one flight Buffalo 1 (MU-) at Kuantan, together with Blenheim 1f. 1942, Blenheim 4f (MU-) at Asansol. 1942, Hurricane F.2c (MU-). 1945, Thunderbolt F.B.2 (MU-), Spitfire F.R.14e, F.R.18 (MU-) at Kemajoran, Tengah. 1951, last unit to fly Spitfire— F.R.18—on operations. In Malaya, with one flight at Kai Tak. 1953, Vampire, F.B.5. Jan. 1955, at Tengah. C.O. S/L A. D. C. Webbe. 1955, Venom F.B.1, F.B.4. 1960, Meteor N.F.14. 1961, Javelin FAW.9. At Tengah.

No. 61 'Lincoln' Squadron

Formed 2 Aug. 1917, at Rochford for Home Defence with sixteen Pups. 1918, received twenty-four S.E.5s and also used Camels. Operated from Rochford and disbanded there in 1919. Reformed 8 March, 1937, at Hemswell with Hind. Also received Audax, Anson and Blenheim 1L (LS-). 1940, Hampden B.1 (LS-, QR-). 1941, Manchester B.1a (QR-). July 1942, Lancaster B.1, B.2, B.3, B.10 (QR-). At Yerston. Oct. 1942, Skellingthorpe. 1944, Coningsby. V.C. won by F/L W. Reid on 3 Nov. 1943. 1947, at Waddington with Lincoln B.2 (QR-). 1954, in Kenya on anti-Mau Mau operations. Reformed Dec. 1954, at Wittering with Canberra B.2. C.O. S/L J. H. Gaston. 1956, at Upwood. Disbanded 1958, reformed with Vulcan B.1.

No. 62 'Northampton' Squadron

Formed 8 Aug. 1916, at Filton with B.E.2c. May, 1917, re-equipped with F2b and went to France as a fighter-bomber unit on 23 Jan. 1918. Oct. 1918, at Bellevue. Disbanded 31 July, 1919. Reformed 12 April, 1937, from 'B' Flight of No. 40 Squadron, with Hind. 1937, Blenheim 1L (JO-) at Cranfield. Sept. 1939, in Far East. April, 1942, renumbered from No. 139 Squadron at Akyab. June, 1942, Hudson G.R.3, Vengeance. Engaged on reconnaissance and bombing. Sept. 1943, Dakota C.3, C.4 (OFB-, ODE-, MODC-, MOFC-) for transport and supply-dropping in India and Burma.

No. 63 Squadron

Formed 31 Aug. 1916, at Stirling with B.E.2d, G-100 Elephant, Bristol

Scout D. 13 Aug. 1917, at Basra with R.E.8 for reconnaissance. 1917, D.H.4. 1918, Spad S-7 C.1. Oct. 1918, at Samarra and Tikrit. Feb. 1919, one flight at Kazvin until disbanding of squadron on 29 Feb. 1920. Aug. 1920, one flight again sent to Kazvin until March, 1921. Reformed 15 Feb. 1937, at Upwood from 'B' Flight of No. 12 Squadron with Hind 1, Audax. 1937, Battle 1 (ON-, NE-), with Anson (NE-) for training. June, 1942, Mustang F.1 (NE-, UB-) for army co-operation. April, 1944, Hurricane F.2c (UB-). May, 1944, Spitfire LF.5b, L.F. 16e (FJ-, UB-). Disbanded 1945. Reformed Jan. 1946, Spitfire L.F.16e (UB-). Re-equipped with Meteor F.3, F.4, T.7 (UB-). 1952, Meteor F.8 at Waterbeach. C.O. Jan. 1954, S/L F. W. Doherty. Vampire T.11. June, 1955, detached to Culdrose. 1957, Hunter F.6 at Waterbeach. C.O. S/L S. Walker.

No. 64 Squadron

Formed 1 Aug. 1916, at Sedgeford. June, 1917, D.H.5. To France 15 Oct. 1917. Jan. 1918, S.E.5a. Oct. 1918, fighter at le Hameau and Aniche. Disbanded 31 Dec. 1919. Reformed 1 March, 1936, at Heliopolis with Demon and Hart (T). Later at Martlesham and Church Fenton. 1939, at Gatwick with Blenheim 1f (XQ-, GR-, SH-). 1940, Spitfire F.1 (GR-) at Croydon, Kenley, Coltishall. 1941, Spitfire F.2a, F.5b (GR-, SH-) at Hornchurch. C.O. S/L J. Rankin. 1943, Spitfire F.9 (SH-). 1944, at Coltishall with Mustang F.1, F.3, F.B.4 (SH-). May, 1946, first squadron to fly Hornet F.1, F.3 (SH-). At Horsham St. Faith, Church Fenton, Linton-on-Ouse. Mosquito T.3 (SH-). 1952, at Duxford with Meteor F.8, T.7. C.O. S/L H. Bennett. 1957, night-fighting with Meteor N.F.14. 1958, Javelin FAW.7 at Duxford. Javelin FAW.9. 1966, Lighting F.3.

No. 65 'East India' Squadron

Formed 1 Aug. 1916, at Wyton. Used G.-W. Type 15 for training. Went to France 27 Oct. 1917, with Camel F.1 and Avro 504. C.O. Capt. E. R. L. Corballis. Oct. 1918, fighter at Petite Synthe. Disbanded 25 Oct. 1919, at Yatesbury. Reformed 1 Aug. 1934, at Hornchurch with Demon. C.O. S/L F. O. Soden. Dec. 1936, Gauntlet. C.O. S/L C. F. H. Grace. Dec. 1937, Gladiator. C.O. S/L D. Cooke. March, 1939, Spitfire F.1 (YT-, FZ-). 1940, Spitfire F.2a (YT-, FZ-). Sept. 1940, at Turnhouse. 1941, Spitfire L.F. 5b (YT-, FZ-) at Tangmere. Training and resting at Debden until Feb. 1942. Training Oct. 1942, until May, 1943, then to Fairlop. 1943, Spitfire F.9b (YT-). 1944, Spitfire F.14 (DW-). 25 June, 1944, to Normandy. Aug. 1944, Belgium. Sept. 1944, to England. 1944, Mustang F.3 (YT-). Jan. 1945, to Peterhead. April, 1945, Mustang F.B.4 (YT-). 1946, Spitfire L.F.16e (YT-). 1947, at Church Fenton with Hornet F.1, F.3 (YT-), Mosquito T.3 (YT-) as daylight low-level in-

truder. 1948, Acklington. 1952, day-fighter at Duxford with Meteor F.8.
C.O. S/L V. R. L. Evans. 1957, Hunter F.6. At Duxford.

No. 66 Squadron

Formed 30 June, 1916, at Filton. 6 March, 1917, Pup. 17 March, 1917,
to France. 21 June, 1917, until 6 July, 1917, at Calais on Home Defence while No. 56 Squadron was in England on similar duties. Oct.
1917, Camel F.1. 22 Nov. 1917, to Italy. 30 March, 1918, V.C. won by
Lt. A. Jerrard. Oct. 1918, fighter-bomber at St. Pietro-in-Gu. Disbanded 25 Oct. 1919. Reformed 20 July, 1936, at Duxford with Gauntlet 2. Dec. 1939, Spitfire F.1 (RB-). 1940, Spitfire F.2, F.2a (LZ-) at
Coltishall. 1942, Spitfire F5b (LZ-). Nov. 1943, Spitfire F.9 (LZ-).
Nov. 1944, Spitfire L.F. 16e (LZ-). 1944, Mustang F.3 (LZ-). Dis-
banded April, 1945. Reformed Sept. 1946, Meteor F.3 (HI-, LZ-).
1951, Meteor F.4, T.7 (HI-, LZ-). 1951, Meteor F.8 at West Raynham.
Dec. 1953, Sabre F.4 at Linton-on-Ouse. 1956, Hunter F.4, F.5. 1957,
Hunter F.6. 1958, at Acklington. 1959, C.O. S/L P. Bairsto. Hunter
FGA.9. 15 Sept. 1961, Belvedere H.C.1—first unit—at Odiham. C.O.
S/L J. R. Dowling.

No. 67 Squadron

Formed June, 1916, at Heliopolis, as No. 1 Squadron, Australian Flying
Corps. B.E.2c, B.E.2e, B.E.12a, R.E.8, G–100 Elephant, D.H.6, Avro
504k, Bristol Scout D. Sept. 1916, became No. 67 (Australian) Squadron.
Served in Palestine. On 6 Feb. 1918, became No. 1 Squadron, Australian
Flying Corps. 1918, F2b. Also received one O/400. V.C. won by Lt. F. H.
McNamara on 20 March, 1917. Reformed March, 1941, with Buffalo
F.1 (RD-). 1942, Hurricane F.1, F.2, F.4 (DR-). Feb. 1944, Spitfire
F.8 (RD-). Disbanded Aug. 1945. Reformed in 2nd T.A.F. with Vampire
F.B.5. May, 1953, became first to use Sabre F.4. 1956, Hunter F.4.

No. 68 Squadron

Formed Oct. 1916, at Heliopolis with Australian personnel. To France
21 Sept. 1917, flying D.H.5. Jan. 1918, S.E.5a. On 19 Jan. 1918,
became No. 2 Squadron, Australian Flying Corps. Reformed Jan. 1941,
for night-fighting with Blenheim 1f (WM-). C.O. G/C Hon. M. Aitken.
May, 1941, Beaufighter N.F.1f (WM-). 1943, Beaufighter N.F.6f
(WM-). July, 1944, Mosquito N.F.13, N.F.17, N.F.19 (WM-). 1945,
Mosquito N.F.30, N.F.36 (WM-), Oxford T.2 (WM-). Disbanded
April, 1945. Reformed 1950 in 2nd T.A.F. at Wahn, Germany, for
night-fighting with Meteor N.F.11, T.7. 1955, C.O. W/C E. James.
1958, Javelin FAW.6. In 2nd T.A.F. 1959, became No. 5 Squadron.

No. 69 Squadron

Formed Sept. 1916, in Egypt and went to France on 9 Sept. 1917, with

R.E.8. Stationed at Savy. On 19 Jan. 1918, became No. 3 Squadron, Australian Flying Corps. Reformed Jan. 1941, from No. 431 G.R. Flt. at Malta with Maryland B.1 (G5–), Baltimore B.3, Hurricane F.1, Wellington B.1c, G.R.13, Sunderland G.R.2. Disbanded April, 1944. Reformed May, 1944, Spitfire P.R.11, Wellington P.R.10, at Northolt. 8 Aug. 1945, renumbered from No. 613 Squadron, with Mosquito F.B.6, B.16, B.35 (W1–). 1 April, 1946, renumbered from No. 180 Squadron. Disbanded Nov. 1947. Reformed for service in 2nd T.A.F. and stationed at Laarbruch in July, 1955, with ten Canberra P.R.3. 1956, Canberra P.R.7. 1958, Canberra P.R.9. July, 1958, became No. 39 Squadron.

No. 70 Squadron

Formed 22 April, 1916, at Farnborough. 24 May, 1916, 'A' Flt. to France; 29 June, 1916, 'B' Flt. to France; 30 July, 1916, 'C' Flt. to France. Equipped with One-and-a-half Strutter at Fienvillers. Aircraft transferred from R.N.A.S.—first squadron to use the type in the R.F.C. and on 1 July, 1916, had eight on strength. 1916, C.O. Maj. A. W. Tedder. July, 1917, first to fly Camel F.1. March, 1918, at Marieux. Oct. 1918, fighter at Droglandt North. Disbanded 22 Jan. 1920, at Spittle-gate. Reformed 1 Feb. 1920, from No. 58 Squadron at Heliopolis, with Vimy, O/400. Flew airmail service from Cairo to Baghdad. 1922, Vernon at Hinaidi. 1925, redesignated as bomber-transport squadron. 1928, at Baghdad. 1926, Victoria 5. 1929, participated in Kabul evacuation. 1930, at Hinaidi. 1934, Valentia 1—first to fly the type. At Dhibban. 1939, Valentia 1 (DU–), at Heliopolis. April, 1940, Wellington B.1a, B.1c. Took part in operations during Iraq rising in 1941. March, 1943, Wellington B.3, B.10. Jan. 1945, Liberator B.2, B.3, B.6. Disbanded and reformed 15 April, 1946, by renumbering No. 178 Squadron with Lancaster B.1. Disbanded Feb. 1948. Reformed June, 1948, by re-numbering No. 215 Squadron with Dakota C.4. 1949, flew in 'Plainfare' Aden food-dropping. 1952, Valetta C.1. 1955, Hastings C.1.

No. 71 'Eagle' Squadron

Formed Dec. 1916. To France 18 Dec. 1917, with Camels. On 19 Jan. 1918, became No. 4 Squadron, Australian Flying Corps. Oct. 1918, Snipe. Part of Army of Occupation. Reformed Sept. 1940, at Church Fenton with Anson T.1, Master T.1a. Received Buffalo F.1 (XR–) for trials. 1940, equipped with Hurricane F.1, F.2c (XR–). 1941, Spitfire F.5b, F5c (XR–) as first American 'Eagle' Squadron. Disbanded Sept. 1942, and transferred to 334th Squadron, U.S.A.A.F. Reformed Oct. 1950, Vampire F.B.5. In 2nd T.A.F. 1953, Sabre F.4. 1955, at Bruggen with Hunter F.4.

No. 72 'Basutoland' Squadron

Formed 8 July, 1917, at Netheravon. 'A' Flt. equipped with Spad S–7 C.1, D.H.4, S.E.5, 'B' Flt. with G–100 Elephant, 'C' Flt. with Bristol M.1c. March, 1918, to Mesopotamia, one flight going to Hamadan, one to Mirjana. Also used Avro 504 and Pup. 1918, Camel F.1 added to 'A' Flt. Oct. 1918, fighter at Ginzina. Disbanded 22 Sept. 1919. Reformed 22 Jan. 1937, at Church Fenton with Gladiator 2 under S/L B. H. Rogers. 1939, Spitfire F.1 (SD–, RN–). 1940, Buffalo F.1 for trials. 1940, Spitfire F.2a, F.5b, F.5c (RN–). Aug. 1940, at Acklington. 22 Feb. 1943, equipped with twenty-four Spitfire F.B.9e (RN–). Disbanded Dec. 1946. Reformed 1946 with Vampire F.1, F.3 (FG–). 1951, at North Weald with Vampire F.5 (FG–, WB–). C.O. S/L D. E. Kingaby. 1952, Meteor F.8. 1956, at Church Fenton. 1957, Meteor N.F.12, N.F.14. 1960, Javelin F.A.W.7. 1962, transport with Belvedere H.C.1. Wessex H.C.2.

No. 73 Squadron

Formed 1 July, 1917, at Upavon, as a fighter squadron and went to France with Camel F.1. on 9 Jan. 1918. March, 1918, at Champion. Oct. 1918, at Hiervilly. Disbanded 2 July, 1919. Reformed 15 March, 1937, at Mildenhall with Fury 2. Later received Gauntlet 2, then Gladiator (HV–). June, 1937, to Debden. 9 Nov. 1937, to Digby. Sept. 1939, to France with A.A.S.F. at Rouvres with Hurricane F.1 (HV–, TP–). Aug. 1940, at Church Fenton. 1941, Hurricane F.2c, Tomahawk F.2b. Engaged in night-fighting at Tobruk and El Alamein. Shot down 50 E/A in two weeks. July, 1943, Spitfire F.5c, F.9c. In Egypt, Malta, Italy. April, 1945, as fighter-bomber with Balkan Air Force. 1946, at Malta with Spitfire F.9c, later using F.21, F.22. Oct. 1948, Vampire F.3. 1952, Vampire F.B.5. 1953, left Malta. Arrived May, 1953, at Habbaniya. July, 1954, Vampire F.B.9. Nov. 1954, Venom F.B.1. Left Habbaniya on 2 May, 1955. March, 1957, at Akrotiri with Canberra B.2. 1966, Canberra B.15.

No. 74 'Trinidad' Squadron

Formed 1 July, 1917, at Northolt and went in the same month to London Colney. 30 March, 1918, to France with S.E.5a. Oct. 1918, fighter at Clairmarais. C.O. Maj. K. Caldwell. Destroyed 140 E/A with 85 'probables'. Maj. E. Mannock, V.C., served with the squadron. Disbanded July, 1919. Reformed 3 Sept. 1935, at Hornchurch. Received Demons. 1936, in Malta. April, 1937, Gauntlet at Hornchurch. 1938, Gladiator. 1940, Spitfire F.1, F.2, F.2a (JH–, ZP–). Aug. 1940, at Hornchurch. C.O. S/L Mungo Park. 1941, at Biggin Hill. C.O. W/C A. G. Malan. 1944, Spitfire F.5b, F.9 (JH–, ZP–, 4D–), Hurricane F.2 (ZP–). 1946, Meteor F.3, F.4 (4D–) at Bentwaters. 1951, Meteor F.8,

T.7 (4D-), Oxford T.2 (4D-). At Horsham St. Faith. C.O. 1952–53, Maj. G. W. Milholland, U.S.A.F. 1955, C.O. S/L W. J. Johnston. 1957, Hunter F.4, F.6. C.O. S/L K. N. Haselwood. 1959, at Coltishall. C.O. G/C H. A. C. Bird-Wilson. 1960, first unit with Lightning F.1. 1961, Lightning F.1A, T.4. At Coltishall. 1967, Lightning F.6.

No. 75 'New Zealand' Squadron

Formed 1 Oct. 1916, for Home Defence with H.Q. at Goldington and flights at Yelling, Old Weston and Therfield. Equipped with B.E.2c. 1918, flying single-seat Avro 504, F2b, Camel. 1918, at Elmswell. June, 1918, at North Weald. Oct. 1918, at Bury St. Edmunds. Disbanded 13 June, 1919. Reformed 15 March, 1937, at Driffield from 'B' Flight of No. 215 Squadron with Harrow B.1, B.2 (FO-) and Anson 1. 1939, Wellington B.1c (AA-). 1940, Wellington B.3 (AA-). Oct. 1940, Stirling B.1, B.3 (AA-). At Mepal. March, 1944, Lancaster B.1, B.3 (AA-, JN-). May, 1945, at Spilsby.

No. 76 Squadron

Formed 15 Sept. 1916, for Home Defence. H.Q. at Ripon; flights at Copmanthorpe, Helperby and Catterick. Equipped with B.E.12, B.E.12a, B.E.12b, R.E.7, D.H.6, B.E.2c, B.E.2e. 1918, single-seat Avro 504, F2b, R.E.8. 1919, at Tadcaster. Disbanded 13 June, 1919. Reformed 12 April, 1937, at Finningley and was first to receive Wellesley 1 (NM-). 1939, Hampden B.1, Anson. Disbanded 22 April, 1940. Reformed May, 1941, Whitley B.4, B.5 (MP-), Halifax B.1 (MP-). 1942, Halifax B.2, B.2/1, B.3, B.6 (MP-). At Holme-on-Spalding. Aug. 1945, transport with Dakota C.4 (MP-). Disbanded 1 Sept. 1946. Reformed as bomber squadron. 1954, Canberra B.2. 1955, at Wittering. C.O. S/L J. G. Wynne. 1959, C.O. S/L J. F. G. Stonham.

No. 77 'Lancaster' Squadron

Formed 1 Oct. 1916, for Home Defence, operating from Edinburgh, Whiteburn and New Haggerston. Used B.E.12, B.E.12b, B.E.2c. 1917, D.H.6, R.E.8. 1918, single-seat Avro 504, F2b. Oct. 1918, night-fighting from Penston. Disbanded 13 June, 1919. Reformed 14 June, 1937, at Honington from 'B' Flight of No. 102 Squadron with Audax, Wellesley 1 (ZL-). 1939, Whitley B.3. 1940, Whitley B.4, B.5 (KN-). 1942, shipping patrols with Whitley G.R.7 (KN-). Oct. 1942, Halifax B.2/1, B.2/1a, B.3 B.5 (KN-, TB-). At Elvington, Full Sutton. 1944. Halifax B.6 (TB-), Dakota C.4 (KN-). 1 Nov. 1946, became No. 31 Squadron. 1 Dec. 1946, renumbered from No. 271 Squadron for transport in India with Dakota C.3, C.4 (YS-, DV-, MOFB-). Reformed Aug. 1958, at Feltwell with Thor IRBM as first Missile Unit. C.O. G/C A. Willan.

No. 78 'Preston' Squadron

Formed 1 Nov. 1916, for Home Defence at Harrietsham with B.E.2c. H.Q. at Hove; flights at Telscombe Cliffs, Gosport and Chiddingstone Causeway. Oct. 1917, One-and-a-half Strutter. Dec. 1917, F.E.9(1). July, 1918, Camel F.1. Oct. 1918, night-fighting from Hornchurch. Disbanded 31 Dec. 1919. Reformed 1 Nov. 1936, at Dishforth with Whitley B.1 (EY-). 1939. Whitley B.3, B.5 (EY-, YY-). Oct. 1941, Halifax B.2 (EY-). 1943, Halifax B.2/1a (EY-). 1945, Halifax B.3(EY-) at Breighton. July, 1945, transport with Dakota C.3, C.4 (EY-, ODJ-). 1950, Valetta C.1. 1956, to Aden with Pioneer C.C.1. 1958, Twin Pioneer C.C.1—first unit. 1967, Wessex H.C.2.

No. 79 'Madras Presidency' Squadron

Formed 1 Aug. 1917, at Gosport under Capt. Williams. 8 Aug. 1917, to Beaulieu. C.O. Maj. M. W. Noel. Training until 15 Dec. 1917, when Dophins were received. To le Havre on 18 Feb. 1918. 20 Feb. 1918, to St. Omer. 22 Feb. 1918, to Estrée Blanche. 5 March, 1918, to Champion. 22 March, 1918, shot down its first E/A. 22 March, 1918, at Cachy. 24 March, 1918, to Beauvais. 16 May, 1918, at St. Marie Cappel. 23 June, 1918, C.O. Maj. A. R. Arnold. 22 Oct, 1918, to Rechem. 26 Oct. 1918, to Nivelles. 20 Dec. 1918, to Bickendorf. Disbanded 15 July, 1919, at Bickendorf. Destroyed 64 E/A, together with 9 balloons. Reformed 22 March, 1937, at Biggin Hill from 'B' Flt. of No. 32 Squadron. C.O. S/L A. W. B. McDonald. Equipped with Gauntlet in 'A' and 'B' Flts. 26 April, 1937, C.O. S/L N. A. P. Pritchett. 20 June, 1938, C.O. S/L G. D. Emms. Dec. 1938, Hurricane F.1 (AL-, NV-). 20 Jan. 1939, C.O. S/L C. C. McMullen. Also used one Hart(T). 12 Nov. 1939, at Manston. 21 Nov. 1939, shot down first E/A for No. 11 Group. 28 Feb. 1940, C.O. S/L R. V. Alexander. 10 May, 1940, to Merville, France. 22 May, 1940, to Biggin Hill. 24 May, 1940, C.O. S/L J. D. C. Joslin. 27 May, 1940, to Digby. 5 June, 1940, to Biggin Hill. 2 July, 1940, to Hawkinge. 11 July, 1940, C.O. S/L J. H. Hayworth. 11 July, 1940, to Sealand. 13 July, 1940, to Acklington. 27 Aug. 1940, to Biggin Hill. 8 Sept. 1940, to Pembrey. 14 June, 1941, to Fairwood Common. 25 June, 1941, C.O. S/L G. D. Haysom. June, 1941, Hurricane F.2a, F.2b (NV-). 27 Sept. 1941, C.O. S/L G. L. Sinclair. 19 Nov. 1941, C.O. S/L C. D. Smith. 24 Dec. 1941, C.O. S/L A. V. Clowes. 27 Dec. 1941, to Baginton. Squadron destroyed 76 E/A, 44 probably destroyed and 15 damaged, before going overseas. 24 Feb. 1942, C.O. S/L C. A. Jones. 20 June, 1942, at Bombay. Hurricane F.2c (NV-). 27 June, 1942, Kanchrapara. 8 Jan. 1943, Dohazari. 21 Jan. 1943, Ramu. 29 May, 1943, Comilla. 20 July, 1943, Ranchi. 1 Oct. 1943, Alipore. 6 Dec. 1943, Chittagong. 27 Jan. 1944, Dohazari. 11 Feb. 1944, C.O. S/L D. O. Cunliffe. 26 May, 1944, Yolahanka. June, 1944, Thunderbolt F.B.2

(NV-). July, 1944, C.O. F/L K. G. Hemingway. 17 Sept. 1944, Arkonam. 19 Oct. 1944, Manipur Road. 19 Nov. 1944, Wangjing. 8 Dec. 1944, C.O. S/L R. D. May. 19 April, 1945, Myingyan North. 1 May, 1945, Tennant. 6 May, 1945, Myingyan North. 7 June, 1945, Meiktila. 9 Aug. 1945, C.O. S/L R. A. Stout. 28 Oct. 1945, C.O. F/L H. A. Rogers. Disbanded 31 Dec. 1945. While in Far East the squadron destroyed 4 E/A, with 2 'probables'. Reformed 15 Nov. 1951, in 2nd T.A.F. for fighter reconnaissance with Meteor F.R.9 (T-), T.7 (T-). Re-constituted at Buckeburg, then at Gütersloh until July, 1954. Then to Buckeburg and to Laarbruch. 1956, Swift F.R.5. C.O. S/L N. A. McCullen. 1961, renumbered No. 4 Squadron with Hunter F.6 and re-equipped with Hunter F.R.10.

No. 80 Squadron

Formed 1 Aug. 1917, with Camel F.1. To France 27 Jan. 1918. March, 1918, at Champion. Oct. 1918, fighter at Bouvincourt. Feb. 1919, Snipe. 1919, to Egypt. Disbanded 1 Feb. 1920, in Egypt and renumbered No. 56 Squadron. Reformed 8 March, 1937, at Debden with Gauntlet 2. June, 1937, Gladiator 2 (GK-). Sept. 1939, to Egypt. 1940, in Greece. March, 1941, Hurricane F.1, F.2b. 12 April, 1943, Spitfire F.5c (EY-), Spitfire F.9 (W2-), Typhoon F.1b (W2-). Aug. 1944, Tempest F.5 (W2-). 1946, Tempest F.6. 1948, Spitfire F.24 (W2-). 1953, at Kai-Tak with Hornet F.3. C.O. S/L H. G. Cullen. Disbanded April 1955. Reformed 1956 with Canberra P.R.3 at Laarbruch. 1959, Canberra P.R.7.

No. 81 Squadron

Formed Sept. 1918, with Snipe. In Nov. 1918, became No. 1 Squadron, Canadian Air Force, at Upper Heyford in No. 1 Canadian Wing. Disbanded 1920. Reformed Aug. 1939, as communication squadron. Disbanded 15 June, 1940. Reformed 29 July, 1941, with Hurricane F.1, F.2b (FK-). Went to Russia as part of No. 151 Wing. Dec. 1941, Spitfire F.5b, F.5c (FL-). Sept. 1942, first in North Africa with Spitfires. Jan. 1943, Spitfire F.9 (FL-). Nov. 1943, Spitfire L.F.8 (FL-). Disbanded 1945. Reformed June, 1945, from No. 123 Squadron in Burma with Thunderbolt F.B.2 (FL-). Disbanded June, 1946. Reformed Sept. 1946, from No. 684 Squadron with Mosquito P.R.16, P.R.34a, T.3, Anson C.19/2. Aug. 1947, Spitfire F.R.18, P.R.19 added from No. 34 Squadron. Engaged on anti-bandit operations from Seletar. 15 Dec. 1955, made last operational sortie by R.A.F. Mosquito. 1 April, 1954, last R.A.F. Spitfire operational sortie by C.O. S/L W. P. Swaby. One flight at Kai-Tak. Nov. 1953, Meteor P.R.10. C.O. S/L G. McCreith. 1956, Pembroke C.(P.R.)1. 1958, Canberra P.R.7.

No. 82 'United Provinces' Squadron

Formed 7 Feb. 1917, at Doncaster, and went to France 20 Nov. 1917, with F.K.8. Oct. 1918, reconnaissance from Proven West. Disbanded 30 June, 1919. Reformed 14 June, 1937, from 'B' Flight of No. 142 Squadron, with Hind. 1938, at Cranfield with Blenheim 1L, 4L (OZ-). June, 1942, in India with Vengeance B.3, Hudson G.R.5. June, 1944, in Burma equipped with Mosquito F.B.6 from No. 47 Squadron. Disbanded 15 March, 1946. Reformed Oct. 1946, at Benson from No. 541 Squadron with Spitfire P.R.19. Jan. 1947, at Eastleigh, East Africa. June, 1948, at Takoradi, West Africa. Jan. 1950, at Nairobi, Southern Rhodesia. 1952. Lancaster P.R.1/F.E. (OT-). Engaged in photographic survey in Africa. 1952, stationed at Benson. Last Bomber Command Lancaster squadron in Nov. 1953. C.O. W/C S. G. Wise. Also used Dakota C.4. 1953, Canberra P.R.3. Dec. 1954, at Wyton. Canberra B.2.

No. 83 Squadron

Formed 7 Jan. 1917, at Montrose, for night-bombing with F.E.2b. To France 4 March, 1918. Oct. 1918, at la Houssoye. Disbanded 31 Dec. 1919. Reformed 4 Aug. 1936, at Scampton with Hind. Nov. 1938, Hampden B.1 (QQ-, OL-). C.O. S/L D. A. Boyle, 1941. March, 1942, Manchester B.1, B.1a (OL-) at Scampton. May, 1942, Lancaster B.1 (OL-) in Pathfinder Force. Aug. 1942, at Wyton. April, 1944, at Coningsby. 1946, Lancaster B.1, B.3 (OL-). Nov. 1946, to Hemswell with Lincoln B.2 (OL-). 1953, C.O. S/L W. C. Sinclair. Aug. 1953, until July, 1954, in Malaya. Disbanded 1 Jan. 1956. 21 May, 1957, at Waddington, first unit to receive Vulcan B.1. 1960, renumbered No. 44 Squadron. 1960, reformed at Waddington as first unit with Vulcan B.2. Oct. 1960 at Scampton. C.O. W/C R. J. Davenport.

No. 84 Squadron

Formed Jan. 1917, at Beaulieu. Equipped with S.E.5, S.E.5a and crossed to France 23 Sept. 1917. March, 1918, at Flez. Oct. 1918, at Bouvincourt. V.C. won by Capt. A. W. Beauchamp-Proctor on 30 Nov. 1918. Disbanded 30 Jan. 1920. Reformed 13 Aug. 1920, as a bomber unit at Baghdad with D.H. 9a. 1928, at Shaibah with Wapiti 2a. Also used Wapiti on floats. 1934, Vincent. 1939, Blenheim 1L (UR-, VT-). 1941, Blenheim 4f (UO-, VT-). One Audax also on strength. C.O. S/L D. G. Lewis. 1942, Mosquito F.B.6 (VT-). Aug. 1943, Vengeance (VT-), Beaufighter T.F.10. 1950, Brigand B.1, Buckmaster T.1 in Malaya. 1954, transport in Middle East with Valetta C.1, Pembroke C.1. C.O. S/L H. Jenkins. 1958, Beverley C.1. At Khormaksar on communications. C.O. S/L E. W. Talbot. 1960, C.O. S/L H. W. Guile. 1960, Valettas transferred to form No. 233 Squadron.

No. 85 Squadron

Formed Aug. 1917, with Dolphin and went to France on 22 May, 1918. 1918, S.E.5a. June, 1918, C.O. Maj. E. Mannock. Oct. 1918, fighter at Estrées-en-Chaussée. Disbanded July, 1919. Reformed 1938 at Debden with Gladiator. Sept. 1938, Hurricane F.1 (NO-, VY-), Master T.1. 1940, with Air Component at Lille. Aug. 1940, at Martlesham. Feb. 1941, Defiant N.F.1 (VY-). 1941, Havoc N.F.1, N.F.2 Intruder (VY-) at West Malling. 1942. Mosquito N.F.12, N.F.17 (VY-), Boston B.2 (VY-). 1945, Mosquito N.F.30, T.3 (VY-). 1950, Mosquito N.F.36 (VY-), at West Malling. 1952, Meteor N.F.11. C.O. S/L J. D. Hawkins. 1953, Meteor N.F.12. June, 1954, Meteor N.F.14. C.O. S/L B. J. Scandrett. 1957, at Church Fenton. Disbanded 1958. Reformed 1958 from No. 89 Squadron at Stradishall with Javelin FAW.2, FAW.6. 5 Aug. 1959, to West Malling. C.O. W/C G. A. Martin. 1960, Javelin FAW.8. 1967, Canberra B.2, T.11.

No. 86 Squadron

Formed Nov. 1917, but was not operational and disbanded in 1918. Reformed 1940 with Blenheim 4 (BX-) for general reconnaissance. 1941, Beaufort G.R.1, G.R.2 (BX-) at St. Eval. Also used Anson G.R.1 (BX-). 1942, Fortress G.R.2, Liberator G.R.3, G.R.5, G.R.6, C.6, C.8 (XQ-). 1945, engaged in transport. June, 1956, Meteor N.F.11. C.O. W/C L. W. G. Gill.

No. 87 'United Provinces' Squadron

Formed 1 Sept. 1917, with Pup. To France 26 April, 1918. Used Dolphin and Camel F.1. Oct. 1918, fighter at Soucamb. Disbanded 24 June, 1919. Reformed 15 March, 1937, at Debden with Fury 2. June, 1937, Gladiator. C.O. S/L J. Rhys-Jones. July, 1938, Hurricane F.1 (PD-, LK-), Master T.1. 1940, with Air Component at Lille. Aug. 1940, at Exeter. Jan. 1943, Hurricane F.2a, F.2b, F.2c, N.F.2c (LK-). Sept. 1943, Spitfire L.F.5b (LK-), L.F.5c (LK-), F.8. (LK-). Aug. 1944, Spitfire F.9b, F.9c (LK-). Disbanded 1946. Reformed 1952 with Meteor N.F.11, T.7. 1955, at Wahn in 2nd T.A.F. 1957, first unit in 2nd T.A.F. with Javelin FAW.1.

No. 88 'Hong Kong' Squadron

Formed March, 1918, at Harling Road as two-seat fighter squadron with F2b. 31 March, 1918, to Kenley. 2 April, 1918, to Capelle, France. Oct. 1918, at Serny. Destroyed 164 E/A. Disbanded 10 Aug. 1919. Reformed 7 June, 1937, at Boscombe Down with Hind. Dec. 1937, Battle 1 (HY-, RH-). 1939, with A.A.S.F. at Mourmelon. Shot down first E/A, an Me.109. Aug. 1940, returned to England. Re-equipped with Blenheim 4L (RH-). July, 1941, first to operate Boston B.2, B.3, B.3a (RH-).

On anti-shipping operations. Also used Mitchell B.3 (RH–). 6 June, 1944, laid D-Day smoke-screen, then operated with 2nd T.A.F. Aug. 1944, Boston B.4 (RH–). Disbanded May, 1945. Reformed 1 Sept. 1946, from No. 209 Squadron for transport from Hong Kong to Japan with Sunderland G.R.5. 1950, carried out 467 sorties on reconnaissance in Korea and 165 sorties in Malaya. April, 1954, to Trincomalee, Ceylon. Disbanded Oct. 1954, at Seletar. Reformed 1956, at Wildenrath, Germany, under W/C J. A. Holmes and was first to receive Canberra B.(I)8. 17 Dec. 1962, became No. 14 Squadron.

No. 89 Squadron

Formed July, 1917, as a training unit with B.E.12a, R.E.8. 1918, Avro 504, Pup, Camel. Disbanded June, 1918. The squadron was to have had S.E.5s for service as a fighter unit in France. It is recorded that the personnel were so resentful at the disbanding that they burnt all of the equipment on a huge bonfire. It is further noted that 'their morale was very high'. Reformed Sept. 1941, for night-fighting with Beaufighter N.F.1f, N.F.4 with A.I. In Egypt. 1942, C.O. W/C G. H. Stainforth killed. April, 1945, Mosquito F.B.6, N.F.13, Harvard T.2b, Walrus A.S.R.2. Disbanded 1 May, 1946. Reformed July, 1947, with Mosquito N.F.36 as all-weather fighter unit. 1954, Venom N.F.3. 1956, Javelin FAW.2. 1958, first unit to operate Javelin FAW.6. 1958, became No. 85 Squadron.

No. 90 Squadron

Formed 8 Oct. 1917, at Shotwick for Home Defence. Received single-seat Avro 504, Dolphin, F.E.2b. Disbanded 3 Aug. 1918. Reformed 14 Aug. 1918, again for Home Defence, with Pup. 1919, Camel 2F.1, single-seat Avro 504k. Disbanded 13 June, 1919. Reformed 15 March, 1937, at Bicester with Hind. 1937, Blenheim 1L, 4L (TW–). 1939, Blenheim 4L (XY–, WP–). Disbanded April, 1940. Reformed 7 May, 1941, being first to fly Fortress B.1 (WP–). Disbanded Sept. 1942. Reformed Dec. 1942, with Stirling B.1 (WP–). May, 1943, Stirling B.3 (WP–). July, 1944, Lancaster B.1, B.3, B.1(F.E.) (XY–, WP–) at Tuddenham. 1946, Lincoln B.2 (WP–). Oct. 1950, Washington B.1 (WP–). C.O. 1952, S/L W. R. Sloane. 1954, Canberra B.2. May, 1957, at Honington with Valiant B.1—seventh squadron to fly the type. C.O. W/C C. B. Owen.

No. 91 'Nigeria' Squadron

Formed Nov. 1917, but was non-operational and disbanded July, 1919. Reformed Jan. 1941, with Hurricane F.2, Spitfire F.2a (BP–). March, 1941, Spitfire F.5b (DL–). 1942. Spitfire F.5c, F.14 (DL–). 1946, Spitfire F.21 (DL–). 1947, Meteor F.4 (DL–). Meteor F.8 (DL–).

No. 92 'East India' Squadron

Formed Sept. 1917, and went to France 1 July, 1918, as a fighter unit with S.E.5a. Oct. 1918, at Estrées-en-Chaussée. Disbanded Aug. 1919. Reformed 10 Oct. 1939, with Blenheim 1f, Hurricane F.1. Aug. 1940, at Pembrey. 8 Sept. 1940, to Biggin Hill with Spitfire F.1, F.2, F.2b (QJ-). C.O. S/L J. A. Kent. Aug. 1941, C.O. S/L J. Rankin. 1942, to Middle East with Spitfire F.5b, F.5c (QJ-). C.O. S/L Wedgwood. At Sidi Barani and Msus. C.O. S/L Morgan. At Elchel and Tamet. 1944, Spitfire H.F.7, F.B.8, F.9 (QJ-). At Medanie and Malta. Then to Marcianese. C.O.s S/L Harper, S/L Humphries, S/L Mackie, S/L Cox. Disbanded Aug. 1946. Reformed with Meteor F.3 (8L-, DL-) at Linton-on-Ouse. 1951, Meteor F.4 (8L-, DL-). 1953, Meteor F.8, T.7 (8L-, DL-). Jan. 1954, Sabre F.4. 1956, Hunter F.4. C.O. S/L R. W. G. Freer. 1956, Hunter F.6—first unit. 1957, at Middleton St. George. 1959, C.O. S/L R. H. B. Dixon. 1961, S/L B. Mercer. At Leconfield. 1967, Lightning F.2.

No. 93 Squadron

Formed Sept. 1917, but was non-operational and was disbanded in Aug. 1918. Reformed Sept. 1940, from No. 430 Flt. as an experimental unit. Used Harrow B.1, Battle 1, Wellington B.1c (HN-), (1 flight), and was first squadron to have Havoc N.F.1 (HN-), with Pandora aerial mine interception, which equipped two flights. At Middle Wallop. 1 June, 1942, as fighter unit with Spitfire F.B.9 (HN-). Spitfire L.F.16e (HN-), Beaufighter F.1, F.5c (HN-). Disbanded 5 Sept. 1945. Reformed Jan. 1946, by renumbering No. 237 Squadron with Mustang F.3. Disbanded 30 Dec. 1946. Reformed 1950, at Celle, Vampire F.B.5. 1954, C.O. S/L R. N. G. Allen. 1955, at Jever with Sabre F.4. C.O. S/L D. F. M. Browne. Jan. 1956. Hunter F.4. 1960, Hunter F.6. C.O. S/L M. O. Bergh.

No. 94 'MacRobert' Squadron

Formed Aug. 1917. June, 1918, S.E.5a. To France 31 Oct. 1918, and stationed at Senlis. Disbanded 30 June, 1919. Reformed 26 March, 1939, at Aden with Gladiator 2, Vincent 1 (ZG-). 22 April, 1940, partly equipped with Hurricane F.2c. Also used Tomahawk F.1. Dec. 1940, completely re-equipped Hurricane F.2c. Jan. 1942, Kittyhawk F.1a. C.O. S/L Mason. April, 1942, Mustang F.3. March, 1944, Spitfire F.5c, April, 1944, Spitfire F.9. July, 1944, Spitfire F.5c. 18 Feb. 1945, Spitfire F.9. Disbanded 20 April, 1945. Reformed in 2nd T.A.F. 1953. Vampire F.B.5. July, 1954, Venom F.B.1. C.O. Oct. 1954, S/L Bower. 1956, at Celle. 1957. C.O. S/L D. G. L. Heywood.

No. 95 Squadron

Formed Sept. 1917, but was non-operational and was disbanded July,

1918. Reformed 16 Jan. 1941, with Sunderland G.R.1, G.R.2, G.R.3 (SE-, DQ-). At Bathurst and Freetown for maritime reconnaissance.

No. 96 Squadron

Formed Sept. 1917, but was non-operational and disbanded in June, 1918. Reformed 18 Dec. 1940, incorporating No. 422 Flt., with Hurricane F.1, N.F.1, N.F.2c (ZJ-). Night-fighting at Speke, Atchem. Feb. 1941, Defiant N.F.1 (ZJ-). Jan. 1942, Defiant N.F.1a (ZJ-). March, 1942, Defiant N.F.2 (ZJ-). June, 1942, Beaufighter F.2, N.F.2f, N.F.6f (ZJ-). July, 1942, Beaufighter F.6. June, 1943, Mosquito N.F.13, T.3, at Honily. Mosquito N.F.17 (ZJ-), Oxford T.2 (ZJ-). Disbanded 12 Dec. 1944. Reformed 30 Dec. 1944, for transport in S.E.A.C. with Halifax C.3 (6H-), Dakota C.3, C.4 (6H-). Disbanded 15 June, 1946, at Kai-Tak and renumbered No. 110 Squadron. Reformed in 2nd T.A.F. with Meteor N.F.11. Aug. 1955, at Ahlhorn.

No. 97 'Straits Settlements' Squadron

Formed 1 Dec. 1917, at Waddington with S11 Shorthorn, D.H.4. To France 4 Aug. 1918, joining Independent Air Force on 9 Aug. 1918. 1918, O/400. Oct. 1918, night-bomber at Xaffrévilliers. 1919, D.H.10 Amiens. Disbanded 1 April, 1920, and renumbered No. 60 Squadron. Reformed 16 Sept. 1935, at Mildenhall with Heyford 2. Later at Leconfield. Feb. 1939, Whitley B.2 (MR-). 1940, Whitley B.3, B.4, B.5 (OF-), Anson 1. Disbanded April, 1940. Reformed Feb. 1941, Wellington B.1c (OF-). 1941, Manchester B.1a (OF-). 1941, Hampden B.1 (OF-). Feb. 1942, Lancaster B.1, B.3 (OF-). Second unit to fly Lancaster. At Woodhall Spa. April, 1943, with Pathfinder Force. At Bourn. April, 1944, at Coningsby. 1945, Lincoln B.2 (OF-). 1952, C.O. S/L T. Helfer. 1958, at Hemswell. C.O. W/C P. C. Lambert.

No. 98 'Derby' Squadron

Formed 30 Aug. 1917, at Harlaxton from flt. of No. 4 Training Squadron, with B.E.2c, B.E.2e, D.H.4, F.K.8, Sopwith Scout, Avro 504. C.O. Lt. D. V. D. Marshall. 31 Aug. 1917, at Old Sarum. 21 Sept. 1917, C.O. Maj. E. L. M. Gower. 14 Dec. 1917, C.O. Capt. E. A. B. Rice. 19 Dec. 1917, C.O. Capt. R. G. Gould. 18 Jan. 1918, C.O. Capt. E. A. B. Rice. 19 Feb. 1918, C.O. Maj. H. MacD. O'Malley. Feb. 1918, D.H.9, Camel. 1 March, 1918, at Lympne. 1 April, 1918, to St. Omer. 3 April, 1918, at Clairmarais. 13 April, 1918, at Alquines. 25 May, 1918, at Coudekerque. 5 June, 1918, C.O. Maj. E. T. Newton-Clare. 6 June, 1918, at Ruisseauville. 21 June, 1918, at Drionville. 14 July, 1918, at Chailly. 3 Aug. 1918, at Blangermont. 26 Aug. 1918, C.O. Maj. P. C. Sherren. 27 Oct. 1918, at Abscon. 27 Dec. 1918, at Marquain. 19 Jan. 1919, at Alquines. Jan. 1919, ferrying with D.H.4. 20 March, 1919, at

D

Shotwick. 24 June, 1919, disbanded at Shotwick. Reformed 17 Feb. 1936, at Abingdon from part of No. 15 Squadron, with six Hinds. 21 Aug. 1936, at Hucknall. 21 Sept. 1936, C.O. S/L P. J. A. Hume-Wright. 3 Aug. 1937, C.O. S/L R. H. Donkin. 10 March, 1938, at Scampton. June, 1938, Battle 1, Anson 1 (QF-, OE-). 15 Sept. 1938, at Hucknall. 6 Sept. 1939, C.O. W/C F. W. Dixon-Wright. 11 Oct. 1939, C.O. W/C D. F. Anderson. 7 March, 1940, at Scampton. 25 March, 1940, C.O. W/C G. R. Ashton. 25 March, 1940, at Finningley. 19 April, 1940, at Nantes. 10 June, 1940, at Gatwick. 31 July, 1940, to Kaldadarness, Iceland. 31 March, 1941, C.O. F/L H. C. G. Wilcox. June, 1941, Hurricane F.1. Disbanded 15 July, 1941, at Kaldadarness. 12 Sept. 1942, reformed at West Raynham. Oct. 1942, first squadron to use Mitchell B.2 (EV-, VO-). C.O. W/C L. A. Lewer. 15 Oct. 1942, at Foulsham. 18 Aug. 1943, C.O. W/C A. M. Phillips. 18 Aug. 1943, at Dunsfold. 26 March, 1944, at Swanton Morley. 9 April, 1944, C.O. W/C R. K. F. Bell-Irving. 10 April, 1944, at Dunsfold. 15 May, 1944, C.O. W/C G. J. C. Paul. 16 Sept. 1944, C.O. W/C L. G. Hamer. Sept. 1944, Mitchell B.3 (EV-, VO-). 16 Oct. 1944, at Melsbroek. 16 Jan. 1945, C.O. W/C K. Gray. 25 Feb. 1945, C.O. W/C V. E. Marshal. 30 April, 1945, at Osnabrück. 17 Sept. 1945, at Melsbroek. Nov. 1945, Mosquito B.16 (EV-, VO-), Mosquito T.3, Oxford T.2. 9 Feb. 1946, C.O. W/C E. W. Thornewill. 15 March, 1946, at Wahn. 12 Feb. 1947, C.O. W/C D. B. Gericke. 5 Nov. 1947, C.O. S/L P. W. Cook. Aug. 1948, Mosquito B.35 (VO-). 25 July, 1949, C.O. S/L D. R. M. Frostick. 17 Sept. 1949, at Celle. 29 Aug. 1950, C.O. S/L J. M. Rumsey. 1 Nov. 1950, at Fassberg Feb. 1951, Vampire F.B.5 (L-), Meteor T.7. 15 March, 1951, C.O.S/L A. S. R. Strudwick. Aug. 1953, Venom F.B.1 (L-), Vampire T.11. 31 Aug. 1953, C.O. S/L J. H. Smith-Carrington. March, 1955, first in 2nd T.A.F. with Hunter F.4. 19 March, 1955, at Jever. 10 Dec. 1955, C.O. S/L D. T. Adamson. Disbanded at Jever 15 July, 1957. Reformed 1 Nov. 1959, at Driffield with Thor I.R.B.M. C.O. S/L P. G. Coulson. May, 1961, C.O. S/L S. Hudson. Disbanded 18 April, 1963. 19 April, 1963, reformed at Tangmere from No. 245 Squadron with Canberra B.2, T.4, for radar calibration. C.O. S/L A. Musker. 1 Oct. 1963, at Watton. 17 Aug. 1964, C.O. S/L P. W. Shaw. 10 Oct. 1966, C.O. S/L L. J. Wright. 16 Jan. 1967, C.O. S/L A. E. Sadler.

No. 99 'Madras Presidency' Squadron

Formed 15 Aug. 1917, at Yatesbury with D.H.6, B.E.2e. March, 1918, received eighteen D.H.9s. To France 25 April, 1918, joining Independent Air Force in May, 1918. At St. Omer, then to Tantonville and Azelot. C.O. Maj. L. A. Pattinson. Sept. 1918, D.H.9a. May, 1919, to India. 1 April, 1920, renumbered as No. 27 Squadron. Reformed 1 April, 1924, at Netheravon and was only unit to receive Aldershot for bombing. April, 1926, first to fly Hyderabad. 1928, at Bircham Newton. 1929, first to receive Hinaidi. 1930, at Upper Heyford. Nov. 1933, first to fly Heyford 2. At Upper Heyford. 14 April, 1937, 'B' Flt. detached to form No. 149 Squadron. Later at Mildenhall. 1939, Wellington B.1c (VF-). Sept. 1939, at Newmarket Heath. 1940, Wellington B.1a, B.2 (LN-). Engaged in leaflet-dropping and anti-shipping operations. April, 1940, at Salon, France. 1941, attacked *Tirpitz*. Also bombed Ruhr, Berlin, *Gneisenau* and *Scharnhorst*. 1942, in India. June, 1944, supply-dropping. 1944, Liberator C.6. June, 1945, in Cocos Islands. Disbanded 15 Nov. 1945. Reformed Nov. 1947, for transport with Hastings C.1 at Lyneham. Also used York C.1 (MOYB-), Hastings C.2. 1959, first to operate Britannia C.1. C.O. W/C W. E. F. Gray. At Lyneham.

No. 100 Squadron

Formed Feb. 1917, at Hingham, for Home Defence under Maj. M. G. Christie. Received twelve F.E.2b, one F.E.2c, four B.E.2c, B.E.2e, B.E.2g. 28 March, 1917, to France as the first night-bomber squadron. Joined Independent Air Force on 11 Oct. 1917, at Ochey. 13 Aug. 1918, received O/400. Oct. 1918, at Xaffrévilliers. Disbanded March, 1919, Reformed 1 Feb. 1920, at Baldonnel, Ireland, with F2b. Engaged on anti-Sinn Fein operations. C.O. Maj. F. Sowrey. Redesignated as a bomber squadron in March, 1920, receiving eighteen D.H.9a. Also used Avro 504k. 1922, to Spittlegate with 'D' Flt. using Vimy. Aug. 1924, until 1926, at Eastchurch with Fawn. 1928, service trials with Antelope and Hart. 1928, at Bicester with Horsley. 3 Nov. 1930, to Donibristle. C.O. W/C G. S. M. Insall, V.C. 1932, Vildebeest 1 and 2. Sept. 1933, to Seletar. 1933, Vildebeest 3 and 4 (RA-, HJ-). 1941, Blenheim 4, Albacore, Wellington B.3 (HJ-). C.O. S/L R. F. C. Markham. Feb. 1942, Beaufort G.R.1 (HJ-). Reformed at Waltham in U.K. Dec. 1942, as bomber with Lancaster B.1, B.3 (HJ-, HW-). At Grimsby. 1943, at Waltham. C.O. W/C R. V. MacIntyre. 1945, at Elsham Wolds. June, 1946, Lincoln B.2 (HW-, AS-), at Lindholme. May, 1950, to Malaya on anti-bandit operations. Code FZ- allocated but not used. Dec. 1950, returned to U.K. 1953, 'A' Flt. to Eastleigh, Nairobi. April, 1954, at Wittering with Canberra B.2. C.O. S/L C. P. H. Kunkler. Canberra B.6, B.(I)8. 1959, C.O. S/L R. A. McPhie. 1966, Victor B.2.

No. 101 Squadron

Formed 12 July, 1917, at Farnborough for night-bombing. Received eighteen F.E.2b and went to France on 25 July, 1917, based at St. André aux Bois. Later at Morville and in Oct. 1918, at Proyart East. Disbanded 31 Dec. 1919, at Filton. Reformed April, 1928, at Bircham Newton

with Sidestrand 2 and 3. Only unit to fly the type. C.O. S/L J. C. P.
Wood. 1930, at Andover. 1934, converted to Overstrand 1. Was the
only squadron to use the Overstrand and the first to operate with power-
driven turrets. 1938, Blenheim 1L (LU–) at Bicester. 1941, Blenheim
4L (SR–). April, 1941, at Manston on anti-shipping operations. Also
using Wellington B.1c, B.3 (SR–). Oct. 1942, Lancaster B.1, B.3, B.10
(SR–). June, 1943, at Ludford Magna. 1946, Lincoln B.2 (SR–). Code
MW–allotted but not used. June 1941, Canberra B.1. at Binbrook. First
to use Canberra. C.O. S/L E. Cassidy. June, 1954, first to fly Canberra
B.6. C.O. S/L W. D. Robertson. Disbanded 1957. 1958, reformed at
Finningley as second unit to fly Vulcan B.1. C.O. W/C A. C. L. Mackie.
Vulcan B.2.

No. 102 'Ceylon' Squadron

Formed Aug. 1917, at Hingham, for night-bombing with F.E.2b. Went to
France 24 Sept. 1917. Oct. 1918, at Famechon. Disbanded 3 July,1919.
Reformed 1 Oct. 1935, at Honington from 'B' Flt. of No. 7 Squadron with
Heyford 2. 1939, Whitley B.1, B.3, B.4, B.5 (TQ–, DY–). Jan. 1942.
Halifax B.2/1 (DY–). June, 1944, at Pocklington with Halifax B.2/1a,
B.3, B.6 (DY–), Liberator C.6, C.8 (EF–). Disbanded Feb. 1946. Re-
formed Oct. 1954, in 2nd T.A.F., at Gütersloh with Canberra B.2.
Aug. 1956, became No. 59 Squadron.

No. 103 'Swindon' Squadron

Formed 1 Sept. 1917 at Beaulieu. To France 12 May, 1918, with D.H.9
for day-bombing. Oct. 1918, at Serny. Disbanded 1 Oct. 1919. Reformed
10 Aug. 1936, at Andover with Hind. 1937, at Usworth with Battle 1
(GV–). Sept. 1939, with A.A.S.F. at Bethenville. Oct. 1940, Wellington
B.1c, B.3 (PM–), Whitley B.5, Blenheim 4L (PM–). June, 1942, Halifax
B2/1a (PM–). Nov. 1942, Lancaster B.1, B.3 (PM–) at Elsham Wolds.
1944, Liberator C.6, C.8 (PM–). Disbanded 25 Nov. 1945. Reformed
1954 with Canberra B.2. Disbanded Aug. 1956. Reformed 1959 from
No. 284 Squadron at Nicosia with Sycamore H.R.14 and Whirlwind
H.A.R.2. C.O. S/L J. L. Price. 1967, at Seletar with Whirlwind
H.A.R.10.

No. 104 Squadron

Formed 4 Sept. 1917, at Andover from part of No. 20 T.S. To Inde-
pendent Force on 19 May, 1918, with D.H.9. 1918, D.H.10 Amiens.Oct.
1918, at Azelot. Disbanded 10 June, 1919. Reformed 7 Jan. 1936, from
'C' Flight of No. 40 Squadron, at Abingdon with Hind. Later at
Hucknall. May, 1938, Blenheim 1 (PO–, EP–). 1939, Battle 1 (PO–).
Disbanded April, 1940. Reformed March, 1941, at Driffield, with
Wellington B.1c. 1942, Wellington B.1a, B.2, B.3 (EP–), Lancaster B.1,

B.7(F.E.) (EP–), Liberator B.6 (EP–). April, 1947, disbanded. Reformed March, 1955, with Canberra B.2.

No. 105 Squadron

Formed Sept. 1917, at Andover, and was stationed in Ireland with R.E.8 in April 1918. Oct. 1918, at St. Omer on artillery observation. Dec. 1918, F2b. Disbanded Feb. 1920. Reformed 26 April, 1937, with Audax 1, using, in 1938, Battle 1 (MT–) at Harwell. 1939, Battle 1 (KB–, GB–) with A.A.S.F. at Villeneuve. 1941, Blenheim 4L (BG–) at Malta. 1942, first unit to fly Mosquito B.4 (KB–). At Bourn. On night-intruder operations from May, 1943. Later equipped with Mosquito F.B.6, B.9. B.16 (GB–) using Oboe in Pathfinder Force. Disbanded 1 Feb.1946. Reformed and, in 1952, flying Vampire F.B.5. 1955, Canberra B.2. Feb. 1962, Argosy C.1. At Aden.

No. 106 Squadron

Formed 30 Sept. 1917, at Andover, with R.E.8 and served in Ireland. Oct. 1918, on reconnaissance from Fermoy with F2b. Disbanded 8 Oct. 1919. Reformed from 'A' Flight of No. 15 Squadron 1 June, 1938, with Hind. Later received Battle 1. June, 1939, Hampden B.1 (XS–). 1940, Hampden B.1 (ZN–). 1942, Manchester B.1a (ZN–) at Coningsby. June, 1942, Lancaster B.1, B.3 (ZN–). First squadron to use the Mk. 14 bombsight. 1 Oct. 1942, at Syerston. Nov. 1943, at Metheringham. 26 April, 1944, V.C. won by W/O N. C. Jackson.

No. 107 Squadron

Formed 15 May, 1918, at Lake Down with D.H. 9. To France 9 June, 1918, for day-bombing. Oct. 1918, at Ecoivres. Disbanded June, 1919, Reformed at Upavon 10 Aug. 1936, with Hind. 1937, at Harwell with Blenheim 1L (BZ–). 1941, Blenheim 4f, 4L (OM–). C.O. S/L B. Embry. March, 1942, Boston B.3 (OM–). Feb. 1943, Mosquito F.B.6 (OM–). 1949, renumbered as No. 11 Squadron. Reformed with Canberra B.2.

No. 108 Squadron

Formed 11 Nov. 1917 at Stonehenge. To France 22 July, 1918, for day-bombing with D.H.9. Oct. 1918, at Capelle. Disbanded 3 July, 1919. Re-formed 4 Jan. 1937, with Hind at Cranfield. 1938, Blenheim 1L (MF–). Disbanded April, 1940. Reformed in Egypt Aug. 1941, with Wellington B.1c (LG–). Later used Wellington B.1, B.2, B.3 (LG–). Dec. 1941, Liberator B.2 temporarily in use in Egypt. Later fully re-equipped with Wellington B.1c. 1942, Halifax C.8 (LG–). Disbanded Dec. 1942. Reformed March, 1943, for night-fighting with Beaufighter F.1, F.6 Feb. 1944, Mosquito N.F.13, Liberator B.2.

No. 109 Squadron

Formed 1 Dec. 1940, at Boscombe Down from W.I.D.U. Wellington B.1c, B.3, B.10 (ZP-), Whitley B.4. (ZP-), Anson T.1 (ZP-). 1942, Wellington B.6a (HS-), Tiger Moth 2, Oxford T.2, Mosquito B.4, B.16, B.9, P.R.16, P.R.31, B.35 (HS-), Anson T.1 (HS-). 1 Oct. 1945, renumbered from No. 627 Squadron with Mosquito B.16 (HS-). 1953, flying Canberra B.2. at Hemswell. C.O. S/L Hill. 1955, Canberra B.6 at Binbrook.

No. 110 'Hyderabad' Squadron

Formed 1 Nov. 1917, at Rendcombe, receiving B.E.2d, B.E.2e, R.E.8, F.K.8, D.H.4, D.H.6, G-100 Elephant. June, 1918, first to fly D.H.9 and D.H.9a. To France 31 Aug. 1918, joining Independent Air Force. Oct. 1918, day-bombing from Bettoncourt. Disbanded 27 Aug. 1919. Reformed 18 May, 1937, at Waddington with Hind. 1938, Blenheim 1, 4L (AY-). Sept. 1939, Blenheim 4L (AY-, VE-) at Wattisham. 4 Sept. 1939, carried out first R.A.F. raid of war from Ipswich Airport. March, 1942, in Burma with Vengeance B.3. 1944, Mosquito F.B.6. 1944, re-equipped with Vengeance. 1945, Mosquito F.B.6. Disbanded April, 1946. Reformed June, 1946, from No. 96 Squadron for transport with Halifax B.3, Dakota C.4. 1953, Valetta C.1 at Changi. 1959, reformed from Nos. 155 and 194 Squadrons at Kuala Lumpur with Sycamore H.R.13 and Whirlwind H.A.R.4. C.O. S/L F. Barnes. 1961, Whirlwind H.A.R.10.

No. 111 Squadron

Formed 1 Aug. 1917, in Palestine. Bristol Bullet D (1), Bristol M.1c(2), D.H.2 (4), Vickers Bullet (5), Nieuport 17C-1 (7). Oct. 1917, S.E.5 (10). Fighter unit in Palestine, Syria, Egypt. Oct. 1918, at Ramleh. Feb. 1919, F2b (6), Snipe. 1 Feb. 1920, renumbered No. 14 Squadron. Reformed 1 Oct. 1923, at Duxford with Grebe. June, 1924, Siskin 3. 1925, Siskin 3a and Dual Siskin. 1930, at Hornchurch. 1931, Bulldog 2a. C.O. S/L E. P. Mackay. 15 July, 1934, to Northolt. July, 1934, Gauntlet 2. Dec. 1937, first to fly Hurricane 1. 10 Feb. 1938. C.O. S/L J. Gillan made record flight at over 400 m.p.h. from Turnhouse to Northolt in 48 mins. Hurricanes coded TM-, JU-. Left Northolt Sept. 1939. Feb. 1940, at Wick. Aug. 1940, at Croydon. April, 1941, Spitfire F.5b, F.5c (JU-). Nov. 1942, in North Africa, then Malta, Italy, Corsica, France. 1944, Spitfire F.9c (JU-, SW-). Disbanded May, 1947, in Italy. Reformed 1952, with Meteor F.8. Aug. 1955, at North Weald with Hunter F.2. C.O. S/L R. L. Topp. 1956, Hunter F.4. 1959, C.O. S/L P. Latham. 1959, Hunter F.6. 1961, third unit with Lightning F.1. At Wattisham. 1961, Lightning F.1A, T.4. C.O. S/L K. A. C. Wirdnam. 1967, Lightning F.3.

No. 112 Squadron

Formed 30 July, 1917, and stationed at Throwley, Faversham for Home Defence. C.O. Maj. C. J. Q. Brand. Received Pup initially and, in May, 1918, Camel F.1. 1919, Snipe. Disbanded 13 June, 1919. Reformed 6 May, 1939, with Gladiator 1 and 2 (XO–, GA–). 1940, in Egypt and Greece. 1941, Tomahawk F.1 (GA–). 1943, Tomahawk F.2b (GA–). C.O. S/L Morello. 1943, Kittyhawk F.1a, F.B.3 (GA–). 1944, Kittyhawk F.4 (GA–). 1944, Mustang F.3, F.B.4 (GA–). Disbanded 30 Dec. 1946. Reformed with Vampire F.B.5 (A–). Oct. 1954, Sabre F.4 (A–). C.O. S/L F. H. Hegerty. In 2nd T.A.F. at Bruggen. 1956, Hunter F.4.

No. 113 Squadron

Formed 1 Aug. 1917, at Ismailia. 27 Oct. 1917, B.E.2e(8), R.E.8 (5), Nieuport 17C–1 (1 flight). Jan. 1918, at Deiran and Sarona. Oct. 1918, one flight at Haifa. Nov. 1918, sixteen B.E.2e. Disbanded 1 Feb. 1920, and renumbered No. 208 Squadron. Reformed 18 May, 1937, for day-bombing with Hind at Grantham. 1939, Blenheim 1L (VA–, BT–) in Egypt. 1941, Blenheim 4L (VA–). March, 1941, in Greece. Blenheim B.5d. 1943, Hurricane F.B.2b in Assam. 1945, Thunderbolt F.1, F.B.2. Disbanded Oct. 1945. Reformed Sept. 1946, from No. 620 Squadron for transport in Middle East with Halifax A.7, A.9 (MOHC–). Disbanded April, 1947. Reformed Sept. 1947, with Dakota C.4.

No. 114 'Hong Kong' Squadron

Formed Sept. 1917, at Lahore from part of No. 31 Squadron for reconnaissance with B.E.2c, B.E.2e, H. Farman F.20. One flight at Aden from end of 1918 until 1920. April, 1920, renumbered No. 28 Squadron. Reformed 12 Dec. 1936, at Wyton for day-bombing with Hind. March, 1937, first squadron to fly Blenheim 1. Dec. 1939, with Blenheim 4L (FD–) in A.A.S.F. at Condé. 1942, Blenheim 4L (FD–, RT–), Blenheim B.5d (RT–). March, 1943, Boston B.3. (RT–). Dec. 1943, Boston B.4, B.5 (RT–). Mosquito F.B.6, T.3 (RT–). April, 1945, Boston B.4, B.5 (RT–) in Italy. Disbanded Nov. 1945, and renumbered No. 8 Squadron. Reformed 1 Aug. 1947, for transport with Dakota C.4. 1950, in Middle East with Valetta C.1. Disbanded 31 Dec. 1957, at Nicosia. Reformed 1958, in Cyprus with Chipmunk T.1. 1958, Hastings C.1 at Colerne. 1962, first Argosy C.1 unit at Benson.

No. 115 Squadron

Formed 1 Dec. 1917, at Catterick. April, 1918, O/400. Joined Independent Air Force 31 Aug. 1918. Oct. 1918, night bombing from Roville. Disbanded Oct. 1919. Reformed 28 June, 1937, from one flight of Hendons from No. 38 Squadron. Later received Harrow 1 (BK–) at Marham. 1938, Whitley B.5 (BK–). 1939, Wellington B.1c, B.2, B.3

(KO–). March, 1943, Lancaster B.1, B.2, B.3, B.1(F.E.), B.10 (KO–, A4–, 1L). At East Wretham. Aug. 1943, Little Snoring. Nov. 1943, Witchford. Also used Stirling B.1. 1949, re-equipped with Lincoln B.2 (KO–). Aug. 1950, Washington B.1 (KO–) at Marham. C.O. S/L G. E. R. Alford. 1953, C.O. S/L L. B. Holmes. Feb. 1954, Canberra B.2. 1959, at Tangmere with Varsity T.1. for radio calibration.

No. 116 Squadron

Formed Nov. 1917, but did not see service and was disbanded Nov. 1918. Reformed 17 Feb. 1941, for radar calibration with Lysander 2 (LI–, II–), Oxford T.2, Hurricane F.1 (II–), Anson 1, Defiant N.F.1, Master T.2, Mustang F.1. Disbanded 26 May, 1945. Reformed for special duties 1953, Anson C.19/1, Lincoln B.2. 1956, at Watton with Varsity T.1. Hastings C.1.

No. 117 Squadron

Formed Jan. 1918, as a day-bomber unit but did not see any service and was disbanded Oct. 1919. Reformed April, 1941, for communications with Dakota C.1, C.2, D.C.2, Hudson C.6, Bombay. June, 1943, in Middle East with Dakota C.3, C.4, Lodestar C.4, Lodestar C.1, C.2, D.H.86b. Moved to Far East for supply dropping.

No. 118 Squadron

Formed Jan. 1918, as a light night-bomber unit with F.E.2b. Disbanded Nov. 1918. Reformed Feb. 1941, as a fighter squadron with Spitfire F.2, F.2a (NK–). At Filton, Colerne, Warmwell, Ibsley. 1944, Spitfire F.5a, F.5b, L.F.5b, H.F.6, F.9c, Mustang F.3, F.B.4 (NK–). Disbanded March, 1946. Reformed in 2nd T.A.F. with Vampire F.B.5. Re-equipped with Venom F.B.1. June, 1955, flying Hunter F.4 at Jever. C.O. S/L C. M. Gibbs.

No. 119 Squadron

Formed Jan. 1918, but did not see service and was disbanded Nov. 1918. Reformed 13 March, 1941, from 'G' Flt. which had been formed in 1940 with three militarized Short S.26/M Grenadier class flying boats— *Golden Fleece*, *Golden Hind* and *Golden Horn*. Based at Islay for reconnaissance, convoy-escort and mail-carrying. April, 1941, Short S.23 *Clio* and *Cordelia*. July, 1941, at Pembroke Dock. Disbanded 6 Dec. 1941. Reformed April, 1942, at Loch Erne with Catalina G.R.1, Sunderland G.R.1, Anson G.R.1. Disbanded 17 April, 1943. Reformed July, 1944, from No. 415 Squadron, R.C.A.F., at Manston with Albacore 1 (NH–). Based in Belgium on anti-submarine duties. Jan. 1945, at Bircham Newton with Swordfish 1 (NH–).

No. 120 'Punjab' Squadron

Formed Jan. 1918, with eighteen D.H.9. and also the D.H.10 Amiens.

Based at Lympne for carriage of airmail to the Rhine. Disbanded Oct.
1919. Reformed 6 June, 1941, at Nutts Corner, as first unit with
Liberator G.R.1, G.R.2, G.R.3, G.R.5. Later used Liberator G.R.6
fitted with Leigh-Light in 1944. Disbanded 4 June, 1945. Reformed
1 Oct. 1946, from No. 160 Squadron with Liberator G.R.8 (BS–), Lancaster G.R.3 (BS–). 1948, at Leuchars. Oxford T.2 (BS–). 1952,
Shackleton M.R.1. 1955, at Aldergrove with Shackleton M.R.2. 1958,
Shackleton M.R.3.

No. 121 'Eagle' Squadron

Formed Jan. 1918, as a day-bomber unit but did not see service and was
disbanded Nov. 1918. Reformed May, 1942, as second 'Eagle' Sauadron
with Spitfire F.5b, F.5c (AV–), Hurricane F.2b (AV–). Disbanded
29 Sept. 1942, and became 335th Squadron, U.S.A.A.F.

No. 122 'Bombay' Squadron

Formed Jan. 1918, for day-bombing but was disbanded in Nov. 1918,
without seeing service. Reformed May, 1941, with Spitfire F.2a, F.5b,
L.F.5b (MT–). 1943, Spitfire F.9b, F.9c, L.F.16e (MT–). 1944, Mustang F.3, F.B.4 (MT–). Disbanded April, 1946. Reformed 1947, with
Spitfire F.21 (MT–).

No. 123 'East India' Squadron

Formed Feb. 1918, for day-bombing but disbanded at Shoreham in
Oct. 1918, without service. Reformed Nov. 1918, as No. 2 Squadron,
Canadian Air Force, at Upper Heyford in No. 1 Canadian Wing. Dis-
banded Feb. 1920. Reformed May, 1941, as a fighter squadron with
Spitfire F.1b, F.2a (XE–). 1942, in Middle East with Hurricane F.2.
May, 1943, Spitfire F.5b (XE–) in North Africa. 1944, Thunderbolt F.1,
F.B.2 in Madras. June, 1945, renumbered No. 81 Squadron.

No. 124 'Baroda' Squadron

Formed in Jan. 1918, but did not see any service and was disbanded in
Oct. 1918. Reformed May, 1941, as a day-fighter unit with Spitfire F.1
(ON–), Tiger Moth T.2 (ON–). Later received Spitfire F.5a, F.5b, F.6,
H.F.7, H.F.9e, F.9c, L.F.16e (all ON–). Took part in attacks on Ger-
man rocket sites on Continent. Received Meteor F.3 (ON–) and on 1
April, 1946, was renumbered No. 56 Squadron.

No. 125 'Newfoundland' Squadron

Formed Feb. 1918, but did not see any service and was disbanded Sept.
1918. Reformed June, 1941, for night-fighting with Defiant N.F.1
(VA–), N.F.2 (VA–). At Colerne and Church Fenton. 1942, Beaufighter F.2 (VA–), Hurricane N.F.2c. Sept. 1942, Beaufighter N.F.6f

(VA–). Jan. 1944, Mosquito N.F.17 (VA–). March, 1945, Mosquito
N.F.30, T.3 (VA–), Mosquito N.F.36. Disbanded Nov. 1945, and renumbered No. 219 Squadron. Reformed with Venom N.F.3. Later
used Meteor N.F.14.

No. 126 Squadron

Formed Feb. 1918, and disbanded in July, 1918, without seeing service.
Reformed June, 1941, for day-fighting with Hurricane F.2b, F.2c.
April, 1942, Spitfire F.5b, F.B.5b (TD–), F.B.5c (TD–). 1943, Spitfire
F.B.9, F.B.9b, F.B.9e, L.F.9c (all 5J–). Disbanded March, 1944. Re-
formed April, 1944, with Mustang, F.3, F.B.4 (5J–).

No. 127 Squadron

Formed Jan. 1918, for day-bombing, but was disbanded in July, 1918,
without service. Reformed June, 1941, for day-fighting with Hurricane
F.1, F.2b and Gladiator 2. Feb. 1943, Spitfire F.5b, F.5c. Oct. 1943,
Hurricane F.2c. April, 1944, Spitfire F.9 (9N–). Jan. 1945, Spitfire
L.F.16e (9N–).

No. 128 Squadron

Formed 1 Feb. 1918, and disbanded in July, 1918, without service. Re-
formed Oct. 1941, at Hastings, Sierra Leone, for fighter, air-sea rescue,
army co-operation, convoy-escort and photo-reconnaissance duties.
Used Hurricane F.1, F.2b (WG–) and Hudson G.R.2. Disbanded
March, 1943. Reformed Sept. 1944, at Wyton with Mosquito B.16
(M5–) and Mosquito B.20. 1 April, 1946, renumbered No. 14 Squadron.

No. 129 'Mysore' Squadron

Formed March, 1918, but disbanded July, 1918, without seeing any
service. Reformed June, 1941, with Spitfire F.5b (DV–) and F.2a (DV–).
1944, Spitfire F.14 (DV–). 1946, Spitfire F.9c, F.14, L.F.16e (DV–) and
Mustang F.3 (DV–).

No. 130 'Punjab' Squadron

Formed March, 1918, but did not see any service and was disbanded in
July, 1918. Reformed June, 1941, as long-range fighter unit with Hur-
ricane F.1 (PJ–) and Spitfire F.2a (PJ–). 1943, Spitfire F.5b (PJ–, AP–).
Disbanded Feb. 1944. Reformed 15 April, 1944, from No. 186 Squadron
for army co-operation with Spitfire F.R.14 (AP–). Also used Spitfire
F.9e, F.16e, L.F.16e (all AP–). Re-equipped with Vampire F.1. (AP–).
Jan. 1947, renumbered No. 54 Squadron. Reformed Dec. 1953, in 2nd
T.A.F. with Sabre F.4. At Bruggen. C.O.S/L Megor. 1956, Hunter F.4.

No. 131 'County of Kent' Squadron

Formed March, 1918, with F.E.2b. Disbanded Sept. 1918. Reformed

June, 1941, as a fighter squadron with Hurricane F.1 (NX-) and Spit-
fire F.1, F.2a (NX-). Dec. 1941, Spitfire F.5b, H.F.7, L.F.8, F.9c
(NX-). 26 June, 1945, renumbered from No. 134 Squadron with
Thunderbolt F.B.2 (NX-).

No. 132 'City of Bombay' Squadron

Formed March, 1918, but was disbanded in Nov. 1918, without seeing
any service. Reformed June, 1941, with Spitfire F.1, F.2b, F.5b (FF-).
Also used Spitfire F.8, F.9, F.9c, L.F.5b, F.9b, F.B.9e, F.R.14 (all
FF-). Served in North Africa and Italy.

No. 133 'Eagle' Squadron

Formed March, 1918, but was disbanded in July, 1918, without seeing
service. Reformed 1 Aug. 1941, as third American 'Eagle' Squadron.
Used Spitfire F.5b (MX-). Was also equipped with Hornet Moth 2,
Hurricane F.2c, Spitfire F.5b, F.9c, H.F.7 (all MD-). 29 Sept. 1942,
became 336th Squadron, U.S.A.A.F.

No. 134 Squadron

Formed 1 March, 1918, from part of No. 17 Squadron but was dis-
banded in July, 1918, without seeing any service. Reformed 31 July,
1941, and was first British squadron in Russia, flying Hurricane F.2b
(GV-). Jan. 1942, in Western Desert with Spitfire F.8, F.9c. Later used
Thunderbolt F.B.2. Disbanded 26 June, 1945, and became No. 131
Squadron.

No. 135 Squadron

Formed 1 March, 1918, but did not see service and was disbanded in
July, 1918. Reformed 15 Aug. 1941, as a fighter unit with Hurricane
F.2b and also used Lysander 2. Served in the Far East and was equipped
later with Thunderbolt F.1 and F.B.2.

No. 136 Squadron

Formed 1 April, 1918, but was disbanded in July, 1918, without service.
Reformed 20 Aug. 1941, as a fighter squadron with Hurricane F.1, F.2b,
F.2c (HM-). Later used Tomahawk F.2b (HM-). 1945, Spitfire F.5c,
L.F.8, F.R.14e (HM-). Fought in India, Burma and Cocos Islands.

No. 137 Squadron

Formed April, 1918, but did not see any service and was disbanded in
July, 1918. Reformed Nov. 1941, at Charmy Down as the second
squadron to be equipped with Whirlwind F.B.1 (SF-). Also used
Hurricane F.B.2b, F.4 (SF-), Spitfire F.2a (SF-). 1942, Typhoon
F.1b (SF-). Engaged in European operations. Reformed with Javelin
F.A.W.5.

No. 138 Squadron

Formed Nov. 1918, at Chingford for fighter-reconnaissance with F2b.
Disbanded Feb. 1919. Reformed 25 Aug. 1941, from No. 1419 Flt. at
Tempsford for special duties. C.O. W/C Knowles. Engaged in dropping
agents in occupied Europe and in picking them up. Used Whitley B.4,
B.5 (NF–), Lysander 3 (AC–), Wellington B.1. (NF–). March, 1942,
Halifax B.1, B.2, B.2/1a, B.2/1(Spec.), B.2/2, B.5/1, B.5/2 (all NF–).
C.O. S/L R. E. Hockey. Engaged in night-bombing when not on special
duties. Also used Oxford T.2. (AC–, NF–). Aug. 1944, Stirling B.1, B.3,
G.T.4 (NF–), Liberator B.2 (NF–). 1945, at Tuddenham. March, 1945,
Lancaster B.1, B.3, B.1(F.E.) (AC–, NF–). 1946, Lincoln B.2 (NF–) at
Wyton. Disbanded Sept. 1950. Jan. 1955 at Gaydon became first
squadron to receive Valiant B.1—12 aircraft. Also used Canberra T.3—3
aircraft. C.O. W/C R. G. W. Oakley. Sept. 1955, to Wittering.

No. 139 'Jamaica' Squadron

Formed 3 July, 1918, at Villaverla from 'Z' Flt. of No. 34 Squadron.
Engaged on fighter-reconnaissance with F2b and also used Camel F.1.
At Grossa and Arcade. Disbanded 7 March, 1919, at Caldiero. Reformed 3 Sept. 1936, at Wyton for day-bombing with Hind. 1938,
Blenheim 1L (SD–, SY–). 1939, Blenheim 4L (XD–). N6215 carried
out first sortie of the War on 3 Sept. 1939, by reconnoitring German
fleet at Wilhelmshaven. Went to France with A.A.S.F. at Bethienville
and Plivot. 1940, Horsham St. Faith. 1941, Hudson G.R.3 at Akyab
and Chittagong. 1942, Lysander 2. 1942, Blenheim B.5d. Disbanded
April, 1942, and renumbered No. 62 Squadron. Reformed June, 1943,
and was second unit to receive Mosquito B.4 (XD–). At Horsham St.
Faith and Marham. Flew with Pathfinder Force. C.O. W/C Shand.
1943, Mosquito B.9, T.3, B.20, B.25 (XD–). Moved to Upwood. 1944,
Mosquito B.16, Oxford T.2 (XD–). 1946, Mosquito B.16, B.35 (XD–)
at Hemswell and Coningsby. 1935, Canberra B.2 at Hemswell. C.O.
S/L T. Pearce. 1955. Canberra B.6. C.O. S/L A. Ashworth. Feb. 1962, at
Wittering, first squadron with Victor B.2.

No. 140 Squadron

Formed in 1918, at Biggin Hill for night-fighting with F2b. Disbanded
1919. Reformed Sept. 1941, for photo-reconnaissance with night flight
of Blenheim 4 and day flight of Spitfire P.R.4. Aug. 1943, Ventura G.R.1.
Spitfire P.R.11 used temporarily. Mosquito N.F.2, P.R.16. April, 1944,
at Northolt.

No. 141 Squadron

Formed 1 Jan. 1918, from a flight of No. 61 Squadron for Home Defence. Received initially Dolphin, and in March, 1918, F2b. F.B.26

Vampire (1). Oct. 1918, at Biggin Hill. Disbanded Feb. 1920. Reformed
4 Oct. 1939, with Gladiator 2 (TW-). Also received Defiant N.F.1
(TW-) and Blenheim 1 and N.F.1f (TW-). At Gatwick, Turnhouse and
Gravesend. Aug. 1940, at Prestwick. Sept. 1940, to Biggin Hill. 1940,
Spitfire F.2 (TW-). 1942, Beaufighter F.1, N.F.1f, N.F.6f (TW-) at
Digby. 1944, Mosquito N.F.2, F.B.6, N.F.30, T.3 (TW-). Disbanded
7 Sept. 1945. Reformed Aug. 1953 with Mosquito N.F.36. 1953, Meteor
N.F.11. 1954, at Coltishall. Meteor N.F.14. 1955, Venom N.F.3. C.O.
W/C P. L. Chilton. Feb. 1957, became second to fly Javelin and first to
receive FAW.4 version. On 16 Jan. 1958, became No. 41 Squadron.

No. 142 'Worcester' Squadron

Formed 2 Feb. 1918, in Palestine with B.E.12a, F.K.8 (7), R.E. (5),
G-100 Elephant. At Julis. Oct. 1918, on reconnaissance from Affuli.
Disbanded 1 Feb. 1920, and renumbered No. 55 Squadron. Reformed
1 June, 1934, for day-bombing with Hart at Netheravon. 1938, at An-
dover with Battle 1 (KB-). Sept. 1939, in France with A.A.S.F. at
Berry-au-Bac. Also flew Blenheim 4L (WV-). 1940, Wellington B.1c,
B.3 (WV-, QT-). Disbanded 5 Oct. 1944. Reformed 25 Oct. 1944 for
photo-reconnaissance with Mosquito P.R.16, P.R.34 (4H-). Disbanded
25 Sept. 1945. Reformed Feb. 1959 at Aden with Venom F.B.4. C.O.
S/L R. Ramirez. 1 April, 1959, became No. 208 Squadron.

No. 143 Squadron

Formed Jan. 1918, for Home Defence with S.E.5a and Camel. Oct.
1918, on night-fighting at Detling. Disbanded Oct. 1919. Reformed 15
June, 1941, for coastal-reconnaissance with Beaufighter F.1c, F.6c
(HO-). Disbanded Nov. 1941. Reformed March, 1942, with Blenheim
4 and operated temporarily as an O.T.U. June, 1944, at North Coates
with Beaufighter T.F.10 (HO-) for anti-shipping duties. Dec. 1944,
Mosquito F.B.6 (HO-). C.O. W/C E. H. McHardy. 1 June, 1945,
renumbered from No. 14 Squadron.

No. 144 'Grimsby' Squadron

Formed 20 March, 1918, at Port Said with B.E.12 and R.E.8. April,
1918, B.E.2e, S7 Shorthorn, D.H.6, G-100 Elephant. Aug. 1918, D.H.9.
14 Aug. 1918, to Junction Station for day-bombing. Oct. 1918, one flight
of R.E.8 at Haifa. Disbanded 4 Feb. 1919, at Ford Junction. Reformed 11
Jan. 1937, at Hemswell with Blenheim 1. Sept. 1939, at Leuchars with
Hampden B.1 (NV-, PL-), Anson G.R.1 (PL-). Engaged in torpedo-
dropping. 1942, Manchester B.1. 1942, Beaufighter T.F.6c, T.F.10
(PL-).

No. 145 Squadron

Formed June, 1918, as a fighter unit with S.E.5. 14 Aug. 1918, one flight

to Ramleh. Supported General Allenby against the Turks. Disbanded
Sept. 1919. Reformed 10 Oct. 1939, with Blenheim 1f (SO-). Aug. 1940,
at Westhampnett with Hurricane F.1 (SO-). Jan. 1941, Spitfire F.2a.
F.2b (SO-). June, 1942, Spitfire F.5b (SO-) at Msus. June, 1944, Spit-
fire F.5b, F.5c, L.F.8, F.9, L.F.9. C.O. S/L Kallio. C.O. S/L N. Duke.
In Sicily. Sept. 1944, C.O. S/L Daniels. Disbanded 19 Aug. 1945.
Reformed in 2nd T.A.F. with Vampire F.B.5. May, 1954, at Celle with
Venom F.B.1. Oct. 1954, C.O.S/L Johnson.

No. 146 'Assam' Squadron

Formed Oct. 1941, as long-range day-fighter unit in the Far East.
Hurricane F.2, Audax 1. Later re-equipped with Thunderbolt F.1.

No. 147 Squadron

Formed May, 1918, but did not see service and was disbanded in
March, 1919. Reformed 5 Sept. 1944, at Croydon for transport duties.
Used Dakota C.3, C.4 (ODF-), Liberator B.1. Code 5F- not used.
Disbanded 15 Sept. 1946. Reformed from No. 1 Long-range Ferry
Unit with Hastings C.1. C.O. S/L T. Stephenson in 1953. 1956, C.O.
S/L B. Foskett. From 8 Dec. 1952, until 19 Dec. 1953, ferried 376
Sabres from Canada in 'Becher's Brook' operation. 1956, at Benson. In
1956, re-equipped—in conjunction with No. 167 Squadron—2nd T.A.F.
squadrons with Swift F.R.5 and Hunter.

No. 148 Squadron

Formed 10 Feb. 1918, for night-bombing at Andover with F.E.2b. To
France 26 April, 1918. Also used Camel F.1. Oct. 1918, at Sainles Pernes.
Disbanded 30 June, 1919. Reformed 7 June, 1937, at Stradishall with
Audax 1. Later received Wellesley 1 (BS-). Nov. 1938, Heyford 2. Sept.
1939, training with Wellington B.1c, Anson 1 (BS-). Disbanded 4 April,
1940. Reformed 14 Dec. 1940, with sixteen Wellington B.1c. Also used
Wellington B.2, B.3, Lysander 3. Disbanded 14 Dec. 1942. Reformed 14
March, 1943, from No. 108 Squadron for special duties. Served in
Middle East and Balkans with Liberator B.6 (FS-) receiving four, and
Halifax B.2/1a (FS-) receiving fourteen. Disbanded, then reformed
4 Nov. 1946, for bombing with Lancaster B.1, B.3, B.1(F.E.) (AU-)
Re-equipped with Lincoln B.2 (AU-). 1957, at Marham with Valiant B.1.

No. 149 'East India' Squadron

Formed 3 March, 1918, at Yapton for night-bombing with F.E.2b.
2 June, 1918, to St. Omer. Oct. 1918, at Clairmarais. Was only F.E. unit
to go to Germany, returning to England in March, 1919. Disbanded
1 Aug. 1919, at Tallaght in Ireland. Reformed 12 April, 1937, at Mildenhall from 'B' Flt. of No. 99 Squadron with Heyford 2. March, 1939,

Wellington B.1c, B.1a, B.1, B.3 (OJ–, LY–). 4 Sept. 1939, attacked German fleet at Brunsbüttel. 18 Jan. 1940, on leaflet raids 15 June, 1940, one flight to Salon, France. Returned to Mildenhall 17 June, 1940. 1941, Stirling B.1, B.3 (OJ–, TK–) at Methwold. April, 1942, engaged in mine-laying. 28 Nov. 1942, V.C. won by F/S R. H. Middleton. Aug. 1943, Lancaster B.1, B.3, B.1(F.E.) (OJ–, TK–) at Methwold and Tuddenham. Re-equipped 1944 with Lancaster B.1. (OJ–), then re-equipped with Lincoln B.2 (OJ–). Nov. 1950, first squadron to fly Washington B.2 (OJ–) at Marham. 1954, Canberra B.2. Sept. 1954, moved to Ahlhorn, Germany, and was first to go abroad with Canberra B.2. C.O. S/L R. E. R. Adams. 1956, at Gütersloh.

No. 150 Squadron

Formed 1 April, 1918, at Salonika from one flight of No. 17 Squadron and one flight of No. 47 Squadron. C.O. Maj. W. R. B. McBain. Used B.E.12, Bristol M.1c, S.E.5a, Camel F.1 and 2F.1, Nieuport 17C-1. Oct. 1918, at Kirec, Macedonia. Disbanded 18 Sept. 1918. Reformed 8 Aug. 1938, with Battle 1 (DG–, JN–). 1939, Blenheim 4L (JN–). To France with A.A.S.F. at Ecury. 1940, Wellington B.1, B.3, B.10 (JN–). Disbanded Oct. 1944. Reformed Nov. 1944, with Lancaster B.1, B.3 (JN–, IQ–) at Hemswell.

No. 151 Squadron

Formed 12 June, 1918, at Hainault from parts of Nos. 44, 78 and 112 Squadrons which had been engaged on Home Defence. The new squadron was equipped with the Camel, its first C.O. being Maj. G. W. Murlis-Green. To France and was stationed at Fontaine-sur-Maye from 23 June, 1918. 27 June, 1918, 'A' flight was detached to join No. 101 Squadron at Famechon on special intruder flying. The squadron was the first night-flying fighter unit. 1 July, 1918, C.O. Maj. C. J. Q. Brand. 8 Oct. 1918, to Bancourt. After Armistice the squadron went to Gullane, Scotland. Disbanded 10 Sept. 1919. While active 21 E/A were destroyed with 5 probably destroyed. Reformed 4 Aug. 1936, at North Weald with Gauntlet 2 (GG–). Nov. 1938, Hurricane F.1, N.F.2 (GG–, DZ–). 1939, C.O. S/L E. M. Donaldson. 1940, S/L Gordon. 1940, S/L West. 17 May, 1940, to Abbeville, France. Returned to Manston, but again went to France, based at Vitry. 19 May, 1940, to North Weald. 1940, Digby, Bramcote. 1940–43, at Wittering. Nov. 1940, Defiant N.F.1, N.F.2 (DZ–). 23 May, 1942, Mosquito F.2, N.F.2 (DZ–). 1943, Colerne, Middle Wallop. 1943–44, Colerne. July, 1943, Mosquito F.B.6, N.F.12 (DZ–). 1944, Predannack, Castle Camps. 1944–45, Hunsdon. Sept. 1945, Mosquito N.F.30 (DZ–). 1945–46, Predannack. 1946, Exeter. 1946, Mosquito N.F.36 (DZ–). 1946, Weston Zoyland. During the war, the squadron destroyed 132 E/A, probably destroyed 24 and damaged 55.

Disbanded 10 Oct. 1946, and merged with No. 23 Squadron to become No. 23/151 Squadron. Reformed 15 Sept. 1951, at Leuchars with Vampire N.F.10 under S/L A. D. Boyle. April, 1953, Meteor N.F.11. Also had Meteor F.8, T.7. 7 Sept. 1953, C.O. S/L D. B. Ainsworth. 1956, Venom N.F.3. Javelin F.A.W.4. June, 1957, Javelin F.A.W.5—first unit.

No. 152 'Hyderabad' Squadron

Formed Oct. 1918, as a night-flying fighter unit. Went to France 18 Oct. 1918, with Camel F.1. At Karvin. Disbanded 30 June, 1919. Reformed 1 Oct. 1939, with Hart and Gladiator 2 (SN-). 1940, Hurricane F.1, Spitfire F.1, F.2, F.2a, F.5b, H.F.7 (SN-). 1943, Spitfire F.5c (UM-, SN-). Feb. 1946, Spitfire F.R.14 (UM-). Disbanded 10 March, 1946. Reformed 10 June, 1946, in Burma with Spitfire F.8 (UM-). 1946, Tempest F.2 (UM-). Disbanded 31 Jan. 1947. Reformed for night-fighting with Meteor N.F.14. 1955, at Wattisham. 1958, at Stradishall. 1960, Pembroke C.I. Twin Pioneer C.C.1.

No. 153 Squadron

Formed Dec. 1918, at Hainault Farm but did not see any service and was disbanded in June, 1919. Reformed 14 Oct. 1941, at Ballyhalbert with Defiant F.1. 1 April, 1943, Beaufighter N.F.1f. 1943, Mosquito N.F.12. Disbanded 5 Sept. 1944. Reformed 2 Oct. 1944, at Scampton with Lancaster B.1, B.3 (P4-). Disbanded 23 Sept. 1945. Reformed Feb. 1955, with Meteor F.8. in use in July, 1955. At West Malling. Sept. 1955, Meteor N.F.12. Later used Meteor N.F.14. July, 1958, became No. 25 Squadron.

No. 154 'Motor Industries Gift' Squadron

Formed Nov. 1941, as a day-fighter unit. Spitfire F.5b (HT-). Mustang F.1. Disbanded Oct. 1944. Reformed 16 Nov. 1944, with Spitfire F.5b, F.9 (QV-). Feb. 1945, Mustang F.4 (QV-).

No. 155 Squadron

Formed 1918, at Chingford for night-fighting and was disbanded in 1919. Reformed 4 April, 1942, with Mohawk F.B.1 (DF-). Served in Far East. 1943, Spitfire F.8 (DG-). Disbanded Aug. 1946. Reformed and flying Whirlwind H.A.R.4 in Malaya in 1955. At Kuala Lumpur, with Sycamore H.R.13. 1959, became No. 110 Squadron.

No. 156 Squadron

Formed 1 Feb. 1918, but was disbanded in Nov. 1918, without service. Reformed 14 Feb. 1942, from part of No. 40 Squadron at Alconbury with Wellington B.1c (GT-), Manchester B.1a (GT-). Flew with Pathfinder Force with Lancaster B.1. B.3 (GT–). At Warboys. 1944, Upwood. 1945, Wyton.

No. 157 Squadron

Formed July, 1918, at Upper Heyford as a fighter unit but was disbanded on 1 Feb. 1919, without service. Reformed 13 Dec. 1941, with Mosquito B.4 (RS–). Later used Mosquito N.F.2, N.F.19 (RS–). 1944, in Pathfinder Force with Mosquito N.F.30 (RS–). Also used Anson T.1 (RS–).

No. 158 Squadron

Reformed 14 Feb. 1942, as a bomber unit with Wellington B.1c. June, 1942, Halifax B.1, B.3, B.2, B.2/1a, B.6 (NP–). At Lissett. 1945, Stirling B.1, C.5 (DK–), Halifax B.3 (DK–).

No. 159 Squadron

Formed 2 Jan. 1942, at Molesworth as first heavy-bomber unit in Middle East, India and Burma. Used Liberator B.2, C.6, C.8. Operated as Pathfinder.

No. 160 Squadron

Formed 16 Jan. 1942, at Thurleigh and served in Ceylon and Burma. Flew Liberator B.2, G.R.5b, G.R.5c in 1943 on photo-reconnaissance. 1944, Liberator G.R.6, G.R.8 (BS–). 1 Oct. 1946, became No. 120 Squadron.

No. 161 Squadron

Formed 15 Feb. 1942, at Tempsford from King's Flight for special duties. C.O. W/C E. H. Fielden. Lysander 3 (MA–), Whitley B.4, B.5 (MA–), Wellington B.1c (MA–). Engaged in agent dropping and picking up. C.O. G/C P. C. Pickard. Wellington B.3 (MA–), Hudson 3a (MA–), Havoc 1 (MA–). Dec. 1942, Halifax B.1, B.2, B.2/1, B.2/1a, B.5/1, B.5/1a MA(–), Ventura B.1 (MA–), Albermarle G.T.1/1 (MA–). Sept. 1944, Stirling B.1, B.3, G.T.4 (MA–).

No. 162 Squadron

Formed early 1942 for special duties. Investigated enemy radar and also engaged in gunning land forces in Middle East. Used Wellington B.3, Blenheim 4, Hart, Blenheim B.5d, Savoia Marchetti S.79, Lodestar, Magister, Wellington B.1c, Baltimore B.3. Disbanded 25 Sept. 1944. Reformed Sept. 1944, as a light-bomber unit. Used Mosquito F.B.6, B.20, B.25 (CR–), Wellington B.1c, B.3, B.10, Baltimore B.3, Magister, Spitfire F.5b. Disbanded July, 1946. Reformed in Transport Command. Code GK– not used.

E

No. 163 Squadron

Formed 10 July, 1942, in Middle East at Suez for transport with Hudson C.6. Disbanded June, 1943. Reformed 25 Jan. 1945, as a light-bomber unit with Mosquito B.25 and B.16. Disbanded 20 Aug. 1945. Reformed for transport with Warwick C.3.

No. 164 'Argentine-British' Squadron

Formed 6 April, 1942, with Spitfire F.5b (FJ-). 1943, Hurricane F.2d, F.B.4 (FJ-). 1944, Typhoon F.1b (FJ-). Attacked German transport in Europe. 1946, Spitfire F.9, L.F.16e (UB-).

No. 165 'Times of Ceylon' Squadron

Formed 6 April, 1942, with Spitfire F.5b (SK-). Later used Spitfire F.9c, L.F.9c, L.F.16e, Mustang F.3 (all SK-). Operated in Europe. Disbanded 1 Sept. 1946. Reformed and in 1957 was flying Meteor N.F.14 as a night-fighter unit.

No. 166 'Huddersfield' Squadron

Formed 13 June, 1918. Nov. 1918, F.E.2b for bombing. Based at Bircham Newton with the V/1500 of which three had been delivered by the Armistice. These were intended for the bombing of Berlin. Disbanded 31 May, 1919. Reformed 1 Nov. 1936, from 'A' Flight of No. 97 Squadron for bombing with Heyford 2 (GB-). At Leconfield. Sept. 1939, Whitley B.3, B.4 (AS-, GB-). Disbanded 6 April, 1940, Reformed 27 Jan. 1943, with Wellington B.3, B.10 (AS-). Sept. 1943, Lancaster B.1, B.3 (AS-) at Kirmington.

No. 167 'Gold Coast' Squadron

Formed Nov. 1918, for bombing with V/1500 from Bircham Newton. Disbanded 21 May, 1919. Reformed 3 April, 1942, as a fighter squadron with Spitfire F.5b (VL-). 12 June, 1943, became No. 322 (Dutch) Squadron. Reformed 21 Oct. 1944, for transport with Warwick C.1, C.3, Anson 1, Dakota C.4, Lancaster B.1 (VL-). Disbanded 1 Feb. 1946. Reformed Jan. 1953, at Benson from No. 1 Overseas Ferry Unit with Valetta C.1. Oct. 1954, C.O. S/L H. D. Byrne. Re-equipped 2nd R.A.F. with Hunters in conjunction with No. 147 Squadron.

No. 168 Squadron

Formed 15 June, 1942, for reconnaissance with Tomahawk F.2. Nov. 1942, Mustang F.R.1a. 2 Oct. 1944, Typhoon F.1b (QC-). Operated with 2nd T.A.F.

No. 169 Squadron

Formed 15 June, 1942, for intruder duties with Mustang F.R.1a (VI-). Disbanded Sept. 1943. Reformed 1 Oct. 1943, with Stirling B.3. Also used Mosquito N.F.2, T.3, F.B.6, B.9, N.F.19 (VI–), Beaufighter N.F.1f, N.F.6f (VI–).

No. 170 Squadron

Formed 15 June, 1942, for army co-operation at Weston Zoyland with Mustang F.R.1a. Disbanded 15 Jan. 1944. Reformed 15 Oct. 1944, as a bomber unit with Lancaster B.1, B.3 (TC–). At Hemswell. Nov. 1944, at Dunholme Lodge. March, 1945, at Hemswell. C.O. S/L P. D. Hackforth. Participated in Operations Manna, Exodus and Dodge.

No. 171 Squadron

Formed 15 June, 1942, with Tomahawk F.1, Mustang F.1a. Disbanded 7 Dec. 1942. Reformed 8 Sept. 1944, at Foulsham with Halifax B.3, B.6, G.T.3, G.T.5/1a (EX–, 6Y–). At North Creake. Also used Stirling B.3 (6Y–).

No. 172 Squadron

Formed 8 March, 1942, for anti-submarine duties with Wellington G.R.14 (WN–). First unit to use Leigh-Light Wellington. Wellington G.R.8, G.R.11, G.R.12, G.R.13, G.R.18 (all OQ–). At Limavady. 1945, Dakota C.3 (OQ–).

No. 173 Squadron

Formed 4 July, 1942, for communications with Lodestar, Proctor. Magister, Boston B.1, Audax, Dakota C.3, C.4, Hurricane F.1. Disbanded 29 Feb. 1944. Reformed 1 Feb. 1953, with Provost T.1, Varsity C.1.

No. 174 'Mauritius' Squadron

Formed March, 1942, as a fighter unit with Hurricane F.B.2b (XP–). April, 1943, Typhoon F.1b (XP–) and engaged in rocket-firing attacks on German targets in Europe. Disbanded April. 1945. Reformed Aug. 1945, with Tempest F.5/2 (JJ–).

No. 175 Squadron

Formed March, 1942, as a fighter unit with Hurricane F.1, F.2b (HH–), Served in 2nd T.A.F. in 1944 with rocket-firing Typhoon F.1b.

No. 176 Squadron

Formed 14 Jan. 1943, and served as a night-fighter unit in India with Beaufighter F.1, N.F.6f, Hurricane N.F.2c, Mosquito N.F.19.

No. 177 Squadron

Formed Jan. 1943, as a fighter unit in the Far East. Engaged in intruder operations with Beaufighter F.1, F.6.

No. 178 Squadron

Formed 15 Jan. 1943, at Shandur, for strategical heavy bombing. Received Liberator B.2, B.3, B.6, B.8, Halifax B.2 and Lancaster B.1. In 1944, its Liberators made flights to Warsaw to help the Polish Home Army under General Bor. Disbanded 15 April, 1946, and became No. 70 Squadron.

No. 179 Squadron

Formed Sept. 1942, for anti-shipping duties. Used Wellington G.R.8, G.R.13 and the G.R.14 with Leigh-Light (OZ–). Was also equipped with Warwick G.R.5 (OZ–) and Lancaster G.R.3, A.S.R.3 (OZ–). Operated from Gibraltar and was second unit to have Leigh-Lights.

No. 180 Squadron

Formed 13 Sept. 1942, for bombing at West Raynham with Mitchell B.1 (VO–). Based at Great Massingham and Foulsham. C.O. W/C Hodder. Later used Mitchell B.2 (VO–, EV–) and Mosquito B.16 (VO–, EV–). Disbanded March, 1946, and became No. 69 Squadron.

No. 181 Squadron

Formed Sept. 1942, and engaged in army air support with Typhoon F.1b (EL–) and Hurricane F.2c. Made attacks on targets in Europe.

No. 182 Squadron

Formed Sept. 1942, as a fighter-bomber unit with Hurricane F.10 (XM–) and Typhoon F.1a, F.1b (XM–). Engaged in attacking targets in Europe.

No. 183 'Gold Coast' Squadron

Formed Nov. 1942, as a fighter unit with Typhoon F.1b (HF–). Made rocket attacks on Europe and took part in assault on Walcheren.

No. 184 Squadron

Formed Dec. 1942, and engaged in anti-tank operations with Hurricane F.2b, F.2d, F.4 (BR–). Jan. 1944, Typhoon F.1b (BR–). Attacked targets in Europe.

No. 185 Squadron

Formed 19 Oct. 1918, at East Fortune for service on H.M.S. *Argus* as a torpedo-bomber unit with Cuckoo. Disbanded 14 April, 1919. Reformed 1 March, 1938, from 'B' Flight of No. 40 Squadron at Abingdon for day-bombing with Hind. Later received Battle 1, Hampden B.1. (ZM–, GL–) Anson and one flight of Hereford B.1 (GL–). Disbanded 5 April, 1940. Reformed May, 1941, for service in Malta as a fighter squadron with Hurricane F.1, F.2, F.2b, F.2c (GL–). June, 1942, Spitfire F.5b (GL–). 1944, Spitfire F.5c, F.8, F.9, F.B.9e (GL–). 14 Aug. 1945, disbanded at Campo Formido. Reformed 15 Sept. 1951, in Malta with Vampire F.B.5.

No. 186 Squadron

Formed 11 April, 1943, as a fighter unit at Drem with Spitfire F.5b, Hurricane F.2, F.4, Typhoon F.1b (all AP–). Disbanded 15 April, 1944, and renumbered No. 130 Squadron for army co-operation. Reformed 5 Oct. 1944, as a heavy-bomber unit from 'C' Flt. of No. 90 Squadron with Lancaster B.1, B.3 (AP–, XY–). At Tuddenham. Dec. 1944, at Stradishall.

No. 187 Squadron

Formed Feb. 1945, for transport with Halifax C.8 (PU–), Dakota C.3, C.4 (PU–, OFT–). Took part in Arnhem landings. Code 5L– not used. Disbanded Dec. 1946. Reformed for ferry and transport and in 1953 had six Ansons at Aston Down. C.O. S/L G. Smythe. Was originally No. 2 Ferry Pool formed in Sept. 1945, under S/L W. Cooke, which became No. 2 Ferry Unit and then No. 187 Squadron in 1953. Also used Varsity T.1. Ferried Sabres in Operation 'Bechers' Brook' in 1953-54, Hunters to 2nd T.A.F. in 1954 and Auster A.O.P.9s in March, 1955.

No. 189 Squadron

Formed 15 Oct. 1944, as a heavy-bomber unit at Bardney with Lancaster B.1, B.3 (CA–). Stationed at Fulbeck and, in 1945, at Bardney.

No. 190 Squadron

Formed 1 March, 1943, for coastal and convoy patrol with Catalina G.R.1b (G5–). 1943, used Stirling G.T.4 and engaged in glider-towing, parachute-dropping and supply-dropping. Disbanded 1 Jan. 1944. Reformed 5 Jan. 1944, with Catalina G.R.1b, Stirling G.T.4, Halifax A.3, A.7 (G5–, L9–), Horsa 1, 2.

No. 191 Squadron

Formed 12 May, 1943, for service in South-East Asia as general-reconnaissance flying-boat unit with Catalina G.R.4b.

No. 192 Squadron

Formed Jan. 1943, for special duties investigating enemy radar and radio. Stationed at Feltwell with Wellington B.3, B.10, Anson 1, Halifax B.2, Mosquito B.4, Halifax B.3, Mosquito P.R.16 (all DT–). Dec. 1943, at Foulsham. Squadron surveyed Norwegian coast. Reformed and at Watton in 1959. Canberra B.2. 1959, became No. 15 Squadron.

No. 193 'Fellowship of the Bellows' Squadron

Formed Dec. 1942, as a fighter-bomber unit with Typhoon F.1b (DP-).
Engaged in attacks on German troops in Europe.

No. 194 Squadron

Formed Oct. 1942, at Lahore with sixteen Hudson C.6 for communica-
tions. 1943, Dakota C.3, C.4. Disbanded Feb. 1946. Reformed in 1950
as a flight only with four Dragonfly H.C.2 for casualty evacuation in
Malaya. At Changi, then Kuala Lumpur. Reformed March, 1953, as
R.A.F.'s first helicopter squadron. C.O. S/L G. R. G. Henderson. 1955,
Sycamore H.R.13, Whirlwind H.A.R.4. C.O. S/L C. R. Turner. At
Kuala Lumpur. 1959, became No. 110 Squadron.

No. 195 Squadron

Formed 16 Nov. 1942, at Duxford with Typhoon F.1b (JE-). Dis-
banded Feb. 1944, then reformed 1 Oct. 1944, from 'C' Flt. of No. 115
Squadron at Witchford with Lancaster B.1, B.3 (A4-, JE-, IL-). Later at
Wratting Common.

No. 196 Squadron

Formed 7 Nov. 1942, at Driffield for parachute-dropping and bombing.
Used Wellington B.3. 1943, Stirling B.3, G.T.4, C.5 (ZO-).

No. 197 Squadron

Formed Nov. 1942, as a fighter unit with Typhoon F.1b (OV-). Engaged
in attacking targets in Europe.

No. 198 Squadron

Formed Dec. 1942, as a fighter unit with Typhoon F.1b (JE-, TP-).
Attacked targets in Europe with rockets.

No. 199 Squadron

Formed 7 Nov. 1942, for minelaying and bombing at Blyton with
Wellington B.3 and Stirling B.3 (EX-). Based at Lakenheath. 1945, at
Foulsham with Halifax B.3, B.6 (EX-). 1946, Lincoln B.2. 1956, Canberra B.2. 1957, using Valiant B (K.) 1 on special duties. Renumbered 1959
as No. 18 Squadron at Honington.

No. 200 Squadron

Formed May, 1941, for anti-shipping patrols from West Africa with
Hudson G.R.5 and Liberator G.R.5 fitted with Leigh-Light. Disbanded 1 May, 1945. Reformed from No. 8 Squadron for supply-
dropping in Malaya and Sumatra.

No. 201 Squadron

Formed 16 Oct. 1914, at Fort Grange, Gosport, as No. 1 Squadron, R.N.A.S. C.O. S/C A. M. Longmore. Used Bristol Scout D, Bristol T.B.8 (4), Avro 504 (8 in Dec. 1914), Tabloid, F.B.5, Blériot XI, Voisin Biplane, H. Farman F20, Curtiss J, B.E.2c, Wight Seaplane, S11 Shorthorn Seaplane, Morane Bullet, Morane Parasol. Its 504s took part in raid on Friedrichshafen and its Tabloids raided Cologne. The unit went to Ostend in 1914 and was at Dunkirk in Feb. 1915. 1916, received Nieuport 17C-1, Nieuport 2-seater, Caudron G.4, Pup. 7 June, 1915, F/S/L R. A. J. Warneford won V.C. 15 Feb. 1917, attached to R.F.C. until 2 Nov. 1917, as No. 1 Wing and 'A' and 'B' Squadrons. 'A' Squadron then became No. 1 Squadron, R.N.A.S. again. 1917, Triplane, Camel F.1. 1918, Camel 2F.1, Snipe. 27 March, 1918, was again attached to R.F.C. 1 April, 1918, became No. 201 Squadron, R.A.F. Aug. 1918, at Bertangles. Oct. 1918, at Baizeux. 27 Oct. 1918, V.C. won by Maj. W. G. Barker. Disbanded 31 Dec. 1919. 1922, F.2a and was known until 1929 as No. 230 Squadron/No. 480 Flight Jan. 1929, reformed as No. 201 Squadron from No. 480 Flt. with Southampton 2 at Calshot. 1936, first to use London 1, 2. At Calshot with six aircraft. Sept. 1938, at Invergordon. Sept. 1939, at Sullom Voe. March, 1940, at Invergordon. Londons coded VQ-, ZM-. April, 1940, Sunderland G.R.1, G.R.2, G.R.3. G.R.4, G.R.5 (ZM-, NS-, A-). At Pembroke Dock and Castle Archdale. Sank 5 U-boats during the war. 1946, used Seaford for a period and then reverted to Sunderland G.R.5 (A-). 1952, C.O. S/L R. A. N. McCready. 1948, flew in Berlin airlift and was stationed at Alness. 1954 in Middle East. 1955, at Pembroke Dock. Disbanded 31 Jan. 1957. Reformed 10 Oct. 1958, with Shackleton M.R.3, from No. 220 Squadron.

No. 202 Squadron

Formed 17 Oct. 1914, at Eastchurch as No. 2 Squadron, R.N.A.S. C.O. S/C E. L. Gerrard. To Ostend in 1914, with B.E.2c, Nieuport 17C-1, Nieuport 2-seater, Avro 504, Bristol Scout D. 1916, Pup, One-and-a-half Strutter, H. Farman F20, Short 225, Morane Parasol. 1917, D.H.4. 1918, D.H.9. April, 1918, at St. Pol on reconnaissance. Oct. 1918, at Beurques on day-bombing. Disbanded 22 Jan. 1920. Reformed 29 Jan. 1929, from No . 481 Coastal Reconnaissance Flight as No. 202 Squadron with Fairey 3d. 1932, Fairey 3f at Malta. 1934, Fairey 3f on floats. 1935, Scapa. Nov. 1937, London 2 (UU-). Sept. 1939, at Gibraltar. 1941, Catalina G.R.1b, G.R.4a, G.R.4b (AX-), Swordfish Floatplane (TQ-). Dec. 1941, Sunderland G.R.1 (AX-). Disbanded June, 1945. Reformed 1946, from No. 518 Squadron for long-range meteorological flights with Halifax

G.R.5/1a, G.R.6, Met. 6 (Y3–, A–). At Gibraltar, then Aldergrove. 1953, Hastings Met. 1 (Y3–), Oxford T.2 (Y3–). 1967, Whirlwind H.A.R.10.

No. 203 Squadron

Formed originally in Nov. 1911, at Eastchurch as the first Naval Air Unit. 27 Aug. 1914, to Ostend under S/C C. R. Samson. Used Avro 504, B.E.2 (3), B.E.2a, B.E.2c, B.E.8, Blériot XI (2), Sopwith 3-seater Biplane (2), Tabloid, Bristol T.B.8, Short Landplane 42, Short Admiralty No. 3. *Astra Torres* 3. Feb. 1915, became No. 3 Squadron, R.N.A.S. 24 March, 1915, to Tenedos, Dardanelles. 1915, Nieuport 17C–1, F.B.5, Bréguet Biplane, S11 Shorthorn. 19 Nov. 1915, V.C. won by S/C R. Bell Davies. 1916, to France, with Pup, Nieuport 2-seater, Short Bomber, H. Farman F20. 1 Feb. 1917, attached to R.F.C. until 15 June, 1917. Returned to Dunkirk 15 June, 1917. July, 1917, Camel F.1. 1918, F2b. March, 1918, Camel 2F.1. Rejoined R.F.C. 3 March, 1918. 1 April, 1918, became No. 203 Squadron, R.A.F. Oct. 1918, at le Hameau. 1919, Nightjar. Disbanded 21 Jan. 1920. Reformed June, 1920, at Leuchars with Nightjar. Disbanded 1 April, 1923. Reformed 1 Jan. 1929, at Cattewater from No. 482 Coastal Reconnaissance Flight as No. 203 Squadron with Southampton 2. Served in Iraq, Aden. 1930, Basrah. 1931, first unit to fly Rangoon, three of which flew in 1934 from Basrah to Melbourne and back. 1935, Singapore 3 (PP–). Sept. 1939, at Aden. 1940, Blenheim 1L, 4L, Beaufort G.R.2. 1941, at Shaibah. 1942, Maryland B.1 from No. 39 Squadron. Dec. 1942, Baltimore B.1, B.2, B.3, B.4. Dec. 1943, Wellington G.R.8, G.R.11, G.R.13. Sept. 1944, Liberator G.R.6, G.R.8 (CJ–). 1946, Lancaster B.3 (CJ–). 1947, Lancaster G.R.3, A.S.R.3 (CJ–). 1948, at Leuchars. Jan. 1953, at Topcliffe and third squadron to receive Neptune M.R.1 (B–). C.O. S/L T. W. Morton. 1958, Shackleton M.R.3.

No. 204 Squadron

Formed 25 March, 1915, as No. 4 Squadron, R.N.A.S. Used Avro 504, B.E.2c. 1916, Morane Biplane, Bristol Scout D, F.B.5, Caudron G.4, Nieuport 2-seater. March, 1916, One-and-a-half Strutter. In France. March, 1917, at Bray Dunes with Pup. March, 1918, Camel 2F.1. 3 March, 1918, attached to R.F.C. 24 Oct. 1918, became No. 204 Squadron, R.A.F. Oct. 1918, fighter at Teteghem. Disbanded 31 Dec. 1919. Reformed 1 Feb. 1929, at Mount Batten with Southampton 2. 1935, Scapa. 1936, Perth. 1937, London 2 (RF–). Sept. 1939, Sunderland G.R.1, G.R.2, G.R.3 (RF–, KG–). Helped to rescue crew of *Kensington Court* in Sept. 1939. 1941, to West Africa for anti-submarine operations. Disbanded June, 1945. Reformed with Dakota C.4, Valetta C.1, Mosquito, at Linton-on-Ouse. June, 1955, at Ballykelly with Shackleton M.R.2. C.O. S/L G. Young.

No. 205 Squadron

Formed 31 Dec. 1916, as No. 5 Squadron, R.N.A.S. at Petite Synthe from 'B' Squadron. Received One-and-a-half Strutter, Caudron G.4. April, 1917, D.H.4. 3 March, 1918, joined R.F.C. 1 April, 1918, became No. 205 Squadron, R.A.F. Aug. 1918, D.H.9a. Oct. 1918, day-bomber at Moislains. Disbanded at Hucknall 22 Jan. 1920. Reformed April, 1920, with D.H.9a. Disbanded 1 April, 1923. Reformed April, 1920, with D.H.9a. Disbanded 1 April, 1923. Reformed 8 Jan. 1929, at Singapore from Far East Flight as No. 205 Squadron with Southampton 2. 1935, Singapore 3 (KM–) at Seletar. 1941, Catalina G.R.1 (FV–). 1942, Catalina G.R.1b, G.R.4b (FV–) in Ceylon. 1943, squadron Catalina made first flight non-stop from Ceylon to Australia. July, 1945, Sunderland G.R.5. 1954, to Seletar. Engaged on operations in Korea and anti-bandit in Malaya. 1955, at Seletar as No. 205/209 Squadron and last unit with flying-boats in the R.A.F. 1958, Shackleton M.R.2, M.R.3. 1959, C.O. W/C R. A. N. McCready. 1959, at Changi.

No. 206 Squadron

Formed 31 Dec. 1916, at Petite Synthe as No. 6 Squadron, R.N.A.S. 15 March, 1917, attached to R.F.C. with Nieuport 17C-1. June, 1917, Camel F.1. At la Bellevue. C.O. S/C J. J. Petre. Disbanded 27 Aug. 1917. Reformed at Dover 1 Jan. 1918, with D.H.4 and rejoined R.F.C. on 31 March, 1918. 1 April, 1918, became No. 206 Squadron, R.A.F. Re-equipped with D.H.9. Oct. 1918, at St. Marie Cappel on day-bombing. 1919, to Egypt. Disbanded 1 Feb. 1920, and renumbered No. 47 Squadron. Reformed 15 June, 1936, at Bircham Newton for general reconnaissance with Anson G.R.1 (WD–, VX–). April, 1940, Hudson G.R.1, G.R.2, G.R.3 (VX–). C.O. S/L J. C. Roberts. Oct. 1942, Fortress G.R.1, G.R.2, G.R.2a (VX–, 2V–). April, 1944, Liberator G.R.5, G.R.6, G.R.8 (VX–, PQ–, 2V–) with Leigh-Light. Operated from the Azores. 1945, Liberator C.6, C.8, York C.1 (MOYG–), Dakota C.4. Code TJ– not used. Disbanded 25 April, 1946. Reformed at St. Eval with Shackleton M.R.1a (B–). C.O. S/L J. D. Beresford in May, 1954. 1958, Shackleton M.R.3.

No. 207 'Leicester' Squadron

Formed Nov. 1916, as No. 7 Squadron, R.N.A.S. from 'B' Squadron, R.N.A.S. with Short Bomber, One-and-a-half Strutter, Nieuport 2-seater, B.E.2c. 1917, Caudron G.4. April, 1917, O/100. At Coudekerque. 3 Sept. 1917, one flight of O/100s sent to Redcar, then went to Manston on 2 Oct. 1917, to form nucleus of 'A' Squadron. Squadron joined R.F.C. 3 March, 1918. 1 April, 1918, became No. 207 Squadron, R.A.F. Oct. 1918, night-bomber at Ligéscourt. July, 1919, O/400. Disbanded 20 Jan. 1920 at Uxbridge. Reformed 1 Feb. 1920, at Bircham Newton with

D.H.9a. 1922-23, at Constantinople. 1928, Fairey 3f. 1930, at Bircham Newton and Eastchurch. 1933, at Bircham Newton with Gordon. C.O. S/L R. J. Rodwell. 1935 in Sudan. April, 1936, Vincent. C.O. S/L Lissett. At Worthy Down. Sept. 1936, Gordon. Sept. 1937, Wellesley 1 at Worthy Down. May, 1938, Battle 1 (NJ-). C.O. S/L J. N. D. Anderson. 1940, Manchester B.1a (EM-) and was first unit to fly the type. C.O. W/C N. C. Hyde, W/C J. N. D. Anderson. 1941, partly re-equipped with Hampden B.1 (EM-). Aug. 1941, Manchester B.1 (EM-). 1942, Lancaster B.1, B.3, B.1(F.E.) (EM-) at Bottesford, Langar and Spilsby. 1948, at Stradishall. 1949, Lincoln B.2 (EM-), Martinet T.T.1 (EM-). Disbanded Feb. 1950. Reformed 29 May, 1951, with Washington B.1. C.O. S/L G. O'N. Fisher. 1954, at Marham with Canberra B.2. 1956, Valiant B.1.

No. 208 Squadron

Formed 25 Oct. 1916, as No. 8 Squadron, R.N.A.S. from Dunkirk R.N.A.S. units with one flight each of Pups (6), Nieuport 17C-1 (6) and One-and-a-half Strutters (5). Attached to R.F.C. at Vert Galand. C.O. S/C G. R. Bromet. Dec. 1916, first unit to be completely equipped with Pups. 1 Feb. 1917, Pups transferred to No. 3 Squadron, R.N.A.S. 1 Feb. 1917, to St. Pol to form Nos. 8 and 9 (Naval) Squadrons. 27 March, 1917, again attached to R.F.C. at Auchel under S/C G. R. Bromet, using Triplanes. Also received R.E.8. July, 1917, Camel F.1. With R.F.C. until 1 March, 1918. March, 1918, re-equipped in England with Camel 2F.1. C.O. Maj. C. Draper. 1 April, 1918, became No. 208 Squadron, R.A.F. Oct. 1918, fighter at Estrées-en-Chaussée with Snipe. Disbanded 7 Nov. 1919. Reformed 1 Feb. 1920, from No. 113 Squadron for army co-operation with F2b. Oct. 1922, to Dardanelles. 1928, to Ismailia. 1939, Atlas 1. 1930, at Heliopolis. 1937, Audax. 1939, Lysander 1 (GA-). 1940, Lysander 2, 3 (GA-) two flights, Hurricane F.1, F.2 (GA-) one flight. 1940, in Greece. March, 1942, one flight of Tomahawk F.1 in Palestine. March, 1944, Spitfire F.B.9c (RG-) in Italy. Also Spitfire F.5b, L.F.16e (GR-). Jan. 1947, Spitfire F.R.18. 1948, in Egypt. Aug. 1950, at Abu Sueir with Meteor F.R.9. 1955, S/L T. F. Neil. Disbanded 1958. Reformed 5 Jan. 1958, at Tangmere from No. 34 Squadron with Hunter F.6. C.O. S/L J. H. Granville-White. March, 1958, to Nicosia. 1 April, 1959, disbanded at Nicosia. Reformed 1 April, 1959, at Aden from No. 142 Squadron with Venom F.B.4. C.O. S/L R. Ramirez. 1959 at Eastleigh, Nairobi. 1960, to Stradishall with Hunter F.G.A.9. 1961, at Khormaksar. C.O. S/L M. R. Goodfellow.

No. 209 Squadron

Formed 1 Feb. 1917, at St. Pol, Dunkirk, as No. 9 Squadron, R.N.A.S.

Received six Pups, nine Triplanes and a flight of Nieuport 17C–1. C.O. S/C H. Fawcett. Attached to R.F.C. at Flez from 15 June, 1917, until 28 Sept. 1917. 13 July, 1917, Camel F.1. Dec. 1917, Camel 2F.1. At Poulainville and Bruille. Rejoined R.F.C. 27 March, 1918. 1 April, 1918, became No. 209 Squadron, R.A.F. 21 April, 1918, Capt. A. R. Brown claimed to have shot down von Richthofen. C.O. Maj. C. H. Butler. Oct. 1918, fighter at le Hameau. Disbanded 24 June, 1919, at Scopwick. Reformed 15 Jan. 1930, at Mount Batten and was first to fly Iris 3. Jan. 1934, first unit to receive Perth. 1935, at Felixstowe. 1936, Singapore 3. 1938, Stranraer 1 (FK–, W9–) at Invergordon. Jan. 1940, first to use Lerwick G.R.1 (WQ–). At Oban. April, 1941, at Loch Erne. Aug. 1941, Iceland. Oct. 1941, Pembroke. 1941, Catalina G.R.1, G.R.2, G.R.2a (WQ–), one of which located the *Bismarck*. 1942, Madagascar. 1944, Sunderland G.R.5 (WQ–) at Kai-Tak. Disbanded 1 Sept. 1946, and renumbered No. 88 Squadron. Reformed with Sunderland G.R.5 and saw service in Korea. 1954, to Seletar. 1955, combined with No. 205 as No. 205/209 Squadron. Disbanded and reformed in 1960 from No. 267 Squadron with Pioneer C.C.1, Pembroke C.1.

No. 210 Squadron

Formed Feb. 1917, as No. 10 Squadron, R.N.A.S. Received Nieuport 17C-1, Nieuport 2-seater, One-and-a-half Strutter. May, 1917, Triplane (15). Attached to R.F.C. from 15 May, 1917, until 20 Nov. 1917. Aug. 1917, Camel F.1. March, 1918, Camel 2F.1. Rejoined R.F.C. 27 March, 1918. 1 April, 1918, became No. 210 Squadron, R.A.F. Disbanded 24 June, 1919. Reformed 1 Feb. 1920, with Cuckoo at Gosport. Disbanded 1 April, 1923. Reformed 1 March, 1931, Southampton 2. May, 1935, at Pembroke Dock. July, 1935, Rangoon. Sept. 1935, at Gibraltar. 1935, Singapore 3. Aug. 1936, at Pembroke Dock. Sept. 1937, Algeria. Dec. 1937, Pembroke Dock. Sept. 1938, Sunderland G.R.1. (VG–, DA–). Sept. 1939, C.O. S/L F. J. Fressanges. April, 1941, Catalina G.R.1, G.R.2 (DA–) engaged on photo-reconnaissance. 8 U-boats sunk by Squadron. 17 July, 1944, V.C. won by F/L J. A. Cruikshank. Later used Catalina G.R.1b, G.R.4a, G.R.4b (DA–). Disbanded June, 1945. Reformed June 1946. Lancaster M.R.3 (OZ–). 1948, at Leuchars. Dec. 1952, second squadron to receive Neptune M.R.1 (L–) at Topcliffe. 1958, Shackleton M.R.2.

No. 211 Squadron

Formed 8 March, 1917, as No. 11 Squadron, R.N.A.S. Equipped with Triplane, Pup, Nieuport 17C–1, Sopwith Baby Seaplane. Disbanded Aug. 1917. Reformed at Petite Synthe. March, 1918, D.H.9 for day-bombing. Later used O/400. 1 April, 1918, became No. 211 Squadron, R.A.F. Oct. 1918, at Petite Synthe. Disbanded 24 June, 1919.

Reformed 14 June, 1937, at Grantham with Audax and Hind. Also received Wellesley 1 (LJ–). 1937, Blenheim 1 (UQ–). Sept. 1939, in Egypt. 1941, Blenheim 1L, 4L (UQ–), Wellington B.1c. Disbanded March, 1942. Reformed Aug. 1943, with Beaufighter T.F.10. Later used Mosquito F.B.6.

No. 212 Squadron

Formed June, 1917, at Dover for marine operations. Used F2a, D.H.4, D.H.9, D.H.9a, Camel 2F.1 from Great Yarmouth. Disbanded Feb. 1920. Reformed early 1940 for co-ordination of activities of Photographic Development Unit based at Heston and its detachments operating on the Continent with Spitfire H.F.7. Disbanded mid-1940. Reformed Oct. 1942, with Catalina G.R.1b, nine aircraft being received for general reconnaissance and air-sea rescue in India.

No. 213 'Ceylon' Squadron

Formed June, 1917, as St. Pol Seaplane Defence Flight. Received Sopwith Baby Seaplane and Pup. Sept. 1917, expanded to become St. Pol Seaplane Defence Squadron with addition of Camel 2F.1. Jan. 1918, became No. 13 Squadron, R.N.A.S. 1 April, 1918, became No. 213 Squadron, R.A.F. Oct. 1918, on sea operations from Beurques. Disbanded 31 Dec. 1919. Reformed 8 March, 1937, at Northolt with Gauntlet 2 (AK–). 10 June, 1937, to Church Fenton. 18 May, 1938, to Wittering. March, 1939, Hurricane F.1 (AK–). Aug. 1940, at Exeter. 1942, Hurricane F.2b, F.2c (AK–). Feb. 1944, Spitfire F.8, F.9 (AK–). June, 1944, Mustang F.B.4 (AK–). Later used Tempest F.6 (AK–), Harvard T.2a (AL–). June, 1954, in Middle East with Vampire F.B.5, F.B.9, Meteor T.7. 1955, Venom F.B.1. Reformed 1956 at Ahlhorn, Germany, as only squadron to receive Canberra B.(I)6. 1960, C.O. W/C P. J. Bayley. At Bruggen. 1966, Canberra B.16.

No. 214 'Federated Malay States' Squadron

Formed 9 Dec. 1917, as No. 14 Squadron, R.N.A.S. from No. 7a Squadron, R.N.A.S. Night-bomber with O/400. 1 April, 1918, became No. 214 Squadron, R.A.F. Oct. 1918, at St. Inglevert. 2 Aug. 1919, to Cairo. Disbanded 1 Feb. 1920. Reformed 16 Sept. 1935, with Virginia X. April, 1937, first to fly Harrow 1, 2 (UX–) at Feltwell. Sept. 1939, Wellington B.1c (UX–). 1940, Wellington B.1c, B.2, B.3 (BU–). April, 1942, Stirling B.1, B.3 (BU–). Jan. 1944, Fortress B.2 (BU–). Also used Lancaster B.1(F.E.), B.7(F.E.) (QN–), Liberator B.8. 31 March, 1946, became No. 37 Squadron. Reformed at Upwood with Lincoln B.2 (QN–). C.O. S/L K. R. Bowhill. Six Lincolns sent to Kenya for anti-Mau Mau operations from 10 June, 1954, until Jan. 1955. 1956, at Marham with Valiant B.1. C.O. W/C L. H. Trent, V.C. 1967, Victor B.1, B.1a.

No. 215 Squadron

Formed 10 March, 1918, at Coudekerque as No. 15 Squadron, R.N.A.S. with O/100. Became No. 215 Squadron, R.A.F. on 1 April, 1918. 19 May, 1918, equipped with O/400 (10). Joined Independent Air Force on 4 July, 1918. Oct. 1918, night-bomber at Xaffrévillier. Disbanded 18 Oct. 1919. Reformed 7 Oct. 1935, with Virginia X. 1937, Anson 1. 1938, Harrow 1, 2 (BH-) at Driffield. Aug. 1939, Wellington B.1c (BH-). Disbanded April, 1940, to become No. 11 O.T.U. Reformed Dec. 1941, for night-bombing with Wellington B.3, B.10. June, 1944, Liberator B.3, C.6. April, 1945, Dakota C.3, C.4 for transport in Burma. Disbanded 15 Feb. 1946, and became No. 48 Squadron at Singapore. Reformed 1947 with Dakota C.3, C.4, Valetta C.1. Disbanded June, 1948, and re-numbered No. 70 Squadron. Reformed May, 1956 at Dishforth with Pioneer C.C.1. 1 Sept. 1958, became No. 230 Squadron. 1967, Argosy C.1.

No. 216 Squadron

Formed 5 Oct. 1917, at Manston as 'A' Squadron from a flight of No. 7 Squadron, R.N.A.S. with four O/400s. 17 Oct. 1917, to France to join Independent Air Force at Ochey. Also used Camel F.1. In 162 raids on Germany dropped 176·5 tons of bombs. 8 Jan. 1918, became No. 16 Squadron, R.N.A.S. 1 April, 1918, became No. 216 Squadron, R.A.F. 1918, D.H.10 Amiens. Oct. 1918, night-bombing from Autreville. After Armistice carried mail to Cologne and Valenciennes. July, 1919, to Egypt. Oct. 1919, using six O/400s on mail and passenger transport to Cairo. June, 1921, carrying airmail between Cairo and Baghdad with D.H.10 and Vimy. 1928, at Heliopolis. 1930, bomber-transport with Victoria 5. Surveyed Central Africa route to Takoradi. 1935, Valentia 1 (VT-). Oct. 1939, Bombay 1 (SH-). 1940, at Maaton Bagush and Mer-sah Matruh. 1941, D.H.86b. Later in Tunis, Sicily and Italy. July, 1942, Hudson C.3a, C.6 (LO-, LD-), Lodestar. April, 1943, Dakota C.2, C.3, C.4. 1944, India and Burma on transport. Later in Mediterranean, Aden and Nairobi. Nov. 1954, at Fayid with eleven Valetta C.1. C.O. S/L W. J. Swift. 10 Nov. 1955, to Lyneham to receive two Comet T.2 and eight Comet C.2 C.O. W/C B. D. Sellick. C.O. W/C R. G. Churcher. 1967, Comet C.4.

No. 217 'Exeter' Squadron

Formed 30 Oct. 1914, as Seaplane Base, R.N.A.S., Dunkirk. 1915, Wight Seaplane, S11 Shorthorn, Sopwith Baby Seaplane. 1916, Short 225. 1917, D.H.4. 11 July, 1917, one Curtiss H.12 Large America and two Camels as escort for H.12. Base closed Jan. 1918. Reformed 17 Jan. 1918, as No. 17 Squadron, R.N.A.S. with D.H.4 for anti-submarine patrols from Bergues. 1 April, 1918, became No. 217 Squadron, R.A.F.

Disbanded 18 Oct. 1919, at Driffield. Reformed 15 March, 1937, at Boscombe Down for general reconnaissance with Anson 1 (YQ–), Tiger Moth. Sept. 1939, at Wormwell. Oct. 1939, at St. Eval. 1940, Anson G.R.1 (MW–), Beaufort G.R.1, G.R.2 (MW–). Aug. 1942, in Ceylon with Hudson. June, 1943, Beaufort. July, 1944, Beaufighter T.F.10 at Vavuniya. Disbanded Sept. 1945. Reformed 13 Jan. 1952, at St. Eval with Neptune M.R.1 (A–), being first squadron to fly the type. C.O. S/L M. A. Ensor. April, 1952, to Kinloss. March, 1954, C.O. S/L P. H. Stembridge. June, 1955, C.O. W/C D. R. Hutchings.

No. 218 'Gold Coast' Squadron

Formed 24 April, 1918, at Dover as No. 18 Squadron, R.N.A.S. for day-bombing with D.H.9. 17 Oct. 1918, became No. 218 Squadron, R.A.F. Oct. 1918, at Fretnum. Disbanded 24 June, 1919. Reformed 16 March, 1936, at Upper Heyford with Hind from 'A' Flight of No. 57 Squadron. 1938, Battle 1 (SV–). 2 Sept. 1939, to France with A.A.S.F. at Auberive. 1940, Blenheim 1, 4L (HA–). Nov. 1940, Wellington B.1c (HA–). Jan. 1942, Stirling B.1, B.3 (HA–) at Chedburgh. Detachment at Downham Market. Aug. 1944, Lancaster B.1, B.3 (HA–) at Woolfox Lodge and Methwold. Feb. 1945, at Chedburgh.

No. 219 'Mysore' Squadron

Formed Aug. 1918, for anti-submarine patrols from R.N.A.S. West-gate with Short 240, Curtiss H.12 Large America, Sopwith Baby Seaplane, Avro 504. Disbanded 7 Feb. 1920. Reformed Oct. 1939, for night-fighting with Blenheim 4. C.O. G/C R. L. R. Atcherley. 1940, Blenheim 4f (FK–) at Catterick. Oct. 1940, Beaufighter N.F.1f, N.F.2f (FK–). Jan. 1944, Mosquito N.F.30, T.3 (FK–). 1945, Mosquito N.F.36 (FK–). Nov. 1945, renumbered from No. 125 Squadron. 1953, Meteor N.F.11. June, 1954, in Middle East with Meteor N.F.13. 1957, Venom N.F.3.

No. 220 Squadron

Formed 1916 as 'C' Flight, R.N.A.S. Imbros, with One-and-a-half Strutter. 1 Jan. 1917, became 'C' Squadron. 1917, D.H.4. 1918, D.H.9 and Camel 2F1. Sept. 1918, became No. 220 Squadron, R.A.F. Disbanded Dec. 1918. Reformed 17 Aug. 1936, at Bircham Newton for general reconnaissance with Anson G.R.1. (HU–, NR–). Sept. 1939, Hudson G.R.3, G.R.5 (NR–). June, 1942, Fortress G.R.2, G.R.2a (2–, ZZ–). Oct. 1944, Liberator G.R.3, G.R.6 (ZZ–). Liberator C.6, C.8 (8D–). Disbanded June, 1946. Reformed and in 1952 was flying Shackleton M.R.1. C.O. S/L A. E. W. Laband. 1955, at St. Eval. 1958, Shackleton M.R.3. 10 Oct. 1958, became No. 201 Squadron.

No. 221 Squadron

Formed 1916 in Aegean as 'D' Flight, R.N.A.S. Stavros, with One-and-a-half Strutter. 1 Jan. 1917, became 'D' Squadron. 1917, D.H.4. 1918, Camel F.1, 2F.1, D.H.9, D.H.9a. 1 April, 1918, became No. 221 Squadron, R.A.F. Jan. 1919, at Petrovsk. March, 1919, at Batum and Baku. Disbanded 1 Sept. 1919. Reformed 11 Nov. 1940, for general reconnaissance with Anson G.R.1. and torpedo-dropping with Wellington G.R.8, G.R.13.

No. 222 'Natal' Squadron

Formed 1916 as 'A' Flight R.N.A.S. Thasos, with One-and-a-half Strutter. 1 Jan. 1917, became 'A' Squadron. 1917, D.H.4. 1918, D.H.9, Camel 2F.1. 1 April, 1918, became No. 222 Squadron, R.A.F. Disbanded Feb. 1919. Reformed Oct. 1939, as a fighter unit with Hurricane F.1, Blenheim 1f (ZD-). Aug. 1940, at Kirton-in-Lindsey. 1940, Spitfire F.1, F.2a, F.5b (ZD-). Later used Spitfire F.9b, F.9c (ZD-). 1940, C.O. S/L H. W. Mermagen. 1945, Tempest F.5 (ZD-). 1946, Meteor F.3 (ZD-). 1951, Meteor F.4 (ZD-). 1953, Meteor F.8, T.7 (ZD-). Dec. 1954, at Leuchars with Hunter F.1 and was second unit to fly the Hunter. C.O. G/C H. Edwards, V.C. Later re-equipped with Hunter F.4.

No. 223 Squadron

Formed 1917 as 'B' Flt., R.N.A.S. at Lemnos with One-and-a-half Strutter, D.H.4. 1918, F.H.9, Camel 2F.1. 1 April, 1918, became No. 223 Squadron, R.A.F. Oct. 1918, day-bombing at Otranto. Disbanded May, 1919. Reformed 15 Dec. 1936, for day-bombing with Gordon at Nairobi. Feb. 1937, Vincent (6). June, 1938, Wellesley 1, 2 (QR-), Gladiator 2, Blenheim 4L. Sept. 1939, to Massawa. 1941, operated temporarily as an O.T.U. with Maryland B.1. Jan. 1942, first to fly Baltimore B.1, B.2, B.3 (6G-). Oct. 1942, Boston B.2, Baltimore B.3, 3a. Disbanded 12 Aug. 1944, becoming No. 30 Squadron, S.A.A.F. Reformed 23 Aug. 1944, with Baltimore B.3a, B.4, B.4a, Fortress B.3 (6G-), Liberator B.6, B.8 (6G-).

No. 224 Squadron

Formed 1917, as R.N.A.S., Otranto, with One-and-a-half Strutter, D.H.4. 1918, D.H.9, Camel 2F.1 (6). Engaged on day-bombing. 1 April, 1918, became No. 224 Squadron, R.A.F. Disbanded at Taranto, May, 1919. Reformed 1 Feb. 1937, at Manston for general reconnaissance with Anson G.R.1 (PW-). Later at Thornaby, Leuchars, Gosport. 1939, first to receive Hudson G.R.1, G.R.2, G.R.3 (QA-). Gladiator 2. 1941, Blenheim 4f. Feb. 1943, Liberator G.R.5 (XB-). C.O. S/L A. E. Clouston. At Beaulieu and St. Eval. 1944, Liberator G.R.6 (XB-). Sank 11 U-boats during the war. 1946, Liberator G.R.6, G.R.8 (XB-). Added one

flight of Halifax G.R.6 (XB–) from No. 518 Squadron. 1947, Lancaster
G.R.3 (XB–). At Gibraltar. Last Halifax G.R.6 retired 17 March, 1952.
1952, Shackleton M.R.1. C.O. S/L J. G. Roberts. 1955, Shackleton
M.R.2. C.O. S/L J. D. E. Hughes.

No. 225 Squadron

Formed 1917 as R.N.A.S., Otranto, with One-and-a-half Strutter,
D.H.4. 1918, D.H.9, Camel 2F.1 (6). 1 April, 1918, became No. 225
Squadron, R.A.F. Oct. 1918, D.H.9a. Disbanded at Otranto Dec. 1918.
Reformed Odiham 3 Oct. 1939, for army co-operation with Lysander 2.
Was engaged in coastal reconnaissance. Became fighter unit. Aug. 1941,
Hurricane F.B.2b, F.B.2c, Mustang F.1a. 1943, Spitfire F.5, F.B.9,
F.5b. Engaged in N. Africa, Italy, invasion Southern France. Disbanded
Camp Formido in Jan. 1947. Reformed Jan. 1960 in Transport Com-
mand with Whirlwind H.A.R.2, H.A.R.4, Sycamore H.R.14. 1960,
Odiham. C.O. S/L A. Twigg. 1961, Whirlwind H.A.R.10. Twin Pioneer
C.C.1.

No. 226 Squadron

Formed 1917, as R.N.A.S., Taranto, with One-and-a-half Strutter,
D.H.4. 1918, D.H.9, Camel 2F.1 (6). Engaged on day-bombing. 1 April,
1918, became No. 226 Squadron, R.A.F. Disbanded 18 Dec. 1918 at
Taranto. Reformed 15 March, 1937, with Audax and Battle 1 (KP–) at
Harwell. 2 Sept. 1939, to France with A.A.S.F. at Rheims. Battle 1
(MQ–), Blenheim 4L (MQ–). 1943, Boston B.3 (MQ–). 1943, Mitchell
B.2, B.3 (MQ–), Oxford T.2, Proctor C.3.

No. 227 Squadron

Formed 1917, as R.N.A.S., Taranto, with One-and-a-half Strutter,
D.H.4. 1918, D.H.9, Camel 2F.1. Engaged on day-bombing. 1 April,
1918, became No. 227 Squadron, R.A.F. Disbanded 9 Dec. 1918. Reformed 20 Aug. 1942, at Luqa from No. 235 Squadron with Beaufighter F.1, F.6c, F.11, Halifax B.1. Disbanded 12 Aug. 1944, at Bioferno,
becoming No. 19 Squadron, S.A.A.F. Reformed 7 Oct. 1944, with
Lancaster B.1, B.3 (9J–) at Balderton. 1945, at Strubby.

No. 228 Squadron

Formed 15 April, 1913, as R.N.A.S., Great Yarmouth. 1914, B.E.2c.
Later known as Boat Flt. in April, 1917, with Curtiss H.12 Large
America. 1918, Curtiss-Porte H.16, F.2a, D.H.4, Short 320, Camel 2F.1
flown from lighters. 20 Aug. 1918, became No. 228 Squadron, R.A.F.
Disbanded 30 June, 1919. Reformed 15 Dec. 1936, at Pembroke Dock
with London 2. Also used Scapa and Singapore 3. 1936, first to fly
Stranraer 1 (TO–). 1940, C.O. W/C E. N. Nicholetts. In Middle East.

1941, Sunderland G.R.1, G.R.2, G.R.3 (TO–, NM–, DG–, WH–). Disbanded June, 1945. Reformed with Shackleton M.R.2. At St. Eval in 1955. C.O. W/C K. M. Murray. Reformed from No. 275 Squadron with Sycamore H.R.14.

No. 229 Squadron

Formed 1917, as R.N.A.S., Oudezeele. 1918, D.H.9, S.E.5a. Sept. 1918, became No. 229 Squadron, R.A.F. 1919, Fairey 3c. Disbanded 31 Dec. 1919. Reformed Oct. 1939, with Blenheim 4f. 1940, Hurricane F.1, F.2a, F.2c (HB–). 26 Sept. 1940, until Nov. 1940, at Northolt. Disbanded May, 1942. Reformed Aug. 1942, with Spitfire F.5b, F.5c (9R–). Later used Spitfire F.9, F.14, L.F.16e (9R–). Jan. 1945, disbanded and became No. 603 Squadron. Reformed and, in 1947, flying Meteor F.4 (HB–).

No. 230 Squadron

Formed 15 April, 1913, as R.N.A.S., Felixstowe. Feb. 1915, Curtiss H.4. 1917, F.2a, F.5, Short 320. 1918, Camel 2F.1. Sept. 1918, became No. 230 Squadron, R.A.F. Later known as No. 480 Flt. at Calshot. Disbanded April, 1923. Reformed Dec. 1934, at Pembroke Dock as first unit to fly Singapore 3. 1934 to 1936, at Alexandria. 1936-38, at Seletar. 1941, Sunderland G.R.1, G.R.2, G.R.3 (FV–, 4X–). Also used Dornier Do.22 and Sea Otter A.S.R.2 (4X–). 1948, on Berlin airlift with Sunderland G.R.5 (B–). 1948, at Alness. 1954, at Pembroke Dock. C.O. S/L E. C. Bennett. Disbanded 31 Sept. 1957. Reformed 1 Sept. 1958, from No. 215 Squadron with Pioneer C.C.1 at Dishforth. C.O. S/L W. J. Simpson. 1959, Twin Pioneer C.C.1. at Upavon. 1960, Odiham. 1967, Whirlwind H.A.R.10.

No. 231 Squadron

Formed 15 April, 1915, as R.N.A.S., Felixstowe. Aug. 1918, became No. 231 Squadron, R.A.F. Operated with F.3, F.5. Disbanded July, 1919. Reformed July, 1940, for fighter-reconnaissance with Lysander 2, Mustang F.1, Tomahawk F.1, F.2b (MV–). Disbanded Jan. 1944. Reformed Sept. 1944, and flew Coronado G.R.1 for transport. Was only unit to fly the type. Also used Liberator C.2, Hudson, Dakota, Skymaster C.1, Lancaster B.3.

No. 232 Squadron

Formed 15 April, 1913, as R.N.A.S., Felixstowe. Engaged on anti-submarine and anti-Zepplein patrols with F.3, F.5. Aug. 1918, became No. 232 Squadron, R.A.F. Disbanded Jan. 1919. Reformed July, 1940, with Hurricane F.1, F.2b (EF–). Aug. 1940, one flight at Sumburgh, rest of squadron at Turnhouse. Later in Far East. Disbanded March,

F

1942. Reformed April, 1942, in Middle East with Spitfire F.5c, F.9. Disbanded Oct. 1944. Reformed Nov. 1944, for transport in India with Liberator C.6, C.7, C.8, C.9, Wellington C.15, C.16, Skymaster C.1, Dakota C.3, York C.1.

No. 233 Squadron

Formed Nov. 1914, as R.N.A.S. Seaplane Base, Dover, with Wight Seaplane (2), H. Farman F.20 (2), Avro 504 (5). 1915, Short 225, Sopwith Baby Seaplane, White and Thompson Flying-boat, Bristol Scout D. 1916, Fairey Hamble Baby Seaplane. 1917, F.2a. 1918, Camel 2F.1, D.H.9. Sept. 1918, became No. 233 Squadron, R.A.F. Disbanded 15 May, 1919. Reformed 18 May, 1936, at Thornaby for general reconnaissance with Anson G.R.1 (EY-). 1940, at Gibraltar with Hudson G.R.1, G.R.2, G.R.3, G.R.4 (QX-). 1944, Dakota C.3, C.4 (5T-, OFU-). 1945, Liberator G.R.5, G.R.6 (5T-, QX-), Skymaster C.1 (5T-). 1960, reformed at Khormaksar with Valetta C.1. from No. 84 Squadron.

No. 234 'Madras Presidency' Squadron

Formed 26 Feb. 1917, as R.N.A.S., Tresco. Operated with Short 225 (2), Curtiss H.12 Large America, F.2a, F.3. From 1 April, 1918, was an R.N.A.S. unit of the R.A.F. Aug. 1918, became No. 234 Squadron, R.A.F. Engaged on anti-submarine patrols from the Scillies. Disbanded 15 May, 1919. Reformed 30 Oct. 1938, at Leconfield receiving two Magisters, followed by Blenheim 1f (AZ-). Also used Tutor, Gauntlet 2 and Battle 1. 1940, Spitfire F.2a, F.2b, L.F.5a, L.F.5b, F.5b (AZ-). Aug. 1940, at St. Eval. Sept. 1944, Mustang F.3, F.4 (AZ-). Also flew Spitfire F.9e, F.B.9e, L.F.16e (FX-). June, 1946, Meteor F.3 (FX-). Disbanded 1 Sept. 1946, becoming part of No. 245 Squadron. Reformed 1 Aug. 1952, in 2nd T.A.F. at Oldenburg with Vampire F.B.5 (W-), F.B.9 (W-). C.O. S/L R. M. Chatfield. Dec. 1953, in 2nd T.A.F. received Sabre F.4. Also used Vampire T.11, Meteor T.7. May, 1956, at Geilenkirchen with Hunter F.4.

No. 235 Squadron

Formed originally as R.N.A.S., Newlyn, for anti-submarine patrol with Short 240. Aug. 1918, became No. 235 Squadron, R.A.F. Disbanded Dec. 1919. Reformed Oct. 1939, in Coastal Command with Battle 1, Blenheim 1f (WR-). 1941, Blenheim 4f (QY-, LA-). Nov. 1941, Beaufighter F.1c, F.6c, T.F.10 (WR-). Engaged on anti-submarine duties. 20 Aug. 1942, became No. 227 Squadron. Reformed July, 1944, Mosquito F.B.6. Disbanded July, 1945. Reformed with Sunderland G.R.5, and, in 1948, took part in Berlin airlift.

No. 236 Squadron

Formed in 1917 as R.N.A.S., Mullion, for anti-submarine patrol with S.S.Z. and C Type airships. 1918, One-and-a-half Strutter, D.H.6, D.H.9. Aug. 1918, became No. 236 Squadron, R.A.F. Nov. 1918, using S.S.T. Mullion Twin Type airship. Disbanded May, 1919. Reformed 31 Oct. 1939, for anti-shipping duties with Blenheim 4f (MB-). 1942, Beaufighter F.1c, T.F.6c, T.F.10 (MB-, ND-) at North Coates. Also used Beaufort G.R.1.

No. 237 'Rhodesia' Squadron

Formed July, 1917, as R.N.A.S., Cattewater, for anti-submarine patrol with Short 240. Aug. 1918, became No. 237 Squadron, R.A.F. Disbanded 15 May, 1919. Reformed April, 1940, for shipping escort with Lysander 2, Audax 1, Hardy, Gladiator 2, Hart 2. C.O. S/L R. R. S. Tuck. 1941, Hurricane F.2c (GO-, DV-). Dec. 1943, Spitfire F.5b, F.9 (DV-), Mustang F.3, F.B.4 (DV-). Jan. 1946, renumbered No. 93 Squadron.

No. 238 Squadron

Formed 1917, as R.N.A.S., Cattewater, for anti-submarine duties with Short 240, Sopwith Baby Seaplane, F.5. Aug. 1918, became No. 238 Squadron, R.A.F. Disbanded 1919. Reformed May, 1940, with Hurricane F.1, F.2b, F.2c (EM-, KC-). Aug. 1940, at Middle Wallop. Later used Spitfire F.9 (KC-), Havoc N.F.1, Boston B.1. Disbanded Oct. 1944. Reformed Dec. 1944, from No. 525 Squadron for transport with Dakota C.3, C.4 (FM-, ODC-, OFR-, MODD-, WF-) in Burma.

No. 239 Squadron

Formed Aug. 1918, for marine operations at Torquay with Short 225 but did not see any service and was disbanded in May, 1919. Reformed Sept. 1940, with Lysander 1, 2, 3, Tomahawk F.1, F.2a, Mustang F.1, Battle 1 (all HB-). 1942, Beaufighter F.1, Anson T.1, Hurricane F.1, F.2c, F.10 (all HB-). C.O. W/C W. F. Gibb. 1944, Mosquito F.B.6, N.F.2, N.F.30, Spitfire F.2.

No. 240 Squadron

Formed April, 1913, as R.N.A.S., Calshot. Operated on anti-submarine patrol with Short 225, 320, Curtiss H.12 Large America, F.2a. Aug. 1918, seaplane and flying-boat units at Calshot became No. 240 Squadron, R.A.F. Disbanded 15 May, 1919. Reformed 30 March, 1937, at Calshot with Scapa. Nov. 1938, Singapore 3. 1940, London 2 (SH-, BN-). Sept. 1939, at Invergordon. Nov. 1939, in the Shetlands. Jan. 1940, at Invergordon. March, 1940, Shetlands. June, 1940, at Pembroke Dock. 1941, Stranraer 1 (BN-). One Lerwick G.R.1 for trials. 1941, Catalina

G.R.2 (BN–), one of which shadowed the *Bismarck*. Later used Sunderland G.R.5. 21 March, 1944, 'B' Flt. became No. 628 Squadron. Unit later operated in India and Far East. Disbanded March, 1946. Reformed and, in 1952, was flying Shackleton M.R.1. 1955, at Ballykelly.

No. 241 Squadron

Formed originally as R.N.A.S., Portland, for anti-submarine patrol with Short 225, Short 240 (4), Wight Seaplane. Aug. 1918, became No. 241 Squadron, R.A.F. Also used Campania. Disbanded 18 June, 1919. Reformed Sept. 1940, for reconnaissance with Lysander 2 (FZ–). 1942, Tomahawk F.2a (RZ–), Mustang F.1 (RZ–). 1943, Mustang F.3 (RZ–), Hurricane F.2b, F.2c (RZ–). 1944, Spitfire F.5b, F.8, F.9c, F.B.9e (RZ–). Disbanded Aug. 1945. Reformed as an O.C.U. squadron with Hastings C.1, Dakota C.3, C.4 (ODK–, HC–).

No. 242 'Canadian' Squadron

Formed originally as R.N.A.S., Newhaven, with Short 240 for sea patrol. Aug. 1918, became No. 242 Squadron, R.A.F. Disbanded 15 May, 1919. Reformed Oct. 1939, with Hurricane F.1, F.2a, F.2b, F.2c (LE–). Served in France until May, 1940, when returned to Biggin Hill. June, 1940, to France with A.A.S.F. C.O. W/C D. R. S. Bader. Aug. 1940, at Coltishall. Disbanded Feb. 1942. Reformed April, 1942, with Spitfire F.5b. 1944, Spitfire F.9 (LE–). Disbanded Nov. 1944. Reformed Nov. 1944, with Wellington C.16 (KY–), Stirling C.5 (KY–), York C.1 (KY–, OYF–, MOYF–). Hastings C.1 also used later.

No. 243 Squadron

Formed originally as R.N.A.S., Cherbourg, in 1917. Seaplane patrols with Short 260, Wight Seaplane. Disbanded 15 March, 1919. Reformed March, 1941, as a fighter unit with Buffalo F.1 for use in Far East. Re-equipped with Spitfire F.5b. Disbanded Oct. 1944. Reformed Dec. 1944, for transport with Dakota C.4, Stirling G.T.4, Liberator C.8.

No. 244 Squadron

Formed July, 1918, at Bangor for marine operations with D.H.6, engaging in anti-submarine operations in co-operation with R.N. and airship station at Llangefni. Disbanded Jan. 1919. Reformed Nov. 1940, for reconnaissance in Far East with Vincent 1. At Shaibah in 1941, using Valentia 5. Also equipped with Blenheim 4L, Blenheim 5D, Wellington B.1c, Catalina G.R.3.

No. 245 'Northern Rhodesia' Squadron

Formed 1917, as R.N.A.S., Fishguard, for anti-submarine patrol with Short 260. Aug. 1918, became No. 245 Squadron, R.A.F. Disbanded

10 May, 1919. Reformed Oct. 1939, with Blenheim 1, Magister. C.O. S/L J. W. C. Simpson. At Scapa, then Rouen. 1940, Hurricane F.1, F.2a, F.2c (DX–, MR–). Aug. 1940, at Aldergrove. Also used Spitfire F.2. 1942, Typhoon F.1b, rocket-firing (MR–). Disbanded Aug. 1945. Reformed from No. 504 Squadron Sept. 1945, with Meteor F.3 (MR–). Re-equipped Meteor F.4 (MR–). June, 1950, Meteor F.8, T.7. At Horsham St. Faith. First Meteor F.8 day-fighter squadron and last to fly the type. April, 1957, Hunter F.4, F.6. 1959, Canberra B.2, T.4, at Tangmere on high-level radar calibration.

No. 246 Squadron

Formed 1917, as R.N.A.S., Seaton Carew, for anti-submarine patrol. with F.E.2b from No. 36 Squadron, R.F.C. April, 1918, Kangaroo. Aug. 1918, became No. 246 Squadron, R.A.F. Disbanded May, 1919. Reformed Aug. 1942, for transport with Halifax C.2. Also used Liberator B.1, C.3, C.6, C.7, C.8. Disbanded May, 1943. Reformed Oct. 1944, with Sunderland G.R.3. Later transport with York C.1 (VU–, OYB–), Skymaster C.1.

No. 247 'China-British' Squadron

Formed 1917, as R.N.A.S., Felixstowe, for anti-submarine patrol. Operated with Sopwith Baby Seaplane, F.2a, F.3, F.5, Curtiss H.12 Large America. Aug. 1918, became No. 247 Squadron, R.A.F. Disbanded Jan. 1919. Reformed Nov. 1939, with Gladiator 2 (ZY–). Aug. 1940, one flight at Roborough. 1940, Hurricane F.1, F.2a, F.2c (ZY–). 1943, Typhoon F.1a (ZY–). Nov. 1943, fighter-bomber with Typhoon F.1b (ZY–). April, 1944, rocket-firing Typhoon F.1b (ZY–). 1945, Tempest F.5, F.2 (ZY–). 1946, Vampire F.1 (ZY–)—first unit. 1950, Vampire F.3 (ZY–). 1952, Vampire F.B.5. 1953, at Tangmere with Meteor F.8. 1955, Hunter F.1, F.4 at Odiham. C.O. S/L L. S. Lawton. 1957, Hunter F.6.

No. 248 Squadron

Formed 1917, as R.N.A.S., Hornsea, for anti-submarine patrol with Short 225, Sopwith Baby Seaplane. Aug. 1918, became No. 248 Squadron, R.A.F. Disbanded 6 March, 1919. Reformed Oct. 1939, at Hendon with Blenheim 1f, 4f (WR–). Later at Northolt. Re-equipped with Beaufighter T.F.1c, T.F.6c, T.F.10 (WR–, NE–) for anti-shipping duties. 1944, Mosquito F.B.6 (DM–, NE–), F.B.18 (WR–). 1946, Brigand B.1. Oct. 1946, disbanded and renumbered No. 36 Squadron.

No. 249 'Gold Coast' Squadron

Formed 1917, as R.N.A.S., Killingholme. April, 1917, Curtiss H.12 Large America, Short 225, 320. Also used F.2a, F.3, F.5. 18 Aug. 1918, became No. 249 Squadron, R.A.F. at Dundee. Disbanded 8 Oct. 1919. Reformed May, 1940, with Hurricane F.2 (GN–). Aug. 1940, at Church Fenton. 16 Aug. 1940, V.C. won by F/L J. B. Nicolson. 1941, Spitfire F.5b, F.5c (GN–). At Malta. F/O G. Buerling joined squadron in June, 1942, and shot down 27 E/A in 14 days, his total being 32 E/A. April, 1943, Mustang F.3 (GN–). July, 1943, Spitfire F.9 (GN–). Nov. 1943, at Taranto. Later used Mustang F.4 (GN–), Tempest F.B.6 (GN–), Mosquito F.B.6, F.B.26 (GN–). Disbanded 23 Oct. 1945. Reformed 23 Oct. 1945, from No. 500 Squadron for photo-survey with Baltimore B.5 (GN–). 1952, at Deversoir with Meteor T.7. June, 1954, Vampire F.B.5, F.B.9, T.11 at Amman. Oct. 1954, Venom F.B.1. C.O. S/L Gough. 1957, at Akrotiri with Canberra B.2. 1966, Canberra B.15.

No. 250 'Sudan' Squadron

Formed 1917, as R.N.A.S., Padstow, for anti-submarine patrol with D.H.6, Curtiss J.N.4. May, 1918, became No. 250 Squadron, R.A.F. 1918, D.H.9. Disbanded May, 1919. Reformed April, 1941, with Hurricane F.1. (LD–), Tomahawk F.1, F.2 (LD–). 1943, Kittyhawk F.1a, F.3, F.B.4 (LD–). 1944. Mustang F.3, F.4 (LD–).

No. 251 Squadron

Formed 1917, as R.N.A.S., Hornsea, for anti-submarine patrol with Short 225. Aug. 1918, became No. 251 Squadron, R.A.F. Disbanded 30 June, 1919. Reformed Aug. 1944, for meteorological reconnaissance and air-sea rescue with Hudson G.R.5 (AD–), Fortress G.R.1, G.R.2a, G.R.5 (AD–).

No. 252 Squadron

Formed 1917, as R.N.A.S., Tynemouth, for anti-submarine patrols with D.H.6, Short 225. 1 April, 1918, became No. 252 Squadron, R.A.F. Disbanded 30 June, 1919. Reformed Nov. 1940, with Blenheim 4f for coastal patrol. Also received Beaufighter F.1c (PN–) and was first Coastal Beaufighter unit. 1941, to Egypt. Oct. 1943, received Beaufighter F.6c, T.F.10, F.11c from No. 603 Squadron.

No. 253 'Hyderabad' Squadron

Formed in 1916 as R.N.A.S., Bembridge, with four Short 240 for antisubmarine patrols. Aug. 1918, became No. 253 Squadron, R.A.F. Disbanded 5 May, 1919. Reformed Oct. 1939, with Blenheim 4 as a fighter unit. Feb. 1940, at Northolt. Aug. 1940, at Turnhouse with Hurricane F.1, F.2c (GD–, SW–). Later used Spitfire F.5b, F.5c, F.8, F.9 (SW–) on fighter-bomber duties. Disbanded May, 1947. Reformed with Venom N.F.2a and was at Waterbeach in 1956.

No. 254 Squadron

Formed 1917, as R.N.A.S., Prawle Point, for anti-submarine patrol with One-and-a-half Strutter, D.H.6, Short 225. May, 1918, became No. 254 Squadron, R.A.F. Disbanded Jan. 1919, Reformed Oct. 1939, for coastal duties with Blenheim 1, 4f. July, 1942, Beaufighter F.6c, T.F.10 'Torbeau' (QM–) at North Coates. Later used Mosquito F.B.18 (QM–). 1946, Brigand B.1. Disbanded Oct. 1946, and became No. 42 Squadron.

No. 255 Squadron

Formed 1917, as R.N.A.S., Pembroke, for anti-submarine patrols with One-and-a-half Strutter, D.H.6, Short 225, C. and S.S.Z. Type airships. Disbanded 14 Jan. 1919. Reformed Nov. 1940, for night-fighting with Defiant N.F.1. Also used Hurricane F.2 (YD–), Beaufighter F.1, N.F.2f, N.F.6f (YD–), Mosquito N.F.12 (YD–).

No. 256 Squadron

Formed originally as R.N.A.S., Seahouses, for convoy duties with F.2a. June, 1918, became No. 256 Squadron, R.A.F. Disbanded 30 June, 1919. Reformed 23 Nov. 1940, for night-fighting with Defiant N.F.1, N.F.2 (JT–), Battle 1, Hurricane F.2d. At Squires Gate and Woodvale. Later used Beaufighter N.F.1f, N.F.6f (JT–), Blenheim 4. Oxford T.2 for training, together with Battle. 1943, on intruder operations with Mosquito N.F.12 (JT–). April, 1944, Spitfire F.2. 1945, Mosquito B.16, N.F.13, N.F.19, N.F.30 (JT–). Disbanded Sept. 1946, in Middle East. Reformed for night-fighting in 2nd T.A.F. and in 1955 was flying Meteor N.F.11. 1956, at Ahlhorn. 1958, Javelin F.A.W.6. 1959, became No. 11 Squadron.

No. 257 'Burma' Squadron

Formed April, 1914, as R.N.A.S., Dundee. Operated on anti-submarine patrols with Sopwith Baby Seaplane, Short 225. Aug. 1918, became No. 257 Squadron, R.A.F. Disbanded 30 June, 1919. Reformed June, 1940, at Hendon as a fighter unit with Spitfire F.2. July, 1940, Hurricane F.1 (DT–). Aug. 1940, at Northolt. Also used Hurricane F.2a, F.2c (DT–), F.2b (FM–). June, 1942, Typhoon F.1b (FM–). Disbanded March, 1945. Reformed 1947 with Meteor F.3, F.4 (A6–). 1952, at Wattisham with Meteor F.8, T.7 (A6–). Dec. 1954, Hunter F.2, being first to receive F.2. Later used Hunter F.6. 1955, C.O. Maj. N. H. Tanner, U.S.A.A.F. on exchange posting.

No. 258 Squadron

Formed originally as R.N.A.S., Luce Bay, for anti-submarine patrol with D.H.6 and S.S. Zero airship. Aug. 1918, became No. 258 Squadron, R.A.F. Disbanded Dec. 1918. Reformed Nov. 1940, at Tengah with Hurricane F.1, F.2a (ZT–). 1944, Thunderbolt F.B.2 in Far East.

No. 259 Squadron

Formed originally in 1913 as R.N.A.S., Felixstowe. Later engaged in marine operations with F.2a, F.3, F.5, Curtiss H.12 Large America. Aug. 1918, became No. 259 Squadron, R.A.F. Disbanded Sept. 1919. Reformed Feb. 1943, for general reconnaissance with Catalina G.R.3 and also used Sunderland G.R.5.

No. 260 Squadron

Formed 1916 as R.N.A.S., Westward Ho! for anti-submarine patrol with D.H.6, Short 225. Aug. 1918, became No. 260 Squadron, R.A.F. Disbanded 22 Feb. 1919. Reformed Nov. 1940, with Hurricane F.2. (HS–) and served with Desert Air Force. 1941, Tomahawk F.1 (HS). May, 1942, Kittyhawk, F.2, F.3 (HS–). March, 1944, Mustang F.3 (HS–).

No. 261 Squadron

Formed originally in 1913, as R.N.A.S., Felixstowe, for marine operations. Later used F.3, F.5. Aug. 1918, became No. 261 Squadron, R.A.F. Disbanded Sept. 1918. Reformed June, 1940, at Hal Far, Malta, with Sea Gladiators of which *Faith*, *Hope* and *Charity* became famous for their defence of the island. 2 Aug. 1940, twelve Hurricanes arrived as reinforcements. Those used by the squadron included Hurricane F.1, F.2, F.B.2b, F.2d (XJ–, FJ–, HA–). March, 1944, Thunderbolt F.B.2 (FJ–).

No. 262 Squadron

Formed Sept. 1942, for service in S.E.A.C. with Catalina G.R.3 and also used Lancaster B.1 (KL–). Disbanded 15 Feb. 1945, and re-numbered No. 35 Squadron, S.A.A.F.

No. 263 'Fellowship of the Bellows' Squadron

Formed March, 1918, in the Mediterranean for coastal reconnaissance with Sopwith Baby Seaplane and F.3. Disbanded 16 May, 1919. Reformed 2 Oct. 1939, at Filton with Gladiator 2 (HE–). 23 April, 1940, to Norway in H.M.S. *Glorious*. Based on Lake Lesjaskog and at Aandalsnes. C.O.s W/C Whitney Straight and S/L Donaldson. May, 1940, at Bardufoss. Also used Hurricane F.1, F.2 (HE–). June, 1940, first unit to fly Whirlwind F.1 (HE–). At Drem. C.O. S/L H. Eeles. Aug. 1940 to Exeter. 1944, Typhoon F.1b (HE–). Disbanded Aug. 1945. Reformed Sept. 1945. 1946, Meteor F.3 (HE–). 1950, Meteor F.4, T.7 (HE–). 1951, at Wattisham with Meteor F.8. Feb. 1955, Hunter F.2, being second squadron to receive F.2. C.O. S/L Aytoun. Later used Hunter F.5. 1957, Hunter F.6. 1958, became No. 1 Squadron at Stradishall.

No. 264 'Madras Presidency' Squadron

Formed April, 1918, for anti-submarine operations in the Aegean with Short 225. Disbanded 1 March, 1919. Reformed 30 Oct. 1939, with Battle 1, Magister. On 27 May, 1940, shot down 37 E/A over Dunkirk with Defiant F.1 (PS-). Based at Manston. Later night-fighting with Defiant N.F.1 (PS-), N.F.2 (PS-). At Duxford and Hornchurch. April, 1942, Mosquito N.F.2, N.F.13 (PS-) at Rochford. May, 1944, Mosquito N.F.12, T.3 (PS-), Oxford T.2 (PS-). At Cherbourg and in U.K. Disbanded 28 Aug. 1945, after 148 E/A destroyed, 13 probably destroyed and 40 damaged. Reformed 20 Nov. 1945, at Church Fenton from No. 135 Squadron with Mosquito N.F.30 (PS-). Later used Mosquito N.F.36 (PS-, VA-). 1952, Meteor N.F.11. April, 1954, at Linton-on-Ouse with Meteor N.F.12, N.F.14. C.O. S/L H. M. H. Tudor. 1956, C.O. S/L J. C. Forbes. 1957, at Middleton St. George. 1957, disbanded and became No. 33 Squadron. 1 Dec. 1958, reformed with Bloodhound at North Coates as first Air Defence Missile Squadron.

No. 265 Squadron

Formed April, 1918, for sea operations in the Mediterranean with Short 225. Disbanded 1919. Reformed 11 March, 1943, as a flying-boat unit in S.E.A.C. with Catalina G.R.3 (TR-).

No. 266 'Rhodesia' Squadron

Formed April, 1918, at Calafrana for anti-submarine patrols in the Aegean with Short 320, Curtiss H.4, F.3, F.B.A. Flying-boat. March, 1919, to Petrovsk. Disbanded 1 Sept. 1919. Reformed 30 Oct. 1939, with Battle 1 at Sutton Bridge. Aug. 1940, at Wittering with Spitfire F.2b. 1941, Spitfire F.5b. 1942, Typhoon F.1a, F.1b (ZH-). 1944, Tempest F.5 (ZH-). In 2nd T.A.F. Disbanded 31 July, 1945. Reformed 1 Sept. 1946, from No. 234 Squadron with Meteor F.3, F.4 (FX-). Disbanded 11 Feb. 1949, and became No. 43 Squadron. Reformed 2 July, 1952, in 2nd T.A.F. with Vampire F.B.5 and based at Wunstorf. 1953, Venom F.B.1. 1955, C.O. S/L W. J. T. Henderson. May, 1956, Venom F.B.4.

No. 267 'Pegasus' Squadron

Formed Nov. 1918, in the Mediterranean for reconnaissance. Used F.2a, F.3, Short 225. 1921, Fairey 3c. In 1922, one flight of 3c was sent to the Dardanelles with H.M.S. *Pegasus* until 1 Aug. 1923, when the squadron was disbanded. Reformed 19 Aug. 1940, as a transport unit with Audax, Proctor, Q.6 Petrel, Hudson C.6 (KW-), Lodestar,

Bombay. 1944, Dakota C.3 in Burma. Also used Gipsy Moth and Liberator C.2. Disbanded 21 July, 1946. Reformed for transport with Dakota C.3 and in Dec. 1954, was at Kuala Lumpur. Received four Pioneer C.C.1 as a support flight. C.O. S/L Hickmott. 1956, using Pembroke C.1, Auster A.O.P.9, Harvard T.2b. C.O. S/L T. W. G. Godfrey. 1960, renumbered No. 209 Squadron. 1967, at Benson with Argosy C.1.

No. 268 Squadron

Formed Nov. 1918, at Malta, for anti-submarine and convoy protection with Short 320. Disbanded 11 Oct. 1919. Reformed at Westley from 'B' Flts. of Nos. 2 and 26 Squadrons. 30 Sept. 1940, with Lysander 2 (NM–), Tiger Moth, Magister. May, 1941, tactical fighter-reconnaissance with Tomahawk F.1 (NM–). April, 1942, Mustang F.1a (NM–), Spitfire F.R.14e. 1944, Mustang F.3, Typhoon F.1b. 19 Sept. 1945, renumbered from No. 487 Squadron with Mosquito F.B.6.

No. 269 Squadron

Formed originally at Port Said as the Anglo-French Seaplane Unit for the defence of the Suez Canal with Nieuport Seaplane. Jan. 1916, aircraft of the *Ben-my-Chree, Anne, Empress, Raven* 2, French Seaplane Base at Port Said and the British Depot at Port Said formed into one squadron, using Short 225 (2), Sopwith Baby Seaplane (4). 6 Oct. 1918, became No. 269 Squadron for bombing with D.H.9 and B.E.2e. Disbanded 15 Nov. 1919. Reformed Dec. 1936, at Bircham Newton with Anson G.R.1 (WP–, UA–). Later at Abbotsinch. 1941, in Iceland with Hudson G.R.3 (UA–). 1944, Hudson, Spitfire F.5b, Martinet, Walrus A.S.R.2, Warwick G.R.1 on air-sea rescue duties. Disbanded 10 March, 1946. Reformed for maritime reconnaissance with Shackleton M.R.1 (B–). 1952, at Ballykelly.

No. 270 Squadron

Formed 1918 for sea operations in the Mediterranean with Short 225. Disbanded 1919. Reformed Nov. 1942, as a flying-boat unit in West Africa for general reconnaissance with Catalina G.R.3 and Sunderland G.R.1.

No. 271 Squadron

Formed April, 1918, as a seaplane unit with Short 225 but did not see any service and was disbanded 9 Dec. 1918. Reformed March, 1940, at Doncaster from No. 1680 Flt. Used Ford 5–AT–D, Bombay, Harrow 3 ('Sparrow') (BJ–) as a transport unit. 1941, Albatross (BJ–). 1942, Hudson (BJ–). Jan. 1944, Dakota C.3, C.4 (YS–, L7–, OFB–, ODN–, OFV–). Thirty Dakotas in use for glider-towing. 19 Sept. 1944, V.C.

won at Arnhem by F/L D. S. A. Lord. Disbanded 1 Dec. 1946, and renumbered No. 77 Squadron.

No. 272 Squadron

Formed July, 1918, at Machrihanish for marine operations but did not see any service and was disbanded in Dec. 1918. Reformed Aug. 1940, for anti-shipping operations with Blenheim 4f. 1941, Beaufighter F.1c, F.6c, T.F.10.

No. 273 Squadron

Formed Aug. 1918, at Burgh Castle from No. 534 Flt., R.N.A.S. Received B.E.2c, D.H.9a, Camel 2F.1 (1). D.H.9 (5) detached to Covehithe, D.H.4 (2) detached to Manston. Marine operations. Disbanded 5 July, 1919. Reformed Aug. 1939, and went to Far East in Sept. 1939. Equipped with Fulmar for drogue-towing, Seal, Vildebeest 4 (HH–). Aug. 1942, Hurricane F.2. 1944, Spitfire F.9.

No. 274 Squadron

Formed April, 1918, at Bircham Newton for marine operations but experimented as a multi-engine night-bomber unit with O/400, V/1500, Vimy and Braemar and was disbanded in 1919. Reformed 19 Aug. 1940, and was first Hurricane unit in the Western Desert. Used Hurricane F.1, F.2b (YK–, NH–). C.O. S/L P. H. Dunn. Later equipped with Spitfire F.5c, F.9, F.9c (NH–, JJ–) and Typhoon F.1b (JJ–). 1944, Tempest F.5 (JJ–).

No. 275 Squadron

Formed Oct. 1941, for air-sea rescue with Lysander A.S.R.3a, Walrus A.S.R.1. May, 1942, Defiant A.S.R.1, 1a. Sept. 1943, Walrus A.S.R.2 (PV–). Also used Anson A.S.R.1, Magister. 1944, Spitfire A.S.R.2c, Warwick A.S.R.1. Disbanded 15 Feb. 1945. Reformed 1 March, 1953, at Linton-on-Ouse for air-sea rescue in Fighter Command with Sycamore H.R.13, only two of which were built for the unit. Also equipped with Sycamore H.R.14. 1955, C.O. S/L B. A. Primavesi. 1955, at Thornaby. Renumbered No. 228 Squadron.

No. 276 Squadron

Formed Oct. 1941, at Harrowbeer for air-sea rescue with Anson A.S.R.1 (AQ–), Lysander A.S.R.3a (AQ–), Walrus A.S.R.2 (AQ). Also equipped with Spitfire A.S.R.2c (AQ–) and Warwick A.S.R.1 (AQ–) which carried Mk. 1a lifeboat. Until Sept. 1944, the unit was operating in the south-western area from Portreath and Harrowbeer. In Sept. 1944, the squadron landed in Normandy at Querqueville, near Cherbourg. The Spitfires and Walruses were taken to France, but the

Warwicks were left behind at Portreath. 20 Sept. 1944, moved to
Amiens Glissy, staying there for a month. 27 Oct. 1944, arrived at
Bruges and operated with the aircraft dispersed at St. Denis Westrem
and Ursel. 13 Dec. 1944, to Knocke-Zoute, with some Spitfires detached
at Ghent. 1 Jan. 1945, squadron shot up on the ground by Me. 109s
and F.W.190s. 18 Feb. 1945, the unit made its 300th rescue. A few
Sea Otter A.S.R.2 (AQ-) were used in early 1945. June, 1945, the
squadron returned to England and was dispersed at Andrewsfield,
Essex, one flight of Spitfires going to Norway for a short while. Finally
disbanded in Sept. 1945.

No. 277 Squadron

Formed Dec. 1941, for air-sea rescue with Walrus A.S.R.1, 2 (BA-),
Defiant A.S.R.1, 2 (BA-). 1942, Lysander A.S.R.3a (BA-). 1943, Spitfire A.S.R.2c (BA-), Hudson A.S.R.3, Warwick A.S.R.3.

No. 278 Squadron

Formed Sept. 1941, for air-sea rescue with Anson A.S.R.1, Lysander
A.S.R.3a (MY-). 1942, Walrus A.S.R.2 (MY-). 1944, Tiger Moth 2
(MY-). 1945, Sea Otter A.S.R.2, Spitfire A.S.R.2c, Warwick A.S.R.1
(MY-).

No. 279 Squadron

Formed Nov. 1941, for air-sea rescue with Hudson A.S.R.3, 3a, 5, 6
(FI-), Anson A.S.R.1. 1944, at Bircham Newton with Warwick A.S.R.1
(FI-), Hurricane F.2c, F.4, Martinet T.T.1 (FI-).

No. 280 Squadron

Formed Dec. 1941, for air-sea rescue with Hudson A.S.R.3 (MF-),
Anson A.S.R.1 (MF-, YF-). 1943, first to use Warwick A.S.R.1 (MF-,
YF-). In East Anglia with Lysander A.S.R.3a, Defiant A.S.R.1, Well-
ington A.S.R.1 (MF-).

No. 281 Squadron

Formed March, 1942, for air-sea rescue with Defiant A.S.R.1, 2,
Lysander A.S.R.3a (FA-). Aug. 1943, Walrus A.S.R.2, Anson A.S.R.1
(FA-). 1944, Warwick A.S.R.1 (B4-, FA-), Hudson A.S.R.3, Sea
Otter A.S.R.2 (FA-).

No. 282 Squadron

Formed 1 Jan. 1943, for air-sea rescue with Anson A.S.R.1, Walrus
A.S.R.2, Wellington A.S.R.1 (B4-). Feb. 1944, Warwick A.S.R.1 (B4-).
1945, Sea Otter A.S.R.2.

No. 283 Squadron

Formed April, 1943, for air-sea rescue with Walrus A.S.R.2, Warwick A.S.R.1, Hurricane F.2c, Spitfire F.9. In North Africa.

No. 284 Squadron

Formed 7 May, 1943, for air-sea rescue with Walrus A.S.R.2, Warwick A.S.R.1. In North Africa. Disbanded 21 Sept. 1945. Reformed Nov. 1956, at Nicosia for rescue work with twelve Sycamore H.R.14, Whirlwind H.A.R.2. 1949, renumbered No. 103 Squadron. C.O. S/L J. L. Price.

No. 285 Squadron

Formed 1 Dec. 1941, for anti-aircraft co-operation and used Blenheim 1, Lysander, Hudson, Defiant T.T.1, T.T.3, Oxford T.2, Martinet T.T.1, Beaufighter F.1, Hurricane F.2, N.F.2c, Anson T.1, Mustang F.1 (all VC–). Based at Woodvale.

No. 286 Squadron

Formed 17 Nov. 1941, for anti-aircraft co-operation, receiving Oxford T.2, Defiant T.T.1, 2, 3, Master, Hurricane F.2, F.4, Martinet T.T.1, Beaufighter F.1, Spitfire L.F.16e (all NW–). At Exeter Aug. 1943. April, 1944, Winkleigh. Sept. 1944, Weston Zoyland.

No. 287 Squadron

Formed Nov. 1941, for anti-aircraft co-operation and operated with Lysander T.T.3a, Anson T.1, Hurricane F.2, Beaufighter N.F.2f, N.F.6f, Defiant N.F.1, N.F.2, Oxford T.2, Martinet T.T.1, Spitfire L.F.16e, Tempest F.5 (all KZ–). Based at Croydon in 1941.

No. 288 Squadron

Formed 18 Nov. 1941, for anti-aircraft co-operation with Hudson, Lysander, Hurricane N.F.1, F.2c, Defiant F.1, F.2, T.T.2 (all RP–). 1945, Vengeance T.T.2/2, T.T.4, Oxford T.2, Spitfire F.5b, F.5c, F.9c, L.F.16e (all RP–). Disbanded 15 June, 1946. Reformed and used Balliol T.2.

No. 289 Squadron

Formed 20 Nov. 1941, for anti-aircraft co-operation at Turnhouse with Blenheim 4, Lysander, Hudson, Defiant T.T.1, 2, 3, Oxford T.2, Hurricane F.1, F.2c, F.4, Martinet T.T.1, Vengeance T.T.2, Spitfire F.5c (all YE–).

No. 290 Squadron

Formed 1 Dec. 1943, for anti-aircraft co-operation and used Martinet T.T.1, Oxford T.2, Hurricane F.2, Spitfire F.5b, L.F.16e (all X6–).

No. 291 Squadron

Formed 1 Dec. 1943, for anti-aircraft co-operation with Martinet T.T.1.

No. 292 Squadron

Formed 1 Feb. 1944, for air-sea rescue and received Walrus A.S.R.2, Warwick A.S.R.1, Sea Otter A.S.R.2, Liberator B.6.

No. 293 Squadron

Formed Nov. 1943, from detachments of Nos. 283 and 284 Squadrons, and based at Bone, French North Africa, with Walrus A.S.R.2, Warwick A.S.R.2, G.R.2 (ZE-). Operated on air-sea rescue. April, 1944, at Pomigliano.

No. 294 Squadron

Formed Oct. 1943, for air-sea rescue with nine Walrus A.S.R.2 and twenty-five Warwick A.S.R.1 and Wellington A.S.R.1c, Blenheim 4. Served in Middle East.

No. 295 Squadron

Formed Aug. 1942, for transport of airborne forces with Horsa 1 and 2. 1943, Whitley B.4, G.T.5 (PX-), Stirling G.T.4 (8E-, 8Z-), Halifax B.5, A.5/1a, G.T.3, A.7, A.9 (8E-, 8Z-, MLHC-). Jan. 1943, first unit to fly Albemarle G.T.2 (8Z-). Disbanded 28 Feb. 1946. Reformed 10 Sept. 1947, as a transport unit.

No. 296 Squadron

Formed Jan. 1942, for transport of airborne forces with Hotspur, Hart, Whitley G.T.5, 10 (XH-), Albemarle G.T.2 (9W-). May, 1945, Halifax G.T.3, C.8, A.5/1a (7C-, 9W-), Horsa 1, 2.

No. 297 Squadron

Formed 15 Feb. 1941, at Netheravon, for transport of airborne forces. Operated with Whitley G.T.5, 10, Albemarle G.T.1, G.T.2 (L5-, P5-), Halifax G.T.3 (CS-), Halifax A.5/1a (P5-), Halifax A.5/1a (L5-), Halifax A.7, A.9 (CS-), Halifax C.8 (MOHA-), Horsa 1, 2. Took part in Arnhem and Rhine operations. Nov. 1948, Hastings C.1.

No. 298 Squadron

Formed Aug. 1942, but did not see any service and was disbanded Oct. 1942. Reformed Nov. 1943, for transport of airborne forces with Halifax G.T.3, G.T.5/1a, A.7 (8A-, 8T-), Hamilcar 1, Horsa 1, 2. 1945, engaged in transport in India with one flight of Halifax B.3 and also used Halifax A.7 (8T-), about thirty aircraft being on strength.

No. 299 Squadron

Formed 4 Nov. 1943, for transport of airborne forces with Ventura 2 (XG–, 5G–), Whitley B.2, Horsa 1, 2, Wellington G.T.10 (MZ–). July, 1945, transport with Stirling G.T.4 (XG–, 5G–).

No. 300 'Masovian' (Polish) Squadron

Formed 1 July, 1940, at Bramcote, as a bomber unit with Battle 1 (BH–). Later re-equipped with Wellington B.1c, B.4 (BH–). Jan. 1943, Wellington B.3 (BH–). Sept. 1943, Wellington B.10 (BH–). 1943, Lancaster B.1, B.3 (BH–). Based at Ingham. 1 Jan. 1944, at Faldingworth and was only Polish Lancaster squadron. Disbanded Jan. 1947.

No. 301 'Pomeranian' (Polish) Squadron

Formed 22 July, 1940, at Bramcote as a bomber unit with Battle 1 (GR–). 1941, Wellington B.1c, B.3, B.4 (GR–). 1943, Warwick C.1, C.3 (GR–), Halifax B.2/1a, B.5, C.8 (OO–, GR–) at Chedburgh. 1 Sept. 1943, received three Liberator B.6 (GR–) and was later incorporated with a British unit as No. 1586 Special Duty Flight with Halifax and Liberator. Disbanded 18 Dec. 1946.

No. 302 'Poznan' (Polish) Squadron

Formed 13 July, 1940, for fighting with Hurricane F.1, F.2 (WX–) at Northolt. Later used Spitfire F.5c, F.9c, L.F.16e (WX–). 1944, Mosquito N.F.30. Disbanded 18 Dec. 1946.

No. 303 'Warsaw-Kosciusco' (Polish) Squadron

Formed 2 Aug. 1940, at Northolt as a fighter unit with Hurricane F.1, F.2a (RF–). C.O. W/C R. G. Kellett. 1940, Spitfire F.2a, F.5b, L.F.5b (RF–). 1942, Spitfire F.9c (RF–, PD–). 1946, Mustang F.B.4 (RF–, PD–). Disbanded 11 Dec. 1946.

No. 304 'Mazonia' (Polish) Squadron

Formed 22 Aug. 1940, at Bramcote, for bombing with Battle 1 and Wellington B.1c, B.3 (QO–, NZ–). 7 May, 1942, became coastal reconnaisance unit. Dec. 1942, Wellington B.10. July, 1943, Wellington G.R.12, G.R.13, G.R.14, C.15 (QD–, NZ–). 1945, Warwick C.3 (QD–), Mosquito B.16, Halifax C.8 (QD–). At Chedburgh. Disbanded 18 Dec. 1946.

No. 305 'Pomeranian' (Polish) Squadron

Formed 1 Sept. 1940, at Bramcote, as a bomber unit with Battle 1 (SM–). Nov. 1940, Wellington B.1c (SM–). July, 1941, Wellington B.2, B.3 (SM–). July, 1942, Wellington B.4 (SM–). June, 1943, Wellington B.10 (SM–). Nov. 1943, Mitchell B.2 (SM–). 1944, Mosquito F.B.6, T.3 (SM–). Disbanded 6 Jan. 1947.

No. 306 'Torun' (Polish) Squadron

Formed 29 Aug. 1940, for fighting with Hurricane F.1, F.2a (UZ-) at Northolt. 1941, Spitfire F.5b (UZ-). 1943, Spitfire F.9c (UZ-). 1946, Mustang F.3, F.4. Disbanded 6 Jan. 1947.

No. 307 'Lwow' (Polish) Squadron

Formed 5 Sept. 1940, at Kirton-in-Lindsey for night-fighting with Defiant N.F.1 (EW-). Nov. 1940, at Jurby. Jan. 1941, at Squires Gate. April, 1941, at Exeter. 1942, Beaufighter N.F.1f, N.F.2f, N.F.6f (EW-). 1943, Mosquito N.F.2, F.B.6, N.F.12 (EW-). 1944, Mosquito N.F.30 (EW-), Oxford T.2 (EW-). Disbanded 2 Jan. 1947.

No. 308 'Krakow' (Polish) Squadron

Formed 5 Sept. 1940, as a fighter unit with Hurricane F.1 (ZF-). At Northolt. 1942, Spitfire F.2a, F.2b (ZF-). 1942, Spitfire F.5b (ZF-). 1943, Spitfire F.9c (ZF-), L.F.16e (ZF-). Disbanded 18 Dec. 1946.

No. 309 'Ziemia Czerwienska' (Polish) Squadron

Formed 8 Oct. 1940, for army co-operation with Lysander 2, 3. 1944, fighter unit with Hurricane F.2c (WC-) at Turnhouse. 1946, Mustang F.1, F.3 (WC-). Disbanded 6 Jan. 1947.

No. 310 (Czecho-Slovak) Squadron

Formed 10 July, 1940, as a fighter unit with Hurricane F.1, F.2a (NN-). 1941, Spitfire F.2a, F.5b, F.5c (NN-). Later used Spitfire F.9c, L.F.16e (NN-). Disbanded 15 Feb. 1946.

No. 311 (Czecho-Slovak) Squadron

Formed 29 July, 1940, at Honington, for bombing with Wellington B.1, B.1a, B.1c (KX-, PP-). Later used Liberator G.R.5, G.R.6, C.6 (PP-), Courier (PP-). Disbanded 15 Feb. 1946.

No. 312 (Czecho-Slovak) Squadron

Formed 29 Aug. 1940, as a fighter unit with Hurricane F.1, F.2a (DU-). 1941, Spitfire F.2a, F.5b, F.9c (DU-). Disbanded 15 Feb. 1946.

No. 313 (Czecho-Slovak) Squadron

Formed 10 May, 1941, as a fighter unit and was equipped with Spitfire F.1, F.2, F.5b, L.F.5b, F.9b, F.9c (RY-). Disbanded 15 Feb. 1946.

No. 315 'Deblin' (Polish) Squadron

Formed 21 Jan. 1941, for fighting with Hurricane F.1 (PK-, SZ-). At Northolt. Later equipped with Spitfire F.2a, F.5b, L.F.5b, F.9 (SZ-).

1944, Mustang F.1, F.3 (SZ–). 1944, Mosquito N.F.30 (SM–). Disbanded 14 Jan. 1947.

No. 316 'Warsaw' (Polish) Squadron

Formed 15 Feb. 1941, as a fighter unit with Hurricane F.1 (PK–). 1942, at Northolt with Spitfire F.5b, F.9c, L.F.16e (PK–). 1943, Mustang F.3 (PK–). Disbanded 11 Dec. 1946.

No. 317 'Wilno' (Polish) Squadron

Formed 22 Feb. 1941, for long-range photographic-reconnaissance with Hurricane F.1, F.2. Also received Magister T.1 (JH–), Spitfire F.5b, F.9c, L.F.16e (JH–). 1944, Mosquito N.F.30. 1946, Hornet F.3. Disbanded 18 Dec. 1946.

No. 318 'Danzig-Gdansk' (Polish) Squadron

Formed 1 April, 1943, as a fighter unit with Hurricane F.2 (LW–). Later used Spitfire F.5b, F.B.9c (LW–). Disbanded 12 April, 1946.

No. 320 (Dutch) Squadron

Formed 1 June, 1940, at Pembroke Dock, for maritime general reconnaissance with Fokker T.8W (TD–), Anson G.R.1. June, 1941, Short S. 21 *Mercury*. 1940, Hudson G.R.2, G.R.3 (TD–, NO–). 18 Jan. 1941, joined by No. 321 Squadron. March, 1943, Mitchell B.2, B.3 (NO–) at Attlebridge and in 2nd T.A.F. Disbanded 2 Aug. 1945.

No. 321 (Dutch) Squadron

Formed 1 June, 1940, for maritime general reconnaissance with Anson G.R.1, Hudson G.R.2, G.R.3. Disbanded 18 Jan. 1941, and merged with No. 320 Squadron. Reformed July, 1943, at China Bay, Java, with five Dornier Do.24K and also used Catalina G.R.4b for reconnaissance. July, 1945, Liberator G.R.6, G.R.8. Disbanded 1945.

No. 322 (Dutch) Squadron

Formed 12 June, 1943, at Hornchurch from No. 167 Squadron with Spitfire F.5b (3W–). 1943, Spitfire F.R.14 (3W–). 1944, Spitfire F.9c (3W–). Nov. 1944, Spitfire L.F.16e (3W–). Disbanded 7 Oct. 1945.

No. 326 (Free-French) Squadron

Formed 1 Dec. 1943, as a day-fighter unit with Spitfire F.9 (9I–). Also used Blenheim 4, Marauder B.1, Wellington G.R.11 (9I–). Disbanded Nov. 1945.

No. 327 (Free-French) Squadron

Formed 1 Dec. 1943, as a day-fighter unit with Spitfire F.5b, F.9.

G

Received also Blenheim 4, Maryland B.1, Marauder B.1. Disbanded Nov. 1945.

No. 328 (Free-French) Squadron

Formed 1 Dec. 1943, as a day-fighter unit with Spitfire F.5b, F.9c (S8–). Disbanded Nov. 1945.

No. 329 (Free-French) Squadron

Formed 5 Jan. 1944, as a day-fighter unit with Spitfire F.9c, F.16 (5A–). Disbanded 17 Nov. 1945.

No. 330 (Norwegian) Squadron

Formed April, 1941, in Canada and operated from Aug. 1941 from Iceland with Northrop N3P-B (GS–) on reconnaissance and convoy-escort. "A" Flt. at Fossvogur, "B" Flt. at Akureyri, "C" Flt. at Budareyri. Re-equipped with Sunderland G.R.1 (GS–). Aug. 1942, six Catalina G.R.2 (WH–). Jan. 1943, to Oban except "C" Flt. which joined at Oban April, 1943. Also used Sunderland G.R.3 (WH–). April, 1945, Sunderland G.R.5. Disbanded Nov. 1945.

No. 331 (Norwegian) Squadron

Formed 21 July, 1941, at Catterick as the first Norwegian fighter unit and received Hurricane F.2b (FN–). Aug. 1941, at Castledown. Sept. 1941, at Skaebrae, with detachments at Dyce and Sumburgh. Nov. 1941, Spitfire F.5a, F.5b, L.F.5b, F.9, F.9c, L.F.9, F.9e (FN–). Disbanded 21 Nov. 1945.

No. 332 (Norwegian) Squadron

Formed Jan. 1942, at Catterick as a fighter unit with Hurricane F.1 (AH–). 3 May, 1942, to North Weald. Re-equipped with Spitfire F.2, F.2a, F.5a, F.5b, F.5c, F.9c, L.F.9 (AH–). Disbanded 21 Nov. 1945.

No. 333 (Norwegian) Squadron

Formed originally as Norwegian detachment of No. 210 Squadron at Woodhaven with Catalina (1). Engaged in special duties and anti-submarine patrol. 1 Feb. 1943, became No. 1477 Flt. 10 May, 1943, became No. 333 Squadron with "A" Flt. at Woodhaven for maritime reconnaissance with Catalina G.R.4a (KK–), and "B" Flt. at Leuchars with Mosquito F.B.6 (KK–). "B" Flt. to Banff in Sept. 1944. 30 May, 1945, provided ten aircraft for the formation of No. 334 Squadron. Disbanded 21 Nov. 1945.

No. 334 (Norwegian) Squadron

Formed 30 May, 1945, from "B" Flt. of No. 333 Squadron with ten Mosquito F.B.6. Disbanded 21 Nov. 1945.

No. 335 (Greek) Squadron

Formed 10 Oct. 1941, as a day-fighter unit and operated in the Western Desert with Hurricane F.1, F.2b, F.2c, (FG–). Also used Walrus A.S.R.2 (FG–). 1943, Spitfire F.5b in Italy. Disbanded 31 July, 1946.

No. 336 (Greek) Squadron

Formed 25 Feb. 1943, for day-fighting with Hurricane F.1, F.2. 1943, Spitfire F.5b. Disbanded 30 June, 1946.

No. 340 'Île de France' (Free-French) Squadron

Formed 7 Nov. 1941, and was first of the Free-French units in U.K. Fighter squadron with Spitfire F.2a, F.5a, F.5c, F.9c, L.F.16e (GW–). Disbanded 27 Nov. 1945.

No. 341 'Alsace' (Free-French) Squadron

Formed 15 Jan. 1943, for day-fighting at Turnhouse with Spitfire F.5b (NL–). C.O. Comdt. Mouchotte. Later at Biggin Hill with Spitfire F.9, F.9c, L.F.16e (NL–). Disbanded 27 Nov. 1945.

No. 342 'Lorraine' (Free-French) Squadron

Formed 24 Sept. 1941, in Damascus with Blenheim 4L (OA–). 1943, Boston B.3, B.3a, B.4 (OA–), Mitchell B.3 (OA–). Disbanded 2 Dec. 1945.

No. 343 (Free-French) Squadron

Formed 29 Nov. 1943, for reconnaissance with Sunderland G.R.3. Disbanded Nov. 1945.

No. 344 (Free-French) Squadron

Formed 29 Nov. 1943, for medium-range reconnaissance with Halifax B.3 at Elvington. Disbanded Nov. 1945.

No. 345 (Free-French) Squadron

Formed Feb. 1944, as a day-fighter unit with Spitfire F.5b, F.9, F.9b (2Y–). Also used Spitfire F.16 (2Y–) and Mustang F.3 (2Y–). Disbanded 27 Nov. 1945.

No. 346 'Guyenne' (Free-French) Squadron

Formed 16 May, 1944, at Elvington as a bomber unit with Halifax B.2/1a, B.5 (H7–). July, 1944, Halifax B.3 (H7–). March, 1945, Halifax B.7 (H7–) at Elvington. Disbanded 15 Nov. 1945.

No. 347 'Tunisie' (Free-French) Squadron

Formed 20 June, 1944, at Elvington for bombing with Halifax B.5 (L8–). July, 1944, Halifax B.3 (L8–). March, 1945, Halifax B.6, B.7 (L8–) at Elvington. Disbanded 15 Nov. 1945.

No. 349 (Belgian) Squadron

Formed June, 1943, as a fighter unit with Tomahawk F.1. June, 1943.
Spitfire F.2a, F.5a (GE-). 1943, Spitfire F.5b (GE-). Feb. 1944, Spit-
fire F.9, F.9c, F.14, L.F.16e (GE-). 1944, Tempest F.5, Spitfire F.9
(GE-). Disbanded 24 Oct. 1946.

No. 350 (Belgian) Squadron

Formed Nov. 1941, for fighting with Spitfire F.5a, F.5b (MN-). Feb.
1942, at Northolt. 1943, Spitfire F.2b, L.F.5b, L.F.5c, F.9, F.9c (MN-).
1944, Spitfire F.14, L.F.16e (MN-). Disbanded 24 Oct. 1946.

No. 351 (Yugo-Slav) Squadron

Formed 1 July, 1944, as a day-fighter unit with Hurricane F.2, F.4.
Disbanded 15 June, 1945.

No. 352 (Yugo-Slav) Squadron

Formed 22 April, 1944, as a day-fighter unit with Hurricane F.2, F.4.
Also used Spitfire F.5b, F.8. Disbanded 15 June, 1945.

No. 353 Squadron

Formed 1 June, 1942, for transport in India with Hudson C.6. 1943,
'C' Flt. became No. 52 Squadron. 1943, Dakota C.3, C.4, Liberator C.6
for general reconnaissance and transport.

No. 354 Squadron

Formed 10 May, 1943, for long-range general reconnaissance in
S.E.A.C. with Liberator G.R.6.

No. 355 Squadron

Formed 18 Aug. 1943, at Salbani as a heavy-bomber unit in S.E.A.C.
with Liberator B.2, B.6, B.8, and used also Wellington B.3, Halifax B.3.

No. 356 Squadron

Formed 15 Jan. 1944, at Salbani as a heavy-bomber unit in S.E.A.C. with
Liberator B.6, B.8, C.6.

No. 357 Squadron

Formed 1 April, 1944, from No. 1576 Flt. for parachute and supply-
dropping with Hudson 3a, one flight of Liberator C.6, Catalina, one
flight of Dakota C.4. 1945, one flight of Lysander 3. In 1945, equipped
with one flight each of Liberator, Dakota, Lysander.

No. 358 Squadron

Formed 8 Nov. 1944, at Kolar as a heavy-bomber unit with Liberator B.6
at Jessore, Calcutta. 1945, on special duties.

No. 400 Squadron, R.C.A.F.

Formed originally in 1933 at Toronto. 1940, Lysander 3 (SP–). 1941, Tomahawk F.1 (SP–). 1942, Mustang F.1a, F.R.1 (SP–) for photographic-reconnaissance. Later used Spitfire P.R.11 and F.12, together with Mosquito P.R.16 for the same duties.

No. 401 'Ram' Squadron, R.C.A.F.

Formed originally in 1937 as No. 1 Squadron, R.C.A.F. with Siskin 3. 1940, renumbered No. 401 Squadron with Hurricane F.1 (YO–). At Odiham, March, 1940, until Oct. 1940, then to Northolt as a day-fighter unit. 1942, Spitfire F.2a, F.5b, L.F.5b (YO–). Also used Spitfire H.F.6, H.F.7, F.9, F.9b, F.9c, F.14e, L.F.16e (YO–). Disbanded June, 1945. Reformed 1948 with Vampire F.B.5. 1956, Sabre F.5 at Montreal.

No. 402 'Winnipeg Bear' Squadron, R.C.A.F.

Formed March, 1941, as a day-fighter unit with Hurricane F.1, F.2a, F.2b, F.B.2b (AE–). Later used Spitfire F.5b, F.5c, F.9, F.9b, F.14e, L.F.16e (AE–).

No. 403 'Wolf' Squadron, R.C.A.F.

Formed 1941 for army co-operation with Tomahawk F.1, F.2a (KH–). Also operated with Spitfire F.1, F.2a, F.5a, F.5b, F.9, F.9b, L.F.16e (KH–).

No. 404 Squadron, R.C.A.F.

Formed 15 April, 1941, at Thorney Island for maritime reconnaissance and coastal-strike duties with Blenheim 1f and 4f (EE–). June, 1941, at Castletown. July, 1941, at Skitten. Oct. 1941, at Dyce. Dec. 1941, at Sumburgh. Sept. 1942, Beaufighter F.2f (EE–). March, 1943, Beaufighter T.F.11c. Aug. 1943, Beaufighter T.F.10 (EE–). March, 1945, Mosquito F.B.6. 1952, Lancaster M.R.10 (AF–) at Greenwood, Nova Scotia. C.O. W/C B. H. Moffit. 1955, Neptune M.R.1. 1959, second squadron with Argus CL-28.

No. 405 'Vancouver' Squadron, R.C.A.F.

Formed 23 April, 1941 at Driffield, for bombing with Wellington B.1c, B.2 (LQ–). 1942, at Pocklington with Halifax B.1, B.2, B.2/1, B.2/1a (LQ–). Aug. 1943, Lancaster B.1, B.3, B.3 (Special), B.10 in Pathfinder Force at Gransden Lodge. May, 1945, at Linton-on-Ouse. Disbanded Sept. 1945 at Scoudouc. Reformed 31 March, 1950, at Greenwood for maritime reconnaissance with Lancaster M.R.10. 1955, Neptune M.R.1. 1958, first unit with Argus CL-28.

No. 406 'Lynx' Squadron, R.C.A.F.

Formed May, 1941, as a night-fighter unit with Blenheim N.F.1f, N.F.4f (HU–). June, 1941, Beaufighter N.F.1f, N.F.2f (HU–). 1942, Beaufighter N.F.6f (HU–). July, 1944, Mosquito N.F.12, N.F.30 (HU–). 1952, Mitchell.

No. 407 Squadron, R.C.A.F.

Formed May, 1941, for maritime reconnaissance with Blenheim 4f (RR–). June, 1941, Hudson G.R.1, 2, 3, 5, 6 (RR–). 1943, Wellington G.R.10, G.R.8, G.R.11, G.R.12, G.R.14. 1953, Lancaster M.R.10 for maritime reconnaissance. Sept. 1958, Neptune M.R.1.

No. 408 'Goose' Squadron, R.C.A.F.

Formed 24 June, 1941, at Lindholme and equipped as a bomber unit with Hampden B.1, Manchester B.1a (EQ–). Later used Lancaster B.1, B.2, B.10 (EQ–). Disbanded Sept. 1945. Reformed Jan. 1946 at Rockcliffe. 1953, photographic-survey and reconnaissance with Lancaster M.R.10. March, 1954, twenty Otter, Dakota.

No. 409 'Nighthawk' Squadron, R.C.A.F.

Formed June, 1941, as a night-fighter unit with Defiant N.F.1 (KP–). Aug. 1941, Beaufighter N.F.2f (KP–). June, 1942, Beaufighter N.F.4, N.F.6f (KP–). Feb. 1944, Mosquito N.F.13 (KP–).

No. 410 'Cougar' Squadron, R.C.A.F.

Formed June, 1941, for night-fighting with Defiant N.F.1, N.F.2 (RA–) at Ayr. Aug. 1941, at Drem. Later at Acklington and Ouston. 1942, Beaufighter N.F.2f (RA–). Oct. 1942, Mosquito N.F.2, F.B.6 (RA–). Nov. 1943, Mosquito N.F.12, N.F.13, N.F.30 (RA–). Disbanded June, 1945. Reformed and was at North Luffenham in 1952 with No. 1 Fighter Wing flying Sabre F.4 (AM–). C.O. S/L D. Warren. Jan. 1955, Sabre F.5 at Baden-Soellingen, then to Marville.

No. 411 'Grizzly Bear' Squadron, R.C.A.F.

Formed June, 1941, as a fighter squadron with Spitfire F.1a, F.2, F.2a, F.5b, F.9, F.9b, F.9e, F.14, L.F.16e (all DB–). 1944, Typhoon F.1b (DB–).

No. 412 'Falcon' Squadron, R.C.A.F.

Formed July, 1941, as a fighter unit with Spitfire F.2a, F.5b, F.5c, F.9, F.9b, F.9c, F.9e, F.14, L.F.16e (all VZ–). 1948, transport with Dakota C.4 (AO–). 1952, Expediter (AO–), Canadair C–5, Norseman 4. 1953, C–119c Packet, Comet 1a.

No. 413 Squadron, R.C.A.F.

Formed July, 1941, for general reconnaissance with Catalina G.R.1, G.R.1b, G.R.4b (QL–), based in Ceylon. Nov. 1941, Short S.23 *Cordelia*. Disbanded 15 Feb. 1945. Reformed for photographic-survey and in 1948 was using Norseman 4, Canso 1, Lancaster P.R.10 (all AP–). 1953, fighter unit with Sabre F.4 (AP–). At Zweibrucken.

No. 414 'Imperial' Squadron, R.C.A.F.

Formed 12 Aug. 1941, for fighter-reconnaissance and operated with Tomahawk F.1, F.2a, F.2b, Lysander 1, 3a, Mustang F.1a, F.R.1, Battle 1, Spitfire L.F.9, F.12, F.R.12, F.R.14e (all RU–). Disbanded 7 Aug. 1945. Reformed as a fighter unit with Sabre F.4, which was being flown in 1953. At Baden-Soellingen. 1957, Sabre F.6.

No. 415 'Swordfish' Squadron, R.C.A.F.

Formed 20 Aug. 1941, for torpedo-bombing at Thorney Island with Beaufort G.R.1 (GX–) and Blenheim 4 (GX–). Jan. 1942, Hampden T.B.1 (GX–). 1943, Wellington G.R.12, G.R.13 (NH–), Albacore 1 (NH–, 6U–). Disbanded July, 1944, to form No. 119 Squadron for anti-submarine duties. Reformed 12 July, 1944, for bombing with Halifax B.3, B.5, B.7 (BM–, NH–, 6U–). Disbanded 15 May, 1945. Reformed 1 May, 1961, at Summerside for maritime-reconnaissance with Argus.

No. 416 'City of Oshawa' Squadron, R.C.A.F.

Formed Nov. 1941, as a fighter unit with Spitfire F.2a, F.2b, F.5b, F.9, F.9b, F.9c, F.14e, L.F.16e (DN–). 1944, Typhoon F.1b (DN–). Disbanded March, 1946. Reformed and in 1952 was flying Sabre F.4. C.O. S/L J. Mackay. To Grostenquin, France. Disbanded Feb. 1957. Reformed Feb. 1957, at St. Hubert with CF–100.

No. 417 'City of Windsor' Squadron, R.C.A.F.

Formed Nov. 1941, as a fighter unit with Hurricane F.1, F.2b, F.2c (AN–). 1942, Spitfire F.2a, F.5b, F.5c (AN–). Sept. 1943, Spitfire F.8 (AN–), F.B.9. (AN–).

No. 418 'City of Edmonton' Squadron, R.C.A.F.

Formed 15 Nov. 1941, for intruder duties at Debden with Boston B.1, B.3 (TH–). Also used Mosquito N.F.2, F.B.6, T.3 (TH–). Disbanded Sept. 1945 at Volkel. Reformed April, 1946, at Edmonton as fighter-bomber squadron. Used Mitchell B.3, Harvard T.2b. March, 1958, for transport and search with Expediter, Otter.

No. 419 'Moose' Squadron, R.C.A.F.

Formed 15 Dec. 1941, as a bomber unit at Mildenhall with Blenheim 4. 1942, Wellington B.1c, B.3, B.10/423 (VR–). 1943, Lancaster B.1, B.3,

B.10 (VR–, NA–). 12 June, 1944, V.C. won by P/O A. C. Mynarski. At Middleton St. George. 1944, Halifax B.2/1a (VR–). Disbanded June, 1945. Reformed at North Bay, Ont. 15 March, 1954 with CF–100. 1957, CF–100/4B. At Baden-Soellingen.

No. 420 'Snowy Owl' Squadron, R.C.A.F.

Formed 19 Dec. 1941, at Waddington for bombing with Hampden B.1 (PT–), Manchester B.1a (PT–), Wellington B.3, B.10. Later equipped with twenty Halifax B.1, B.3, B.7 (PT–). April, 1945, Lancaster B.3, B.10 (PT–) at Tholthorpe. Disbanded Sept. 1945. Reformed 1948 at London, Ont. as auxiliary with Harvard T.2b, Mustang F.4. 1955, CL–30 Silver Star.

No. 421 'Red Indian' Squadron, R.C.A.F.

Formed April, 1942, as a fighter unit and operated with Spitfire F.5a, F.5b, F.9, F.9a, F.8b, F.16, L.F.16e (all AU–). Disbanded July, 1945. Reformed and in 1952 was flying Sabre F.4 (AX–). At Grostenquin. 1957, Sabre F.6.

No. 422 Squadron, R.C.A.F.

Formed April, 1942, for general reconnaissance with Catalina G.R.1b (QL–, DG–), Lerwick G.R.1 (DG–). Nov. 1942, Sunderland G.R.3 (QL–, DG–). Also used Liberator C.6, C.8. Disbanded Sept. 1945. Reformed as a fighter unit and in 1953 was using Sabre F.4. At Baden-Soellingen. 1956, Sabre F.6.

No. 423 Squadron, R.C.A.F.

Formed May, 1942, at Oban for general reconnaissance with Sunderland G.R.2 (YI–, AB–). Also used Sunderland G.R.3 (YI–) and Liberator C.6, C.8. Disbanded Sept. 1945. Reformed June, 1953, at St. Hubert and was second unit to receive CF–100. Feb. 1957, to Grostenquin. CF–100/4B.

No. 424 'Tiger' Squadron, R.C.A.F.

Formed 15 Oct. 1942, at Topcliffe for bombing, and used Wellington B.3, B.10/423, B.10 (QB–). 1944, Halifax B.3, B.7 (QB–). Jan. 1945, at Skipton with Lancaster B.1, B.3, B.10 (QB–). Disbanded 15 Oct. 1945, at Skipton-on-Swale. Reformed 15 April, 1946, as auxiliary squadron. In turn bomber, fighter, transport and rescue, using Harvard T.2b, Mustang F.4, CL–30 Silver Star, D.H.C.3 Otter, Expediter.

No. 425 'Alouette' Squadron, R.C.A.F.

Formed 25 June, 1942, for bombing at Dishforth with Wellington B.3, B.10/423, B.10 (KW–). 1943, received Halifax B.2, B.3, B.3a, B.7 (KW–, LO–) at Tholthorpe. May, 1945, Lancaster B.1(F.E.), B.10 (KW–).

No. 426 'Thunderbird' Squadron, R.C.A.F.

Formed 15 Oct. 1942, as a bomber unit at Dishforth with Wellington
B.3, B.10 (OW-) and Hampden B.1 (EQ-). June, 1943, at Linton-on-
Ouse with Lancaster B.2 (EQ-, OW-). 1944, Halifax B.3a, B.7 (OW-).
1945, Liberator C.6, C.8 (OW-). Disbanded Jan. 1946. Reformed
and in 1952 was flying Dakota, Expediter, Norseman 4, Canadair C-5.
1953, C-119c Packet. July, 1950, until June, 1954, Korean airlift. 1954,
at Dorval. 1961, CC-106 Yukon.

No. 427 'Lion' Squadron, R.C.A.F.

Formed 7 Nov. 1942, for bombing at Croft with Wellington B.3, B.10
(ZL-). 1942, Halifax B.2, B.3, B.5/1 Special (ZL-). 1943, at Middleton
St. George. Feb. 1945, Lancaster B.1, B.3, B.7 (ZL-). Disbanded May,
1946. Reformed as a fighter unit and in 1952 was flying Sabre F.4. 1953,
at Zweibrucken. 1957, Sabre F.6. Dec. 1962, first CF-104 R.C.A.F.
Squadron.

No. 428 'Ghost' Squadron, R.C.A.F.

Formed 7 Nov. 1942, for bombing at Dalton with Wellington B.3, B.10
(NA-). Later received Halifax B.2/1a, B.5/1a (SE-, NA-), Lancaster
B.10 (NA-) at Middleton St. George. Disbanded June, 1945. Reformed
with CF-100.

No. 429 'Bison' Squadron, R.C.A.F.

Formed 7 Nov. 1942, as a bomber unit at East Moor, with Wellington
B.3, B.10 (AL-). 1943, at Leeming Bar with Halifax B.2, B.2/1a, B.3a,
B.5/1a (AL-). Feb. 1943, Lancaster B.1, B.3 (AL-). 1967, reformed with
Buffalo.

No. 430 Squadron, R.C.A.F.

Formed Jan. 1943, as a fighter squadron with Tomahawk F.2 (G9-).
Later used Mustang F.R.1, F.3, Spitfire F.12, F.14. Disbanded Aug.
1945. Reformed and in 1952 was flying Sabre F.4. At Grostenquin.
1957, Sabre F.6 (BH-).

No. 431 'Iroquois' Squadron, R.C.A.F.

Formed 11 Nov. 1942, as a bomber unit at Burn with Wellington B.3,
B.10 (SE-). 1943, Halifax B.2, B.3, B.3a, B.5/1a (WL-, SE-). Oct. 1944,
Lancaster B.3, B.10 (SE-) at Croft.

No. 432 'Fox'/'Leaside' Squadron, R.C.A.F.

Formed 1 May, 1943, for bombing at Skipton-on-Swale with Wellington
B.10 (QO-). Later used Halifax B.3, B.7 (QO-). Nov. 1943, Lancaster
B.2, B.3 (QO-) at Eastmoor. Disbanded June, 1945. Reformed 1 Oct.
1955, at Bagotville, P.Q., with CF-100.

No. 433 'Porcupine' Squadron, R.C.A.F.

Formed 25 Sept. 1943, as a bomber unit at Skipton-on-Swale with Halifax B.2, B.3a, B.7 (FD–, BM–). Dec. 1944, Lancaster B.1, B.3 (BM–) at Skipton and engaged in mine-laying. Disbanded Oct. 1945. Reformed 1955, at Cold Lake, Alta., with CF-100.

No. 434 'Bluenose' Squadron, R.C.A.F.

Formed 13 June, 1943, for bombing at Tholthorpe with Halifax B.2, B.3, B.5/1a (DH–, WL–). 1944, Lancaster B.1, B.10 (IP–, WL–) at Croft. Disbanded June, 1945. Reformed with Sabre F.4. 1953, at Zweibrucken. 1957, Sabre F.6.

No. 435 'Edmonton' Squadron, R.C.A.F.

Formed Oct. 1944, as a fighter unit with Spitfire F.9 (SW–, 8J–). Disbanded March, 1946. Reformed 1952, for transport with Dakota C.3, C.4, Expediter, Norseman 4. 1953, C-119c Packet. At Toronto.

No. 436 'Montreal' Squadron, R.C.A.F.

Formed Oct. 1944, for transport in S.E.A.C. with Dakota C.3, C.4 (FM–, U6–, ODM–). Disbanded June, 1946. Reformed for transport with C-119c and C-119f Packet.

No. 437 Squadron, R.C.A.F.

Formed Sept. 1944, as a transport unit with Dakota C.3, C.4 (Z2–, OFA–, ODD–, ODO–), Anson.

No. 438 Squadron, R.C.A.F.

Formed 15 Nov. 1943, as a fighter squadron with Hurricane F.2, F.B.4 (F3–). 1944, Typhoon F.B.1b (F3–). Disbanded 26 Aug. 1945. Reformed 1948 with Vampire F.B.5. 1956, Sabre F.5 at Montreal.

No. 439 'Sabre-Toothed Tiger' Squadron, R.C.A.F.

Formed 1 Jan. 1944, as a fighter unit with Hurricane F.B.4 (5V–) and Typhoon F.B.1b (5V–). Disbanded 26 Aug. 1945. Reformed and in 1952 was flying Sabre F.4 at North Luffenham with No. 1 Fighter Wing. Feb. 1955, to Marville with Sabre F.5. 1957, Sabre F.6.

No. 440 Squadron, R.C.A.F.

Formed 27 Jan. 1944, as a fighter unit with Hurricane F.B.4 (I8–) and Typhoon F.B.1b (I8–). Disbanded April, 1945. Reformed 1955 at Bagotville, P.Q., with CF-100. 1957, CF-100/4B. At Zweibrucken.

No. 441 'Silver Fox' Squadron, R.C.A.F.

Formed Feb. 1944, as a fighter squadron with Spitfire F.5b (9G–).

10 June, 1944, to France. April, 1945, Spitfire F.9, L.F.9, H.F.9, F.9b, F.9e (9G–). June, 1945, Mustang F.3 (9G–). Disbanded Aug. 1945. Reformed March, 1945, at St. Hubert with Vampire F.B.5. 1952, at North Luffenham with No. 1 Fighter Wing flying Sabre F.4 (BT–). Dec. 1954, at Zweibrucken. Feb. 1955, at Marville, using Sabre F.5 (BT–). 1957, Sabre F.6 (BT–).

No. 442 'Caribou' Squadron, R.C.A.F.

Formed Feb. 1944, as a fighter unit with Spitfire F.5b (Y2–). March, 1944, Spitfire F.9b, F.9e (Y2–). 10 June, 1944, to France. March, 1945, Mustang F.3, F.B.4 (Y2–).

No. 443 'Hornet' Squadron, R.C.A.F.

Formed 13 Feb. 1944, as a fighter unit with Spitfire F.5b, F.9b, F.14, L.F.16e (2I–). 10 June, 1944, to France.

No. 444 Squadron, R.C.A.F.

Formed as a fighter unit and in 1953 was flying Sabre F.4. At Baden-Soellingen. 1957, Sabre F.6.

No. 445 Squadron, R.C.A.F.

Formed 1 April, 1953 as an all-weather fighter squadron with CF–100/3 (SA–) at North Bay, Ont., and was first unit to fly CF–100. Later at Uplands, Ont. CF–100/4A. Nov. 1956, to Marville with CF–100/4B.

No. 450 Squadron, R.A.A.F.

Formed Feb. 1941, for ground attack with Hurricane F.1 (PD–, OK–) and also had Magister and one Audax. Later used Kittyhawk F.1, F.2, F.3, F.4 (OK–).

No. 451 Squadron, R.A.A.F.

Formed 1941, as a day-fighter and army co-operation unit with Hurricane F.1, F.2c and Lysander 2 (BQ–). Nov. 1943, Spitfire F.5b, F.5c (NI–). Dec. 1943, Spitfire F.9, F.9c (BQ–, NI–), F.R.14e (NI–).

No. 452 Squadron, R.A.A.F.

Formed 8 April, 1941, for fighting with Spitfire F.1, F.2a, F.5b, F.5c, F.9b, F.9c (UD–, FU–).

No. 453 Squadron, R.A.A.F.

Formed originally in Far East for service in Malaya with Buffalo 1 (FU–). Reformed 15 June, 1942, at Drem with Spitfire F.5b, F.5c (FU–). 1943, Spitfire F.9c, F.14 (FU–). 1944, to France and later in Germany.

No. 454 Squadron, R.A.A.F.

Formed April, 1942, as a bomber squadron in Middle East with Blenheim 4 and 5. 1943, Marauder B.1. Sept. 1943, Baltimore B.4, B.5.

No. 455 Squadron, R.A.A.F.

Formed 6 June, 1941, as first Australian bomber squadron in U.K. 26 April, 1942, at Leuchars for torpedo-bombing with Hampden T.B.1 (UB-). 1943, Beaufighter T.F.1c, T.F.6c, T.F.10 (UB-).

No. 456 Squadron, R.A.A.F.

Formed June, 1941, for night-fighting with Defiant N.F.1 (PZ-). Oct. 1941, Beaufighter N.F.2f. July, 1942, Beaufighter N.F.6f. Nov. 1943, Mosquito F.2, F.B.6, N.F.17 (RX-). Dec. 1944, Mosquito N.F.12, N.F.30 (RX-).

No. 457 Squadron, R.A.A.F.

Formed 16 June, 1941, at Jurby with Spitfire F.1, F.2, F.2a, F.5b, F.5c (BP-) as a fighter unit. Later used Spitfire F.9c (KU-).

No. 458 Squadron, R.A.A.F.

Formed 8 July, 1941, for bombing with Wellington B.4. At Holme-on-Spalding Moor. 1942, in Middle East for general reconnaissance with Wellington B.1c, G.R.8, G.R.13, G.R.14 fitted with Leigh-Light.

No. 459 Squadron, R.A.A.F.

Formed 10 Feb. 1942, for general reconnaissance with Blenheim 4L, Hudson G.R.3, Ventura 1, Baltimore B.3, Beaufighter T.F.10 (all BP-).

No. 460 Squadron, R.A.A.F.

Formed 15 Nov. 1941, at Molesworth as a bomber unit with Wellington B.1c, B.4 (UV-). Later used Halifax B.2/1a. At Breighton. Nov. 1942, Lancaster B.1, B.3, B.7 (AR-, UV-). June, 1943, at Binbrook. 1944, Lancaster B.1 (F.E.) (AR-).

No. 461 Squadron, R.A.A.F.

Formed April, 1942, for transport and reconnaissance with Sunderland G.R.1, G.R.2, G.R.3 (UT-).

No. 462 Squadron, R.A.A.F.

Formed 7 Sept. 1942, at Fayid as a bomber unit from detachments of Nos. 10/227 and 76/462 squadrons with Halifax B.2/1a (Z5-). At Driffield. 3 March, 1944, became No. 614 Squadron. Reformed 12 Aug. 1944, at Driffield. 1944, at Foulsham with Halifax B.3, B.6 (Z5-).

No. 463 Squadron, R.A.A.F.

Formed 25 Nov. 1943, at Waddington from 'C' flight of No. 467 Squadron with Lancaster B.1, B.3 (PO-, JO-) for bombing.

No. 464 Squadron, R.A.A.F.

Formed 1 Sept. 1942, at Feltwell for reconnaissance with Hudson G.R.3 (SB-). Later used Ventura B.1, B.2 (SB-). July, 1943, at Sculthorpe. 1944, Mosquito B.4, F.B.6 (SB-).

No. 466 Squadron, R.A.A.F.

Formed 15 Oct. 1942, at Driffield, for bombing with Wellington B.3, B.10 (HD-). 1943, Halifax B.2/1a, B.3, B.6 (HD-) at Driffield. 1944, Lancaster B.1 (HD-).

No. 467 Squadron, R.A.A.F.

Formed 7 Nov. 1942, at Scampton as a bomber unit with Wellington B.3, B.10 (PO-) at Blyton. June, 1943, Lancaster B.1, B.3 (PO-). 1944, at Waddington. May, 1945, at Metheringham.

No. 485 Squadron, R.N.Z.A.F.

Formed March, 1941, at Redhill as a fighter unit with Spitfire F.1, F.2a (OU-). Later used Spitfire F.5b, F.5c, F.9b, L.F.5b, F.9c, H.F.7, L.F.16e (OU-), Mustang F.1 (OU-).

No. 486 Squadron, R.N.Z.A.F.

Formed March, 1942, as a fighter squadron with Hurricane N.F.2 (SA-). 1943, Typhoon F.1b (SA-). Jan. 1944, Tempest F.5 (SA-). 1944, Typhoon F.5 (SA-), Spitfire F.5b (SA-).

No. 487 Squadron, R.N.Z.A.F.

Formed 15 Aug. 1942, at Feltwell for bombing with Ventura B.1, B.2 (EG-). 3 May, 1943, V.C. won by S/L L. H. Trent. June, 1943, Mosquito F.B.6 (EG-, SY-) for intruder operations. July, 1943, at Sculthorpe. Disbanded 19 Sept. 1945, at Celle and became No. 16 Squadron. 16 Oct. 1945, became No. 268 Squadron.

No. 488 Squadron, R.N.Z.A.F.

Formed originally with Buffalo F.1 for service in Malaya. Reformed June, 1942, with Hurricane F.1, Beaufighter N.F.2f (ME-). March, 1943, Beaufighter N.F.6f (ME-). Aug. 1943, Mosquito N.F.12, N.F.13 (ME-). Sept. 1944, Mosquito N.F.30, T.3 (ME-).

No. 489 Squadron, R.N.Z.A.F.

Formed Aug. 1941, for torpedo-bombing with Beaufort G.R.2 (P6-).

Jan. 1942, Blenheim 4L (XA–). March, 1942, Hampden T.B.1 (XA–) at Wick. Feb. 1943, Beaufighter T.F.10 'Torbeau' (P6–). Also used Mosquito F.B.6.

No. 490 Squadron, R.N.Z.A.F.

Formed March, 1943, for general reconnaissance with Catalina G.R.1b. 1944, Sunderland G.R.3.

No. 500 'County of Kent' Squadron

Formed 16 March, 1931, at Manston in the Special Reserve with Virginia X. 25 May, 1936, became part of Auxiliary Air Force. 1936, Hart. Re-equipped with Hind, Tutor. 7 Nov. 1938, became general reconnaissance unit. 1940, Anson G.R.1 (SQ–, MK–). May, 1941, Blenheim 1L, 4L (MK–). Nov. 1941, Hudson G.R.3 (MK–). 1943, Ventura B.1. Aug. 1944, Baltimore B.5a, B.5c. Disbanded 23 Oct. 1945, and became No. 249 Squadron. Reformed June, 1946, at West Malling as an Auxiliary night-fighter unit with Mosquito. N.F.30, T.3 (RAA–), Oxford T.2 (RAA–). C.O. S/L P. Green. 1950, day-fighter with Meteor F.3, T.7 (RAA–), S7–), Harvard T.2b (S7–). 1952, Meteor F.8. C.O. S/L D. de Villiers. Oct. 1954, C.O. S/L D. M. Clause. Dec. 1955, C.O. S/L D. H. M. Chandler.

No. 501 'County of Gloucester' Squadron

Formed 14 June, 1929, at Filton in the Special Reserve with D.H.9a, Avro 504k. 1 May, 1930, designated City of Bristol. 1932, Wapiti 2a. 1 May, 1936, became part of Auxiliary Air Force. 1934, first unit to fly Wallace 1 and 2. 1936, Hart. 1938 Hind. 1939, Hurricane F.1. (ZH–, SD–) in France, together with Anson. Aug. 1940, at Gravesend. 1941, Spitfire F.1b, F.2 (SD–). 1942, Spitfire F.5a, F.5b, F.9 (SD–). 1944, Tempest F.5 (SD–) at Hawkinge and shot down over 100 V.1s. Disbanded April, 1945. Reformed May, 1946, at Filton as a day-fighter unit Auxiliary with Spitfire L.F.16e (RAB–), Harvard T.2b (SD–, RAB–). C.O. S/L C. D. Griffiths. Converted to jet fighters with Vampire F.1 (SD–, RAB–) and Meteor T.7 (SD–). 1951, Vampire F.B.5. July, 1955, C.O. S/L M. C. Collins.

No. 502 'County of Ulster' Squadron

Formed 15 May, 1925, at Aldergrove in the Special Reserve for night-bombing with Vimy. Avro 504n for training. 1928, Hyderabad. Re-equipped with Virginia X, followed by Wapiti 2a. 1936, Wallace 2. 1936, Heyford 2. 1 July, 1937, became part of Auxiliary Air Force, using Hinds. 27 Nov. 1938, became general reconnaissance unit. 1939, Blenheim 4 (YG–) and Anson G.R.1 (KQ–, YG–). 1940, Botha 1 (YG–). Sept. 1940, at Chivenor with Whitley B.4, B.5, G.R.7 (YG–).

1944, Halifax B.2, G.R.3 (YG–), Halifax G.R.9 (V9–), Hampden B.1, Liberator G.R.6. Disbanded May, 1945. Reformed June, 1946, at Aldergrove as an Auxiliary light-bomber unit with Mosquito F.B.6 (RAC–), Oxford T.2 (RAC–). C.O. S/L W. H. McGiffin. 1949, fighter unit with Spitfire F.22 (V9–, RAC–), Harvard T.2b (V9–, RAC–). 1951, Vampire F.B.5 (V9–). 1955, C.O. S/L N. G. Townsend.

No. 503 'County of Lincoln' Squadron

Formed Nov. 1926, in the Special Reserve as a bomber unit with Fawn and Avro 504k at Waddington. 1929, night-bomber with Hyderabad. Re-equipped with Virginia X and Hinaidi. 1935, Wallace 1 and 2. 1 May, 1936, became part of the Auxiliary Air Force with Hart, followed by Hind in 1938. Disbanded 1 Nov. 1938, to become No. 616 Squadron.

No. 504 'City of Nottingham' Squadron

Formed 26 March, 1928, in the Special Reserve as a bomber unit with Horsley at Hucknall. 1935, Wallace 2. 18 May, 1936, became part of the Auxiliary Air Force. 1938, Hind, Gauntlet. 31 Oct. 1938, became fighter unit. 1939, Hurricane F.1 (AW–, TM–, HX–). Aug. 1940, at Castletown. 1941, Spitfire F.5b (HX–). 1942, Spitfire F.9c (TM–). March, 1945, second unit to receive Meteor F.3 (TM–). Became No. 245 Squadron Aug. 1945. Reformed June, 1946, as an Auxiliary with Mosquito N.F. 30, T.3 (RAD–) at Hucknall and Syerston. C.O. S/L A. H. Rook. 1950, fighter unit with Meteor F.4, T.7 (HX–, TM–), Oxford T.2 (RAD–), Harvard T.2b (TM–, RAD–). 1952, Meteor F.4. Oct. 1954, at Wymeswold, C.O. S/L P. J. Briggs.

No. 510 Squadron

Formed 15 Oct. 1942, at Hendon as a transport unit to augment No. 24 Squadron. Used many different types, including Dakota, Tiger Moth 2, Hudson, Lockheed 12a, Spitfire, Lysander, Proctor 1, Vega Gull, Anson, Hornet Moth 2, Stinson Reliant 1, Oxford T.2, Miles Mohawk, Hart and Dominie 1. Disbanded 11 April, 1944. Reformed in 1944 as the Metropolitan Communication Squadron with Proctor 1. Disbanded July, 1948, and became No. 31 Squadron.

No. 511 Squadron

Formed Oct. 1942, for transport with Liberator C.2, C.3, C.6. Feb. 1943, Albemarle 1. Nov. 1943, York C.1. March, 1944, Dakota C.3, C.4. Aug. 1944, fully equipped with York C.1 (OYC–, MOYC–), being first unit to do so. Also using Liberator C.7. Code BC– not used. 1955, at Lyneham with Hastings C.1, C.2. 1957, at Colerne. 1 Sept. 1958, renumbered No. 36 Squadron. Reformed 15 Dec. 1959, at Lyneham as second Britannia C.1 Squadron. C.O. W/C A. W. G. Le Hardy.

No. 512 Squadron

Formed Aug. 1943, for transport with Dakota C.3, C.4 (HC–, ODK–).

No. 513 Squadron

Formed 15 Sept. 1943, for bombing with Stirling B.3.

No. 514 Squadron

Formed 1 Sept. 1943, at Foulsham with Lancaster B.1, B.2, B.3 (A2–, JI–) equipped with 'G.H.' bombing aid. C.O. W/C A. J. Sampson. Nov. 1943, to Waterbeach.

No. 515 Squadron

Formed 1 Oct. 1942, at Northolt with Beaufighter F.1 (P3–). 1943, Mosquito B.16 (P3–), Defiant T.T.3, N.F.2.

No. 516 Squadron

Formed 28 July, 1943, for transport with Mustang F.3, Blenheim 4, Lysander, Anson C.1, Proctor 1, Hurricane F.2, Master T.2, Tiger Moth 2.

No. 517 Squadron

Formed Aug. 1943, for meteorological reconnaissance with Hampden Met.1, incorporating No. 1404 Flt. Dec. 1943, Hudson Met.1. Feb. 1944, Fortress Met.2. Feb. 1944, Halifax Met.3, Met.6, A.7 (X9–), using 24 aircraft. Also using Stirling Met.4 (X9–) from Brawdy.

No. 518 Squadron

Formed July, 1943, for meteorological reconnaissance at Tiree with Hudson Met.3 (Y3–) and incorporated No. 1405 Flt. Sept. 1943, Halifax Met. 5/1a (Y3–, YS–), receiving 16 aircraft. April, 1945, re-equipped with Halifax Met.6 (Y3–), Oxford T.2 (YS–). Dec. 1945, at Aldergrove. Disbanded 1 Oct. 1946, one flight being renumbered No. 202 Squadron, and one becoming No. 224 Squadron.

No. 519 Squadron

Formed Aug. 1943, for long-range meteorological reconnaissance with Hampden Met. 1 (Z9–), incorporating No. 1408 Flt. 1943, Spitfire H.F.7, Hudson Met.3, twelve Ventura Met.5 (Z9–). At Wick. 1944, Fortress Met.2, Met.2a (Z9–), Halifax Met.6, A.7 (Z9–).

No. 520 Squadron

Formed Sept. 1943, at Gibraltar for meteorological reconnaissance with Gladiator 2, Hudson Met.3, Hurricane F.1 (2M–), Halifax Met.2/1a, Met.5/1a (2M–), Spitfire F.5b, Martinet T.T.1 (2M–).

No. 521 Squadron

Formed Nov. 1941, for meteorological reconnaissance with Gladiator 2, Spitfire F.5c, F.6, F.9 (50–), Blenheim 4 (50–), Hudson Met.3 (50–). April, 1942, Mosquito P.R.1 (50–). June, 1942, absorbed No. 1401 Met. Flt. (THUM and PRATA). To Manston, Aug. 1943. 1943, incorporated No. 1403 Flt., Hampden Met.1, Ventura Met.5, Halifax Met.6 (50–). May, 1945, Fortress Met.2, Met.2a, Hurricane F.2c (50–).

No. 524 Squadron

Formed Oct. 1943, at Oban for general reconnaissance with Mariner G.R.1. Disbanded Dec. 1943. Reformed April, 1944, for the same duties with Wellington G.R.13. March, 1945, Wellington G.R.14.

No. 525 Squadron

Formed Sept. 1943, for transport with Warwick C.3 (WF–). June, 1944, Dakota C.3, C.4 (WF–, ODP–). Code 8P– not used. Disbanded Dec. 1944, and renumbered No. 238 Squadron.

No. 526 Squadron

Formed 15 June, 1943, for radar calibration with Oxford T.2, Blenheim 4, Hornet Moth 2 and Dominie.

No. 527 Squadron

Formed June, 1943, for radar calibration with Hurricane F.1, F.10, Blenheim 4L, Wellington B.3, Spitfire F.5b, Dominie, Oxford T.2, Beaufighter 1f, N.F.2f (all WN–), Auster A.O.P.4, Harvard T.2b. Disbanded April, 1946. Reformed as a special duties squadron, and in 1953 was using Anson C.19, Lincoln B.2.

No. 528 Squadron

Formed 28 June, 1943, for radar calibration with Blenheim 4, Hornet Moth 2.

No. 529 Squadron

Formed 15 June, 1943, at Athalton from No. 1448 Flt., with C.30 and C.40 Rota (KX–), Hornet Moth 2 (KX–), Auster A.O.P.1 (KX–). Aug. 1944, Hoverfly 1 (KX–). 19 Aug. 1944, to Henley. Engaged on radar calibration.

No. 530 Squadron

Formed 2 Sept. 1942, for night-fighting with Turbinlite Havoc 1.

No. 531 Squadron

Formed 2 Sept. 1942, for night-fighting with Turbinlite Havoc 1.

H

No. 532 Squadron
Formed 2 Sept. 1942, for night-fighting with Turbinlite Havoc 1.

No. 533 Squadron
Formed 2 Sept. 1942, for night-fighting with Turbinlite Havoc 1.

No. 534 Squadron
Formed 2 Sept. 1942, for night-fighting with Turbinlite Havoc 1.

No. 535 Squadron
Formed 2 Sept. 1942, for night-fighting with Turbinlite Havoc 1.

No. 536 Squadron
Formed 2 Sept. 1942, for night-fighting with Turbinlite Havoc 1.

No. 537 Squadron
Formed 2 Sept. 1942, for night-fighting with Turbinlite Havoc 1.

No. 538 Squadron
Formed 2 Sept. 1942, for night-fighting with Turbinlite Havoc 1.

No. 539 Squadron
Formed 2 Sept. 1942, for night-fighting with Turbinlite Havoc 1.

No. 540 Squadron
Formed Oct. 1942, for photographic-reconnaissance with Mosquito P.R.1, P.R.4, P.R.9, P.R.16, P.R.34, T.3 (DH–, OT–). Disbanded Oct. 1946. Reformed and in 1953 was flying Canberra P.R.7 at Wyton.

No. 541 Squadron
Formed Oct. 1942, for photographic-reconnaissance with Spitfire P.R.11, P.R.19, Martinet T.T.1, Harvard T.2b (ES–, WY–). Disbanded Oct. 1946 and became No. 82 Squadron. Reformed for the same duties with Meteor F.R.9, P.R.10 (WY–) in use in 1952. C.O. S/L Thompson. 1953, first to fly Canberra P.R.3. At Benson. May, 1957, to 2nd T.A.F. at Wunstorf. Last to fly Meteor P.R.10.

No. 542 Squadron
Formed 19 Oct. 1942, for photographic-reconnaissance with Spitfire P.R.4, P.R.11, P.R.19. Disbanded 27 Aug. 1945. Reformed for same duties with Canberra P.R.7 which was being flown in June, 1954. C.O. S/L A. J. Picknett.

No. 543 Squadron
Formed 19 Oct. 1942, for photographic-reconnaissance with Spitfire

P.R.11. Disbanded 17 Sept. 1944. Reformed April, 1945, at Wyton and was first to receive Valiant B. (P.R.)1. C.O. W/C R. E. Havercroft. 1966, Victor B. (S.R.)2 for photographic-reconnaissance.

No. 544 Squadron

Formed Oct. 1942, for photographic-reconnaissance and anti-shipping duties. Used Anson G.R.1, Wellington G.R.8, three Spitfire P.R.11, Mosquito P.R.16. April, 1944, detachment to Northolt for mail-carrying to Moscow.

No. 547 Squadron

Formed Oct. 1942, for torpedo-bombing with Wellington G.R.11. Later equipped with Halifax G.R.6. 1945, Liberator G.R.5, G.R.6, G.R.8 (2V-) with Leigh-Light.

No. 548 Squadron

Formed 15 Dec. 1943, in Australia as a fighter unit with Spitfire F.9.

No. 549 Squadron

Formed 15 Dec. 1943, in Australia as a fighter unit with Spitfire F.9.

No. 550 Squadron

Formed 25 Nov. 1943, at Waltham from 'C' Flight of No. 100 Squadron. At North Killingholme as a bomber unit with Lancaster B.1, B.3 (BQ-) from Jan. 1944.

No. 567 Squadron

Formed 1 Dec. 1943, for target-towing and army co-operation with Hurricane F.2, Oxford T.2, Tiger Moth 2, Battle 1, Martinet T.T.1, Spitfire F.9, Vengeance T.T.2, T.T.4, Barracuda, Defiant T.T.1, T.T.3, Avenger T.B.3, Wellington B.1c, Spitfire F.5b, L.F.16e, Swordfish (all I4-).

No. 569 Squadron

Formed 10 Jan. 1944, for transport but did not become operational.

No. 570 Squadron

Formed Nov. 1943, as an airborne carrier unit with Albemarle G.T.1, G.T.2 (E7-, V8-). July, 1944, Stirling G.T.4 (E7-, V8-). Operated with 2nd T.A.F.

No. 571 Squadron

Formed 7 April, 1944, at Downham Market for Pathfinder Force duties with Mosquito B.16 (8K-). 20 July, 1945, to Warboys.

No. 575 Squadron

Formed Feb. 1944, as a troop transport unit with Dakota C.3, C.4 (I9-, OFD-, OFN-, OFS-). Also used Anson T.1 (I9-) and Oxford T.1. (I9-).

No. 576 Squadron

Formed 25 Nov. 1943, from 'C' Flight of No. 103 Squadron at Elsham Wolds as a bomber unit with Lancaster B.1, B.3 (UL-). 1945, at Fiskerton. Participated in Operations Manna, Exodus, Post Mortem and Dodge.

No. 577 Squadron

Formed 1 Dec. 1943, for anti-aircraft co-operation with Hurricane F.2, Oxford T.2, Beaufighter F.1, T.F.10, Spitfire F.5b, L.F.16e, Vengeance T.T.2, T.T.4, Martinet T.T.1 (all 3Y-).

No. 578 Squadron

Formed 14 Jan. 1944, at Snaith from 'C' Flight of No. 51 Squadron as a bomber unit with Halifax B.2/1a, B.3 (LK-). 3 Nov. 1943, V.C. won by P/O C. J. Barton. Also used Mosquito B.16 for Pathfinder duties.

No. 582 Squadron

Formed 18 April, 1944, from 'C' Flights of Nos. 7 and 156 Squadrons. In Pathfinder Force with Lancaster B.1, B.3 (60-). V.C. won by Capt. E. Swales on 23 Feb. 1945. At Little Staughton. 1945, participated in Operations Manna and Exodus.

No. 587 Squadron

Formed Dec. 1943, for anti-aircraft co-operation with Harvard T.2b, Tiger Moth 2, Hurricane F.1, F.2b, F.2c, Oxford T.2, Spitfire L.F.16e, Vengeance T.T.4, Martinet T.T.1 (all M4-).

No. 595 Squadron

Formed 1 Dec. 1943, for anti-aircraft co-operation with Hurricane F.2, F.4, Martinet T.T.1, Vengeance T.T.2, T.T.4, Spitfire F.5b, F.9, T.T.9, F.12, L.F.16e, Oxford T.2, Beaufighter T.T.10 (all 7B-). Was first to use Vampire F.1 for anti-aircraft co-operation. Disbanded 11 Feb. 1949, and renumbered No. 5 Squadron.

No. 597 Squadron

Formed 10 Jan. 1944, for transport but did not become operational.

No. 598 Squadron

Formed 1 Dec. 1943, for anti-aircraft co-operation with Oxford T.2, Lysander T.T.3a, Martinet T.T.2, Hurricane F.2.

No. 600 'City of London' Squadron

Formed 26 Feb. 1925, at Northolt as an Auxiliary for bombing with D.H.9a. C.O. W/C A. W. James. Used Avro 504k and 504n for training. Dec. 1926, to Hendon. 1929, Wapiti 2a. 1933, Hart. C.O. S/L S. B. Collett. Aug. 1934, redesignated as a fighter squadron and received Demons. C.O. S/L P. G. Stewart. Used Tiger Moth, Hart(T) and Tutor for training. 1938, Hind (MV-). C.O. S/L Viscount Carlow. 1939, Blenheim 1f (MV-, BQ-). 25 Aug. 1939, to Northolt. Oxford T.2. 1940, Blenheim 4f (BQ-). C.O. S/L J. Wells. 10 May, 1940, six of the unit's Blenheims were sent to attack Waalhaven. Of this number, only one machine—that flown by F/O Norman Hayes, accompanied by his gunner Corporal G. H. Holmes—survived to return to base from the sortie against the Germans advancing on Rotterdam and from being subsequently attacked themselves by twelve Me. 110s. The crew were awarded respectively the D.F.C. and D.F.M. Aug. 1940, at Manston. 1940, Bolingbroke (BQ-). 1940, Beaufighter N.F.1f (BQ-), Boston 1. 1941, Beaufighter N.F.2f. C.O. W/C G. H. Stainforth. 1942, Beaufighter N.F.6f (BQ-). 1942-45, in North Africa and Italy. 1945, Mosquito N.F.19. C.O. W/C A. H. Drummond. Destroyed 179 E/A, the highest score by a night-fighter squadron. Disbanded in Italy Aug. 1945. Reformed July, 1946, at Biggin Hill as an Auxiliary for day-fighting with Spitfire F.21 (RAG-). C.O. S/L T. N. Hayes. Also used Spitfire F.14, Harvard T.2b (RAG-). 1948, Spitfire F.22 (RAG-). C.O. S/L D. E. Proudlove. 1949, Vampire F.1. 1951, Meteor F.4 (LJ-). C.O. S/L J. Meadows. 1952, Meteor F.8 (LJ-)—eight aircraft. Meteor T.7 (LJ-)—two aircraft. C.O. 1953, S/L J. McR. Cormack.

No. 601 'County of London' Squadron

Formed 1 Aug. 1925, at Northolt as an Auxiliary for bombing with D.H.9a, Avro 504k. Jan. 1927, to Hendon. 1930, Wapiti 2a. Feb. 1933, Hart. Aug. 1934, became a fighter unit with Hart Fighter. C.O. S/L R. G. Shaw. Tutor for training. 1935, Demon. 1938, Gauntlet 2 (YN-). 1939, Blenheim 1f (YN-, UF-). At Tangmere 2 Sept. 1939. 1940, Hurricane F.1, F.2b, F.2c (UF-). 1941, only unit to fly Airacobra 1 (UF-). 1941, Spitfire L.F.5b, F.5c (UF-). Served in Malta, North Africa, Italy. 1944, Spitfire F.9c, F.B.9, L.F.16e (HT-). Disbanded 1945. Reformed June, 1946, at Hendon as an Auxiliary with Spitfire F.21 (RAH-). Day-fighter unit. C.O. S/L Hon. M. Aitken. 1950, at North Weald with Vampire F.3 (HT-), Harvard T.2b (HT-, RAH-). 1951, Meteor F.4. 1952, Meteor F.8—ten aircraft. C.O. S/L C. C. McCarthy-Jones.

No. 602 'City of Glasgow' Squadron

Formed 15 Sept. 1925, at Renfrew as an Auxiliary for bombing with

D.H.9a, Avro 504k. 1928, Fawn, Avro 504n. 1931, Wapiti 2a. 1935, Hart 2. Nov. 1938, became army co-op unit. Hector, Hind (ZT-). At Abbotsinch. Jan. 1939, became fighter unit with Gauntlet, Gladiator. 1939, Spitfire F.1, F.2a (ZT-, LO-). 1940, at Drem. 17 Dec. 1940, at Prestwick. 1943, Spitfire F.5b, L.F.5b, H.F.6, H.F.7, F.8, F.9b, F.9c, F.14, L.F.16e. At Perranporth, Biggin Hill. Later in North Africa and Western Europe. Disbanded May, 1945. Reformed Aug. 1946, at Abbotsinch as an Auxiliary for day-fighting with Spitfire F.R.14e, F.21, F.22, Harvard T.2b, Meteor T.7 (all LO-, RAI-). 1951, Vampire F.B.5, F.B.9 (LO-). 1952, at Renfrew. C.O. S/L J. A. Forrest. 1 Jan. 1954, C.O. S/L R. B. Davidson.

No. 603 'City of Edinburgh' Squadron

Formed 14 Oct. 1925, at Turnhouse as an Auxiliary for bombing with D.H.9a, Avro 504k, 504n. C.O. S/L J. A. McKelvie. 1930, Wapiti 2a. 1934, Hart 2, Tiger Moth, Tutor, Hart(T). March, 1938, Hind. 24 Oct. 1938, became fighter unit. March, 1939, Gladiator 2 (RL-). 1940, Spitfire F.1, F.2a, F.5a, F.5b (XT-). April, 1942, Malta. 1943, Beaufighter F.1c, F.6c, F.6, F.10, F.11c. Jan. 1945, renumbered from No. 229 Squadron with Spitfire L.F.16e (9R-). Disbanded 15 Aug. 1945. Reformed May, 1946, at Turnhouse as an Auxiliary for day-fighting with Spitfire F.21, F.22, L.F.16e (XT-, 9R-, RAJ-), Harvard T.2b (RAJ-). C.O. S/L G. K. Gilroy. May, 1951, Vampire F.B.5, Meteor T.7. C.O. S/L P. J. Anson. March. 1953, C.O. S/L Lloyd Davies. Sept. 1953, S/L R. A. Schofield.

No. 604 'County of Middlesex' Squadron

Formed 17 March, 1930, at Hendon as an Auxiliary for day-bombing with D.H.9a, Avro 504n. 1930, Wapiti 2a. 23 July, 1934, redesignated as a fighter unit with Hart Fighter. 1936, Demon. C.O. S/L C. P. Gabriel. Feb. 1940, at Northolt with Blenheim 1f (WQ-, NG-). Aug. 1940, at Middle Wallop. 1940, night-fighting with Beaufighter N.F.1f, N.F.2f, N.F.6f (NG-). 1944, Mosquito N.F.12, N.F.13, N.F.19 (NG-). Disbanded April, 1945. Reformed June, 1946, at Hendon as an Auxiliary for day-fighting with Spitfire L.F.16e (NG-, RAK-), Harvard T.2b (RAK-). C.O. S/L J. Cunningham. 1950, Vampire F.3 (NG-) at Biggin Hill. 1952, Meteor F.4, F.8. C.O. S/L A. Dettrikh. Sept. 1953, C.O. S/L T. P. Turnbull.

No. 605 'County of Warwick' Squadron

Formed 15 Oct. 1926, at Castle Bromwich as an Auxiliary for day-bombing with D.H.9a, Avro 504k. 1930, Wapiti 2a. 1935, Hart, Tutor. 1938, Hind. 1 Jan. 1939, became fighter unit. May, 1939, fighter unit with Gladiator 2 (HE-, UP-). Sept. 1939, Hurricane F.1, F.2a (UP-). Aug.

1940, at Drem. 1941, Dutch East Indies. June, 1942, intruder duties with Havoc 2, Boston B.2, B.3 (UP-). Feb. 1943, Mosquito N.F.2, F.B.6 (UP-) in 2nd T.A.F. 31 Aug. 1945, renumbered No. 4 Squadron. Reformed June, 1946, at Honiley as an Auxiliary for night-fighting with Mosquito N.F.30, N.F.36 (RAL-). C.O. G/C G. R. Edge. Harvard T.2b (RAL-) for training. 1950, first Auxiliary unit to operate jet aircraft with Vampire F.1, F.B.5 (NR-, RAL-). 1954, C.O. S/L P. M. T. Walton. Dec. 1955, C.O. S/L R. E. Tickner.

No. 607 'County of Durham' Squadron
Formed 17 March, 1930, at Usworth for bombing with Wapiti 2a, Avro 504n. 23 Sept. 1936, redesignated as a fighter unit with Demon. 1937, Gladiator 2 (LW-, AF-). 1939, with Air Component at Vitry, Arras. 1940, Hurricane F.1, F.2b, F.2c. Aug. 1940, at Usworth. 1943, Spitfire F.2, F.5b, F.5c, F.8, F.R.14 (AF-). In Burma. Disbanded Aug. 1945. Reformed June, 1946, at Ouston as an Auxiliary with Spitfire L.F.16e, F.21, F.22 (LA-, RAN-). C.O. S/L J. R. Kayll. Harvard T.2b (LA-, RAN-). 1952, Vampire F.3, F.5b, Meteor T.7. Sept. 1953, C.O. S/L J. A. Stephen.

No. 608 'North Riding' Squadron
Formed 17 March, 1930, at Thornaby as an Auxiliary for bombing with Wapiti 2a, Avro 504n. 1936, Wallace 2. 16 Jan. 1937, redesignated fighter unit with Demon 1 (PG-). 1939, Anson G.R.1 (PG-, OY-). Oct. 1939, first unit to fly Botha G.R.1 (UL-). 1940, Blenheim 4. 1941, Hudson G.R.3, G.R.5 (UL-, OY-, 6T-). July, 1944, Mosquito B.16 (6T-) for Pathfinder duties. Disbanded 24 Aug. 1945. Reformed June, 1946, at Thornaby as an Auxiliary with Mosquito N.F.30, T.3 (RAO-), Oxford T.2 (6T-, RAO-). 1948, Spitfire F.16, F.22 (RAO-). 1950, Vampire F.3, F.B.5 (6T-). Meteor T.7, Harvard T.2b (6T-), RAO-). C.O. S/L F. A. Robinson. 1955, C.O. S/L H. D. Costain.

No. 609 'West Riding' Squadron
Formed 10 Feb. 1936, at Yeadon as an Auxiliary for bombing with Hart, Tutor. 1938, Hind. 8 Dec. 1938, became fighter unit. 1939, fighter unit with Spitfire F.1, F.2a (BL-, PR-). At Catterick. July, 1940, at Northolt. 1941, at Biggin Hill with Spitfire F.5b, F.5c, F.9. May, 1942, Typhoon F.1a, F.1b (PR-) with rockets. C.O. S/L R. P. Beamont. Disbanded Sept. 1945. Reformed May, 1946, at Church Fenton as an Auxiliary for night-fighting with Mosquito N.F.36, T.3 (RAP-). 1950, Spitfire L.F.16e, F.21 (PR-, RAP-), Harvard T.2b (PR-, RAP-), Oxford T.2 (RAP-). 1950, Vampire F.3. 1952, Meteor F.4, F.8, at Church Fenton. Dec. 1953, C.O. S/L E. Evans.

No. 610 'County of Chester' Squadron

Formed 10 Feb. 1936, at Hooton Park as an Auxiliary for bombing with Wallace 2, Tutor. 1937, Hart. 1938, Hind. 1 Jan. 1939, became fighter unit. 1940, Spitfire F.1 (JE-, DW-). July, 1940, at Biggin Hill. S/L J. E. Johnson, who scored 38 victories, flew with the squadron. 1944, Spitfire F.2a, F.5b, F.9, F.R.14 (DW-). 1944, destroyed 50 V.1s. Dec. 1944, in 2nd T.A.F. Disbanded March, 1945. Reformed June, 1946, at Hooton Park as an Auxiliary with Spitfire F.R.14e, F.21, F.22 (DW-, RAQ-), Harvard T.2b (DW-, RAQ-). C.O. S/L P. G. Lamb. 1951, Meteor F.4. 1952, Meteor F.8. C.O. S/L J. E. Storrar. May, 1954, C.O. W/C M. Kellett.

No. 611 'West Lancashire' Squadron

Formed 10 Feb. 1936 at Hendon as an Auxiliary for bombing with Hart, Tutor. May, 1936, to Speke. 1 Jan. 1939, became fighter unit. 1940, Hurricane F.1, Hind(T), Battle 1 (GZ-, FY-). 1940, Spitfire F.1, F.2a (GZ-, FY-). 1941, Spitfire F.5a, F.5b, F.5c (FY-). 1943, at Biggin Hill with Spitfire F.9c (FY-), L.F.5b (FY-). 1944, Mustang F.B.4 (FY-). Disbanded Aug. 1945. Reformed June, 1946, at Speke as an Auxiliary for fighting with Spitfire F.14e, F.22 (FY-, RAR-). C.O. S/L W. J. Leather. Harvard T.2b (RAR-) for training. 1951, Meteor F.4. 1952, Meteor F.8. C.O. S/L S. J. Kirtley. 1955, at Hooton Park.

No. 612 'County of Aberdeen' Squadron

Formed 1 June, 1937, at Aberdeen as an Auxiliary for bombing with Hind. C.O. S/L F. Crerar. 1939, Anson G.R.1 (DJ-), Hector 1 (DJ-). Engaged on anti-submarine patrol. 1939, Whitley B.3, Wellington B.1c, B.5 (WL-). 1942, Whitley G.R.7 (WL-), Wellington G.R.10, G.R.14 (8W-). Disbanded July, 1945. Reformed June, 1946, at Dyce as an Auxiliary for fighting with Spitfire F.R.14e, L.F.16e, F.21 (8W-, RAS-), Harvard T.2b (8W-, RAS-), Meteor T.7 (8W-). 1952, Vampire F.B.5. C.O S/L G. W. Cory. June, 1955, C.O. S/L T. E. Johnson.

No. 613 'East Lancashire—City of Manchester' Squadron

Formed 1 March, 1939, at Ringway as an Auxiliary for bombing with Hind 1 (ZR-), Hind(T), Tutor, Tiger Moth. Oct. 1939, Hector 1, Lysander 2, 3 (SY-). 1941, Tomahawk F.1. 1942, Mustang F.R.1 (SY-). Oct. 1943, Mosquito F.B.6 (SY-) at Lasham. Under W/C R. N. Bateson raided Gestapo H.Q. at The Hague, Copenhagen and Odense in 1944. Disbanded Aug. 1945, and renumbered No. 69 Squadron. Reformed June, 1946, at Ringway as an Auxiliary for fighting with Spitfire F.R.14e, F.21, F.22 (Q3-, RAT-), Harvard T.2b (Q3-, RAT-). 1952, Vampire

F.1, F.B.5, Meteor T.7 (Q3–, RAT–). C.O. S/L J. B. Wales. Chipmunk T.1 for training.

No. 614 'County of Glamorgan' Squadron

Formed 1 June, 1937, at Cardiff as an Auxiliary for bombing with Hind, Tutor. 1938, Hector 1 (YX–). 1939, Lysander 2. 1941, Blenheim 4f, 4L, 5, Wellington B.3. May, 1942, participated in first 1,000 bomber raid on Cologne. In North Africa. Nov. 1943, Halifax B.2/1a, Liberator B.6, B.8. Pathfinder duties in Italy. Bombed Ploesti oilfields. Disbanded Feb. 1944. Reformed 3 March, 1944, from No. 462 Squadron. 1944, Mosquito B.16, B.25. Disbanded July, 1945. Reformed May, 1946, at Llandow as an Auxiliary for fighting with Spitfire L.F.16e, F.22 (7A–, RAU–). 1950, Vampire F.B.5, Meteor T.7, Harvard T.2b (7A–, RAU–).

No. 615 'County of Surrey' Squadron

Formed 1 June, 1937, at Kenley as an Auxiliary with Gauntlet 2 (RR–), Tutor. 1938, Gladiator 2 (RR–, KW–). 1939, with Air Component at Arras. Also used Hector 1. April, 1940, Hurricane F.1, F.2b, F.2c (KW–). 1942, in Far East. Oct. 1943, Spitfire F.5c, F.8 (KW–). 1944, Thunderbolt F.B.2 (KW–). Disbanded Sept. 1945. Reformed June, 1946, at Biggin Hill as an Auxiliary for fighting with Spitfire F.R.14e, F.21, F.22 (V6–, RAV–). C.O. S/L R. G. Kellett. 1951, Meteor F.4 (V6–, RAV–), Harvard T.2b (V6–, RAV–). 1952, Meteor F.8. C.O. S/L F. B. Sowrey. Jan. 1954, C.O. S/L R. A. Eccles.

No. 616 'South Yorkshire' Squadron

Formed 1 Nov. 1938, at Doncaster from No. 503 Squadron as an Auxiliary for bombing with Hind, Tutor, Avro 504n. Also used Gauntlet 2 (QJ–, YQ–), Battle 1 (YQ–). 1940, Spitfire F.1, F.2a, F.5b, H.F.6, F.7, H.F.7, F.9, L.F.9 (YQ–). 21 July, 1944, first jet fighter squadron in R.A.F., and only one to use Meteor F.1 (YQ–) of which twelve were supplied. C.O. S/L A. McDowell. At Culmhead. Dec. 1944, Meteor F.3 (YQ–) in 2nd T.A.F. Disbanded Aug. 1945. Reformed June, 1946, at Finningley as an Auxiliary for night-fighting with Mosquito N.F.30, T.3 (RAW–), Oxford T.2 (RAW–). C.O. S/L K. Holden, 1949, Spitfire F.22 (YQ–), Harvard T.2b (RAW–). 1950, Meteor F.3 (YQ–, RAW–). 1951, Meteor F.4 (YQ–) at Linton-on-Ouse. 1952, Meteor F.8, T.7 (YQ–). Nov. 1954, C.O. S/L W. G. Abel. 1955, at Finningley.

No. 617 Squadron

Formed 21 March, 1943, at Scampton. Became famous for its great exploits in breaching the Möhne, Eder and Sorpe Dams in Operation Chastise on 16 May, 1943, earning it the title of 'The Dam-Busters'. C.O. W/C Guy Gibson awarded V.C. Equipped with Lancaster B.1,

B.1(Spec.) B.3 (AJ–, YZ–). 30 Aug. 1943, at Coningsby. 15 Sept. 1943, attacked Dortmund-Ems Canal, using 12,000 lb. H.C. bombs for first time. 6 June, 1944, flew in Operation Taxable. June, 1944, dropped first 'Tallboy' bombs on Saumur tunnel. Sept./Oct./Nov. 1944, attacked *Tirpitz.* 14 March, 1945, dropped first 22,000 lb. 'Grand Slam' bomb. Jan. 1944, at Woodhall Spa. 1945, Lancaster B.7(F.E.) (YZ–, KC–). 1946, Lincoln B.2 (KC–, YZ–), Oxford T.2 (KC–, YZ–). 1952, Canberra B.2. 1955, Canberra B.6. May, 1955, in Malaya on anti-terrorist duties. Disbanded Dec. 1955. Reformed 1 May, 1958, at Scampton with Vulcan B.1. C.O. W/C D. Bower. 1960, C.O. W/C L. G. Bastard. 1961, Vulcan B.2.

No. 618 Squadron

Formed 1 April, 1943, for special duties with Coastal Command, flying Mosquito B.4.

No. 619 Squadron

Formed 18 April, 1943, at Strubby as a bomber unit with Whitley B.5 (PG–). 1944, Lancaster B.3 (PG–) at Metheringham. 1945, at Skellingthorpe.

No. 620 Squadron

Formed June, 1943, for transport of airborne forces and supplies. Used Stirling G.T.4 (QS–, D4–), Halifax A.7, A.9 (QS–, D4–), Horsa 1 and 2. Disbanded Sept. 1946, and became No. 113 Squadron.

No. 621 Squadron

Formed 12 Sept. 1943, for general reconnaissance with Wellington G.R.12, G.R.13, Warwick A.S.R.5, Lancaster B.3, G.R.3. Served in East Africa. Disbanded 1 Sept. 1946, and became No. 18 Squadron.

No. 622 Squadron

Formed 10 Aug. 1943, as a bomber unit with Stirling B.3 (GI–). Dec. 1943, Lancaster B.1, B.3 (GI–) at Mildenhall. Disbanded Aug. 1945. Reformed Dec. 1950, at Blackbushe as an Auxiliary for transport with Valetta C.1, C.2 (MOVF–).

No. 623 Squadron

Formed 10 Aug. 1943, at Downham Market from a flight of No. 218 Squadron for bombing with Stirling B.3 (IC–).

No. 624 Squadron

Formed 22 Sept. 1943, from No. 1575 Flt. for special duties in the Mediterranean with Halifax B.2/1, B.2/1a, B.5/1a, Ventura, Lysander 1, Stirling B.3. Engaged in agent-dropping. Disbanded 5 Sept. 1944. Reformed 28 Dec. 1944, with Walrus A.S.R.2 for air-sea rescue.

No. 625 Squadron

Formed 1 Oct. 1943, at Kelstern as a bomber unit with Wellington B.10 (CF-), Lancaster B.1, B.3 (CF-). March, 1945, at Scampton.

No. 626 Squadron

Formed 7 Nov. 1943, at Wickenby from 'C' Flight of No. 12 Squadron for bombing with Lancaster B.1, B.3 (UM-).

No. 627 Squadron

Formed 12 Nov. 1943, at Oakington from part of No. 139 Squadron for target-marking and high-level bombing with Lancaster B.1, B.2, B.3 (AZ-) in Pathfinder Force. 1944, Mosquito B.4, B.9, B.16, B.25 (AZ-), Boston B.3 (AZ-). Disbanded Sept. 1945, and renumbered No. 109 Squadron.

No. 628 Squadron

Formed 21 March, 1944, from 'B' Flt., No. 240 Squadron, for special duties in S.E.A.C. with Catalina G.R.4.

No. 630 Squadron

Formed 15 Nov. 1943, at East Kirby from 'B' Flight of No. 57 Squadron for bombing with Lancaster B.1, B.3 (LE-). Flew in Operation Exodus in 1945.

No. 631 Squadron

Formed 1 Dec. 1943, for anti-aircraft co-operation with Hurricane F.2, F.4, Tiger Moth, Vengeance T.T.4, Oxford T.2, Spitfire L.F.5b, L.F.16e, Martinet T.T.1, Henley T.T.3 (all 6D-).

No. 635 Squadron

Formed 20 March, 1944, at Downham Market from 'B' Flight of No. 35 Squadron and 'C' Flight of No. 97 Squadron for target-marking with Lancaster B.1, B.3, B.6 (F2-). Only unit to fly Lancaster B.6. 4 Aug. 1944, V.C. won by S/L I. W. Bazalgette.

No. 639 Squadron

Formed 1 Dec. 1943, for anti-aircraft co-operation with Henley T.T.3, Hurricane F.2, Martinet T.T.1.

No. 640 Squadron

Formed 7 Jan. 1944 at Leconfield from 'C' Flight of No. 158 Squadron for bombing with Halifax B.3, B.6 (C8-). At Leconfield.

No. 644 Squadron

Formed 23 Jan. 1944, at Tarrant Rushton for transport of airborne forces with Halifax B.5 (2P-, 9U-), Halifax G.T.3, G.T.5/1a, A.7, A.9 (2P-, 9U-), Horsa 1 and 2. Disbanded 1 Sept. 1946, in Palestine and became No. 47 Squadron.

No. 650 Squadron

Formed 1 Dec. 1943, for air observation post duties with Auster A.O.P.3.

No. 651 Squadron

Formed Aug. 1941, and was the first air observation post unit. Equipped with Auster A.O.P.1, 3, 5, 6. 1946, engaged in patrolling and tracking illegal immigration shipping to Palestine.

No. 652 Squadron

Formed 1 May, 1942, as an air observation post unit with Auster A.O.P.1, 3, 4, 5, 6 (XM-), Tiger Moth (XM-).

No. 653 Squadron

Formed 20 June, 1942, for air observation post duties with Auster A.O.P.1, 3, 4, Tiger Moth.

No. 654 Squadron

Formed 15 July, 1942, as an air observation post unit with Taylorcraft D, Auster A.O.P.3, 4, Tiger Moth (QD-).

No. 655 Squadron

Formed 8 Dec. 1942, for air observation post duties with Auster A.O.P.1, 3, 4 (PA-, VC-).

No. 656 Squadron

Formed Dec. 1942, at Bury St. Edmunds as an air observation post squadron with Auster A.O.P.1, 3, 4, 5, 6. Served in India, Burma, Java, Malaya and Hong Kong. Disbanded Jan. 1947, one flight becoming No. 1914 Flt. Reformed July, 1948, from Station H.Q., Nos. 1902, 1903, 1907, 1914 Flts. as No. 656 A.O.P. Flt. with Auster A.O.P.6, 7. Nov. 1953, in Malaya. April, 1954, one flight detached to Benta, Malaya, as No. 1914 Flt. Sept. 1955, in Malaya as No. 656 Light Liaison Flt. with Auster A.O.P.9. 1 Sept. 1957, became No. 656 Lt. Aircraft Squadron, Army Air Corps. C.O. Lt.-Col. B. B. Storey. Sept. 1958, No. 16 Recce. Flt. added, making total five flights.

No. 657 Squadron

Formed Jan. 1943, at Woolsington for air observation post duties with Auster A.O.P.1, 2. July, 1943, Auster A.O.P.3, 4, 5 (TS-). Jan. 1943, 'A' and 'B' Flts. formed into No. 1900 A.O.P. Flt. July, 1943, at Algiers with 1st Canadian Corps. March, 1945, in Belgium. Observed 4,444 shoots during the war. 1946, at Andover with Auster A.O.P.6, Hoverfly 1 and 2 (TS-).

No. 658 Squadron

Formed 30 April, 1943, as an air observation post unit with Auster A.O.P. 1, 3, 4, 5.

No. 659 Squadron

Formed 30 April, 1943, for air observation post duties with Auster A.O.P. 3, 5, 6.

No. 660 Squadron

Formed 4 Aug. 1943, as an air observation post squadron with Auster A.O.P.3, 5 (BG-).

No. 661 Squadron

Formed 31 Aug. 1943, as an air observation post unit with Auster A.O.P.3, 4, 5 (OE-). Disbanded 31 Dec. 1945. Reformed 1 May, 1949, at Kenley as an Auxiliary with Auster A.O.P.5, 6 (ROA-), Auster T.7. No. 1957 Flt. at Kenley, No. 1958 Flt. at Hendon, No. 1959 Flt. at Hornchurch, No. 1960 Flt. at Kenley.

No. 662 Squadron

Formed Sept. 1943, for air observation post duties with Auster A.O.P.3, 4, 5 (ET-). Disbanded Dec. 1945. Reformed 1 Feb. 1949 at Colerne with Auster A.O.P.5, 6 (ROB-) as an Auxiliary. No. 1956 Flt. at Colerne, No. 1962 Flt. at Middle Wallop, No. 1963 Flt at Colerne.

No. 663 (Polish) Squadron

Formed 7 Sept. 1944, in Italy as an air observation post unit with Auster A.O.P.4, 5. Disbanded Oct. 1946. Reformed 1 July, 1949, at Hooton Park as an Auxiliary with Auster A.O.P.5, 6 (ROC-), Tiger Moth (ROC-). Jan. 1955, H.Q. and Nos. 1953 and 1955 Flts. at Hooton Park, No. 1951 Flt. at Ringway, No. 1954, Flt. at Castle Bromwich, No. 1952 Flt. at Llandow.

No. 664 Squadron, R.C.A.F.

Formed Dec. 1944, as an air observation post with Auster A.O.P.1, 3, 4, 5 (AW-). Disbanded May, 1946. Reformed 1 Sept. 1949, at Hucknall as an Auxiliary with Auster A.O.P.5, 6 (ROD-), Tiger Moth (ROD-). 1954, C.O. Maj. J. Eaton. March, 1955, C.O. Capt. R. Robertson. No. 1964 Flt. at Yeadon, No. 1965 Flt. at Usworth, No. 1969 Flt. at Wymeswold, No. 1970 Flt. at Hucknall.

No. 665 Squadron, R.C.A.F.

Formed 22 Jan. 1945, as an air observation post unit with Auster A.O.P.4, 5.

No. 666 Squadron, R.C.A.F.

Formed 5 March, 1945, for air observation post duties with Auster A.O.P.4, 5 (BX–). Disbanded July, 1945. Reformed 1 May, 1949, at Scone as an Auxiliary with Auster A.O.P.5, 6 (ROG–), Tiger Moth 2 (ROG–). No. 1966 Flt. at Perth, No. 1967 Flt. at Abbotsinch, No. 1968 Flt. at Turnhouse.

No. 667 Squadron

Formed 1 Dec. 1943, for anti-aircraft co-operation with Hurricane F.2, Oxford T.2, Tiger Moth, Vengeance T.T.2/2, T.T.4, Defiant T.T.1, T.T.3, Blenheim 4, Spitfire L.F.16e (all U4–).

No. 668 Squadron

Formed 16 Nov. 1944, for transport of airborne forces with Dakota C.3, Horsa, Hadrian, Harvard T.2b, Tiger Moth.

No. 669 Squadron

Formed 16 Nov. 1944, for transport of airborne forces with Dakota C.3, Horsa, Hadrian.

No. 670 Squadron

Formed 14 Dec. 1944, for transport of airborne forces with Dakota C.3, Horsa, Hadrian, Tiger Moth.

No. 671 Squadron

Formed 16 Nov. 1944, for transport of airborne forces with Dakota C.3, Horsa, Hadrian, Tiger Moth, Auster A.O.P.5.

No. 672 Squadron

Formed 16 Nov. 1944, for transport of airborne forces with Dakota C.3., Horsa, Hadrian, Tiger Moth, Auster A.O.P.3, 5.

No. 673 Squadron

Formed 27 Jan. 1942, for transport of airborne forces with Dakota C.3, Horsa, Hadrian, Tiger Moth, Auster A.O.P.1.

No. 679 Squadron

Formed 1 Dec. 1943, for anti-aircraft co-operation with Hurricane F.2, Martinet T.T.1.

No. 680 Squadron

Formed 1 Feb. 1943, for photographic-reconnaissance with Spitfire P.R.4, P.R.11, Hurricane F.2, Mosquito P.R.4, P.R.16, P.R.34, Baltimore B.3, Blenheim 4, Lockheed 12a, Fairchild Argus, Lightning 1. Aug. 1946, became No. 13 Squadron.

No. 681 Squadron

Formed 25 Jan. 1943, in Burma for photographic-reconnaissance with Hurricane F.2, Mitchell B.3, Mosquito B.4, F.B.6. 1944, at Alipore, Calcutta, Mingaladon. 1944, Spitfire P.R.4, P.R.11, P.R.19. Jan. 1946, at Seletar. Disbanded 1 Aug. 1946, and became No. 34 Squadron.

No. 682 Squadron

Formed 1 Feb. 1943, for photographic-reconnaissance with Spitfire P.R.11.

No. 683 Squadron

Formed Jan. 1943, for photographic-reconnaissance with Spitfire F.5b, P.R.4, P.R.11, F.R.14. Disbanded Sept. 1945. Reformed and engaged in air-mapping during 1952.

No. 684 Squadron

Formed Sept. 1943, at Calcutta for photographic-reconnaissance with Mitchell B.3, Mosquito F.B.6, Spitfire P.R.11, P.R.19, Mosquito P.R.16, P.R.34. Operated from Alipore, Cox's Bazaar, China Bay, Akyab, Mingaladon, Cocos Islands. 1945, at Kallang, Saigon. Jan. 1946, at Bangkok. Three Beaufighter 10 used as a communication flight. Disbanded Sept. 1946, and became No. 81 Squadron.

No. 691 Squadron

Formed 1 Dec. 1943, for anti-aircraft co-operation with Vengeance T.T.4/1 (5S–), Defiant T.T.3, Tiger Moth, Oxford T.1, T.2, Hurricane F.2c, Gladiator 2, Battle 1, Spitfire F.14, L.F.16e (5S–), Beaufighter T.T.10, Barracuda, Spitfire F.R.18, Harvard T.2b, Martinet T.T.1 (5S–), Mustang F.1 (5S–). Disbanded 11 Feb. 1949, and became No. 17 Squadron.

No. 692 'Fellowship of the Bellows' Squadron

Formed 1 Jan. 1944, at Graveley in Pathfinder Force with Mosquito B.4, B.9, B.16 (P3–). First Mosquito squadron to drop 4,000 lb. bomb on 23 Feb. 1944. 12 May, 1944, first Mosquito squadron to lay mines. June, 1945, at Gransden Lodge.

No. 695 Squadron

Formed 1 Dec. 1943, for anti-aircraft co-operation with Henley T.T.3 (4M–), Lysander 1 (4M–), Martinet T.T.1 (4M–, 8Q–), Hurricane F.2c (4M–, 8Q–), Tiger Moth (4M–), Vengeance T.T.4/2 (4M–, 8Q–), Oxford T.2 (4M–), Spitfire L.F.16e (4M–, 8Q–), Harvard T.2b (4M–), Beaufighter T.T.10 (4M–, 8Q–), Meteor F.4. Disbanded 11 Feb. 1949, and became No. 34 Squadron.

Aircraft used as Equipment or for Service Trials by Squadrons

* denotes first to operate

Airship *Beta*, No. 1
Airship *Gamma*, No. 1
Airship *Delta*, No. 1
Airship *Zeta*, No. 1
Airship *Eta*, No. 1
Airship *Astra Torres*, No. 203
Airship S.S.Z type, Nos. 236, 255, 258
Airship C type, Nos. 236, 255
Airship S.S.T. Mullion Twin type, No. 236
Airspeed Courier, No. 311
Airspeed Oxford T.2, Nos. 1, 5, 9, 17, 21, 24, 34, 41, 68, 74, 96, 98, 109, 116, 120, 138, 139, 202, 226, 256, 264, 285, 286, 287, 288, 289, 290, 307, 500, 502, 504, 510, 518, 526, 527, 567, 575, 577, 587, 595, 598, 600, 608, 609, 616, 617, 631, 667, 691, 695
Airspeed Horsa 1 and 2, Nos. 190, 295, 296, 297, 298, 299, 620, 644, 668, 669, 670, 671, 672, 673
Armstrong Whitworth F.K.3, No. 47
Armstrong Whitworth F.K.8, Nos. 2, 8, 10, 17, *35, 36, 47, 50, 53, 82, 98, 110, 142

Armstrong Whitworth Siskin 3, Nos. *41, 111
Armstrong Whitworth Siskin 3a, Nos. 1, 17, 19, 25, 29, 32, 41, 43, 54, 56, 111
Armstrong Whitworth Siskin— Dual, Nos. 1, 17, 19, 25, 29, 32, 41, 43, 54, 56, 111
Armstrong Whitworth Atlas 1, Nos. 2, 4, 13, 16, *26, 208
Armstrong Whitworth Atalanta, No. 31
Armstrong Whitworth Whitley B.1, Nos. *10, 51, 58, 78, 102
Armstrong Whitworth Whitley B.2, Nos. 10, 97, 299
Armstrong Whitworth Whitley B.3, Nos. 7, 10, 51, 53, 58, 77, 78, 97, 612
Armstrong Whitworth Whitley B.4, Nos. 51, 58, 76, 77, 97, 102, 109, 138, 161, 166, 295, 502
Armstrong Whitworth Whitley B.5, Nos. 10, 51, 76, 77, 78, 97, 102 103, 115, 138, 161, 295, 296, 297, 502, 619
Armstrong Whitworth Whitley G.R.7, Nos. 58, 77, 502, 612
Armstrong Whitworth Whitley 10, Nos. 296, 297

Armstrong Whitworth Ensign, No. 24

Armstrong Whitworth Albemarle G.T.1/1, Nos. 161, *295, 296, 297, 511, 570

Armstrong Whitworth Meteor N.F.11, Nos. 5, 11, *29, 68, 85, 86, 87, 96, 139, 141, 151, 213, 219, 256, 264

Armstrong Whitworth Meteor N.F.12, Nos. 25, 33, 46, 72, 85, 153, 264

Armstrong Whitworth Meteor N.F.13, Nos. 39, 219

Armstrong Whitworth Meteor N.F.14, Nos. 25, 33, 46, 60, 64, 72, 85, 125, 141, 152, 153, 165, 264

Armstrong Whitworth Argosy C.1, Nos. 105, *114, 215, 267

Auster A.O.P.1, Nos. 529, *651, 652, 653, 655, 656, 657, 658, 664, 673

Auster A.O.P.2, No. 657

Auster A.O.P.3, Nos. 650, 651, 652, 653, 654, 655, 656, 657, 658, 659, 660, 661, 662, 664, 672

Auster A.O.P.4, Nos. 527, 652, 653, 654, 655, 656, 657, 658, 661, 662, 663, 664, 665, 666

Auster A.O.P.5, Nos. 651, 652, 656, 657, 658, 659, 660, 661, 662, 663, 664, 665, 666, 671, 672

Auster A.O.P.6, Nos. 651, 652, 657, 659, 661, 662, 663, 664, 666

Auster A.O.P.7, Nos, 656, 661

Auster A.O.P.9, Nos. 267, 656

Avro 500, No. 3

Avro 504, Nos. 1, 3, 4, 5, 13, 23, 33, 36, 43, 45, 51, 53, 65, 72, 75,

76, 77, 89, 90, 98, 201, 202, 203, 204, 219, 233

Avro 504j, No. 5

Avro 504k, Nos. 3, 24, 67, 100, 501, 503, 600, 601, 602, 603, 605

Avro 504n, Nos. 24, 502, 600, 602, 603, 604, 607, 608, 616

Avro Aldershot, No. 99

Avro Bison, No. 3

Avro Antelope, No. 100

Avro Anson, Nos. 7, 24, 31, 35, 42, *48, 51, 58, 61, 63, 71, 75, 76, 86, 97, 98, 109, 116, 119, 144, 148, 157, 167, 185, 187, 192, 206, 215, 217, 220, 221, 224, 233, 239, 269, 275, 276, 278, 279, 280, 281, 282, 285, 287, 320, 321, 437, 500, 501, 502, 510, 516, 527, 544, 575, 608, 612

Avro Tutor, Nos. 24, 234, 500, 600, 601, 603, 605, 609, 610, 611, 613, 614, 615, 616

Avro Rota C.30, No. 529

Avro Rota C.40, No. 529

Avro Manchester B.1 and B.1a, Nos. 44, 49, 50, 57, 61, 83, 97, 106, 144, 156, *207, 408, 420

Avro Lancaster B.1, Nos. 7, 9, 12, 15, 35, *44, 49, 50, 57, 61, 70, 75, 82, 83, 90, 97, 100, 101, 103, 104, 106, 115, 138, 148, 149, 150, 153, 156, 166, 167, 170, 178, 186, 189, 195, 207, 218, 227, 262, 300, 405, 408, 419, 424, 427, 429, 433, 434, 460, 463, 466, 467, 514, 550, 576, 582, 617, 622, 625, 626, 627, 630, 635

Avro Lancaster B.1(F.E.), Nos. 7,

9, 35, 49, 90, 115, 138, 149,
207, 214, 425

Avro Lancaster B.1(Spec.), Nos. 15,
617

Avro Lancaster B.2, Nos. 61, 115,
408, 432, 541, 627

Avro Lancaster B.3, Nos. 7, 9, 12,
15, 21, 35, 44, 49, 50, 57, 61,
75, 83, 90, 97, 100, 101, 103,
106, 115, 120, 138, 148, 149,
150, 153, 156, 166, 170, 189,
195, 203, 207, 218, 227, 231,
300, 405, 419, 420, 424, 426,
427, 429, 431, 432, 433, 460,
463, 467, 514, 550, 576, 582,
617, 619, 621

Avro Lancaster G.R.3, Nos. 18,
179, 203, 621

Avro Lancaster B.3(Spec.), No. 405

Avro Lancaster A.S.R.3, Nos. 37,
179, 203

Avro Lancaster M.R.3, Nos. 37, 38,
210, 224, 404, 405, 407, 408

Avro Lancaster B.6, No. 635

Avro Lancaster B.7, Nos. 9, 35, 40,
57, 104, 214, 427, 460, 617

Avro Lancaster M.R.10, Nos. 61,
101, 115, 405, 408, 420, 424,
425, 428, 431, 434

Avro Lancaster P.R.10, Nos. 413,
419

Avro York C.1, Nos. *24, 40, 51,
59, 99, 206, 232, 242, 246, 511

Avro Lancastrian, No. 24

Avro Lincoln B.2, Nos. 7, 9, 12, 15,
35, 44, 49, 50, *57, 61, 83, 90,
97, 100, 101, 115, 116, 138, 148,
149, 199, 207, 214, 537, 617

Avro Shackleton M.R.1, Nos. 37,
42, 120, 206, 220, 224, 240, 269

Avro Shackleton M.R.2, Nos. 37,
38, 42, 120, 204, 205, 210, 224,
228

Avro Shackleton M.R.3, Nos. 42,
120, 201, 203, 205, 206, *220

Avro Vulcan B.1, Nos. 27, 44, 50,
61, *83, 101, 617

Avro Vulcan B.2, Nos. 9, 12, 27,
35, 50, *83, 101, 617

Avro Andover C.1, Nos. 46, 52

Avro-Canada CF-100, Nos. 416,
419, 423, 428, 432, 433, 440,
*445

Beech Expediter, Nos. 412, 418, 424,
426, 435

Bell Airacobra F.1, No. 601

Blackburn Kangaroo, No. 246

Blackburn Dart, No. 36

Blackburn Iris 3, No. 209

Blackburn Perth, Nos. 204, *209

Blackburn Botha, Nos. 502, *608

Blackburn Beverley C.1, Nos. 30,
34, *47, 53, 84

B.E.1, No. 2

B.E.2, Nos. *2, 3, 4, 6, 7, 8, 9, 16,
203

B.E.2a, Nos. 2, 4, 6

B.E.2b, Nos. 4, 6

B.E.2c, Nos. 2, 3, 4, 5, 6, 7, *8, 9,
10, 12, 13, 14, 15, 16, 17, 19,
21, 23, 26, 30, 31, 33, 34, 35,
36, 39, 42, 43, 50, 51, 52, 53,
56, 62, 67, 75, 76, 77, 78, 98,
100, 114, 201, 202, 203, 204,
207, 228, 273

B.E.2d, Nos. 2, 4, 5, 6, 7, 8, 10, 12,
13, 15, 16, 42, 51, 63, 110

B.E.2e, Nos. 2, 4, 5, 6, 7, 8, 9, 10, 12,

110, 113, *114, 139, 141, 144, 211, 218, 222, 234, 245, 254, 285

Bristol Blenheim 1f, Nos. 17, 23, 25, 27, 29, 30, 60, 64, 92, 143, 235, 248, 404, 600, 601, 604

Bristol Blenheim N.F.1f, Nos. 141, 406

Bristol Blenheim 1L, Nos. 8, 11, 18, 21, 42, 52, 203, 500

Bristol Blenheim 4, Nos. 6, 14, 20, 23, 35, 45, 47, 52, 53, 57, 59, 86, 88, 100, 103, 110, 113, 115, 139, 140, 143, 162, 203, 219, 224, 230, 236, 244, 256, 289, 294, 326, 404, 406, 407, 415, 419, 454, 500, 502, 516, 521, 526, 527, 528, 608, 667, 680

Bristol Blenheim 4f, Nos. 18, 25, 30, 53, 60, 84, 107, 229, 235, 248, 252, 254, 272, 600, 614

Bristol Blenheim N.F.4f, No. 406

Bristol Blenheim 4L, Nos. 8, 11, 13, 14, 15, 21, 34, 39, 40, 42, 52, 55, 82, 90, 101, 105, 142, 150, 211, 218, 223, 342, 459, 489, 500, 614

Bristol Blenheim B.5d, Nos. 13, 18, 42, 47, 113, 114, 139, 162, 244, 614

Bristol Bombay, Nos. 117, *216, 267, 271

Bristol Bolingbroke, No. 600

Bristol Beaufort G.R.1, Nos. *22, 39, 42, 47, 48, 86, 100, 217, 236, 415, 489

Bristol Beaufort G.R.2, Nos. 86, 203

Bristol Beaufighter F.1, Nos. 25, 27, *29, 46, 93, 108, 141, 143, 153, 176, 177, 219, 227, 234, 235, 236, 239, 252, 255, 256, 272, 285, 286, 515, 527, 577, 600

Bristol Beaufighter T.F.1c, Nos. 47, 248, 455, 603

Bristol Beaufighter N.F.1f, Nos. 68, 89, 141, 153, 169, 307, 406, 604

Bristol Beaufighter N.F.1/2, No. 25

Bristol Beaufighter N.F.1/3, No. 25

Bristol Beaufighter F.2, Nos. 68, 96, 125, 219, 410, 456, 600

Bristol Beaufighter F.2f, Nos. 404, 604

Bristol Beaufighter N.F.2f, Nos. 96, 255, 287, 307, 406, 409, 410, 488, 527

Bristol Beaufighter N.F.4, Nos. 89, 409

Bristol Beaufighter 5, No. 29

Bristol Beaufighter 6, Nos. 25, 26, 96, 108, 125, 143, 144, 176, 177, 235, 236, 252, 254, 272, 456, 600, 603

Bristol Beaufighter T.F.6c, Nos. 47, 144, 248, 455, 603

Bristol Beaufighter N.F.6f, Nos. 48, 141, 169, 255, 256, 287, 370, 406, 409, 488, 604

Bristol Beaufighter T.F.10, Nos. 17, 22, 27, 34, 36, 39, 42, 45, 47, 84, 143, 144, 211, 217, 235, 236, 248, 252, 254, 272, 404, 455, 459, 489, 577, 603, 684

Bristol Beaufighter T.T.10, Nos. 5, 595, 691, 695

Bristol Beaufighter T.F.11c, Nos. 47, 227, 252, 404, 603

Bristol Brigand B.1, Nos. 8, 36, 42, 45, *84, 248, 254

Bristol Brigand T.F.1, Nos. 36, 42

Curtiss Tomahawk F.2b, Nos. 73, 136, 231, 414

Curtiss Kittyhawk F.1, Nos. 94, 250, 450

Curtiss Kittyhawk F.1a, Nos. 94, 112, 250

Curtiss Kittyhawk F.2, Nos. 260, 450

Curtiss Kittyhawk, F.3, Nos. 112, 250, 260, 450

Curtiss Kittyhawk F.4, Nos. 112, 250, 450

De Havilland D.H.1A, No. 14

De Haviland D.H.2, Nos. 5, 11, 16, 17, 18, *24, 29, 32, 47, 111

De Havilland D.H.4, Nos. 1(Comm.), 2(Comm.), 18, 25, 27, 30, 49, 51, *55, 57, 63, 72, 97, 98, 110, 202, 205, 206, 211, 212, 217, 220, 221, 222, 223, 224, 225, 226, 227, 228, 273

De Havilland D.H.5, Nos. 24, 32, 41, 64, 68

De Havilland D.H.6, Nos. 67, 76, 77, 99, 110, 144, 236, 244, 250, 252, 254, 255, 258, 260

De Havilland D.H.9, Nos. 17, 18, 27, 47, 49, 55, 98, 99, 103, 104, 107, *110, 120, 144, 202, 206, 211, 212, 218, 220, 221, 222, 223, 224, 225, 226, 227, 229, 233, 236, 250, 269, 273

De Havilland D.H.9a, Nos. 8, 11, 12, 14, 15, 18, 24, 25, 27, 30, 35, 39, 45, 47, 55, 60, 84, 99, 100, *110, 205, 207, 212, 221, 225, 273, 501, 600, 601, 602, 603, 604, 605

De Havilland D.H.10 Amiens, Nos. 60, 97, 104, 120, 216

De Havilland D.H.56 Hyena, No. 4

De Havilland D.H.60 Gipsy Moth, Nos. 24, 267

De Havilland D.H.82a Tiger Moth, Nos. 4, 16, 20, 24, 109, 124, 217, 268, 278, 510, 516, 567, 587, 600, 603, 613, 631, 653, 654, 663, 664, 666, 667, 668, 670, 671, 672, 673, 691, 695

De Havilland D.H.86b Express, Nos. 24, 117, 133, 216

De Havilland D.H.87b Hornet Moth, Nos. 510, 526, 528, 529

De Havilland D.H.89 Dominie, Nos. 4, 24, 510, 526, 527

De Havilland D.H.91 Albatross, No. 271

De Havilland D.H.94 Moth Minor, No. 4

De Havilland D.H.95 Hertfordshire, No. 24

De Havilland D.H.98 Mosquito P.R.1, Nos. 521, 540

De Havilland D.H.98 Mosquito N.F.2, Nos. *23, 25, 140, 141, 151, 157, 169, 239, 264, 307, 410, 418, 456, 605

De Havilland D.H.98 Mosquito T.3, Nos. 13, 19, 23, 25, 29, 39, 41, 58, 64, 65, 81, 85, 96, 98, 114, 125, 139, 141, 169, 219, 264, 305, 418, 488, 500, 504, 540, 608, 609, 616

De Havilland D.H.98 Mosquito B.4, Nos. 21, *105, 109, 139, 157, 192, 464, 618, 627, 680, 681, 692

De Havilland D.H.98 Mosquito
P.R.4, No. 540

De Havilland D.H.98 Mosquito
F.B.6, Nos. 2, 4, 8, 11, 16, 21,
22, 23, 25, 27, 34, 36, 45, 47, 69,
82, 84, 89, 107, 110, 114, 141,
143, 151, 162, 169, 211, 235,
239, 248, 249, 268, 305, 307,
333, 334, 404, 410, 418, 456,
464, 487, 489, 502, 605, 613,
681, 684

De Havilland D.H.98 Mosquito
B.9, Nos. 105, 109, 139, 169,
627, 692

De Havilland D.H.98 Mosquito
P.R.9, No. 540

De Havilland D.H.98 Mosquito
N.F.12, Nos. 29, 85, 151, 153,
256, 264, 307, 406, 410, 456,
488, 604

De Havilland D.H.98 Mosquito
N.F.13, Nos. 25, 68, 89, 96,
108, 256, 264, 409, 410, 488,
604

De Havilland D.H.98 Mosquito
N.F.14, No. 86

De Havilland D.H.98 Mosquito
B.16, Nos. 2, 4, 13, 14, 69, 81,
98, 105, 109, 128, 139, 140, 142,
163, 180, 192, 256, 304, 515,
544, 571, 578, 608, 614, 627,
684, 692

De Havilland D.H.98 Mosquito
P.R.16, Nos. 109, 400, 540, 680

De Havilland D.H.98 Mosquito
N.F.17, Nos. 25, 68, 85, 96,
125, 456

De Havilland D.H.98 Mosquito
F.B.18, Nos. 248, 254

De Havilland D.H.98 Mosquito

N.F.19, Nos. 58, 68, 157, 169,
176, 256, 600, 604

De Havilland D.H.98 Mosquito
B.20, Nos. 128, 139, 162

De Havilland D.H.98 Mosquito
B.25, Nos. 139, 162, 163, 614,
627

De Havilland D.H.98 Mosquito
F.B.26, Nos. 29, 55, 249

De Havilland D.H.98 Mosquito
N.F.30, Nos. 23, 25, 29, 68,
85, 125, 141, 151, 157, 219, 239,
256, 264, 302, 307, 315, 317,
406, 410, 456, 488, 500, 504,
604, 608, 616

De Havilland D.H.98 Mosquito
P.R.31, No. 109

De Havilland D.H.98 Mosquito
P.R.34, Nos. 13, 58, 81, 142,
540, 680, 684

De Havilland D.H.98 Mosquito
B.35, Nos. 14, 69, 98, 109, 139

De Havilland D.H.98 Mosquito
P.R.35, No. 58

De Havilland D.H.98 Mosquito
N.F.36, Nos. 23, 25, 29, 39, 68,
85, 89, 125, 141, 151, 219, 264,
605, 609

De Havilland D.H.103 Hornet F.1,
Nos. 19, 41, *64, 65

De Havilland D.H.103 Hornet F.3,
Nos. 19, 33, 41, 45, 64, 65, 80,
317

De Havilland D.H.103 Hornet F.4,
Nos. 33, 45

De Havilland D.H.100 Vampire
F.1, Nos. 3, 16, 54, 72, 130,
*247, 501, 600, 605, 613

De Havilland D.H.100 Vampire
F.3, Nos. 16, 32, 43, 54, 72,

73, 247, 601, 604, 607, 608, 609

De Havilland D.H.100 Vampire F.B.5, Nos. 3, 4, 5, 6, 11, 16, 20, 26, 28, 32, 54, 60, 67, 71, 72, 73, 93, 94, 98, 105, 112, 118, 145, 185, 213, 234, 247, 249, 266, 401, 438, 441, 501, 502, 602, 603, 605, 607, 608, 612, 613, 614

De Havilland D.H.100 Vampire F.B.9, Nos. 8, 32, 73, 213, 234, 249, 602

De Havilland D.H.113 Vampire N.F.10, Nos. 23, *25, 151

De Havilland D.H.115 Vampire T.11, Nos. 8, 14, 41, 56, 63, 98, 234, 249

De Havilland D.H.112 Venom F.B.1, Nos. 5, 6, 11, 16, 20, 28, 32, 60, 73, 94, 98, 118, 145, 213, 249, 266

De Havilland D.H.112 Venom N.F.2, Nos. 23, 33

De Havilland D.H.112 Venom N.F.2a, No. 253

De Havilland D.H.112 Venom N.F.3, Nos. 11, 23, 33, 89, 125, *141, 151, 219

De Havilland D.H.112 Venom F.B.4, Nos. 5, 6, 8, 45, 60, 142, 208, 266

De Havilland D.H.104 Devon, No. 31

De Havilland D.H.106 Comet 1a, No. 412

De Havilland D.H.106 Comet C.2, Nos. 51, 216

De Havilland D.H.106 Comet T.2, No. 216

De Havilland D.H.106 Comet C.4, No. 216

De Havilland D.H.C.1 Chipmunk T.1, Nos. 31, 114, 613

De Havilland D.H.C.3 Otter, Nos. 408, 418, 424

De Havilland D.H.C.5 CC–115 Buffalo, No. 429

Deperdussin Monoplane, No. 3

Dornier Do.22, No. 230

Dornier Do.24K, No. 321

Douglas Boston B.1, Nos. 173, 223, 238, 418

Douglas Boston B.2, Nos. 23, 85, 88, 605

Douglas Boston B.3, Nos. 13, 18, 23, 24, 39, *88, 107, 114, 226, 342, 418, 605, 627

Douglas Boston B.3a, Nos. 88, 342

Douglas Boston B.4, Nos. 13, 18, 55, 88, 114, 342

Douglas Boston B.5, Nos. 13, 18, 55, 114

Douglas Havoc N.F.1, Nos. 25, *85, 93, 161, 238

Douglas Havoc N.F.2, Nos. *85, 605

Douglas Turbinlite Havoc 1, Nos. 23, 43, 530, 531, 532, 533, 534, 535, 536, 537, 538, 539

Douglas D.C.2, Nos. 31, 117

Douglas D.C.3, No. 31

Douglas Dakota C.1, C.2, C.3, C.4, Nos. 10, 18, 24, 27, 30, 31, 36, 46, 48, 52, 53, 62, 70, 76, 77, 78, 82, 96, 110, 113, 114, 117, 147, 167, 172, 173, 187, 194, 204, 206, 215, 216, 231, 232, 233, 238, 241, 243, 267, 271, 353, 357, 408, 412, 426, 435,

Fairey Albacore, Nos. 36, 100, 119, 415

Fairey Barracuda, Nos. 567, 691

Farman (Henri) F20, Nos. 3, 5, 6, 7, 26, 35, 114, 201, 202, 203, 233

Farman (Maurice) S7 Longhorn, Nos. 1, 2, 3, 4, 5, 6, 9, 16, 18, 25, 30

Farman (Maurice) S11 Shorthorn, Nos. 1, 2, 3, 4, 9, 25, 97, 144, 201, 203, 217

F.B.A. Flying-boat, No. 266

F.E.2a, No. 6

F.E.2b, Nos. 6, 11, 16, 18, *20, 22, 23, 25, 28, 31, 33, 35, 36, 38, 39, 51, 58, 83, 90, 100, 101, 102, 118, 131, 148, 149, 166, 246

F.E.2b Single-seater, No. 36

F.E.2b Dual-control, No. 38

F.E.2c, Nos. 25, 100

F.E.2d, Nos. 20, 25, 33, 36, 51, 57

F.E.8, Nos. 5, 29, *40, 41

F.E.9, No. 78

Felixstowe F.2a, Nos. 201, 212, 228, 230, 233, 234, 240, 247, 249, 256, 259, 267

Felixstowe F.3, Nos. 231, 232, 234, 247, 249, 259, 261, 263, 266, 267

Felixstowe F.5, Nos. 230, 231, 232, 238, 247, 249, 259, 261, 267

Fokker T.8W, No. 320

Ford 5–AT–D Trimotor, No. 271

General Aircraft Cygnet, No. 24

General Aircraft Hotspur, No. 296

General Aircraft Hamilcar, No. 298

Gloster Grebe, Nos. 19, *25, 29, 32, 41, 56, 111

Gloster Grebe 2-seater, No. 56

Gloster Gamecock 1, Nos. 3, 17, 19, *23, 32, 43, 56

Gloster Gauntlet 1, Nos. *19, 111

Gloster Gauntlet 2, Nos. 6, 17, 19, 32, 46, 54, 56, 65, 66, 73, 74, 79, 80, 111, 151, 213, 234, 504, 601, 602, 615, 616

Gloster Gladiator 1 and 2, Nos. 1, 3, 6, 16, 17, 19, 25, 33, 46, 54, 56, 65, 72, 73, 74, 80, 85, 87, 94, 112, 127, 141, 152, 223, 224, 237, 247, 263, 520, 521, 602, 603, 605, 607, 615, 691

Gloster Sea Gladiator, No. 261

Gloster Meteor F.1, No. 616

Gloster Meteor F.3, Nos. 1, 43, 56, 63, 66, 74, 92, 124, 222, 234, 245, 257, 263, 266, 500, 504, 616

Gloster Meteor F.4, Nos. 1, 43, 56, 63, 66, 74, 91, 92, 222, 229, 234, 245, 257, 263, 266, 504, 600, 601, 604, 609, 610, 611, 615, 616, 695

Gloster Meteor T.7, Nos. 1, 5, 41, 43, 56, 63, 64, 66, 68, 74, 79, 87, 92, 98, 151, 213, 222, 234, 245, 249, 257, 263, 500, 501, 504, 600, 602, 603, 607, 608, 612, 613, 614, 616

Gloster Meteor F.8, Nos. 1, 2, 19, 29, 34, 41, 43, 54, 56, 63, 64, 65, 66, 72, 74, 92, 111, 151, 153, 222, *245, 247, 257, 263, 500, 600, 601, 604, 609, 610, 611, 615, 616

Gloster Meteor F.R.9, Nos. 2, 8, 79, 208, 541

Gloster Meteor P.R.10, Nos. 13, 81, 541

Gloster Javelin FAW.1, Nos. *46, 87

Gloster Javelin FAW.2, Nos, 46, 85, 89

Gloster Javelin T.3, No. 46

Gloster Javelin FAW.4, Nos. 3, 5, 11, 23, 33, 41, 46, 72, 89, *141, 151

Gloster Javelin FAW.5, Nos. 41, 137, *151

Gloster Javelin FAW.6, Nos. 5, 29, 46, 68, 85, *89, 256

Gloster Javelin FAW.7, Nos. 3, 23, 25, *33, 64, 72

Gloster Javelin FAW.8, Nos. 25, *41, 85

Gloster Javelin FAW.9, Nos. 23, 25, 29, 60, 64

Grahame-White Type 15, No. 65

Grumman Goose, No. 24

Grumman Avenger T.B.3, No. 567

Handley Page O/100, Nos. 207, 215

Handley Page O/400, Nos. 1(Comm.), 2(Comm.), 58, 67, 70, 97, 100, 115, *207, 211, 214, 215, 216, 274

Handley Page V/1500, Nos. *166, 167, 274

Handley Page Hyderabad, Nos. 9, 10, *99, 502, 503

Handley Page Hinaidi, Nos. 10, *99, 503

Handley Page Heyford 2, Nos. 7, 9, 10, 38, 97, *99, 102, 148, 149, 166, 502

Handley Page Harrow, Nos, 37, 75, 93, 115, *214, 215

Handley Page Hampden B.1, Nos. 7, 44, *49, 50, 61, 76, 83, 97, 106, 144, 185, 207, 408, 415, 420, 426, 455, 489, 502, 521

Handley Page Hampden Met.1, Nos. 517, 519

Handley Page Hereford, Nos. 35, 185

Handley Page Sparrow, No. 271

Handley Page Halifax B.1, Nos. *35, 51, 58, 76, 138, 148, 158, 161, 227, 346, 405, 408, 420

Handley Page Halifax B.2, Nos. 10, 35, 51, 58, 76, 77, 78, 102, 103, 138, 158, 161, 178, 192, 246, 301, 405, 408, 419, 425, 427, 428, 429, 432, 433, 434, 460, 462, 502, 520, 614

Handley Page Halifax B.2/1, Nos. 76, 138, 161, 405, 408, 624

Handley Page Halifax B.2/1a, Nos. 10, 51, 59, 77, 102, 138, 148, 158, 161, 405, 408, 428, 429, 466, 578, 624

Handley Page Halifax B.2/2, No. 138

Handley Page Halifax A.3, No. 190

Handley Page Halifax B.3, Nos. 10, 35, 51, 58, 76, 77, 78, 96, 102, 110, 158, 171, 192, 199, 298, 344, 346, 347, 408, 415, 420, 424, 425, 427, 431, 434, 462, 466, 502, 578, 640

Handley Page Halifax B.3a, Nos. 425, 426, 429, 431, 433

Handley Page Halifax G.T.3, Nos. 171, 295, 296, 297, 298, 644

Handley Page Halifax A.5/1a, Nos. 295, 296, 297

Handley Page Halifax B.5, Nos. 77,

295, 298, 301, 346, 347, 415,
*427, 517, 518, 520, 644

Handley Page Halifax B.5/1, Nos.
138, 161

Handley Page Halifax B.5/1a, Nos.
58, 59, 161, 297, 408, 428, 429,
431, 434, 517, 624

Handley Page Halifax B.5/1(Spec.),
No. 427

Handley Page Halifax G.T.5/1a,
Nos. 171, 644

Handley Page Halifax B.5/2, No.
138

Handley Page Halifax B.6, Nos. 10,
58, 76, 77, 102, 158, 171, 199,
202, 224, 347, 466, 517, 519,
640

Handley Page Halifax G.R.6, No.
547

Handley Page Halifax Met.6, No.
521

Handley Page Halifax A.7, Nos. 58,
113, 190, 295, 298, 346, 347,
408, 415, 420, 424, 425, 426,
432, 433, 517, 519

Handley Page Halifax C.8, Nos.
108, 187, 295, 296, 297, 301,
304

Handley Page Halifax A.9, Nos. 47,
113, 295, 297, 620, 644

Handley Page Halifax G.R.9, No.
502

Handley Page Hastings C.1, Nos.
24, 36, *47, 48, 53, 59, 70, 99,
114, 116, 147, 202, 241, 242,
297, 511

Handley Page Hastings Met.1, No.
202

Handley Page Victor B.1, Nos. *10,
15, 55, 57, 214

Handley Page Victor B.1A, Nos. 55,
57, 214

Handley Page Victor B.(S.R.)2, No.
543

Handley Page Victor B.2, Nos. 100,
139

Hawker Woodcock, Nos. *3, 17

Hawker Horsley, Nos. 11, 15, 33,
36, 100, 504

Hawker Tomtit, No. 24

Hawker Hart, Nos. 5, 6, 11, 12, 15,
18, 21, 24, *33, 39, 52, 57, 60,
100, 142, 152, 162, 237, 296,
500, 501, 503, 510, 600, 601,
602, 603, 604, 605, 609, 610,
611

Hawker Hart(C), No. 24

Hawker Hart(T), Nos. 24, 64, 79,
600, 603

Hawker Fury 1, Nos. 1, 25, *43

Hawker Demon, Nos. 6, 8, *23, 25,
29, 41, 64, 65, 74, 600, 601,
604, 607, 608

Hawker Turret-Demon, Nos. 23, 29

Hawker Audax 1, Nos. 2, *4, 5, 13,
16, 20, 24, 26, 28, 52, 61, 63,
77, 84, 105, 146, 148, 173, 208,
211, 226, 237, 267, 450

Hawker Hardy, Nos. 6, *30, 237

Hawker Hind, Nos. 12, 15, 18, *21,
24, 34, 40, 49, 50, 52, 57, 61,
62, 63, 82, 83, 88, 90, 98, 103,
104, 106, 107, 108, 110, 113,
114, 139, 185, 211, 218, 500,
501, 502, 504, 600, 602, 603,
605, 609, 610, 611, 612, 613,
614, 616

Hawker Hind(T), No. 611

Hawker Osprey, No. 24

Hawker Fury 2, Nos. *25, 41, 73, 87

Hawker Hector, Nos. 2, *4, 13, 16, 26, 53, 59, 602, 612, 613, 614, 615

Hawker Henley T.T.3, Nos. 631, 639, 695

Hawker Hurricane F.1, Nos. 1, 3, 5, 6, 17, 27, 29, 32, 33, 43, 46, 56, 67, 69, 71, 73, 79, 80, 81, 85, 87, 92, 96, 98, *111, 116, 127, 128, 130, 131, 136, 145, 151, 152, 173, 175, 185, 208, 213, 222, 229, 232, 238, 242, 245, 247, 249, 250, 253, 257, 258, 261, 263, 274, 289, 302, 303, 306, 308, 310, 312, 315, 316, 317, 332, 335, 336, 401, 402, 417, 450, 451, 488, 501, 504, 520, 527, 587, 601, 605, 607, 611, 615

Hawker Hurricane N.F.1, No. 288

Hawker Hurricane N.F.1a, No. 96

Hawker Hurricane F.2, Nos. 43, 60, 63, 67, 74, 91, 112, 113, 123, 146, 180, 185, 208, 225, 249, 255, 258, 260, 263, 273, 285, 286, 287, 290, 302, 317, 318, 336, 351, 352, 438, 486, 516, 567, 577, 595, 598, 631, 639, 667, 679, 680, 681

Hawker Hurricane F.2a, Nos. 3, 17, 34, 56, 79, 87, 229, 242, 245, 257, 303, 306, 310, 312, 402, 605

Hawker Hurricane F.2b, Nos. 87, 121, 126, 185

Hawker Hurricane F.B.2b, Nos. 1, 3, 6, 11, 17, 20, 28, 32, 34, 79, 80, 81, 127, 128, 134, 135, 136, 137, 174, 175, 184, 213, 225, 232, 238, 241, 242, 257, 261,

274, 331, 335, 402, 417, 587, 601, 607, 615

Hawker Hurricane F.B.2c, No. 33

Hawker Hurricane F.2c, Nos. 1, 3, 5, 6, 17, 30, 32, 42, 46, 71, 73, 79, 87, 94, 125, 126, 127, 133, 136, 181, 185, 213, 225, 229, 237, 238, 239, 241, 242, 245, 247, 253, 257, 279, 283, 289, 335, 417, 451, 521, 587, 601, 607, 615, 691, 695

Hawker Hurricane F.2d, Nos. 5, 6, 20, 164, 184, 256, 261

Hawker Hurricane N.F.2, No. 151

Hawker Hurricane N.F.2c, Nos. 87, 96, 176, 285, 288

Hawker Hurricane F.4, Nos. 8, 20, 67, 137, 164, 184, 186, 279, 286, 289, 351, 352, 438, 439, 440, 595, 631, 639

Hawker Hurricane F.5c, No. 71

Hawker Hurricane F.10, Nos. 1, 182, 239, 527

Hawker Typhoon F.1a, Nos. 33, *56, 182, 247, 266, 609

Hawker Typhoon F.1b, Nos. 1, 3, 4, 54, 56, 80, 137, 164, 168, 174, 175, 181, 182, 183, 184, 186, 193, 195, 197, 198, 245, 247, 257, 263, 266, 268, 274, 411, 416, 438, 439, 440, 486, 609

Hawker Typhoon F.5, No. 486

Hawker Tempest F.5, Nos. *3, 16, 20, 26, 30, 33, 41, 56, 80, 174, 222, 247, 266, 274, 287, 349, 486, 501

Hawker Tempest F.6, Nos. 3, 6, 8, 16, 39, 56, 80, 213, 249

Hawker Tempest F.2, Nos. 5, 16, 20, 26, 30, 33, *54, 56, 152, 247

Fighter Squadron Markings 1922–1938

No. 1 Fury 1

No. 3 Gladiator 1

No. 17 Woodcock

No. 19 Gauntlet 1

No. 23 Demon

No. 25 Fury 1

No. 29 Siskin 3A

No. 32 Siskin 3A

No. 41 Demon

No. 43 Fury 1

No. 46 Gauntlet. 2

No. 54 (Original Marking) Bulldog 2A

No. 54 (Revised Marking) Bulldog 2A

No. 56 Grebe

Fighter Squadron Markings 1922–1938

No. 64 Demon

No. 65 Gauntlet 2

No. 66 Gauntlet 2

No. 72 Gladiator 2

No. 73 Gladiator 2

No. 74 Gauntlet 2

No. 79 Gauntlet 2

No. 87 Gladiator 2

No. 111 Bulldog 2A

No. 151 Gauntlet 2

No. 213 Gauntlet 2

No. 600 Demon

No. 601 Demon

No. 604 Demon

Fighter Squadron Markings 1946–1959

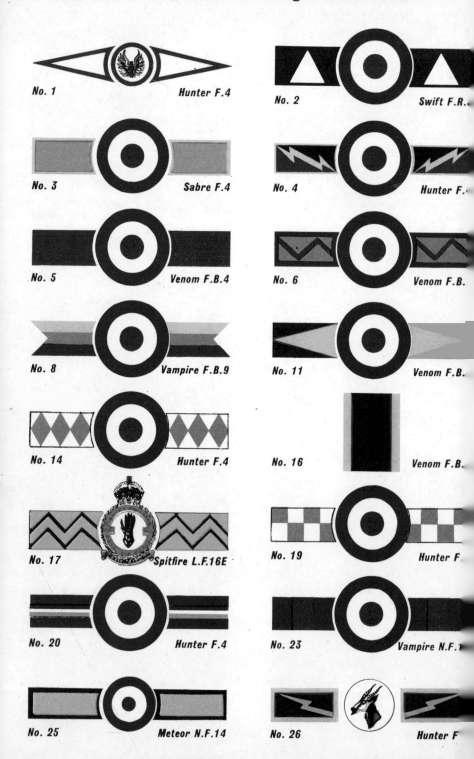

No. 1   Hunter F.4

No. 2   Swift F.R.

No. 3   Sabre F.4

No. 4   Hunter F.

No. 5   Venom F.B.4

No. 6   Venom F.B.

No. 8   Vampire F.B.9

No. 11   Venom F.B.

No. 14   Hunter F.4

No. 16   Venom F.B.

No. 17   Spitfire L.F.16E

No. 19   Hunter F.

No. 20   Hunter F.4

No. 23   Vampire N.F.

No. 25   Meteor N.F.14

No. 26   Hunter F

Fighter Squadron Markings 1946–1959

No. 28 — Venom F.B.1

No. 29 — Meteor N.F.11

No. 32 — Venom F.B.1

No. 33 — Venom N.F.3

No. 34 — Hunter F.5

No. 39 — Meteor N.F.13

No. 41 — Hunter F.5

No. 43 — Hunter F.4

No. 45 — Venom F.B.4

No. 46 — Meteor N.F.14

No. 54 — Hunter F.6

No. 56 — Hunter F.5

No. 60 — Venom F.B.4

No. 63 — Meteor F.8

No. 64 — Meteor F.8

No. 65 — Meteor F.8

Fighter Squadron Markings 1946–1959

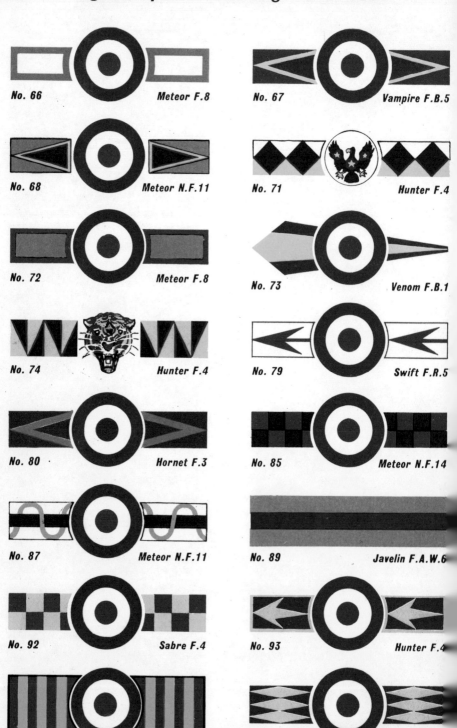

No. 66   Meteor F.8

No. 67   Vampire F.B.5

No. 68   Meteor N.F.11

No. 71   Hunter F.4

No. 72   Meteor F.8

No. 73   Venom F.B.1

No. 74   Hunter F.4

No. 79   Swift F.R.5

No. 80   Hornet F.3

No. 85   Meteor N.F.14

No. 87   Meteor N.F.11

No. 89   Javelin F.A.W.6

No. 92   Sabre F.4

No. 93   Hunter F.4

No. 94   Venom F.B.1

No. 96   Meteor N.F.1

Fighter Squadron Markings 1946–1959

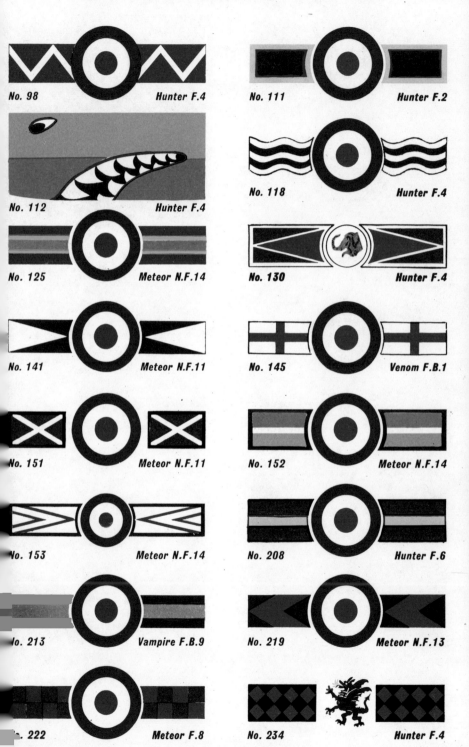

No. 98   Hunter F.4

No. 111   Hunter F.2

No. 112   Hunter F.4

No. 118   Hunter F.4

No. 125   Meteor N.F.14

No. 130   Hunter F.4

No. 141   Meteor N.F.11

No. 145   Venom F.B.1

No. 151   Meteor N.F.11

No. 152   Meteor N.F.14

No. 153   Meteor N.F.14

No. 208   Hunter F.6

No. 213   Vampire F.B.9

No. 219   Meteor N.F.13

No. 222   Meteor F.8

No. 234   Hunter F.4

Fighter Squadron Markings 1946–1959

No. 245   Meteor F.8

No. 247   Hunter F.1

No. 249   Vampire F.B.5

No. 253   Venom N.F.2A

No. 256   Meteor N.F.11

No. 257   Meteor F.8

No. 263   Hunter F.2

No. 264   Meteor N.F.14

No. 266   Venom F.B.1

No. 500   Meteor F.8

No. 501   Vampire F.B.5

No. 502   Vampire F.B.5

No. 504   Meteor F.4

No. 600   Meteor F.8

No. 601   Meteor F.8

No. 602   Vampire F.B.5

Fighter Squadron Markings 1946–1959

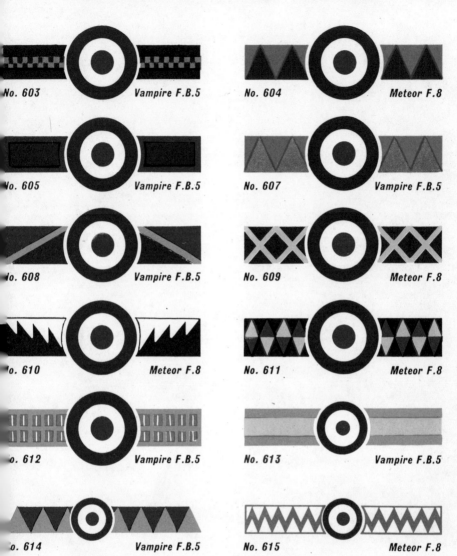

No. 603   Vampire F.B.5

No. 604   Meteor F.8

No. 605   Vampire F.B.5

No. 607   Vampire F.B.5

No. 608   Vampire F.B.5

No. 609   Meteor F.8

No. 610   Meteor F.8

No. 611   Meteor F.8

No. 612   Vampire F.B.5

No. 613   Vampire F.B.5

No. 614   Vampire F.B.5

No. 615   Meteor F.8

No. 616   Meteor F.8

Sopwith Triplane, Nos. 201, 208, 209, 210, 211

Sopwith Dolphin, Nos. *19, 23, 79, 85, 87, 90, 141

Sopwith Camel F.1 and 2F.1, Nos. 3, 17, 28, 36, 37, 43, 44, 45, 46, 47, 50, 54, 61, 65, 66, *70, 71, 72, 73, 75, 78, 80, 87, 89, 98, 112, 139, 143, 148, 150, 151, 152, 189, 201, 203, 204, 206, 208, 209, 210, 212, 213, 216, 217, 220, 221, 222, 223, 224, 225, 226, 227, 228, 230, 233, 273

Sopwith Snipe, Nos. 1, 3, 14, 17, 19, 23, 25, 29, 32, 41, 43, 45, 56, 71, 80, 81, 111, 112, 201, 208

Sopwith Cuckoo, Nos. *185, 210

Spad S-7 C.1, Nos. 17, *19, 23, 30, 60, 63, 72

Spad S-13 C.1, Nos. *19, 23

Stinson Reliant, No. 510

Supermarine Southampton 2, Nos. *201, 203, 204, 205, 210

Supermarine Scapa, Nos. *202, 204, 228, 240

Supermarine Stranraer, Nos. 209, *228, 240

Supermarine Walrus A.S.R.2, Nos. 89, 269, 275, 276, 277, 278, 281, 282, 283, 284, 292, 293, 294, 335, 624

Supermarine Spitfire F.1, Nos. *19, 41, 54, 64, 65, 66, 72, 74, 92, 123, 124, 131, 132, 152, 222, 313, 403, 452, 457, 485, 602, 603, 609, 610, 611, 616

Supermarine Spitfire F.1a, No. 411

Supermarine Spitfire F.1b, Nos. 123, 501

Supermarine Spitfire F.2, Nos. 41, 64, 66, 74, 141, 152, 222, 232, 239, 245, 257, 332, 411, 457, 501, 603, 607

Supermarine Spitfire F.2a, Nos. 19, 41, 54, 64, 65, 66, 72, 74, 91, 92, 118, 122, 123, 129, 130, 131, 137, 145, 152, 303, 308, 310, 312, 313, 315, 332, 340, 349, 401, 403, 411, 412, 416, 452, 457, 485, 603, 609, 610, 611, 616

Supermarine Spitfire F.2b, Nos. 92, 132, 145, 234, 266, 308, 350, 416

Supermarine Spitfire A.S.R. 2c, Nos. 275, 276, 277, 278

Supermarine Spitfire P.R.4, Nos. 140, 542, 680, 681, 683

Supermarine Spitfire F.5, No. 26

Supermarine Spitfire F.5a, Nos. 19, 41, 64, 118, 124, 331, 332, 340, 349, 350, 403, 421, 501, 603, 611

Supermarine Spitfire L.F.5a, No.234

Supermarine Spitfire F.5b, Nos. 19, 32, 41, 43, 54, 63, 64, 65, 66, 71, 72, 74, 81, 87, 91, *92, 111, 118, 121, 123, 124, 126, 127, 129, 130, 131, 132, 133, 145, 152, 154, 162, 164, 165, 167, 185, 186, 208, 222, 225, 229, 234, 237, 241, 242, 243, 249, 253, 266, 269, 288, 290, 303, 306, 308, 310, 313, 315, 317, 318, 322, 327, 328, 331, 332, 335, 336, 341, 345, 349, 350, 352, 401, 402, 403, 411, 412, 416, 417, 421, 441, 442, 443, 451, 452, 453, 457, 485, 486, 501, 504, 519, 520, 527, 567, 577, 595, 601, 602, 603, 607, 611, 683

Supermarine Spitfire L.F.5b, Nos.
122, 234, 350, 611, 622
Supermarine Spitfire F.B.5b, No.
126
Supermarine Spitfire F.5c, Nos. 33,
72, 73, 80, 81, 87, 91, 92, 93,
94, 111, 121, 122, 127, 136,
145, 152, 185, 229, 232, 249,
253, 274, 288, 289, 302, 310,
316, 332, 340, 402, 412, 417,
451, 452, 453, 457, 485, 521,
601, 603, 607, 609, 611, 615
Supermarine Spitfire F.B.5c, No.
126
Supermarine Spitfire L.F.5c, No.
350
Supermarine Spitfire F.6, Nos. 124,
401, 521, 602
Supermarine Spitfire H.F.6, Nos.
118, 616
Supermarine Spitfire F.7, No. 616
Supermarine Spitfire H.F.7, Nos.
32, 92, 124, 131, 133, 152, 212,
401, 485, 519, 602, 615
Supermarine Spitfire F.8, Nos. 11,
17, 20, 28, 43, 54, 67, 81, 87, 92,
131, 132, 134, 138, *145, 152,
155, 185, 213, 241, 253, 352,
417, 602, 607, 615
Supermarine Spitfire F.9, Nos. 1, 6,
19, 33, 43, 54, 56, 64, 65, 66,
73, 74, 80, 81, 87, 92, 93, 94,
111, 127, 132, 145, 154, 164,
165, 185, 213, 222, 225, 229,
232, 237, 238, 241, 242, 249,
253, 273, 274, 283, 303, 306,
308, 315, 316, 317, 318, 322,
326, 327, 331, 341, 345, 349,
350, 401, 402, 403, 412, 416,
417, 421, 435, 441, 451, 453,

501, 521, 548, 549, 567, 595,
601, 602, 609, 610, 616
Supermarine Spitfire F.B.9, No.
126
Supermarine Spitfire F.9a, No. 421
Supermarine Spitfire F.9b, Nos.
122, 132, 313, 345, 401, 402,
403, 411, 412, 416, 421, 441,
442, 443, 452, 485
Supermarine Spitfire F.9c, Nos. 1,
6, 32, 33, 64, 73, 87, 118, 124,
129, 131, 132, 133, 134, 165,
222, 274, 288, 310, 312, 313,
328, 329, 331, 332, 340, 341,
349, 350, 451, 452, 453, 457,
485, 504, 601, 602, 611
Supermarine Spitfire F.9e, Nos. 1,
124, 126, 130, 132, 234, 241,
331, 411, 412, 441, 442
Supermarine Spitfire F.B.9e, Nos.
72, 185, 234
Supermarine Spitfire H.F.9, No. 441
Supermarine Spitfire F.B.9, No. 601
Supermarine Spitfire F.B.9c, No.
208
Supermarine Spitfire T.T.9, Nos. 5,
595
Supermarine Spitfire P.R.11, Nos.
2, 4, 16, 26, 69, 140, 256, 400,
541, 542, 543, 544, 680, 681,
682, 683, 684
Supermarine Spitfire F.12, Nos. 41,
400, 414, 430, 595
Supermarine Spitfire P.R.13, No. 4
Supermarine Spitfire F.R.14, Nos.
2, 11, 16, 17, 20, 28, 41, 60, 65,
91, 129, 130, 132, 136, 152, 229,
322, 349, 350, 402, 411, 412,
430, 443, 453, 600, 602, 607,
*610, 613, 683, 691

Supermarine Spitfire F.R.14e, Nos.
26, 268, 401, 414, 416, 451,
607, 610, 611, 612
Supermarine Spitfire F.16, No. 421
Supermarine Spitfire F.16e, No. 130
Supermarine Spitfire L.F.16e, Nos.
5, 17, 19, 20, 34, 41, 63, 65, 66,
93, 122, 124, 127, 129, 130,
164, 165, 208, 234, 286, 287,
288, 290, 302, 308, 310, 316,
317, 322, 329, 340, 341, 345,
349, 350, 401, 402, 403, 411,
412, 416, 421, 443, 485, 501,
567, 577, 587, 595, 601, 602,
604, 607, 608, 609, 612, 631,
667, 691, 695
Supermarine Spitfire F.R.18, Nos.
11, 28, 32, 60, 81, 208, 691
Supermarine Spitfire P.R.19, Nos.
2, 4, 16, 34, 81, 82, 541, 542,
681, 684
Supermarine Spitfire F.21, Nos. 1,
41, 73, 91, 122, 600, 601, 602,
603, 607, 609, 610, 612, 613, 615
Supermarine Spitfire F.22, Nos. 19,
73, 502, 504, 600, 602, 607, 608,
610, 611, 613, 614, 615
Supermarine Spitfire F.24, No. 80
Supermarine Sea Otter A.S.R.2,
Nos. 230, 276, 278, 281, 282,
292
Supermarine Swift F.1, No. 56
Supermarine Swift F.2, No. 56
Supermarine Swift F.R.5, Nos. *2,
79

Taylorcraft D, No. 654

Vickers Bullet D, Nos. 11, 17, 47,
50, 111

Vickers F.B.5 Gunbus, Nos, 4, 5, 7,
*11, 18, 24, 35, 201, 203, 204
Vickers F.B.9 Gunbus, Nos. 2, 5, 7,
*11, 15, 16, 18
Vickers F.B.26 Vampire, No. 141
Vickers Vimy, Nos. 7, 9, 45, *58,
70, 100, 216, 274, 502
Vickers Virginia X, Nos. *7, 9, 10,
58, 214, 215, 500, 502, 503
Vickers Vespa, No. 4
Vickers Vernon, Nos. *45, 70
Vickers Victoria, Nos. 45, *70, 216
Vickers Vildebeest 1, Nos. 36, 42,
*100
Vickers Vildebeest 2, Nos. 22, 100
Vickers Vildebeest 3, Nos. 22, 36,
42, 100
Vickers Vildebeest 4, Nos. 22, 36,
*42, 273
Vickers Vincent 1, Nos. 5, *8, 31,
45, 47, 55, 84, 207, 223, 244
Vickers Valentia 1, Nos. 31, *70,
216, 244
Vickers Wellesley 1, Nos. 7, 14, 35,
45, 47, *76, 77, 148, 207, 211, 223
Vickers Wellesley 2, No. 14, 45, 47,
223
Vickers Wellington A.S.R.1, No. 280
Vickers Wellington B.1, Nos. 108,
138, 149, 311
Vickers Wellington B.1a, Nos. 7, 38,
99, 104, 149, 311
Vickers Wellington B.1c, Nos. *9,
15, 24, 35, 37, 38, 40, 57, 69,
70, 75, 93, 97, 99, 101, 103, 104,
108, 109, 115, 142, 148, 149,
150, 156, 158, 161, 162, 211,
214 215, 218, 232, 244, 294,
300, 301, 304, 305, 311, 405,
419, 458, 460, 567, 612

Vickers Wellington B.2, Nos. 12, 15, 36, 38, 40, 99, 104, 108, 115, 148, 214, 305, 405

Vickers Wellington B.3, Nos. 9, 12, 37, 40, 57, 70, 75, 100, 101, 103, 104, 108, 109, 115, 142, 148, 149, 150, 161, 162, 166, 192, 196, 199, 214, 215, 300, 301, 304, 305, 355, 419, 420, 424, 425, 426, 427, 428, 429, 431, 466, 467, 527, 614

Vickers Wellington B.4, Nos. 300, 301, 305, 460

Vickers Wellington B.5, No. 612

Vickers Wellington B.6a, No. 109

Vickers Wellington G.R.8, Nos. 172, 179, 203, 221, 407, 458, 544

Vickers Wellington B.10, Nos. 37, 69, 70, 109, 150, 162, 166, 192, 215, 300, 304, 305, 407, 420, 424, 425, 426, 427, 428, 429, 431, 432, 466, 467, 625

Vickers Wellington B.10/Type 423, Nos. 419, 424, 425

Vickers Wellington G.T.10, No. 299

Vickers Wellington G.R.11, Nos. 172, 203, 326, 407, 547

Vickers Wellington G.R.12, Nos. 36, 172, 304, 415, 621

Vickers Wellington G.R.13, Nos. 8, 38, 69, 172, 179, 203, 221, 304, 415, 458, 524, 621

Vickers Wellington G.R.14, Nos. 8, 14, 36, 38, 172, 179, 304, 407, 458, 524, 612

Vickers Wellington C.15, Nos. 24, 232, 304

Vickers Wellington C.16, Nos. 14, 232, 242

Vickers Wellington G.R.18, No. 172

Vickers Warwick 1, Nos. 38, 269, 275, 276, 277, 278, 279, *280, 281, 282, 283, 284, 292, 294, 301, 304, 525

Vickers Warwick C.1, No. 301

Vickers Warwick T.1, No. 167

Vickers Warwick G.R.2, No. 293

Vickers Warwick 3, Nos. 163, 167, 293, 301, 304, 525

Vickers Warwick G.R.5, No. 179

Vickers Warwick A.S.R.5, No. 621

Vickers Valetta C.1, Nos. 24, 30, 48, 52, 70, 78, 84, 110, 114, 167, 204, 215, 216, 233, 622

Vickers Varsity T.1, Nos. 115, 116, 173, 187

Vickers Valiant B.1, Nos. 7, 49, 90, *138, 148, 199, 207, 214

Vickers Valiant B.(K.)1, No. 18

Vickers Valiant B.(P.R.)1, No. 543

Vickers VC-10, No. 10

Voisin Biplane, Nos. 4, 5, 6, 7, 16, 30, 201

Vought-Sikorsky Hoverfly 1, Nos. 529, 657

Vultee Vengeance 1, Nos. 27, 45, 62, 82, 84, 110

Vultee Vengeance T.T.2/2, Nos. 288, 289, 567, 577, 595, 667

Vultee Vengeance T.T.4, Nos. 288, 567, 577, 587, 595, 631, 667, 691, 695

Waco Hadrian, Nos. 668, 669, 670, 671, 672, 673

Westland Walrus, No. 3

Westland Wapiti 2a, Nos. 5, 11, 20, 24, 27, 28, 30, 31, 39, 55, 60, *84, 501, 502, 600, 601, 602, 603, 604, 605, 607, 608

APPENDIX II

Aircraft Specifications

A list of Air Ministry specifications issued to the Industry, showing the number, year, requirement and the aircraft built and projected to each. As an example, F29/27 indicates the 29th specification of the year 1927, the requirement being for a single-seater fighter equipped with the Coventry Ordnance Works gun, to which both Westland and Vickers built aircraft and Bristol submitted a projected machine.

A1A	S/S Fighter	Austin A.F.T.3 Osprey
N1A	S/S Fighter	Mann Egerton H.1 and H.2
N1B	S/S Fighter	Supermarine Baby, Blackburn N.1B, Westland N.1B
N2A	Floatplane	Fairey 3
N2B	Floatplane	Fairey 3B
Type 1	S/S Fighter	Sopwith Snail, Sopwith Snark, Sopwith Snapper, A.W. Ara, Nieuport Nighthawk, B.A.T. F.K.25 Basilisk, Westland Wagtail
Type 7	S/R Night Bomber	Vickers Vimy
Type 21	Fleet Fighter	Fairey Pintail 1, Bristol 35 project
D of R3	Recce.	Bristol 69, D.H.41 projects
D of R3A	Recce.	Bristol 70, D.H.35 projects
D of R12	Torpedo Carrier	D.H.28 project
2/20	Bomber	Avro Aldershot, D.H.27 Derby, Bristol 55 project
3/20	Torpedo Bomber Recce.	H.P.19 Hanley, Blackburn Dart
5/20	Troop Transport	Vickers Victoria, Bristol 56 project
11/20	Postal Biplane	B. & P. Bodmin
1/21	Night Bomber	Vickers Virginia
3/21	Fleet Spotter	Avro Bison, Bristol 68 project

5/21 Day Bomber	Fairey Fawn
9/21 Torpedo Landplane	Specification to 32/22
16/21 Transport	H.P.18, W.8B
18/21 Transport	D.H.24, D.H.32 projects
19/21 2-seater Fighter	Short Springbok 1
6/22 S/S F.A.A. Fighter	Fairey Flycatcher, Parnall Plover
7/22 Corps Recce.	Hawker Duiker
16/22 Coastal Defence Torpedo Bomber	D.H. 36, Avro 556 projects
21/22 Flying-boat	Supermarine Swan
22/22 2-seater Fighter	D.H.42 Dormouse, Vickers 91 Venture 1, Bristol 52 Bullfinch
25/22 S/S Night Fighter	Hawker Woodcock
30/22 M/R Day Bomber	B. & P. Bugle
31/22 Bomber	H.P.24 Hyderabad
32/22 Torpedo Landplane	Blackburn Dart 2 production
33/22 Fleet Spotter	Avro Bison modification
35/22 S/S Fighter	Gloster Mars 6
37/22 Fleet Recce.	Fairey Ferret 1, 2 and 3
38/22 G.P. Recce.	Fairey 3d
40/22 Civil Transport	H.P.29, D.H.54, Avro 550 project
41/22 Civil Transport	H.P.27 Hampstead
44/22 Long-range Recce.	Fairey Freemantle
11/23 Fleet Spotter	Blackburn Blackburn
16/23 Fleet Spotter	Avro Bison production
20/23 Day Bomber	Fairey Fawn 2 and 3 production
21/23 Torpedo Bomber	H.P.31 Harrow, Blackburn Ripon
24/23 S/S F.A.A. Fighter	Fairey Firefly 1
25/23 Torpedo Bomber	H.P.25 Hendon
26/23 Day Bomber	H.P.28 Handcross, Bristol Berkeley, Westland Yeovil, Hawker Horsley
28/23 Night Bomber	Vickers Virginia production
37/23 S/S Fighter	Gloster Gamecock prototype, Gloster Gloster 2

44/23	S/S Communication	D.H.53 Humming Bird
1/24	F.A.A. Fighter/Recce.	Parnall Pike, Short S.6 Sturgeon
2/24	Twin-engine Fighter	Bristol Bagshot
F4/24	C.O.W. Gun Fighter	Bristol Bagshot, Westland Westbury
5/24	Deck-landing Trainer	Vickers Vendace, Parnall Perch, Blackburn Sprat
6/24	Fleet Spotter Recce.	Supermarine Seagull 5
8/24	Army Co-operation	D.H.42A Dingo 1, Bristol Boarhound, Short Springbok 2
9/24	Day Bomber	B. & P. Sidestrand
R12/24	L/R Marine Recce.	Short Singapore 1
R14/24	M/R Marine Recce.	Blackburn Iris 1
15/24	M/R Night Bomber	H.P.24 Hyderabad Mk. 1 production
16/24	Submarine-borne Recce.	Parnall Peto
R18/24	Marine Recce.	Supermarine Southampton 1
19/24	Fleet Recce.	Fairey 3f prototype
20/24	L/R F/Bt.	Beardmore Inverness
23/24	Transport	H.P.32 Hamlet
27/24	S/S/ Fighter	B. & P. Bittern
A30/24	Army Co-operation	Short S.3b Chamois
31/24	Recce. Amphibian	Supermarine Seamew
34/24	Transport	Vickers 134 Vellore 1
1/25	Day Bomber	Fairey Fawn 3 with supercharged Lion
16/25	S/S Metal Fighter	Gloster Goldfinch
17/25	S/S Fleet Fighter	Avro Avocet, Vickers Vireo
18/25	S/S Fighter	Gloster Gamecock production
20/25	Army Co-operation	A.W. Ajax, A.W. Aries
21/25	Day Bomber	Fairey Fox 1 production
22/25	Day Bomber	Hawker Horsley
23/25	Day Bomber Recce.	H.P.34 Hare, Hawker Harrier, Westland Witch, Blackburn Beagle
24/25	Torpedo Bomber	Hawker Horsley, Hawker Harrier, Blackburn Beagle

5/26 High-speed Racing Float-plane	Gloster 4
S6/26 High-speed Racing Float-plane	Supermarine S.5
7/26 High-speed Racing Float-plane	Short-Bristow Crusader
F9/26 S/S Fighter	Gloster S.S.18, Hawker Haw-finch, B. & P. Partridge, A.W.16, Bristol 105 Bull-dog, A.W. Starling 1 and 2
12/26 Day Bomber	Hawker Hart, Avro Antelope, Fairey Fox 2
R14/26 Transport	Short Calcutta
N21/26 Naval Fighter	Parnall Pipit, Gloster Gnat-snapper 1, Hawker Hoopoe, Vickers 141, Fairey Fly-catcher 2, A.W.16
O22/26 Fleet Fighter Recce.	Blackburn Nautilus, Short Gurnard, Fairey Fleetwing, Hawker Osprey, H.P.37 pro-ject, Hawker Hart project
31/26 Gyro Boat-Seaplane	Short/Cierva C.14 project
33/26 Army Co-op.	A.W. Atlas, D.H.56 Hyena, Bristol Boarhound, Vickers Vespa
36/26 G.P. Recce.	Fairey 3f Mk. 4
37/26 General Purpose	Vickers Vivid, Fairey 3f de-velopment
R1/27 L/R Maritime Recce.	Supermarine Southampton 2
1/27 Day Bomber Reconditioning	Fairey Fox 1A
2/27 Day Bomber	Hawker Horsley
R5/27 Maritime Recce. F/Bt.	Blackburn Sydney
F10/27 S/S Fighter	Gloster S.S.19A and S.S.19B, Saunders-Roe A-10
11/27 Day Bomber	Fairey Fox 1a production
M17/27 Torpedo Spotter Recce. Landplane	Hawker Horsley
B19/27 Heavy Bomber	Fairey Hendon, H.P. Heyford, Vickers B19/27, Bristol 108 project, Hawker project,

C20/27 Transport
F20/27 Interceptor Fighter

F20/27a Fighter
21/27 L/R Civil Transport
B22/27 Night Bomber
26/27 General Purpose

27/27 Floatplane
F29/27 S/S Fighter with C.O.W.
       Gun

R32/27 L/R Maritime Recce.
M5/28 Torpedo Bomber

R6/28 L/R Maritime Recce.
9/28 High-speed Racing Float-
     plane
10/28 Recce. F/Bt. Dev't.
15/28 Aerodynamic Test-bed
C16/28 Troop Transport

21/28 Mailplane
1/29 General Purpose
2/29 General Purpose
6/29 Biplane/Monoplane tests

9/29 Day Bomber
12/29 Fleet T/S/Recce.
13/29 Night Bomber

H.P. 33 project, Avro pro-
ject, Vickers 150, 195, 225
H.P.35 Chitral/Clive
Bristol Bullpup, Westland
F20/27, Hawker Hornet,
Fairey Firefly 2M, D.H.77,
A.W.16, Gloster S.S.19B,
Vickers 151 Jockey, Vickers
177, Westland Wizard 1 and
2, Vickers 156 and 157
projects, Bristol 112 project,
Hawker F20/27
Blackburn Blackcock
Short Valetta
D.H.72, B. & P. P.32
Westland Wapiti on floats—to
Spec. 1/29
Fairey 3f 4M
Westland C.O.W. Gun,
Vickers 161, Bristol 112
project
Short Singapore 2
H.P.41 project, Hawker pro-
ject
Short Sarafand
Gloster 6

Supermarine Southampton
Parnall Parasol
H.P.43, Gloster Troop Carrier
T.C.33, Bristol 115 and 116
projects
Gloster project
From 26/27
Blackburn Ripon 2
Blackburn Biplane and Mono-
plane
Hawker Hart 1 production
Fairey Seal
H.P.36 Hinaidi

17/29 Fleet T/S/Recce.	Fairey Seal production
17/29 Torpedo Bomber	All-metal development of Hawker Horsley
R18/29 F/Bt. Dev't.	Short Rangoon 3
M1/30 Fleet Torpedo Bomber	Blackburn B.3, H.P.46, Vickers 207, Vickers Vildebeest, Avro project
M1/30a Fleet Torpedo Bomber	Blackburn B.3 development
M2/30 Fleet Torpedo Bomber	Blackburn project
3/30 Trainer	Avro 621
4/30 Recce. F/Bt. Dev't.	Supermarine Southampton— metal hull
5/30 Mailplane	Vickers 166 Vellore 2
T6/30 Trainer	Avro 504n production
F7/30 S/S Fighter	Gloster Gladiator, Supermarine 224, Bristol 123 and 133, Westland P.V.4, Hawker P.V.3, Blackburn F7/30, Vickers 171 Jockey, Bristol 127, 128 and 129 projects, A.W.35 project, Hawker High-speed Fury
8/30 Communication	D.H.60 Moth
S9/30 Fleet T/S/Recce.	Hawker project, Fairey S9/30, Vickers 218, Gloster T.S.R.38, Gloster F.S.36 project, Avro 632 project
R10/30 Flying-boat	Short Sarafand
C11/30 Civil Transport for India	A.W.15 Atalanta, Avro 642/ 4M
12/30 General Purpose for India	Westland Wapiti
13/30 Interceptor Fighter	Hawker Fury 1 production
14/30 Long-distance	Fairey Long-range Monoplane—second
15/30 Day/Night Fighter	Hawker Hart, Fairey Fox
16/30 F.A.A. Fighter Dev't.	Hawker Nimrod on floats, Gloster Gnatsnapper development
17/30 Aircraft Reconditioning	Fairey Fox 1A
18/30 General Purpose	Fairey Gordon production

19/30	Fleet Fighter Recce.	Hawker Osprey on floats
20/30	Day Bomber	Hawker Hart production
C29/30	G.P. Fighter Recce.	A.W. Siskin 3a for R.C.A.F.
1/31	S/S Fighter	Gloster Gladiator 2
2/31	Torpedo Bomber	Hawker Horsley 2—all-metal production
3/31	General Purpose	Fairey 3f Mk. 4b
G4/31	General Purpose	Bristol 120, Westland P.V.7, Blackburn B.7, Parnall G4/31, Vickers 246 and 253, Fairey F.1, Hawker P.V.4, H.P.47, A.W.19, Bristol 121, 122, 125 and 126 projects
5/31	Heavy Bomber	Vickers Virginia production
6/31	Bomber Transport	Vickers Victoria production
7/31	Army Co-op.	Hawker Audax
8/31	Army Co-op. Dual Control	A.W. Atlas Trainer production
9/31	G.P. Bomber	Hawker Hart for India
10/31	F.A.A. General Purpose	Fairey 3f production
11/31	S/S Fighter	Bristol Bulldog 2a stainless-steel test
12/31	High-altitude Aircraft	—
13/31	General Purpose	Blackburn Ripon 2 production
14/31	Recce. F/Bt.	Supermarine Southampton 2 production
T15/31	Trainer	D.H.60 Moth Mk. 2
16/31	G.P. Army Co-op.	Westland Wapiti 2a production
17/31	Trainer	Westland Wapiti 4 Dual-Control
18/31	Trainer	Avro 621 Tutor
R19/31	F/Bt. Dev't.	Short Rangoon—fourth and subsequent
R20/31	Recce.F/Bt.	Supermarine Scapa
21/31	G.P. Trainer	Fairey 3f
22/31	Torpedo Bomber	Vickers Vildebeest
23/31	Trainer	D.H.82 Tiger Moth production
R24/31	G.P. Recce. F/Bt.	Short S.18 Knuckleduster, Supermarine 227, 230, 235, 237, Saro London A.27

25/31	Day Bomber	Hawker Hart
C26/31	Bomber Transport	Bristol 130 Bombay, H.P.51, Vickers 231, A.W.23
2/32	Conversion	Avro 10 with all-metal wings by Armstrong-Whitworth
6/32	2-seater Fighter	Hawker Demon
8/32	Trainer	Hawker Hart Trainer
B9/32	Medium Bomber	Vickers Wellington, H.P. Hampden, Bristol 131 project
S11/32	Fleet Spotter Seaplane	Fairey Seafox
T12/32	Fighter Trainer	Bristol 124 Bulldog Trainer
13/32	Interceptor Fighter Dev't.	Hawker Fury 1
F14/32	H/S Interceptor Fighter	Hawker High-Speed Fury
15/32	Amphibian Development	Saro A.19 Cloud
16/32	Army Co-op.	Hawker Audax production
17/32	Torpedo Spotter Recce.	Fairey Seal
18/32	Monospar Tests	Saro Cloud test-bed for Monospar
19/32	Conversion Set	Westland Wapiti to Wallace P.V.6
20/32	F/Bt. Dev't.	Blackburn Iris 5/Perth
21/32	Strength of Metal Structures Test Specimens	—
B23/32	Night Bomber	H.P. Heyford
24/32	Trainer Dev't.	Fairey Seal Trainer
25/32	Trainer	Avro 621b Tutor
26/32	Trainer	Avro 621b Sea Tutor on floats
P27/32	Day Bomber	Fairey Battle, A.W.29, Bristol 136 project, Hawker project
R1/33	2-seater Fighter	Westland Pterodactyl 5
R2/33	G.P. F/Bt.	Short Sunderland, Saro A.33, Supermarine 232, 239 and 310 projects
R3/33	G.P. F/Bt. Dev't.	Short Singapore 3—first four
4/33	Torpedo Bomber	Blackburn Ripon fitted with Pegasus
F5/33	2-seater Turret Fighter	Bristol 140 project, A.W.34 project
T6/33	Trainer	D.H.82 Tiger Moth on floats

7/33	General Purpose	Westland Wallace production
8/33	Day Bomber	Hawker Hart production
9/33	General Purpose	Westland Wallace production
10/33	Stainless-steel Dev't.	Hawker Osprey 3
11/33	Stainless-steel Dev't.	Hawker Nimrod 2
12/33	Day Bomber for India	Hawker Hart
13/33	Composite Aircraft	Short/Mayo Maia and Mercury
14/33	General Purpose	Fairey Gordon 2
S15/33	Torpedo Spotter Recce.	Gloster T.S.R.38—from S9/30, Fairey Swordfish T.S.R.2, Blackburn B–6
T17/33	Float Conversion Set	Avro Sea Tutor
18/33	Radio-control Target	D.H.82b Queen Bee Mk. 1
19/33	F/Bt. Recce. Dev't.	Supermarine Scapa
20/33	General Purpose	Vickers 267 Vildebeest 3 production
21/33	General Purpose Dev't.	Vickers 267 Vildebeest
F22/33	Twin-engine Turret Fighter	Bristol 141 project, A.W.33 project
G23/33	General Purpose	Hawker Hardy
24/33	S/S Interceptor Fighter	Gloster Gauntlet 1 production
25/33	Bomber Transport Dev't.	Vickers 260 Victoria 6
26/33	Trainer	D.H.82 Tiger Moth production
27/33	Long-range Monoplane	Fairey project with Junkers Jumo 4 engine
R28/33	G.P. F/Bt.	Project with four Napier Culverin engines
29/33	Day Bomber Dev't.	B. & P. Sidestrands converted to first four Overstrands
1/34	G.P. Fighter for R.A.A.F.	Hawker Demon
2/34	High-altitude Experimental	Bristol 138a
B3/34	Heavy Bomber	A.W.38 Whitley, H.P.54 Harrow, Bristol 144 project
P4/34	Light Day Bomber	Hawker Henley, Fairey P4/34
F5/34	S/S Fighter	Gloster G–38, Bristol 146, Martin-Baker M.B.2, Vickers 279 Venom, Hawker project

6/34	Amphibian Spotter for R.A.A.F.	Supermarine Seagull 5
G7/34	Day Bomber	Hawker Hind
8/34	Fighter Development	Hawker Demon 2 production
9/34	General Purpose	Hawker Audax
10/34	Communication Conversion	Hawker Hart (C)
11/34	G.P. Torpedo Bomber Recce.	Fairey Seal production
12/34	Torpedo Spotter Recce.	Blackburn B.6 Shark
13/34	Fighter Trainer Conversion	Bristol Bulldog
R14/34	F/Bt. Dev't.	Short S.19 Singapore 3—fifth and subsequent
15/34	General Purpose	Vickers 267 Vildebeest 3 production
16/34	General Purpose	Vickers Vincent production
17/34	T.S.R. Dev't.	Blackburn B.5 Baffin
18/34	Day Bomber	Hawker Hart
19/34	General Purpose for India	Hawker Audax
20/34	Heavy Bomber	Fairey Hendon 2 production
21/34	Fleet Recce. Dev't.	Hawker Osprey 4
22/34	General Purpose for S.A.A.F.	Hawker Hartbees
23/34	Medium Day Bomber	B.P. Overstrand 1
24/34	Trainer Dev't.	Avro 621b Tutor
25/34	Amphibian Dev't.	Saro A.19 Cloud—metal hull
26/34	Trainer	Avro 646 Sea Tutor on floats
O27/34	Fighter Dive Bomber	Blackburn Skua, Vickers 280 project, Boulton Paul project, Hawker project, Avro project
28/34	Medium Night Bomber	H.P. Heyford 2
F29/34	S/S Fighter for S.A.A.F.	Hawker Fury
30/34	Bomber Transport	Vickers Valentia production
31/34	Armoured Day Bomber	Hawker Hart
32/34	Trainer	Avro 626b Prefect
34/34	Army Co-op.	Hawker Audax production
F36/34	8-gun Interceptor	Hawker Hurricane
F37/34	8-gun Interceptor	Supermarine 300 Spitfire
S38/34	Torpedo Spotter Recce.	Fairey Swordfish T.S.R.2
A39/34	Army Co-op.	Westland Lysander, Bristol 148 and 148b, Hawker project

40/34	2-seater Fighter	Hawker Demon
B1/35	Heavy Bomber	Vickers Warwick 284, 400, 401, 411, 427, H.P.55 Halifax project with 2 Merlin, A.W. Whitley with A.S. Deerhound, Airspeed A.S.29 project, A.W. project
2/35	F.A.A. General Recce.	Supermarine 307 Seagull 5/ Walrus
R3/35	G.P. Recce. F/Bt.	Saro A.27 London 2
4/35	General Purpose	Hawker Hart modif'n, Hawker Hector initial production
5/35	2-seater Fighter	Hawker Demon 2 modif'n.
6/35	S/S Interceptor Fighter	Hawker Fury 2
T7/35	Trainer	D.H.82 Tiger Moth T.2 production
8/35	Trainer	Hawker Hart(T)
F9/35	2-seater Fighter	B.P. Defiant, Hawker Hotspur, Bristol 147 and 147a projects, A.W.30 project, Fairey project
10/35	S/S D/N Fighter	—
11/35	General Purpose	Hawker Hind G.P. production
R12/35	High-performance Boat-Seaplane	Supermarine 308 project
13/35	T/S/R Dev't.	Blackburn Shark 2´
14/35	S/S Fighter	Gloster Gladiator production
M15/35	Shore-based Torp. Bomber	Bristol 150, Avro 672 and 675—to 10/36
16/35	Autogyro	Avro/Cierva C–30a Rota 1 production
17/35	Recce. F/Bt.	Supermarine Stranraer 2 production
G18/35	G.P. Coastal Recce	Avro 652a Anson prototype, D.H.89M
19/35	S/S Day Fighter	Hawker Fury 2 production
20/35	Radio-control Target	D.H. Queen Bee Mk. 1 production

L

B21/35	Medium Night Bomber	A.W.38 Whitley 2
22/35	L/R G.P. Bomber	Vickers Wellesley 1
P23/35	Light Day Bomber	Fairey Battle production
G24/35	General Recce. Bomber	Bristol Bolingbroke, Avro 672 and 675—to 10/36
25/35	Army Co-op. for India	Hawker Audax 1
26/35	Fleet Spotter Recce.	Hawker Osprey 4 production
27/35	Night Bomber	H.P. Heyford 3 production
B28/35	Medium Bomber Dev't.	Bristol Blenheim 1
B29/35	Heavy Bomber Dev't.	H.P.54 Harrow 2
O30/35	F.A.A. Turret Fighter	Blackburn Roc, B.P. Defiant project
G31/35	General Purpose	Westland Wallace 2
Q32/35	R/C Target Alternatives	Percival Gull-Six P.8 project, Airspeed AS.30 Queen Wasp
33/35	General Recce. for S.A.A.F.	Avro 652a Anson
F34/35	Twin-engine Fighter	Gloster project—became F9/37
F35/35	S/S High-speed Fighter	Bristol 151, G.A.L.28, Airspeed A.S.31, Hawker—all projects
36/35	Medium-range Mailplane	D.H. Albatross project
F37/35	S/S D/N Fighter	Westland Whirlwind, Bristol 153 and 153A projects, Supermarine 313 project, Hawker project
38/35	Special G.P. Defence	Airspeed A.S.27 project
39/35	Communication for S.A.A.F.	Airspeed Convertible Envoy
40/35	Floatplane Dev't.	Fairey Seafox
41/35	General Purpose	Vickers Vildebeest 4 production
R1/36	G.P. F/Bt.	Saro Lerwick, Blackburn B.20, Supermarine 314 project
2/36	Autogyro Dev't.	Avro/Cierva C–30a Rota 2 production
3/36	G.P. Trainer	Avro 652a Anson G.R.2 project
B4/36	Catapulted Heavy Bomber	Short Stirling project
5/36	G.P. Spotter Recce. Dev't.	Supermarine Walrus

T6/36 Single-engine Trainer   Miles Master—originally P.V., D.H.93 Don

M7/36 Torpedo Spotter Recce.   Fairey Albacore layout project

O8/36 Dive Bomber Recce.   Fairey project

S9/36 3-seater Spotter Recce.   Fairey project, Short project

10/36 General Recce. Torp. Bomber   Bristol Beaufort production by Blackburn, Blackburn Botha —from M15/35 and G24/35

11/36 Interim G.P.   Bristol 149 Bolingbroke

B12/36 Heavy Bomber   Short Stirling, Supermarine 316, 317 and 318 projects, projects by H.P., Avro, Hawker, A.W. and Bristol

P13/36 Heavy Bomber   H.P. Halifax H.P.56/57, Avro 679 Manchester, Short Stirling project, Hawker and Bristol projects

14/36 Light Day Bomber   Fairey Battle production

15/36 8-gun Fighter   Hawker Hurricane 1 production

F16/36 8-gun Fighter   Supermarine Spitfire 1 production

17/36 Turret Fighter   Production of Hawker Hotspur 1 by Avro project

18/36 2-seater Fighter   —

S19/36 Torpedo Spotter Recce.   Blackburn Shark 3

20/36 Medium Bomber   A.W. Whitley 3 production

21/36 G.P. Recce. F/Bt.   Development of Saro A.33 to R2/33 project

R22/36 G.P. Recce. F/Bt.   Short Sunderland production

T23/36 Twin-engine Trainer   Airspeed A.S.10 Oxford

24/36 Communication/Trainer   Miles Nighthawk and Mentor production

25/36 F.A.A. Dive Bomber   Blackburn Skua production

26/36 F.A.A. Fighter Dev't.   Blackburn Roc on floats

27/36 G.P. F/Bt.   Saro London 2 production

28/36 Dive Bomber Fighter Dev't.   Hawker Henley project

29/36 Medium Bomber   Vickers Wellington 1 production

B30/36 Medium Bomber	H.P. Hampden production
31/36 General Purpose	Hawker Hind 1
32/36 Light Day Bomber	Fairey Battle built by Austin
33/36 Medium Day Bomber	Bristol Blenheim 1 built by Rootes
34/36 Interim General Purpose	Bristol Bolingbroke redesign and production of Spec. 11/36
R35/36 L/R F/Bt.	Short S.27 Catapulted F/Bt. project
A36/36 G.P. Army Co-op.	Westland Lysander 1, 3 and 3a production
37/36 F.A.A. Spotter Recce.	Supermarine Walrus 1 production
38/36 G.P. Troop Transport	Redesign of Bristol Bombay 1
39/36 G.P. General Recce.	Blackburn Botha—B.P.-built project
T40/36 Trainer	Miles M.14 Magister 1 production
S41/36 Torpedo Spotter Recce.	Fairey Albacore
42/36 General Purpose	Hawker Henley production by Gloster
43/36 F.A.A. Gyroplane	—
B44/36 Medium Bomber	H.P. Hereford 1 production by Short
45/36 G.P. General Recce.	Blackburn Botha production project
46/36 Army Co-op.	Hawker Hind and Demon for R.A.A.F.
47/36 Bomber Troop Transport	Bristol Bombay by Short and Harland
T1/37 2-seater Trainer	Heston, Miles M.15, Parnall 382, 'Percival P.20 project, G.A.L.32a and 32b projects, Airspeed A.S.36 project
2/37 Medium Day Bomber	Bristol Blenheim 1L by Avro and Rootes
T3/37 Link Trainer	—
4/37 G.P. Recce. F/Bt.	Saro London 2 production project

F5/37	2-seater Turret Fighter	B.P. Defiant production
6/37	V.I.P. Transport	Airspeed Royal Envoy 3
T7/37	Communication	Percival P.22, P.23, P.23a and P.23b projects, G.A.L.36 project, Airspeed A.S.38 project, Heston J.A.4 project
Q8/37	High-speed F.A.A. Target	Percival P.21 and P.21a projects, G.A.L.35 project, Airspeed A.S.37 project
F9/37	Twin-engine D/N Fighter	Gloster G–39 and G–39a, Bristol Beaufighter project
10/37	Medium Bomber	Bristol Bolingbroke project—Australia
F11/37	Twin-engine D/N Fighter	Boulton Paul P.92/2 project, Bristol Beaufort fighter project—later Spec. F17/39, Supermarine 319 project, Short project, A.W. project, Hawker project
12/37	Fighter Conversion	Turret conversion of Hawker Demon
13/37	Day Bomber Conversion	Hawker Hind
14/37	Transport	Bristol 143
O15/37	F.A.A. Turret Fighter	Blackburn Roc production
16/37	Communication	Avro 652a Anson production
B17/37	Bomber	Specification became B19/38
F18/37	S/S Fighter	Hawker Tornado, Hawker Typhoon, Supermarine 324 and 325 projects
19/37	Heavy Bomber	Avro Manchester production
20/37	Float Conversion Set	Blackburn Roc production conversion
A21/37	Army Co-op.	—
22/37 (Pt. 1)	Experimental Method of Reinforced Synthetic Spar Construction	—
22/37 (Pt. 2)	Floats for Blackburn Roc Conversion Tests	—

S23/37	F.A.A. Observation	G.A.L.38 Fleet Shadower, Airspeed A.S.39 Fleet Shadower, Percival P.25 project
S24/37	Torpedo Bomber Recce.	Supermarine 322 Dumbo, Fairey Barracuda, Supermarine 380 project, Westland P.11 project, Hawker project, Blackburn B.29 project
B25/37	Heavy Bomber	—
P26/37	High Altitude Med. Bomber	—
27/37	Trainer	Hawker Hind Conversion
28/37	Radio Trainer	D.H.86b
S29/37	Autogyro	Hafner Gyroplane
S30/37	Torpedo Bomber Recce.	G.A.L.39a and 39b projects, Short project
31/37	Torpedo Bomber Recce.	Blackburn Shark 3—Canadian production
32/37	Heavy Bomber	H.P. Halifax production
33/37	Medium Bomber	Vickers Wellington production by Gloster
34/37	General Recce.	Avro 652a Anson production
35/37	G.P. Recce. F/Bt.	Saro London 1 conversion to Mk. 2
F36/37	S/S Fighter	Gloster Gladiator 2 production
T37/37	Trainer	Miles Magister 1 production
T38/37	Communication/Trainer	Miles Mentor production
T39/37	Survey/Trainer	Airspeed Oxford for R.N.Z.A.F.
40/37	Survey	Airspeed Oxford for R.N.Z.A.F.
41/37	Experimental Laminated Wood Spar	—
42/37	Transport	Miles X project
43/37	Engine Flying Test-bed	Folland Test-beds, Percival P.26 and P.26a projects, G.A.L.43a and 43b projects
A1/38	Army Co-op.	Specification to A7/39
F2/38	2-seater Fighter	Specification to F26/39

R3/38	Medium-range F/Bt.	Supermarine 238 project—specification to R5/39
T4/38	Twin-engine Trainer	—
N5/38	2-seater F.A.A. Fighter	Specification to N8/39
N6/38	2-seater F.A.A. Fighter	Specification to N9/39
S7/38	3-seater F.A.A. Amphibian	Supermarine Sea Otter—specification to S14/39
O8/38	2-seater F.A.A. Fighter	Fairey Fulmar
P9/38	Medium Bomber	A.W. project—specification to 17/38 and 18/38
S10/38	F.A.A. Amphibian	—
B11/38	Flying-boat	—
Q12/38	Radio-control Target	—
13/38	Rail-launching Scheme	—
14/38	Transatlantic Civil Land-plane	Short S.32a and S.32b projects, Miles M.26 project, Folland project
15/38	Medium-range Civil Land-plane	G.A.L.40a and 40b, Folland, Fairey F.C.1—all projects
T16/38	Trainer	Miles M.9 Kestrel P.V. production
B17/38	Medium Bomber	Bristol 155 project—to B18/38
B18/38	Reconnaissance Bomber	A.W. Albemarle from Bristol 155, D.H. Flamingo bomber development
B19/38	Twin-engine Bomber	Bristol 157—specification to B1/19—from B17/37
20/38	Communication	Percival Proctor conversion from Vega Gull
21/38	Communication	D.H.89a Dominie conversion from Rapide
A22/38	Army Co-op. Rotorplane	Hafner A.R.4 project
23/38	Dummy Aircraft	Production by various manufacturers
24/38	Communication	Airspeed Colonial Envoy
25/38	Communication	Percival Petrel Q.6 Mk. 5
26/38	F.A.A. Communication	Percival Proctor 1 from Vega Gull 3
27/38	Wooden Wing for Experimental Fighter	Miles project

W28/38	Helicopter	Weir W.6
T29/38	Radio Trainer	D.H. Dominie for No. 2 Radio School
B1/39	Medium/Heavy Bomber	H.P.60a, Avro, Bristol 157 and 149, Vickers 405 and 415, Short S.34 and A.W.48—all projects
2/39	Armament Flying Test-bed	—
T3/39	Twin-engine Communication/Trainer	—
T4/39	Trainer	Airspeed A.S.45
R5/39	Medium-range F/Bt.	$\frac{1}{2}$-scale Saro A.37 Shrimp, Blackburn B.39 project, Saro A.38 project
F6/39	Fighter	Supermarine 334 project
A7/39	Army Co-operation	—
N8/39	F.A.A. Fighter	Fairey project, Hawker project
N9/39	F.A.A. Turret Fighter	Fairey project, Hawker project. Specifications to N5/40
A10/39	Autogyro	Hafner P.D.6 project
B11/39	Light Bomber	Specification to B7/40
G12/39	General Reconnaissance	—
T13/39	Communication	—
S14/39	Recce. Amphibian	Supermarine Sea Otter development — specification to S12/40
S15/39	Torpedo Bomber Recce.	Specification to E28/40
R16/39	Large High-altitude F/Bt.	—
F17/39	Heavy D/N Fighter	Bristol Beaufighter, for four P.V. aircraft
F18/39	S/S Fighter	Martin-Baker M.B.3 and M.B.5, M.B.4 project
19/39	Transport	D.H. Hertfordshire conversion from Flamingo
20/39	Transport Conversion	D.H. Flamingo for communications
21/39	Transport Conversion	D.H. Flamingo for King's Flight project
F22/39	Cannon Fighter	Vickers 414—specification to F16/40

B23/39	High-altitude Bomber	Vickers 407, 421 and 426 Wellington 5
S24/39	F.A.A. Spotter	—
T25/39	Army Communication	—
F26/39	Turret Fighter	—
B27/39	High-speed Bomber	—
E28/39	Experimental Jet Test-bed	Gloster/Whittle Pioneer G.40
B1/40	High-speed Recce. Bomber	D.H. Mosquito 1, Short project
2/40	High-speed Trainer	D.H. Mosquito 3 project
B3/40	Reconnaissance Bomber	Blackburn Botha, A.W. project, Avro project
F4/40	S/S High-altitude Fighter	Westland Welkin 1 revised to F7/41, Hawker P1004 project, G.A.L.46 project, Spitfire 3, 4 and 20
N5/40	2-seater Naval Fighter	Fairey Firefly — specification combination of N8/39 and N9/39
B6/40	Medium Day Bomber	Bristol Bisley 1 (Blenheim 5)
B7/40	Light High-speed Day Bomber	Bristol 161 Beaufighter development Beaumont project, Hawker Henley project, A.W.48 re-design project—from B11/39
8/40	Ambulance Conversion	Airspeed Oxford
F9/40	Experimental Twin-jet Test-bed	Gloster Meteor (Thunderbolt) G.41a
X10/40	Training Glider	G.A.L. Hotspur 1
N11/40	F.A.A. Torpedo Strike Fighter	Blackburn Firebrand, Hawker P1009 Sea Typhoon project
S12/40	G.P. Recce. Amphibian	Supermarine Sea Otter 1
R13/40	Flying-boat	Blackburn B.40 project
R14/40	Large G.P. Recce. F/Bt.	Short S.35 Shetland 1
15/40	Photo-recce.	Heston conversion of Supermarine Spitfire P.R.4
F16/40	High-altitude Cannon Fighter	Vickers 420—completed as 432 to F7/41
B17/40	High-altitude Bomber	Vickers Wellington production

F18/40	Night Fighter	Hawker P1008 project, Miles M.22a project
F19/40	S/S Day Fighter	Miles M.20 Mk. 1 P.V.
B20/40	Day Bomber Conversion	Bristol 162 project, Hawker Henley project as P1006
F21/40	High-speed High-altitude Fighter	D.H. Mosquito N.F.2
X22/40	Glider Dev't.	G.A.L. Hotspur 2 production —first twenty aircraft
23/40	Glider Dev't.	G.A.L. Hotspur 2—subsequent production
T24/40	Fighter Trainer	Airspeed A.S.50, A.S.49 project
X25/40	Troop Glider	Slingsby Hengist 1
X26/40	Troop Glider	Airspeed Horsa 1
X27/40	Tank-carrying Glider	G.A.L. Hamilcar 1
E28/40	F.A.A. Torpedo Bomber Recce.	Folland FO.116 project—from S15/39
F29/40	Night Fighter	Gloster project
N1/41	S/S F.A.A. Fighter	Miles M.20 Mk. 2
B2/41	High-speed Medium Day Bomber	Bristol Buckingham 1, Bristol Beaumont project
X3/41	Glider Bomber	Airspeed Horsa Bomber, Miles-Hooper project
F4/41	Photo-recce.	Supermarine Spitfire P.R.4
B5/41	High-altitude Bomber Dev't.	Vickers Warwick 3 with pressure cabin
E6/41	Jet Fighter Test-bed	D.H. Vampire 1 (Spidercrab)
F7/41	High-altitude Cannon Fighter	Vickers 432, Westland Welkin
B8/41	Heavy Bomber	Short S.36 project
T9/41	Communication/Trainer	Percival Proctor 4
F10/41	Fighter	Hawker Tempest 1
B11/41	Bomber	Miles M.39b ⅝-scale model, D.H.101 project, Hawker P1005 project
12/41	Target Tug	Miles Martinet
C1/42	Interim Transport	Avro York
N2/42	S/S Retractable-hull Fighter	Blackburn B.44 and B.46 projects

E5/42	Jet Fighter	Became Specification E1/44
E5/42	Glider	D.H.G.2 for R.A.A.F.
F6/42	Light Fighter	Folland, English Electric, Hawker Light Tempest and Westland projects
H7/42	D/N Torpedo Fighter	Bristol Brigand, Bristol Buccaneer project—from S7/42
R8/42	G.P. Recce. F/Bt.	Short Sunderland 4 (Seaford)
Q9/42	High-speed Target-tower	Miles Monitor
E10/42	Autogyro	Hafner Rotachute
E11/42	Autogyro	Hafner Rotabuggy
F1/43	S/S Fighter	Supermarine Spiteful 1
F2/43	S/S Fighter	Hawker Fury 1—from F6/42
TX3/43	S/S F.A.A. Fighter	G.A.L. 55, A.S.54 project
N4/43	S/S F.A.A. Fighter	Supermarine Seafire 15 and 17
O5/43	Torpedo Dive Bomber	Fairey Spearfish project
S6/43	Torpedo Bomber Recce.	Short Sturgeon 1, A.W.53 project, Westland project
N7/43	F.A.A. Fighter	Hawker P1022 Sea Fury 10 project to Spec. N22/43
S8/43	Torpedo Strike Fighter	Blackburn Firebrand 3 and 4
F9/43	High-altitude D/N Fighter	Westland Welkin N.F.2a
Q10/43	Radio Control Target	Miles Queen Martinet
S11/43	F.A.A. Recce.	Short S.A.1 Sturgeon P.R.1, Supermarine project, A.W. 54 project
F12/43	S/S Twin-engine Fighter	D.H. Hornet 1, P.V.
13/43	Heavy High-speed Trainer	Bristol Buckmaster
B14/43	Heavy Bomber	Avro Lincoln (Lancaster 4 and 5)
C15/43	Medium-range Civil Transport	H.P.68 Hermes
E16/43	Autogyro	Weir/Cierva W.9b
A17/43	Communication	Miles Messenger 1
C18/43	Long-range Transport	Short Stirling project
F19/43	Jet plus piston-engine Fighter	Folland project to be built by English Electric
TX20/43	Training Glider	Slingsby/Kirby Cadet
T21/43	Torpedo Trainer	Fairey Spearfish Trainer project

B3/42	Heavy Bomber	Vickers Windsor
B4/42	Medium Bomber	D.H.102 Mosquito Mk. 2 project
N22/43	S/S Fighter	Hawker Sea Fury 10 from F2/43
T23/43	Basic Trainer	Percival Prentice, Heston J.C.1 project, Miles M.53 project, D.H.105 project
E24/43	High-speed Research	Miles M.52 project
C25/43	European Transport	Airspeed Ambassador
C26/43	Light Civil Transport	D.H.104 Dove, Airspeed Ambassador project
B27/43	Heavy Bomber	H.P. Halifax 6
S28/43	Torpedo Strike Fighter	Blackburn YA–1 Firecrest
C29/43	Long-range Civil Transport	Avro Tudor 1
E1/44	S/S Jet Fighter	Gloster G.42 Ace—from E5/42
2/44	High-altitude Transport	Bristol Brabazon 1, Miles X-11 project, Short project
C3/44	Transport	H.P. Hastings production, H.P.73 project
X4/44	Powered Tank Transport	G.A.L. Hamilcar 10
N5/44	S/S F.A.A. Fighter	D.H. Sea Hornet 20
E6/44	Jet F/Bt. Fighter	Saro S.R.A.1
N7/44	S/S F.A.A. Fighter	Supermarine Seafire 46 and 47
PR8/44	Long-range Photo-recce.	Bristol Buckingham P.R. project
E9/44	Jet Mailplane	A.W.52
E10/44	Jet Fighter	Vickers Attacker 392 and 397
N11/44	Torpedo Strike Fighter	Westland Wyvern, G.A.L.56 project
12/44	Long-range Civil Transport	Avro Tudor 2, Supermarine project
F13/44	Long-range Escort Fighter	Westland Wyvern development for R.A.F.
S14/44	Air-sea Rescue Amphibian	Supermarine Seagull 381 and 530
N15/44	F.A.A. Fighter Recce.	D.H. Sea Mosquito T.R.33 and T.R.37
C16/44	Long-range Transport	Avro Lancastrian 2
17/44	Medium-range Transport	Vickers Viking 1b

18/44 Civil Transport — Miles Marathon 1, A.W. project, Percival P.41 and P.42 projects

19/44 Interim Transport B.O.A.C. — Avro York

20/44 High speed Mailplane — D.H.106 project

O21/44 Torpedo Spotter Recce. — Fairey project

22/44 Freighter — Bristol Freighter/Wayfarer 2 and 3a project

E1/45 F.A.A. Fighter — Supermarine Attacker conversion

A2/45 Air Observation Post — Auster A.O.P., Heston J.C.6, Miles project

B3/45 Jet Bomber — E.E. Canberra B.1

A4/45 Communication — Scottish Aviation Prestwick Pioneer, Miles M.66 project, G.A.L.58 project, Heston J.C.5 project, Folland project, Cunliffe-Owen project

N5/45 F.A.A. Fighter — Supermarine Seafang 31 and 32

6/45 Civil Transport — Avro 693/21 and A.W. projects

T7/45 Turbo-prop Trainer — Avro Athena 1, B.P. Balliol 1, Blackburn project

TX8/45 A.T.C. Training Glider — Slingsby/Kirby Cadet 20

C9/45 Freighter — Bristol Freighter (Military)

S10/45 F.A.A. Strike Recce. Bomber — Blackburn B.48

F11/45 F.A.A. Jet Fighter — D.H. Sea Vampire 10

N12/45 Torpedo Strike Fighter — Westland Wyvern T.F.2

C13/45 Military Freighter — Airspeed A.S.60 Ayrshire project

GR14/45 Maritime Recce. — Vickers project

C15/45 Transport — H.P.68, H.P.72 project

N16/45 Anti-submarine Turbo-prop — Fairey project

GR17/45 Anti-submarine Strike — Fairey Gannet, Blackburn YA–5 and YB–1, Westland project

E18/45 Tailles Jet Research — D.H.108 Swallow

Q19/45 Target-tower — D.H. Mosquito T.T.39 by G.A.L.

E20/45	Helicopter	Bristol Sycamore
N21/45	2-seater F.A.A. Fighter	D.H. Sea Hornet N.F.21
Q1/46	Target-tower	Short S.A.2 Sturgeon T.T.2
E2/46	Transport	Bristol Brabazon 2
3/46	Helicopter	G.A.L.60 project, Cierva W.12 project
E4/46	Gyrodyne	—
R5/46	Maritime Recce.	Avro Shackleton 1
N7/46	F.A.A. Fighter	Hawker Seahawk P.1040, Short S.41 S.A.3
8/46	Transport	Short S.43 S.A. 5
C9/46	Transport	Vickers Valetta
C10/46	F/Bt. Transport	Saro S.R.45 Princess
F11/46	S/S Fighter	Gloster Meteor 4
12/46	Civil Freighter	Bristol Wayfarer
C13/46	Transport	D.H. Devon C.1 conversion from Dove
B14/46	Heavy Bomber	Short Sperrin
C15/46	Transport	Miles Marathon 2
C16/46	Transport	A.W. Apollo
17/46	Torpedo Strike Fighter	Westland Wyvern T.F.1
18/46	Freighter	Bristol Freighter
E19/46	Helicopter	Cierva W.10 Workhorse
20/46	Trainer	Percival Prentice production
21/46	Trainer	Percival Prentice by Blackburn
22/46	Jet Transport	D.H.106 Comet
23/46	S/S Fighter	Production specification of E1/44
T24/46	Navigation Trainer, Overseas	Avro Anson T.20
T25/46	Navigation Trainer, Home	Avro Anson T.21
T26/46	Radio Trainer	Avro Anson T.22
E27/46	Research	B.P.111 and B.P.111A
E28/46	Transport for B.S.A.A.C.	Avro Tudor 4
29/46	Trainer	B.P. Balliol 2 production
X30/46	Glider	Folland, G.A.L., Scottish Aviation and Short S.48 S.A.9 projects
PR31/46	Photo-recce.	E.E. Canberra P.R.3
32/46	Civil Transport	H.P. Hermes 5

C33/46 Transport	H.P. Hermes 2
E34/46 Helicopter	Bristol Sycamore 2
B35/46 Jet Bomber	H.P. Victor, Avro Vulcan, Vickers Valiant and Short P.D.1
37/46 Transport	H.P. Hermes 4
E38/46 S/S Fighter	Hawker P.1052
39/46 Transport for B.S.A.A.C.	Avro Tudor 5, H.P. Hermes 5
N40/46 F.A.A. Fighter	D.H.110—specification to N14/49
E41/46 S/S Fighter	Supermarine 510 and 535
R42/46 Maritime Recce.	Avro Shackleton 1 production
F43/46 S/S Fighter	Hawker P.1054 project—to F3/48
F44/46 2-seater Fighter	D.H. 110, Gloster Javelin, E.E. Canberra B.8, Hawker project—to F4/48
45/46 F.A.A. Fighter	D.H. Sea Vampire by D.H.
46/46 F.A.A. Fighter	D.H. Sea Vampire by E.E.
T47/46 Advanced Trainer	Avro Athena 2 production
T1/47 Jet Trainer	Gloster Meteor T.7 P.V.
2/47 Transport—Empire	Bristol Britannia 1, Blackburn project, A.W.57 project, Avro project, H.P.83, 84, 85 and 86 projects
3/47 S/S Fighter	D.H. Vampire production
E4/47 Helicopter	Bristol 173
B5/47 Jet Bomber	E.E. Canberra B.2
A6/47 Helicopter	Bristol 171
A7/47 Gyrodyne	—
E8/47 H/S L/R Bomber Research	Bristol 174, ½ scale 172, 3/10 scale 172 as 176 to E8/47/2
N9/47 F.A.A. Fighter	Supermarine 508 and 529, Hawker P1063 project, Westland project
E10/47 High-speed research	Fairey F.D.1
T11/47 Jet Trainer	E.E. Canberra T.4
12/47 Transport	H.P. Marathon production
13/47 Meteorological Recce.	Vickers Valetta Met.

T14/47	Trainer	Avro Athena T.2, B.P. Balliol T.2
15/47	Transport	H.P. Marathon production
E16/47	Gyrodyne	Fairey Gyrodyne
N18/47	F.A.A. Fighter	—
N19/47	F.A.A. Trainer	Hawker Sea Fury T.20
E1/48	Helicopter	Bevan Jet Helicopter
R2/48	M/R Flying-boat	Saro project, Short P.D.2
F3/48	S/S Fighter	Hawker P1067 Hunter F.1 and F.2, Bristol 177
F4/48	2-seater Fighter	D.H.110, Gloster Javelin from Spec. 44/46
E6/48	Research	H.P.88
T8/48	Trainer	D.H. Chipmunk T.10 production
B9/48	Jet Bomber	Vickers Valiant B.1
E10/48	Helicopter	Cierva W.11T
S11/48	F.A.A. Helicopter	Westland Dragonfly S.51
T12/48	Torpedo Strike Fighter	Westland Wyvern — from N11/44
T13/48	Trainer	Vickers Varsity T.1
S14/48	F.A.A. Helicopter	Westland Dragonfly H.R.1
E15/48	Flying-scale Avro Vulcan Jet Bomber	⅓-scale Spec. B35/46—L/S 707 and 707B
T16/48	Trainer	Percival Provost T.1, H.P.R.2, B.P. project, Westland project
B22/48	Jet Bomber	E.E. Canberra B.5
23/48	Freighter	Avro Trader 1
F23/48	S/S Fighter	Hawker P.1082
F24/48	2-seater Night Fighter	Gloster Meteor N.F.11
25/48	F.A.A. Fighter	Hawker Seahawk F.1
T1/49	Trainer	Vickers Valetta T.3
T2/49	Jet Trainer	E.E. Canberra T.4
T3/49	Trainer	Avro Anson
M6/49	A.S.W. Patrol	Short S.B.3
A9/49	Helicopter	Bristol Sycamore H.C.11
E10/49	Flying-scale Avro Vulcan Jet Bomber	⅓-scale Spec. B35/46 H/S 707A
A13/49	Helicopter	Saro Skeeter

N14/49	F.A.A. Fighter	D.H.110 from N40/46
15/49	Fighter/Bomber	D.H. Venom F.B.1
T17/49	F.A.A. Trainer	Percival Sea Prince T.1
C18/49	F.A.A. Transport	Percival Sea Prince C.2
C19/49	Transport	H.P. Hastings C.2 and C.3
A20/49	Air Observation Post	Auster A.O.P.9
F23/49	S/S Fighter	E.E. P.1
26/49	Transport	Replacement for D.H. Rapide
E27/49	H/S Research	Boulton Paul P.120
ER100	Research	Short S.B.5
ER103	H/S Research	Fairey F.D.2, E.E. P.1
F105D2	S/S Fighter	Supermarine 545
UB109	Expendable Bomber	Bristol 182
ER110T	Variable-sweep Research Monoplane	Bristol 183 project
N113D	S/S F.A.A. Fighter	Supermarine 525
N113P	S/S F.A.A. Fighter	Supermarine 544 Scimitar 1 production
N114T	Water-based Fighter	Short P.D.5
C115P	Transport	Hastings C.2
M123D	A.S.W. Patrol	Short Seamew A.S.1
F124T	Rocket Fighter	Bristol 178, Short P.D.7
B126T	Low-level Bomber	Bristol 186, Short P.D.9
ER134	H/S Research	Bristol 188
F138D	Mixed-power Fighter	Saro SR.53
ER143	VTOL Jet Research	Short S.C.1
HR144T	Scout Helicopter	Bristol 190, Short S.B.8, Fairey U/L
HR146	Naval Helicopter	Bristol 190
M148T/ NA39	Tactical Strike Bomber	Blackburn Buccaneer, Hawker P.1108 and Short P.D.13 projects.
HR149	Helicopter for R.C.A.F.	Bristol 193
H150	Helicopter for R.A.F.	Bristol 192
T157D	Jet Trainer	Hawker P.1101 Hunter T.7
FR164D	S/S Fighter	Hawker Hunter F.R.4
OR189D	Research	Hunting H.126
C203	Transport	Short S.C.5/10 Belfast C.1
ER221D	Research	Fairey F.D.2/Bristol 221
OR323	M/R Freighter	Short P.D.16, A.W. Argosy

M

OR329 H/S Interceptor	Hawker P.1103
OR330 Supersonic Bomber	H.P.100, Avro 730 and Vickers projects
GOR339 VTOL Jet Research	E.E./Short P.D.17
OR343 Supersonic Bomber	B.A.C. TSR–2
OR351 Tactical Freighter	Short S.C.5/21 P.D.47, H.S. 681
OR357 Maritime Recce.	Short P.D.69

APPENDIX III

Titles of Squadrons

No. 1	Cawnpore	No. 82	United Provinces
No. 18	Burma	No. 87	United Provinces
No. 21	Norwich	No. 88	Hong Kong
No. 24	Commonwealth	No. 91	Nigeria
No. 26	South African	No. 92	East India
No. 35	Madras Presidency	No. 94	MacRobert
No. 40	Abingdon	No. 97	Straits Settlements
No. 43	China-British	No. 98	Derby
No. 44	Rhodesia	No. 99	Madras Presidency
No. 46	Uganda	No. 102	Ceylon
No. 49	Sheffield	No. 103	Swindon
No. 51	York	No. 110	Hyderabad
No. 56	Punjab	No. 114	Hong Kong
No. 57	Cheltenham	No. 120	Punjab
No. 61	City of Lincoln	No. 121	No. 2 American Eagle
No. 62	Northampton	No. 122	Bombay
No. 65	East India	No. 123	East India
No. 67	No. 1 Australian Flying Corps	No. 124	Baroda
		No. 125	Newfoundland
No. 68	No. 2 Australian Flying Corps	No. 129	Mysore
		No. 130	Punjab
No. 69	No. 3 Australian Flying Corps	No. 131	County of Kent
		No. 132	City of Bombay
No. 71	No. 4 Australian Flying Corps	No. 133	No. 3 American Eagle
		No. 139	Jamaica
No. 71	No. 1 American Eagle	No. 142	Worcester
No. 72	Basutoland	No. 144	Grimsby
No. 74	Trinidad	No. 146	Assam
No. 75	New Zealand	No. 149	East India
No. 77	Lancaster	No. 152	Hyderabad
No. 78	Preston	No. 154	Motor Industries Gift
No. 79	Madras Presidency	No. 164	Argentine-British

No. 165 Times of Ceylon
No. 166 Huddersfield
No. 167 Gold Coast
No. 174 Mauritius
No. 183 Gold Coast
No. 193 Fellowship of the Bellows
No. 207 Leicester
No. 213 Ceylon
No. 214 Federated Malay States
No. 217 Exeter
No. 218 Gold Coast
No. 219 Mysore
No. 222 Natal
No. 234 Madras Presidency
No. 237 Rhodesia
No. 242 Canadian
No. 245 Northern Rhodesia
No. 247 China-British
No. 249 Gold Coast
No. 250 Sudan
No. 253 Hyderabad
No. 257 Burma
No. 263 Fellowship of the Bellows
No. 264 Madras Presidency
No. 266 Rhodesia
No. 267 Pegasus
No. 300 Masovian
No. 301 Pomeranian
No. 302 Poznan
No. 303 Warsaw-Kosciusko
No. 304 Mazonia
No. 305 Pomeranian
No. 306 Torun
No. 307 Lwow
No. 308 Krakow
No. 309 Ziemia Czerwienska
No. 315 Deblin
No. 316 Warsaw
No. 317 Wilno
No. 318 Danzig-Gdansk

No. 340 Île de France
No. 341 Alsace
No. 342 Lorraine
No. 346 Guyenne
No. 347 Tunisie
No. 401 Ram
No. 402 Winnipeg Bear
No. 403 Wolf
No. 405 Vancouver
No. 406 Lynx
No. 408 Goose
No. 409 Nighthawk
No. 410 Cougar
No. 411 Grizzly Bear
No. 412 Falcon
No. 414 Imperial
No. 415 Swordfish
No. 416 City of Oshawa
No. 417 City of Windsor
No. 418 City of Edmonton
No. 419 Moose
No. 420 Snowy Owl
No. 421 Red Indian
No. 424 Tiger
No. 425 Alouette
No. 426 Thunderbird
No. 427 Lion
No. 428 Ghost
No. 429 Bison
No. 431 Iroquois
No. 432 Fox/Leaside
No. 433 Porcupine
No. 434 Bluenose
No. 435 Edmonton
No. 436 Montreal
No. 439 Sabre-toothed Tiger
No. 441 Silver Fox
No. 442 Caribou
No. 443 Hornet
No. 500 County of Kent

No. 501 County of Gloucester/
        City of Bristol
No. 502 County of Ulster
No. 503 County of Lincoln
No. 504 City of Nottingham
No. 600 City of London
No. 601 County of London
No. 602 City of Glasgow
No. 603 City of Edinburgh
No. 604 County of Middlesex
No. 605 County of Warwick
No. 607 County of Durham

No. 608 North Riding
No. 609 West Riding
No. 610 County of Chester
No. 611 West Lancashire
No. 612 County of Aberdeen
No. 613 East Lancashire—City of
        Manchester
No. 614 County of Glamorgan
No. 615 County of Surrey
No. 616 South Yorkshire
No. 692 Fellowship of the Bellows

Cranwell Sword

The Sword of Honour is awarded by the Air Council at the Flight Cadets' passing-out parade to the Cadet who has shown the greatest merit in all categories at the end of the current term at the R.A.F. College, Cranwell.

Dec. 1921.	C. L. Falconer	Dec. 1936.	H. F. Burton
Aug. 1922.	D. MacFadyen	July, 1937.	J. M. N. Pike
Dec. 1922.	N. Carter	Dec. 1937.	P. G. St. G. O'Brian
Aug. 1923.	G. L. Worthington	July, 1938.	B. P. Young
Dec. 1923.	G. C. A. Armstrong	Dec. 1938.	H. F. D. Breese
July, 1924.	H. R. D. Waghorn	July, 1939.	T. N. Stack
Dec. 1924.	G. R. Beamish	April, 1948.	J. E. Y. King
July, 1925.	T. N. McEvoy	April, 1949.	P. V. Pledger
Dec. 1925.	E. B. Webb	July, 1949.	W. J. Herrington
July, 1926.	B. C. Yarde	Dec. 1949.	J. R. E. Edmondson-
Dec. 1926.	J. Clarke		Jones
July, 1927.	F. R. Worthington	April, 1950.	W. F. Knapper
Dec. 1927.	A. W. Hunt	July, 1950.	G. W. F. Charles
July, 1928.	N. E. White	Dec. 1950.	R. T. MacMullen
Dec. 1928.	G. P. Charles	April, 1951.	J. A. Pryer
July, 1929.	K. W. Niblett	July, 1951.	H. A. Merriman
Dec. 1929.	G. R. A. Elsmie	Dec. 1951.	J. M. A. Parker
July, 1930.	P. B. Coote	April, 1952.	R. Parfitt
Dec. 1930.	H. A. V. Hogan	July, 1952.	R. A. Streatfield
July, 1931.	C. W. M. Ling	Dec. 1952.	L. R. Davis
Dec. 1931.	R. H. E. Emson	April, 1953.	P. L. Gray
July, 1932.	A. N. Combe	July, 1953.	P. G. Cock
Dec. 1932.	R. V. Rolph	Dec. 1953.	L. A. Jones
July, 1933.	J. V. C. Bodger	April, 1954.	R. S. Blockey
Dec. 1933.	G. C. Eveleigh	July, 1954.	P. H. Stanning
July, 1934.	P. W. Ashton	Dec. 1954.	G. Wallingford
Dec. 1934.	H. M. Styles	April, 1955.	F. M. A. Hines
July, 1935.	H. E. C. Boxer	July, 1955.	T. R. Morgan
Dec. 1935.	M. P. Skinner	Dec. 1955.	M. J. Griffiths
July, 1936.	P. B. Chamberlain	April, 1956.	A. A. Boyle

July, 1956. J. H. Constable
April, 1957. P. C. Little
July, 1957. T. E. Enright
Dec. 1957. P. S. Martin
April, 1958. C. C. Lane
July, 1958. A. E. Thomson
Dec. 1958. T. V. Spencer
July, 1959. T. F. H. Mermagen
Dec. 1959. T. C. Porteous
July, 1960. P. J. Kemp
Dec. 1960. R. P. Hallam
Aug. 1961. N. R. Hayward

Dec. 1961. D. R. Conran-Smith
July, 1962. R. B. Thomson
Dec. 1962. K. B. Latton
July, 1963. I. D. Macfadyen
Dec. 1963. J. A. Cheshire
July, 1964. C. Mitchell
Dec. 1964. J. W. Lanham
June, 1965. W. F. C. Tyndall
Dec. 1965. R. R. C. Parsley
Aug. 1966. R. P. Slogrove
Mar. 1967. R. M. Joy
May, 1967. M. D. C. Fonfé
Aug. 1967. L. J. Marshall

APPENDIX V

Chronology

1878. Military tests at Woolwich with free and captive balloons, for which an equipment store was set up.

1879. Five balloons in use with Royal Engineers.

24 June, 1880. Balloons used in army manœuvres.

1882. Balloons again used in army manœuvres.

Oct. 1882. Balloon Store transferred to Chatham.

1883. Balloon School, Factory and Depot at Chatham being operated by Royal Engineers.

26 Nov. 1884. Expedition sent to Bechuanaland included R.E. balloon detachment.

15 Feb. 1885. Balloon unit sent to Sudan.

May, 1890. Royal Engineers' Balloon Section and Depot officially sanctioned.

June, 1890. Balloon Factory and School transferred to South Farnborough, the Depot remaining at Chatham.

May, 1891. R.E. Balloon Section transferred to Aldershot.

1892. Balloon Depot and Factory transferred to Aldershot and School of Ballooning formed.

1 Sept. 1899. Balloon Sections Nos. 1 and 2 sent to South African War.

7 March, 1900. Balloon Section No. 3 reached South African War.

1905. Balloon Factory transferred to South Farnborough.

1906. Lt.-Col. J. E. Capper appointed Superintendent of Balloon Factory.

1907. Wireless-telegraphy experiments between air and ground at Balloon School with captive balloons.

2 March, 1911. First Naval flying instruction began at Eastchurch.

1 April, 1911. Air Battalion of Royal Engineers formed, comprising Headquarters and No. 1 Airship Coy. at South Farnborough, and No. 2 Aeroplane Coy. at Larkhill, together with a Reserve.

Dec. 1911. Naval Flying School established at Eastchurch.

Jan. 1912. Admiralty disbanded special airship section.

13 April, 1912. Royal Warrant issued for the formation of the Royal Flying Corps.

13 May, 1912. Royal Flying Corps constituted with Military and Naval Wings, Central Flying School, Reserve and Farnborough Royal Aircraft Factory.

May, 1912. No. 1 Airship Coy. of the Air Battalion became No. 1 Airship and Kite Squadron.

19 June, 1912. Central Flying School opened at Upavon.

5 July, 1912. First fatal R.F.C. flying accident.

Sept. 1912. Naval airship section reformed.

Oct. 1912. Navy decided to set up coastal air stations.

Dec. 1912. Isle of Grain Seaplane Base commissioned.

1913. Calshot, Felixstowe, Yarmouth and Cromarty Seaplane Bases commissioned.

March, 1913. Experimental Branch of R.F.C. Military Wing formed.

Jan. 1914. All airship organization transferred to Naval Wing, together with equipment of No. 1 Squadron.

April, 1914. Dundee Seaplane Base commissioned.

April, 1914. Kingsnorth (Hoo) Airship Base commissioned.

1 July, 1914. Royal Naval Air Service formed from Naval Wing, R.F.C.

18–22 July, 1914. R.N.A.S. in Spithead Fleet Review and Manœuvres.

4 Aug. 1914. War declared on Germany by Great Britain.

10 Aug. 1914. English Channel patrolled by airships.

13–15 Aug. 1914. First R.F.C. squadrons flew to France.

19 Aug. 1914. First R.F.C. aerial reconnaissance.

22 Aug. 1914. First aerial fight and British aircraft shot down.

25 Aug. 1914. First German aircraft brought down from the air.

1 Sept. 1914. R.N.A.S. Base set up at Dunkirk.

15 Sept. 1914. German lines photographed from the air.

16 Sept. 1914. Canadian Aviation Corps set up.

22 Sept. 1914. Airship shed at Düsseldorf attacked by R.N.A.S.

22 Sept. 1914. First artillery observation by R.F.C.

27 Sept. 1914. Headquarters Wireless Section formed.

28 Sept. 1914. National insignia adopted for German aircraft.

8 Oct. 1914. Zeppelin sheds at Düsseldorf and Cologne raided by R.N.A.S. and first Zeppelin destroyed on the ground.

12 Nov. 1914. Red, white and blue roundel adopted as the British aircraft marking.

21 Nov. 1914. Zeppelin sheds at Friedrichshafen raided by R.N.A.S.

29 Nov. 1914. R.F.C. in France reorganized into H.Q., H.Q. Wireless Unit, 1st H.Q. Wing, 2nd H.Q. Wing and Aircraft Park.

21 Dec. 1914. First aeroplane raid on England.

24 Dec. 1914. First enemy bombs dropped on British soil at Dover.

25 Dec. 1914. Cuxhaven airship sheds raided by seaplane and their carriers.

Jan. 1915. Clock code devised for artillery observation.

19 Jan. 1915. Zeppelins L.3 and L.4 made first airship raid on Great Britain.

March, 1915. 'A' aircraft camera first used over enemy lines.

15 March, 1915. First attack on a merchant ship from the air.

26 April, 1915. First air V.C. won by Lt. W. B. Rhodes-Moorhouse.

7 June, 1915. L.Z.37 destroyed by Flt. Sub-Lt. R. A. J. Warneford.

7 June, 1915. L.Z.38 destroyed on the ground at Evere.

25 July, 1915. No. 11 Squadron first British 2-seater fighter squadron in France.

10 Aug. 1915. L.12 brought down by gunfire.

12 Aug. 1915. First seaplane torpedo to sink enemy ship in Dardanelles.

19 Aug. 1915. Col. H. M. Trenchard assumed command of R.F.C. in France.

Jan. 1916. R.F.C. reorganized into Brigades.

Jan. 1916. Start of formation flying in R.F.C.

15 Feb. 1916. Joint Air Committee formed.

16 Feb. 1916. Responsibility for defence of London assumed by War Office.

March, 1916. R.F.C. squadron strength increased from 12 to 18 aircraft.

31 March, 1916. L.15 brought down by gunfire.

April, 1916. Responsibility for defence of British Isles assumed by War Office.

11 May, 1916. Curzon Advisory Air Board formed to succeed Joint Air Committee.

24 May, 1916. No. 70 Squadron first in France with gun interrupter gear.

1 July, 1916. First contact patrols instituted.

2 Sept. 1916. S.L.11 shot down by Lt. W. Leefe-Robinson.

15 Sept. 1916. Air co-operation for first time with tanks.

23 Sept. 1916. L.32 destroyed by 2nd Lt. F. Sowrey.

23 Sept. 1916. L.33 brought down by gunfire.

1 Oct. 1916. L.31 brought down by 2nd Lt. W. Tempest.

9 Nov. 1916. First 500 lb. bomb dropped by Short seaplane.

27 Nov. 1916. L.34 brought down by 2nd Lt. I. V. Pyott.

27 Nov. 1916. L.21 brought down by Sub-Lt. E. L. Pulling.

28 Nov. 1916. First daylight aeroplane raid on London.

24 Jan. 1917. Supply of aircraft taken over by Ministry of Munitions.

6 Feb. 1917. Cowdray Air Board succeeded Curzon Air Board.

13 April, 1917. Felixstowe 'Spider-web' anti-submarine patrol started.

31 April, 1917. Corps Reconnaissance squadrons' establishment raised to 24 aircraft each.

7 May, 1917. First aeroplane raid on London by night.

9 May, 1917. First raid by Handley Page bombers based in Belgium.

14 May, 1917. L.22 shot down by flying-boat flown by Flt. Lt. C. J. Galpin.

20 May, 1917. UC.36 first U-boat sunk from the air.

1 June, 1917. Reserve Squadrons became Training Squadrons.

7 June, 1917. First low-flying aircraft attacks on ground targets.

14 June, 1917. L.43 shot down by flying-boat flown by Flt. Sub-Lt. B. D. Hobbs.

17 June, 1917. L.48 shot down by 2nd Lt. L. P. Watkins.

2 Aug. 1917. Sopwith Pup landed on H.M.S. *Furious* by Sqn. Cdr. E. H. Dunning.

21 Aug. 1917. L.23 shot down by Flt. Sub-Lt. B. A. Smart from H.M.S. *Yarmouth*.

24 Aug. 1917. London Air Defence Area set up.

3 Sept. 1917. First night operations by British single-seat fighters.

20 Sept. 1917. London Balloon Apron set up.

21 Sept. 1917. Aerial Operations Committee set up. Later renamed War Priorities Committee.

1 Oct. 1917. Aircraft launched from gun turret on H.M.S. *Repulse*.

5 Oct. 1917. R.F.C. Palestine Brigade formed.

11 Oct. 1917. Formation of 41st Wing to bomb Germany from Nancy.

29 Nov. 1917. Royal Assent to Air Force (Constitution) Act.

2 Jan. 1918. Formation of Air Ministry.

3 Jan. 1918. Formation of Air Council to replace Air Board.

18 Jan. 1918. Maj.-Gen. J. M. Salmond appointed to command R.F.C. in France.

1 Feb. 1918. 8th Brigade formed to bomb Germany.

24 March, 1918. Six E/A shot down in one day by Capt. J. L. Trollope.

1 April, 1918. R.F.C. and R.N.A.S. combined to form Royal Air Force.

1 April, 1918. Women's Royal Air Force formed.

12 April, 1918. Six E/A shot down in one day by Capt. H. W. Woollett.

May, 1918. Northern Air Defence Area formed.

June, 1918. R.A.F. Nursing Service formed.

6 June, 1918. Maj.-Gen. H. M. Trenchard assumed command of Independent Air Force when it was formed on the same day.

4 July, 1918. Six E/A shot down in one day by Capt. W. G. Claxton.

19 July, 1918. L.54 and L.60 destroyed on the ground by Camels from H.M.S. *Furious*.

2 Aug. 1918. R.A.F. in action in North Russia.

5 Aug. 1918. L.70 destroyed by Maj. E. Cadbury and Capt. R. Leckie.

8 Aug. 1918. First contact patrols carried out with cavalry.

11 Aug. 1918. L.53 shot down by Camel flown by Lt. S. D. Culley and launched from a lighter.

5 Sept. 1918. Royal Canadian Naval Air Service set up.

19–20 Sept. 1918. Turkish 7th Army in Wadi el Far'a destroyed from the air.

30 Sept. 1918. Armistice with Bulgaria.

14 Oct. 1918. Largest British bomb of 1,650 lb. first dropped.

26 Oct. 1918. Inter-Allied Independent Air Force set up under Maj.-Gen. Sir Hugh M. Trenchard.

30 Oct. 1918. Armistice with Turkey.

3 Nov. 1918. Armistice with Austria.

11 Nov. 1918. Armistice with Germany.

29 Nov. 1918. Capt. Ross Smith started on first flight from Cairo to India.

5 Dec. 1918. Royal Canadian Naval Air Service disbanded.

13 Dec. 1918. Maj. A. S. C. MacLaren started on first flight from England to India in H.P. V/1500.

Feb. 1919. Formation by Air Ministry of Department of Civil Aviation.

March, 1919. Commencement of airmail service between Folkestone and Cologne for Army of Occupation.

14–15 June, 1919. Capt. John Alcock and Lt. Arthur Whitten Brown flew the Atlantic in a Vickers Vimy, making first non-stop flight.

2–13 July, 1919. Airship R.34 made return Atlantic flight.

July, 1919. Short Service Commissions introduced.

1 Aug. 1919. First list of post-war R.A.F. commissions.

4 Aug. 1919. New R.A.F. rank titles adopted.

Oct. 1919. Airship Service transferred from Admiralty to Air Ministry.

12 Nov. 1919. Capt. Ross Smith and Lt. Keith Smith left on first flight from England to Australia.

Dec. 1919. Coastal Area Command formed, together with Northern and Southern Commands.

4 Feb. 1920. Wing Cdr. P. Van Ryneveld and Flt. Lt. C. J. Q. Brand left on first flight from England to Cape Town.

5 Feb. 1920. Cranwell R.A.F. College opened.

18 Feb. 1920. Canadian Air Force established.

April, 1920. Northern and Southern Commands combined as Inland Area.

3 July, 1920. R.A.F. Tournament held at Hendon.

9 Aug. 1920. South African Air Force formed.

Jan. 1921. Airship Service of R.A.F. discontinued.

1 April, 1921. Australian Air Force formed.

23 June, 1921. Egypt to Iraq air route opened by R.A.F.

24 Aug. 1921. Airship R.38 lost.

31 Aug. 1921. Prefix Royal granted to Australian Air Force.

1 April, 1922. Prefix Royal granted to Canadian Air Force.

4 April, 1922. R.A.F. Staff College at Andover opened.

1 Oct. 1922. R.A.F. assumed control of Iraq.

9 Feb. 1923. Reserve of Air Force Officers formed.

June, 1923. R.A.F.N.S. became Princess Mary's R.A.F.N.S.

14 June, 1923. New Zealand Air Force formed.

25 June, 1923. Announcement of raising of Home-based R.A.F. to 52 Squadrons.

April, 1924. Formation of Fleet Air Arm.

9 Oct. 1924. Order in Council authorizing setting-up of Auxiliary Air Force.

1 Jan. 1925. Air Defence of Great Britain formed.

1925. Auxiliary Air Force and Special Reserve established.

1925. Parachutes adopted as standard equipment.

22 Oct. 1925. Formation of No. 1 Apprentices Wing at Halton.

27 Oct. 1925. Return flight from Cairo to Kano of D.H.9As commenced under Sqn. Ldr. A. Coningham.

1 March, 1926. Return flight from Cairo to the Cape started under Wing Cdr. C. W. H. Pulford.

1 July, 1926. Around-the-Mediterranean Cruise started of flying-boats under Sqn. Ldr. G. E. Livock from Plymouth to Egypt and return.

16 Sept. 1926. Start of return flight from Cairo to Aden under Air Comm. C. R. Samson.

1 Jan. 1927. Opening of Imperial Defence College.

30 March, 1927. Start of return flight from Cairo to Cape Town under Air Comm. C. R. Samson.

20–23 May, 1927. 3,400-mile non-stop long-distance record set by Flt. Lts. C. R. Carr and L. E. M. Gillman, flying from Cranwell to Persian Gulf.

12 Aug. 1927. Start of Felixstowe to the Baltic Cruise and return by flying-boats under Sqn. Ldr. C. L. Scott.

26 Sept. 1927. Schneider Trophy won by Flt. Lt. S. N. Webster in Supermarine S.5.

17 Oct. 1927. Start of 23,000-mile flight from Plymouth to Singapore of Flying-boat Development Flight under Wing Cdr. H. M. Cave-Brown-Cave.

27 Oct. 1927. Start of return flight from Cairo to Kano under Wing Cdr. F. W. Stent.

Feb. 1928. R.A.F. assumed control of defence of Aden.

1 March, 1928. Start of return flight from Cairo to Cape Town under A.V.M. Sir T. I. Webb-Bowen.

21 May, 1928. Start of cruise by four Southamptons around Australia and to Singapore and Japan.

29 Sept. 1928. Start of return flight from Plymouth to India under Sqn. Ldr. C. L. Scott.

23 Dec. 1928. Start of evacuation of Kabul by R.A.F. aircraft.

12 Feb. 1929. Start of return flight from Cairo to Cape Town under Sqn. Ldr. C. R. Cox.

28 Feb. 1929. Start of flying-boat flight from Plymouth to Basrah under Wing Cdr. T. E. B. Howe.

1929. Survey flights from England to Calcutta and return by flying-boats.

1929. Resignation by C.A.S. Sir Hugh M. Trenchard.

24–26 April, 1929. Non-stop flight of 4,130 miles from Cranwell to Karachi by Sqn. Ldr. A. G. Jones-Williams and Flt. Lt. N. H. Jenkins.

8 May, 1929. Start of return flight from Basrah to Muscat by flying-boats under Air Cdre. C. S. Burnett.

6–7 Sept. 1929. Schneider Trophy won by Flg. Off. H. R. D. Waghorn in Supermarine S.6

7 Oct. 1929. Start of return flight from Felixstowe to Norway by flying-boats under Sqn. Ldr. C. L. Scott.

19 Oct. 1929. Start of return flight from Cairo to West Africa by aircraft under Sqn. Ldr. F. J. Vincent.

11 Jan. 1930. Start of return flight from Cairo to Cape Town under Flt. Lt. C. B. Greet.

22 June, 1930. Start of return flight from Mount Batten to Iceland under Wing Cdr. S. Smith.

29 July, 1930. Start of return flight to Canada by airship R.100.

25 Aug. 1930. Start of return flight from Plymouth to Gibraltar by aircraft under Flt. Lt. L. G. Maxton.

2 Sept. 1930. Start of return flight from Calshot to the Baltic under Gp. Capt. E. R. C. Nanson.

5 Oct. 1930. Airship R.101 wrecked.

19 Oct. 1930. Start of return flight from Khartoum to West Africa under Sqn. Ldr. E. L. Howard-Williams.

2 Nov. 1930. Start of return flight from Delhi to Singapore on the occasion of the visit to Siam of the A.O.C. India, A.M. Sir W. G. H. Salmond.

12 Jan. 1931. Start of return flight from Cairo to Cape Town under Gp. Capt. E. M. Murray.

14 July, 1931. Start of Mediterranean Cruise from Malta under Wing Cdr. F. G. D. Hards.

15 Aug. 1931. Start of return flight by flying-boat sfrom Felixstowe to Middle East.

12 Sept. 1931. Schneider Trophy won outright by Flt. Lt. J. N. Boothman in Supermarine S.6b.

29 Sept. 1931. World's Speed Record of 407.5 m.p.h. set up by Flt. Lt. G. H. Stainforth in Supermarine S.6b.

14 Oct. 1931. Start of return flight from Heliopolis to West Africa under Sqn. Ldr. F. T. Vincent.

27–28 Oct. 1931. First non-stop flight from England to Egypt by Sqn. Ldr. O. R. Gayford and Flt. Lt. D. L. G. Bett.

Dec. 1931. Start of 3,000 sq. mile survey from the air of British Somaliland.

1932. Return flight by flying-boats from Singapore to Port Darwin.

20 June, 1932. Start of return flight from Malta to Khartoum under Sqn. Ldr. H. W. Evens.

5 Sept. 1932. Start of return flight from Felixstowe to the Baltic under Wing Cdr. R. Leckie.

6–8 Feb. 1933. Non-stop long-distance record of 5,340 miles from Cranwell to Walvis Bay set up by Sqn. Ldr. O. R. Gayford and Flt. Lt. G. E. Nicholetts.

1 April, 1933. Indian Air Force formed.

1933. Wessex Bombing Area became Western and Central Bombing Areas.

1934. Flight by three Rangoon flying-boats from Basrah to Melbourne and return.

24 May, 1934. First Empire Air Day held.

July, 1936. A.D.G.B. reorganized into Bomber, Fighter, Coastal and Training Commands.

30 July, 1936. R.A.F. Volunteer Reserve formed.

28 Sept. 1936. World's Height Record of 49,967 ft. set up by Sqn. Ldr. F. R. D. Swain.

1 April, 1937. Royal New Zealand Air Force formed.

30 June, 1937. World's Height Record of 53,937 ft. set up by Flt. Lt. M. J. Adam.

30 July, 1937. Admiralty assumed control of Fleet Air Arm.

20 Jan. 1938. Announcement of the end of the Hendon Air Displays.

10 Feb. 1938. Non-stop flight from Turnhouse to Northolt in 48 min. by Sqn. Ldr. J. W. Gillan at 408 m.p.h. in Hurricane.

5-7 Nov. 1938. World's Long-Distance Record of 7,162 miles non-stop from Ismailia to Darwin set by Wellesleys.

17 Jan. 1939. Auxiliary Air Force Reserve formed.

May, 1939. Control of Fleet Air Arm assumed by Royal Navy.

28 June, 1939. Women's Auxiliary Air Force formed.

1 Sept. 1939. Air Transport Auxiliary formed.

2 Sept. 1939. Ten squadrons of Battles went to France as Advanced Air Striking Force.

3 Sept. 1939. Great Britain declared war on Germany. R.A.F. and Dominion Air Forces mobilized.

4 Sept. 1939. Germany Navy attacked at Heligoland.

1 Oct. 1939. First propaganda leaflet balloons sent to Germany.

16 Oct. 1939. First German aircraft shot down over Britain in 1939-45 War.

13 Nov. 1939. First bombs dropped on Britain in 1939-45 War.

17 Dec. 1939. Empire Air Training Scheme instituted.

26 Dec. 1939. First R.A.A.F. squadron arrived in Britain.

14 Feb. 1940. *Altmark* located by Hudson.

25 Feb. 1940. First R.C.A.F. unit reached Britain.

26 March, 1940. Five Me.109s shot down in France.

9 April, 1940. Norway and Denmark invaded by Germany.

13 April, 1940. First British mines laid from the air.

29 April, 1940. Training under E.A.T.S. began in Australia, Canada and New Zealand.

10 May, 1940. German invasion of Belgium, Holland and Luxembourg.

12 May, 1940. First air V.C.s of World War II won by Flg. Off. D. E. Garland and Sgt. T. Gray.

15 May, 1940. First R.A.F. raids on the Ruhr.

30 May, 1940. Evacuation of Dunkirk started.

5 June, 1940. Airfields in Britain bombed.

8 June, 1940. H.M.S. *Glorious* sunk.

10 June, 1940. War declared by Italy on the Allies.

20 June, 1940. First R.C.A.F. Squadron arrived in Britain.

1 July, 1940. First 2,000 lb. bomb dropped on Kiel.

3 July, 1940. F.A.A. attack on French shipping at Oran.

23 July, 1940. First British aircraft over Berlin.

13 Aug. 1940. Battle of Britain began.

24 Aug. 1940. First bombs dropped on London.

25 Aug. 1940. First R.A.F. raid on Berlin.

8 Aug. 1940. Formation of first Eagle Squadron announced.

11 Nov. 1940. F.A.A. attacked Taranto.

23 Nov. 1940. Italian Air Force raided Britain.

24 Feb. 1941. First operational raid by Manchesters.

6 April, 1941. Invasion of Yugo-Slavia and Greece by Germany.

15 May, 1941. Gloster-Whittle Pioneer flew at Cranwell.

26 May, 1941. *Bismarck* located by Catalina.

22 June, 1941. Russia invaded by Germany.

18 July, 1941. Ferry Command formed.

27 Aug. 1941. U-570 captured by Hudson.

11 Sept. 1941. R.A.F. Wing in Russia became operational.

12 Nov. 1941. H.M.S. *Ark Royal* sunk.

7 Dec. 1941. Japan declared war on Great Britain and U.S.A.

7 Dec. 1941. Great Britain declared war on Finland, Hungary and Rumania.

8 Dec. 1941. Great Britain declared war on Japan.

11 Dec. 1941. War declared between U.S.A. and Germany and Italy.

8 Jan. 1942. Proposed formation of R.A.F. Regiment announced.

1 Feb. 1942. R.A.F. Regiment formed.

11-12 Feb. 1942. Attacks on *Gneisenau* and *Scharnhorst* in the Channel.

30 May, 1942. First 1,000-bomber raid on Germany with 1,046 aircraft.

19 Aug. 1942. Raid on Dieppe.

16 Sept. 1942. Eagle Squadrons transferred to U.S.A.A.F.

8 Nov. 1942. Invasion of North Africa by Allies.

11 March, 1943. Transport Command formed.

16 May, 1943. Möhne, Eder and Sorpe dams attacked.

1 June, 1943. Army Co-operation Command disbanded.

14 June, 1943. Tactical Air Force formed.

24 July, 1943. First use of 'Window'.

8 Sept. 1943. Italy surrendered.

13 Oct. 1943. Italy declared war on Germany.

18 Feb. 1944. Amiens prison attacked.

1 June, 1944. Balkan Air Force formed.

6 June, 1944. D-Day invasion of France by Allies.

10 June, 1944. Allied aircraft operating from Normandy.

13 June, 1944. First V.1s landed in Britain.

14 June, 1944. First V.1 shot down from the air.

12 July, 1944. First British jet fighters in service.

21 July, 1944. First British jet fighters operational.

15 Aug. 1944. Invasion by Allies of Southern France.

8 Sept. 1944. First V.2 fell on Britain.

13 Sept. 1944. Armistice declared between Allies and Rumania.

15 Sept. 1944. *Tirpitz* hit with 12,000 lb. 'Tallboy' bomb.

17 Sept. 1944. Allied landings made at Arnhem.

15 Oct. 1944. A.D.G.B. became Fighter Command.

1 Jan. 1945. Mass German attacks by air on Allied Belgian and Dutch airfields.

14 March, 1945. First 22,000 lb. 'Grand Slam' bomb dropped.

31 March, 1945. Empire Air Training Scheme ended.

2 May, 1945. War in Italy ended.

8 May, 1945. VE-Day—war ended in Europe.

10 May, 1945. Lancaster *Aries* flew over North Pole.

30 July, 1945. Allied Air Forces in Mediterranean disbanded.

6 Aug. 1945. First atom bomb dropped on Hiroshima.

8 Aug. 1945. Russia declared war on Japan.

9 Aug. 1945. Second atom bomb to be dropped fell on Nagasaki.

14 Aug. 1945. Japan surrendered, VJ-Day.

2 Sept. 1945. Armistice signed with Japan.

7 Nov. 1945. World's Speed Record of 606·25 m.p.h. set up by Gp. Capt. H. J. Wilson in Meteor.

27 March, 1946. R.A.F. Reserve Command reconstituted.

2 June, 1946. Announcement of reconstitution of Auxiliary Air Force.

8 June, 1946. Victory-Day fly-past by R.A.F. and F.A.A.

12 July, 1946. High-speed Flight set up.

Sept. 1946. Fleet Air Arm became Naval Aviation.

7 Sept. 1946. World's Speed Record of 615·81 m.p.h. set up by Gp. Capt. E. M. Donaldson, in Meteor.

26 Sept. 1946. High-speed Flight disbanded.

3 Jan. 1947. King's Flight reformed.

16 Dec. 1947. Prefix Royal granted to Auxiliary Air Force.

28 June, 1948. R.A.F. took part in Berlin airlift.

12–14 July, 1948. Six Vampires of No. 54 Squadron made first crossing of Atlantic by jet aircraft.

12 May, 1949. Berlin blockade ended.

1 Nov. 1949. Twenty R.Aux.A.F. fighter squadrons transferred from R.A.F. Reserve Command to Fighter Command.

25 June, 1950. South Korea invaded by North Korea.

7–8 July, 1950. R.A.F. in display at Farnborough.

22 July, 1950. R.A.F. Reserve Command renamed Home Command.

20 May, 1953. Naval Aviation renamed Fleet Air Arm.

17 July, 1953. Coronation Review at Odiham.

7 Sept. 1953. World's Speed Record of 727·6 m.p.h. set up in Hunter by Sqn. Ldr. Neville F. Duke.

25 Sept. 1953. World's Speed Record, of 737·7 m.p.h. set up in Swift by Lt. Cdr. Michael J. Lithgow.

1 April, 1954. Last operational flight by a Spitfire made on photographic-reconnaissance in Malaya.

14 Oct. 1954. Southern Rhodesian Air Force became Royal Rhodesian Air Force.

10 Feb. 1956. M.R.A.F. Lord Trenchard died.

10 March, 1956. World's Speed Record of 1,132 m.p.h. set up in Fairey Delta 2 by Peter Twiss.

31 Oct. 1956. R.A.F. in action against Egyptian Air Force.

1 Sept. 1957. Army Air Corps formed.

Nov. 1958. Announcement of disbanding of Home Command.

1964. Low-level camouflage scheme adopted for Valiant, Vulcan and Victor bombers.

1 April, 1968. 50th. Anniversary of formation of Royal Air Force.

APPENDIX VI

Personnel, Squadrons and Aircraft: Approximate Strengths

Aug. 1914. R.F.C. 147 officers, 1,097 other ranks.
    4 operational squadrons, 1 training.
    179 aircraft.
    R.N.A.S. 50 officers, 550 other ranks.
    1 operational squadron, 2 training.
    93 aircraft, 7 airships.

Dec. 1916. R.F.C. 5,982 officers, 51,915 other ranks.
    3,929 aircraft.
    R.N.A.S. 2,764 officers, 26,129 other ranks.
    1,567 aircraft.

Dec. 1917. R.F.C. 15,522 officers, 98,738 other ranks.
    R.N.A.S. 4,765 officers, 43,050 other ranks.

Jan. 1918. R.F.C. 8,350 aircraft.
    R.N.A.S. 2,741 aircraft.

April, 1918. R.F.C. 18,700 officers, 131,637 other ranks.
    10,000 aircraft.
    R.N.A.S. 5,378 officers, 49,689 other ranks.
    3,000 aircraft.
    R.A.F. formed from R.F.C. and R.N.A.S. with 24,078 officers, 181,326 other ranks.
    13,500 aircraft.
    W.R.A.F. 8,000.
    W.R.N.S. 3,000.

Nov. 1918. R.A.F. 27,333 officers, 263,837 other ranks.
    200 operational squadrons, 199 training.
    22,647 aircraft—including 3,300 first-line.
    103 airships.
    25,400 W.R.A.F.

July, 1919. R.A.F. 10,500 officers, 62,500 other ranks.

Dec. 1919. R.A.F. 4,000 officers, 31,500 other ranks.
    12 squadrons.

March, 1920. R.A.F. 3,280 officers, 25,000 other ranks.
33 squadrons—including 8 forming.
360 aircraft.

March, 1923. R.A.F. 3,000 officers, 27,500 other ranks.
35 squadrons.

Oct. 1924. R.A.F. 43 squadrons.

1926. R.A.F. 64 squadrons.

1930. R.A.F. 72 squadrons.

March, 1932. R.A.F. 75 squadrons.

1934. R.A.F. 30,000 total personnel.
76 squadrons.
732 aircraft.

Jan. 1937. R.A.F. 133 squadrons.
1,565 aircraft.

July, 1937. R.A.F. 1,750 aircraft.

Jan. 1938. R.A.F. 65,000 total personnel.

Sept. 1938. R.A.F. 1,982 first-line aircraft.

Sept. 1939. R.A.F. 118,000 total personnel.
9,343 total aircraft—including 1,911 first-line.

Aug. 1940. R.A.F. 2,913 first-line aircraft.

Dec. 1941. R.A.F. 4,287 first-line aircraft.

March, 1943. R.A.F. 6,026 first-line aircraft.

June, 1944. R.A.F. 8,339 first-line aircraft.

Jan. 1945. R.A.F. 8,395 first-line aircraft.

May, 1945. R.A.F. 1,079,835 total personnel.
540 squadrons.
55,469 total aircraft.

Dec. 1946. R.A.F. 305,000 total personnel.

1947. R.A.F. 100 squadrons, 1,000 first-line aircraft.

1948. R.A.F. 370,000 total personnel.

April, 1950. R.A.F. 202,400 total personnel.

Jan. 1951. R.A.F. 125,700 total personnel.

May, 1953. R.A.F. 278,300 total personnel.

Dec. 1953. R.A.F. 271,500 total personnel.

April, 1954. R.A.F. 265,100 total personnel.

March, 1955. R.A.F. 269,200 total personnel.

1956. R.A.F. 185 squadrons, 2,000 first-line aircraft.

April, 1964. R.A.F. 137,200 total personnel.

Code Lettering

An aircraft's unit may be identified by the fuselage code lettering listed here. In some cases it will be noted that the same combination was used by two or more units. For example, a Hurricane F.1 marked AL will, on reference to the histories of Nos. 79 and 429—both of which used AL— be found to have belonged to No. 79.

A1 A Flt. 1 A.A.C.U
A2 514 Sqn.
A3 1653 H.C.U.
A3 230 O.C.U
A4 115 Sqn.
A4 195 Sqn.
A5 3 L.F.S.
A6 257 Sqn.
A9 Woodbridge
A 112 Sqn.
A 201 Sqn.
A 202 Sqn.
A 217 Sqn.
AA 75 Sqn.
AB 423 Sqn.
AB 1557 Flt.
AC 138 Sqn.
AD 251 Sqn.
AD 60 Sqn.
AD 11 Sqn.
AE 1409 Flt.
AE 402 Sqn.
AE 2 Sqn. R.C.A.F.
AE 130 Sqn. R.C.A.F.
AF 607 Sqn.
AF 404 Sqn.
AF A.F.D.U.
AG C.F.E.
AH 332 Sqn.

AJ 617 Sqn.
AJ North Luffenham
AK 213 Sqn.
AK 1674 H.C.U.
AL 79 Sqn.
AL 429 Sqn.
AM 410 Sqn.
AM 14 O.T.U.
AM 417 Sqn.
AN 13 Sqn.
AN Gt. Dunmow
AO 412 Sqn.
AP 413 Sqn.
AP 186 Sqn.
AP 130 Sqn.
AQ 276 Sqn.
AR 460 Sqn.
AS 166 Sqn.
AS 100 Sqn.
AT 60 O.T.U.
AT 13 O.T.U.
AU 148 Sqn..
AV 121 Sqn.
AW 664 Sqn.
AW 42 Sqn.
AW 504 Sqn.
AX 202 Sqn.
AX 421 Sqn.
AX 413 Sqn.

AX 1 Sqn. S.A.A.F.
AX 77 O.T.U.
AY 110 Sqn.
AY 17 O.T.U.
AZ 627 Sqn.
AZ 234 Sqn.
B1 B Flt. 1 A.A.C.U.
B3 Wyton
B4 282 Sqn.
B4 281 Sqn.
B6 Spilsby
B7 Waddington
B8 Woodhall Spa
B9 1562 Met. Flt.
B 269 Sqn.
B 230 Sqn.
B 206 Sqn.
BA 277 Sqn.
BA 125 Sqn. R.C.A.F.
BB 27 O.T.U.
BB 226 O.C.U.
BC 511 Sqn.
BD 43 O.T.U.
BD 227 O.C.U.
BE 8 O.T.U.
BF 3 Sqn. R.A.A.F.
BF 14 Sqn.
BF 28 Sqn.
BF 54 O.T.U.

BG 660 Sqn.

BH 215 Sqn.

BH 430 Sqn.

BH 300 Sqn.

BI Holme

BJ 1680 Flt.

BJ 271 Sqn.

BK 115 Sqn.

BK Stn. Flt. Sn. Sec.

BL 1656 H.C.U.

BL 609 Sqn.

BL 40 Sqn.

BM 433 Sqn.

BM 415 Sqn.

BN 240 Sqn.

BN 1401 Met. Flt.

BP 457 Sqn.

BP 91 Sqn.

BP 459 Sqn.

BQ 451 Sqn.

BQ 550 Sqn.

BQ 600 Sqn.

BR 184 Sqn.

BS 160 Sqn.

BS 148 Sqn.

BS 1651 C.U.

BS 120 Sqn.

BT 441 Sqn.

BT 113 Sqn.

BT 30 O.T.U.

BU 214 Sqn.

BV 126 Sqn. R.C.A.F.

BW 58 Sqn.

BX 86 Sqn.

BX 666 Sqn.

BY 58 Sqn.

BY 23 O.T.U.

BZ 107 Sqn.

BZ 12 O.T.U.

C5 Tibenham

C6 51 Sqn.

C7 1 Fy. Pl.

C8 640 Sqn.

C 236 O.C.U.

CA 189 Sqn.

CA 3 Sqn. S.A.A.F.

CB 31 Sqn.

CB Met. Com. Sqn.

CC Holmsley Sth.

CE 1668 H.C.U.

CE 5 L.F.S.

CF 625 Sqn.

—

CG Binbrook

CH Swinderby

CJ 203 Sqn.

CL Little Staughton

CM 1333 T.C.U.

CM 107 O.T.U.

CM 42 Gp. Com. Flt.

CP Topcliffe

CR 162 Sqn.

CS Stn. Flt. Upwood

CS 297 Sqn.

CS 13 Sqn. R.A.A.F.

CT 52 O.T.U.

CV 3 Sqn. R.A.A.F.

CV Tuddenham

CX 14 Sqn.

CY Ludford Magna

D4 620 Sqn.

D6 Methel

D8 22 M.U.

DA 210 Sqn.

DA 273 M.U.

DB 2 Sqn. S.A.A.F.

DB 411 Sqn.

DC Oakington

DD 45 Sqn.

DD 22 O.T.U.

DE 61 O.T.U.

DF C.B.E.

DG 422 Sqn.

DG 228 Sqn.

DG 150 Sqn.

DH 540 Sqn.

DH 434 Sqn.

DH 1664 H.C.U.

DI Kemble

DJ 612 Sqn.

DK 158 Sqn.

DL 54 Sqn.

DL 91 Sqn.

DL 92 Sqn.

DM 248 Sqn.

DM 36 Sqn.

DN 416 Sqn.

DP 193 Sqn.

DP 30 Sqn.

DQ 95 Sqn.

DQ 1402 Flt.

DR 67 Sqn.

DR 1555 Flt.

DS Llanbedr

DT 257 Sqn.

DT 192 Sqn.

DU 70 Sqn.

DU 312 Sqn.

DV 129 Sqn.

DV 77 Sqn.

DV 237 Sqn.

DW 610 Sqn.

DX 245 Sqn.

DX 57 Sqn.

DY 102 Sqn.

DZ 151 Sqn.

E1 E Flt. 1 A.A.C.U.

E2 Warboys

E4 Wickenby

E7 570 Sqn.

E9 Westcott

EA 49 Sqn.

EA 145 Sqn. R.C.A.F.

EB 41 Sqn.

EC Odiham

ED 21 O.T.U.

ED 202 C.T.U.

EE 404 Sqn.

EE Elvington

EF 102 Sqn.

EF 15 Sqn.

EF 232 Sqn.

EG 16 Sqn.
EG 487 Sqn.
EG 27 Sqn.
EH 55 O.T.U.
EJ C.C.F.I.S.
EK 1656 H.C.U.
EL 181 Sqn.
EL 10 O.C.U.
EM 207 Sqn.
EM 238 Sqn.
EN 27 O.T.U.
EO 15 O.T.U.
EP 104 Sqn.
EP 84 Gp. Com. Flt.
EQ 57 Sqn.
EQ 408 Sqn.
EQ 426 Sqn.
ER 1552 R.A.T. Flt.
ES 541 Sqn.
ES 229 O.C.U.
ET 662 Sqn.
EU 26 O.T.U.
EV 13 O.T.U.
EV 98 Sqn.
EV 180 Sqn.
EW 47 Sqn.
EW 307 Sqn.
EX 199 Sqn.
EX 171 Sqn.
EX 11 Sqn.
EY 233 Sqn.
EY 78 Sqn.
EY 80 Sqn.
EZ 1380 C.U.
F1 F Flt. 1 A.A.C.U.
F2 635 Sqn.
F3 438 Sqn.
FA 281 Sqn.
FAA 19 F.T.S., R.A.F. College
FAB 19 F.T.S., R.A.F. College
FAC 19 F.T.S., R.A.F. College

FAD 19 F.T.S., R.A.F. College
FAE 19 F.T.S., R.A.F. College
FAG 19 F.T.S., R.A.F. College
FAI 20 F.T.S., 2 F.T.S.
FAJ 20 F.T.S., 2 F.T.S.
FAK 20 F.T.S., 2 F.T.S.
FAL 20 F.T.S., 2 F.T.S.
FAM 20 F.T.S., 2 F.T.S.
FAN 21 F.T.S.
FAO 21 F.T.S.
FAP 21 F.T.S.
FAQ 21 F.T.S.
FAS 16 S.F.T.S., 16 F.T.S.
FAT 16 S.F.T.S., 16 F.T.S.
FAU 16 S.F.T.S., 16 F.T.S.
FAV 16 S.F.T.S., 16 F.T.S.
FAW 16 S.F.T.S., 16 F.T.S.
FAX 16 S.F.T.S., 16 F.T.S.
FAY 16 S.F.T.S., 16 F.T.S.
FB 24 O.T.U.
FB 35 Sqn.
FBA 7 S.F.T.S., 7 F.T.S.
FBB 7 S.F.T.S., 7 F.T.S.
FBC 7 S.F.T.S., 7 F.T.S.
FBD 7 S.F.T.S., 7 F.T.S.
FBE 7 S.F.T.S., 7 F.T.S.

FBG 6 S.F.T.S., 6 F.T.S.
FBH 6 S.F.T.S., 6 F.T.S.
FBI 6 S.F.T.S., 6 F.T.S.
FBJ 6 S.F.T.S., 6 F.T.S.
FBK 6 S.F.T.S., 6 F.T.S.
FBL 6 S.F.T.S., 6 F.T.S.
FBM 6 S.F.T.S., 6 F.T.S.
FBN 6 S.F.T.S., 6 F.T.S.
FBP 3 S.F.T.S., 3 F.T.S.
FBQ 3 S.F.T.S., 3 F.T.S.
FBR 3 S.F.T.S., 3 F.T.S.
FBS 3 S.F.T.S., 3 F.T.S.
FBT 3 S.F.T.S., 3 F.T.S.
FBU 3 S.F.T.S., 3 F.T.S.
FBV 3 S.F.T.S., 3 F.T.S.
FBW 3 S.F.T.S., 3 F.T.S.
FBX 3 S.F.T.S., 3 F.T.S.
FBY 3 S.F.T.S., 3 F.T.S.
FC Kenley
FCA 17 S.F.T.S., 17 F.T.S., 1 F.T.S.
FCB 17 S.F.T.S., 17 F.T.S., 1 F.T.S.
FCC 17 S.F.T.S., 17 F.T.S., 1 F.T.S.

FCD 17 S.F.T.S., 17 F.T.S., 1 F.T.S.
FCE 17 S.F.T.S., 17 F.T.S., 1 F.T.S.
FCF 17 S.F.T.S., 17 F.T.S., 1 F.T.S.
FCG 17 S.F.T.S., 17 F.T.S., 1 F.T.S.
FCI 22 S.F.T.S., 22 F.T.S.
FCJ 22 S.F.T.S., 22 F.T.S.
FCK 22 S.F.T.S., 22 F.T.S.
FCL 22 S.F.T.S., 22 F.T.S.
FCM 22 S.F.T.S., 22 F.T.S.
FCT Empire Fg. Scl.
FCU Empire Fg. Scl.
FCV Empire Fg. Scl.
FCW Empire Fg. Scl.
FCX Empire Fg. Scl.
FCY Empire Fg. Scl.
FD 1659 H.C.U.
FD 114 Sqn.
FD 433 Sqn.
FDA 21(P) A.F.U., 1(P) R.F.U.
FDB 21(P) A.F.U., 1(P) R.F.U.
FDC 21(P) A.F.U., 1(P) R.F.U.
FDD 21(P) A.F.U., 1(P) R.F.U.
FDE 21(P) A.F.U., 1(P) R.F.U.
FDF 21(P) A.F.U., 1(P) R.F.U.
FDG 21(P) A.F.U., 1(P) R.F.U.
FDH 21(P) A.F.U., 1(P) R.F.U.
FDI C.F.S.

FDJ C.F.S.
FDK C.F.S.
FDL C.F.S.
FDM C.F.S.
FDN C.F.S.
FDO C.F.S.
FDQ 8 E.F.T.S.
FDR 8 E.F.T.S.
FDS 8 E.F.T.S.
FDT 8 E.F.T.S.
FDU Beam App. Scl.
FDW Beam App. Scl.
FDW C.F.S.
FDY Scl. Fg. Control, Scl. Air Traffic Control
FE 56 O.T.U.
FEA 1 GTS.
FEB 1 G.T.S.
FEC 1 G.T.S.
FED 1 G.T.S.
FEE 1 G.T.S.
FEG 3 G.T.S.
FEH 3 G.T.S.
FEI 3 G.T.S.
FEJ 3 G.T.S.
FEK 3 G.T.S.
FEL 3 G.T.S.
FEM 3 G.T.S.
FEN 3 G.T.S.
FEP 21 H.G.C.U.
FEQ 21 H.G.C.U.
FER 21 H.G.C.U.
FES 21 H.G.C.U.
FET 21 H.G.C.U.
FF 132 Sqn.
FFA 10 A.G.S.
FFB 10 A.G.S.
FFC 10 A.G.S.
FFD 10 A.G.S.
FFE 11 A.G.S.
FFF 11 A.G.S.
FFG 11 A.G.S.
FFI 5 A.N.S., 1 A.N.S.

FFJ 5 A.N.S., 1 A.N.S.
FFK 5 A.N.S., 1 A.N.S.
FFM 7 A.N.S., 2 A.N.S.
FFN 7 A.N.S., 2 A.N.S.
FFO 7 A.N.S., 2 A.N.S.
FFP 7 A.N.S., 2 A.N.S.
FFR 10 A.N.S.
FFS 10 A.N.S.
FFT 10 A.N.S.
FFU 10 A.N.S.
FFV 10 A.N.S.
FG 335 Sqn.
FG 72 Sqn.
FGA E.A.A.S., R.A.F. Fg. Coll.
FGB E.A.A.S., R.A.F. Fg. Coll.
FGC E.A.A.S., R.A.F. Fg. Coll.
FGE Empire Nav. Scl.
FGF R.A.F. Fg. Coll.
FGG R.A.F. Fg. Coll.
FGI A.A.E.E.
FGJ A.A.E.E.
FGK A.A.E.E.
FGL A.A.E.E.
FGM A.A.E.E.
FGN A.A.E.E.
FGP E.T.P.S.
FGQ E.T.P.S.
FGR E.T.P.S.
FGT A.F.E.E.
FGU A.F.E.E.
FGV A.F.E.E.
FGW A.F.E.E.
FGX A.F.E.E.
FH 53 Sqn.
FH 15 O.T.U.
FH 46 Sqn.
FHA 1 E.F.T.S.
FHB 1 E.F.T.S.

FHC 1 E.F.T.S.
FHE 2 E.F.T.S.
FHF 2 E.F.T.S.
FHG 2 E.F.T.S.
FHI 3 E.F.T.S.
FHJ 3 E.F.T.S.
FHK 3 E.F.T.S.
FHM 4 E.F.T.S.
FHN 4 E.F.T.S.
FHO 4 E.F.T.S.
FHQ 6 E.F.T.S.
FHR 6 E.F.T.S.
FHS 6 E F.T.S.
FHT 6 E.F.T.S.
FHV 7 E.F.T.S.
FHW 7 E.F.T.S.
FHX 7 E.F.T.S.
FHY 7 E.F.T.S.
FI 279 Sqn.
FI 1 A.A.C.U.
FIA 11 E.F.T.S.
FIB 11 E.F.T.S.
FIC 11 E.F.T.S.
FID 11 E.F.T.S.
FIJ 15 E.F.T.S.
FIK 15 E.F.T.S.
FIL 15 E.F.T.S.
FIN 16 E.F.T.S.
FIO 16 E.F.T.S.
FIP 16 E.F.T.S.
FIR 18 E.F.T.S.
FIS 18 E.F.T.S.
FIT 18 E.F.T.S.
FIV 21 E.F.T.S.
FIW 21 E.F.T.S.
FIX 21 E.F.T.S.
FJ 63 Sqn.
FJ 37 Sqn.
FJ 164 Sqn.
FJ 261 Sqn.
FJA 22 E.F.T.S.
FJB 22 E.F.T.S.
FJC 22 E.F.T.S.
FJD 22 E.F.T.S.

FJF 24 E.F.T.S.
FJG 24 E.F.T.S.
FJH 24 E.F.T.S.
FJJ 28 E.F.T.S.
FJK 28 E.F.T.S.
FJL 28 E.F.T.S.
FJN 29 E.F.T.S.
FJO 29 E.F.T.S.
FJP 29 E.F.T.S.
FJQ 29 E.F.T.S.
FJR C.G.S.
FJS C.G.S.
FJT C.G.S.
FJU C.G.S.
FJV C.G.S.
FJW C.G.S.
FJX C.G.S.
FK 81 Sqn.
FK 219 Sqn.
FK 209 Sqn.
FKA 1511 B.A.T. Flt.
FKD 1537 B.A.T. Flt.
FKF 1547 B.A.T. Flt.
FKN F.T.C. Com. Flt.
FKO 21 Gp. Com. Flt.
FKP 23 Gp. Com. Flt.
FKQ 25 Gp. Com. Flt.
FKR 54 Gp. Com. Flt.
FKS Stn. Flt. Cranwell
FL 81 Sqn.
FLA Cambridge U.A.S.
FLV Cambridge U.A.S.
FLB Aberdeen U.A.S.
FLC Edinburgh U.A.S.
FLD Glasgow U.A.S.
FLE Belfast U.A.S.
FLF St. Andrews
        U.A.S.
FLG Liverpool U.A.S.
FLH Manchester
        U.A.S.
FLI Leeds U.A.S.
FLJ Durham U.A.S.

FLK Birmingham
        U.A.S.
FLL Nottingham
        U.A.S.
FLM Bristol U.A.S.
FLN Swansea U.A.S.
FLO London U.A.S.
FLP Southampton
        U.A.S.
FLQ Oxford U.A.S.
FLR Perth U.A.S.
FLS Wolverhampton
        U.A.S.
FLT Derby U.A.S.
FLU Yatesbury U.A.S.
FM 257 Sqn.
FM 436 Sqn.
FM 238 Sqn.
FMA 201 A.F.S.
FMB 201 A.F.S.
FME 202 A.F.S.
FMI 203 A.F.S.
FMJ 203 A.F.S.
FMK 203 A.F.S.
FMO 204 A.F.S.
FN 331 Sqn.
FO 75 Sqn.
FQ 32 O.T.U.
FR Manston
FS 148 Sqn.
FT 43 Sqn.
FT Mildenhall
FU 453 Sqn.
FU 452 Sqn.
FV 205 Sqn.
FV 230 Sqn.
FV 13 O.T.U.
FV 18 Sqn.
FV 1659 C.U.
FW Rivenhall
FX 234 Sqn.
FX 266 Sqn.
FY 4 Sqn.
FY 611 Sqn.

FZ 65 Sqn.
FZ 23 O.T.U.
FZ 100 Sqn.
G2 19 Gp. Com. Flt.
G4 Skellingthorpe
G5 190 Sqn.
G5 69 Sqn.
G7 Br. Comd. Film
  Unit
G8 Wing
G9 430 Sqn.
GA 112 Sqn.
GA 208 Sqn.
GA 16 O.T.U.
GA 204 C.T.U.
GB 166 Sqn.
GB 105 Sqn.
GC Pershore
GD 253 Sqn.
GD Stn. Flt. Horsham
  St. Faith
GE 58 Sqn.
GE 349 Sqn.
GF 56 O.T.U.
GG 151 Sqn.
GG 1667 H.C.U.
GI 622 Sqn.
GJ Duxford
GK 80 Sqn.
GK 162 Sqn.
GL 5 Gp. Pool Sqn.
GL 185 Sqn.
GL 5 Sqn. S.A.A.F.
GL 1529 Flt.
GM 55 Sqn.
GM 42 O.T.U.
GN 249 Sqn.
GN C.B.E.
GO 237 Sqn.
GO A.F.D.U.
GO C.F.E.
GP 1661 C.U.
GQ North Killing-
  holme

GR 1586 Flt.
GR 37 Sqn.
GR 64 Sqn.
GR 301 Sqn.
GS 330 Sqn.
GT 156 Sqn.
GV 103 Sqn.
GV 134 Sqn.
GV 1652 C.E.
GW 340 Sqn.
GX 415 Sqn.
GX Broadwell
GY 1383 C.U.
GZ 611 Sqn.
H1 H Flt. 1 A.A.C.U.
H3 111 O.T.U.
H4 1653 H.C.U.
H7 346 Sqn.
H9 Shepherds Grove
HA 261 Sqn.
HA 218 Sqn.
HA 129 Sqn. R.C.A.F.
HB 229 Sqn.
HB 239 Sqn.
HC 512 Sqn.
HC 241 Sqn.
HD 466 Sqn.
HE 605 Sqn.
HE 263 Sqn.
HF 183 Sqn.
HF 54 Sqn.
HH 273 Sqn.
HH 175 Sqn.
HI 66 Sqn.
HJ 100 Sqn.
HK Ftr. Ldr. Scl.
HL 26 Sqn.
HL Gransden Lodge
HM 136 Sqn.
HM 1677 T.T. Flt.
HN 93 Sqn.
HN 20 Sqn.
HO 143 Sqn.
HP A.F.D.U.

HP Full Sutton
HQ 14 Sqn. R.N.Z.A.F.
HQ 56 O.T.U.
HR 9 O.T.U.
HR Stn. Flt. N.E. Sec.
HS 37 Sqn.
HS 260 Sqn.
HS 109 Sqn.
HT 154 Sqn.
HT 601 Sqn.
HU 220 Sqn.
HV 73 Sqn.
HV East Kirby
HW 100 Sqn.
HX 226 O.C.U.
HX 504 Sqn.
HX 203 A.F.S.
HX 61 O.T.U.
HY 88 Sqn.
HZ 44 Gp. Com. Flt.
I1 116 Sqn.
I2 48 Sqn.
I4 567 Sqn.
I5 1381 C.U.
I6 32 M.U.
I8 440 Sqn.
I8 439 Sqn.
I9 575 Sqn.
IA Syerston
IC 623 Sqn.
IF 84 O.T.U.
II 59 O.T.U.
IK B.C.I.S.
IL 195 Sqn.
IN Valley
IP 434 Sqn.
IP B.C.I.S.
IQ 150 Sqn.
IV Upper Heyford
IW Chilbolton
IY Dunsfold
JI J Flt. 1 A.A.C.U.
J5 3 Sqn.
J6 1521 R.A.T. Flt.

J7 8 M.U.
J8 24 M.U.
J9 1668 H.C.U.
JA 1652 C.U.
JB 138 O.C.U.
JC 11 Gp. Com. Flt.
JD Grimsetter
JE 610 Sqn.
JE 198 Sqn.
JF 39 Sqn.
JF 3 Sqn.
JG 17 O.T.U.
JH 317 Sqn.
JH 203 A.F.S.
JH 74 Sqn.
JI 514 Sqn.
JJ 274 Sqn.
JJ 174 Sqn.
JL 10 O.T.U.
JL 15 Sqn. R.N.Z.A.F.
JM 20. O.T.U.
JN 150 Sqn.
JN 75 Sqn.
JN 30 Sqn.
JO 62 Sqn.
JO 463 Sqn.
JP 21 Sqn.
JP 12 O.T.U.
JQ 2 A.A.C.U.
JQ Breighton
JS 16 O.T.U.
JT 256 Sqn.
JU 111 Sqn.
JV Finningley
JV 6 Sqn.
JV 3 Sqn. R.N.Z.A.F.
JW 44 Sqn.
JW C.F.E.
JX 1 Sqn.
JY 10 O.T.U.
JZ 57 O.T.U.
K1 K Flt. 1 A.A.C.U.
K2 2 Gp. Com. Flt.
K5 Pocklington

K7 236 O.C.U.
K7 6 O.T.U.
K8 Wymeswold
K9 Tain
KA 9 Sqn.
KB 142 Sqn.
KB 105 Sqn.
KB 1662 H.C.U.
KC 238 Sqn.
KD 30 O.T.U.
KD 168 Sqn. R.C.A.F.
KE B.L.E.E.
KG 3 O.T.U.
KG 204 Sqn.
KG 1380 C.U.
KH 403 Sqn.
KH 11 O.T.U.
KI Coningsby
KJ 16 Sqn.
KJ 4 Sqn. S.A.A.F.
KK 333 Sqn.
KK 15 O.T.U.
KL 54 Sqn.
KL 262 Sqn.
KM 205 Sqn.
KM 44 Sqn.
KN 77 Sqn.
KO 2 Sqn.
KO 115 Sqn.
KP 226 Sqn.
KP 409 Sqn.
KQ 502 Sqn.
KQ 204 O.C.U.
KQ 13 O.T.U.
KR 61 O.T.U.
KR 1667 C.U.
KR 226 O.C.U.
KS Tarrant Rushton
KT 32 Sqn.
KU 47 Sqn.
KU 457 Sqn.
KW 615 Sqn.
KW 425 Sqn.
KW 267 Sqn.

KX 1448 Flt.
KX 529 Sqn.
KX 311 Sqn.
KY 242 Sqn.
KY 287 Sqn.
L1 L Flt. 1 A.A.C.U.
L4 27 M.U.
L5 297 Sqn.
L6 1669 H.C.U.
L7 271 Sqn.
L8 347 Sqn.
L9 190 Sqn.
L 210 Sqn.
LA 607 Sqn.
LA 235 Sqn.
LB 34 Sqn.
LB 32 O.T.U.
LC Feltwell
LD 250 Sqn.
LD 216 Sqn.
LE 242 Sqn.
LE 40 Sqn.
LE 630 Sqn.
LF 38 Sqn.
LG 108 Sqn.
LG 13 Gp. Com. Flt.
LH Mepal
LI 116 Sqn.
LJ 211 Sqn.
LJ 600 Sqn.
LK 1 Sqn.
LK 87 Sqn.
LK 578 Sqn.
LK 51 Sqn.
LL 1513 Flt.
LM Elsham Wolds
LN 99 Sqn.
LN 83 Gp. Com. Flt.
LO 425 Sqn.
LO 216 Sqn.
LO 602 Sqn.
LP 8 O.T.U.
LP 237 O.C.U.
LQ 405 Sqn.

LR 56 Sqn.
LR 1667 C.U.
LS 61 Sqn.
LS 15 Sqn.
LT Predannack
LT 7 Sqn.
LT 22 O.T.U.
LT 54 O.T.U.
LU 101 Sqn.
LU M.S.F.U.
LV 57 O.T.U.
LW 607 Sqn.
LW 318 Sqn.
LW 75 Wing
LX 54 O.T.U.
LX Scl. of A/Co-op.
LY 149 Sqn.
LY 1 Flt. P.R.U.
LZ 66 Sqn.
LZ 421 Flt.
LZ 1421 Flt.
M1 M Flt. 1 A.A.C.U
M2 33 M.U.
M4 587 Sqn.
M5 128 Sqn.
M6 83 Gp. Com. Flt.
M7 91 Gp. Com. Flt.
M8 4 Gp. Com. Flt.
M 1 F.T.S.
MA 161 Sqn.
MB 52 Sqn.
MB 326 Sqn.
MC Fiskerton
MD 133 Sqn.
ME 488 Sqn.
MF C.F.E.
MF 108 Sqn.
MF 280 Sqn.
MG 7 Sqn.
MH 51 Sqn.
MJ 1680 Flt.
MK 500 Sqn.
MN 350 Sqn.
MOAY 31 Sqn.

MOAZ Colerne Com. Sqn.
MODA 24 Sqn.
MODA 1 P. & G.T.S.
MODB 53 Sqn.
MODC 24 Sqn.
MODC 27 Sqn.
MODC 62 Sqn.
MODD 238 Sqn.
MODF 30 Sqn.
MOFA 18 Sqn.
MOFB 77 Sqdn.
MOFC 62 Sqn.
MOFG 46 Sqn.
MOGC 242 O.C.U.
MOHA 297 Sqn.
MOHC 113 Sqn.
MOHC 295 Sqn.
MOHD 47 Sqn.
MOKD 24 Sqn.
MORC 240 O.C.U.
MORG 30 Sqn.
MOSC 30 Sqn.
MOVF 622 Sqn.
MOWA 40 Sqn.
MOWB 59 Sqn.
MOYA 51 Sqn.
MOYB 99 Sqn.
MOYC 511 Sqn.
MOYD 24 Sqn.
MOYD 59 Sqn.
MOYF 242 Sqn.
MOYG 206 Sqn.
MOYU Com. Flt. S.C.H.Q. India
MP 76 Sqn.
MQ 226 Sqn.
MR 245 Sqn.
MR 97 Sqn.
MS 23 Sqn.
MS Church Fenton
MS Hornet Con. Flt.
MT 122 Sqn.
MT 105 Sqn.

MU 60 Sqn.
MV 231 Sqn.
MV 63 O.T.U.
MV 600 Sqn.
MW 217 Sqn.
MW 1641 Flt.
MW 101 Sqn.
MX 133 Sqn.
MX Glatton
MY 278 Sqn.
MZ 299 Sqn.
N1 N Flt. 1 A.A.C.U.
N7 Lyneham
N8 Waterbeach
N9 Blackbushe
N Devon, Trpt. Comd.
NA 1 Sqn.
NA 428 Sqn.
NA 419 Sqn.
ND 236 Sqn.
NE 63 Sqn.
NE 248 Sqn.
NE 36 Sqn.
NF 138 Sqn.
NG 604 Sqn.
NH 274 Sqn.
NH 119 Sqn.
NH 38 Sqn.
NH 21 Sqn. R.A.A.F.
NI 451 Sqn.
NJ 207 Sqn.
NK 118 Sqn.
NM 268 Sqn.
NM 228 Sqn.
NM 76 Sqn.
NN 310 Sqn.
NO 320 Sqn.
NO 85 Sqn.
NP 158 Sqn.
NQ 43 Sqn.
NQ 24 Sqn.
NR 605 Sqn.
NS 201 Sqn.
NS 52 O.T.U.

NT 29 O.T.U.
NU 1382 C.U.
NU 240 O.C.U.
NU 242 O.C.U.
NV 79 Sqn.
NV B.L.E.E.
NV 144 Sqn.
NW 33 Sqn.
NW 286 Sqn.
NX 131 Sqn.
NX C.F.E.
NY 33 Sqn.
NY 1665 C.U.
NZ 304 Sqn.
O5 B.S.D.U.
O8 Merryfield
O9 S.F.C.S.
OA 22 Sqn.
OA 342 Sqn.
OB 53 O.T.U.
OB 45 Sqn.
OC Sandtoft
OD 56 O.T.U.
OD 241 Sqn.
ODA 24 Sqn.
ODC 238 Sqn.
ODD 437 Sqn.
ODE 62 Sqn.
ODF 147 Sqn.
ODJ 78 Sqn.
ODK 512 Sqn.
ODM 436 Sqn.
ODN 271 Sqn.
ODO 437 Sqn.
ODP 525 Sqn.
ODR 48 Sqn.
ODS 575 Sqn.
ODT 53 Sqn.
ODU 31 Sqn.
ODV 10 Sqn.
ODW 52 Sqn.
ODY 1333 T.C.U.
OE 98 Sqn.
OE 661 Sqn.

OF 97 Sqn.
OFA 10 Sqn.
OFA 437 Sqn.
OFB 62 Sqn.
OFB 271 Sqn.
OFD 575 Sqn.
OFG 46 Sqn.
OFN 575 Sqn.
OFR 238 Sqn.
OFT 187 Sqn.
OFU 233 Sqn.
OFV 271 Sqn.
OG 1665 C.U.
OI 2 Sqn.
OJ 149 Sqn.
OK 450 Sqn.
OK 3 G.R.S.
OL 83 Sqn.
OM 107 Sqn.
ON 124 Sqn.
ON 56 Sqn.
ON 63 Sqn.
OO 301 Sqn.
OO 1663 H.C.U.
OO 13 Sqn.
OP 3 Sqn.
OP 11 O.T.U.
OQ 5 Sqn.
OQ 172 Sqn.
OQ 52 O.T.U.
OR B.B.U.
OS Sturgate
OT 5 Sqn. R.N.Z.A.F
OT 58 Sqn.
OT 82 Sqn.
OT 540 Sqn.
OU 485 Sqn.
OV 197 Sqn.
OW 426 Sqn.
OX 40 Sqn.
OY 13 O.T.U.
OY 11 Sqn.
OY 48 Sqn.
OY 608 Sqn.

OZ 179 Sqn.
OZ 82 Sqn.
OZ 24 Sqn. S.A.A.F.
OZ 210 Sqn.
P2 Stn. Flt. Marston
　　Moor
P3 515 Sqn.
P3 692 Sqn.
P4 153 Sqn.
P5 297 Sqn.
P6 489 Sqn.
P6 Banff
P8 A.S.W.D.U.
PA 55 O.T.U.
PA 655 Sqn.
PA 5 Sqn. R.N.Z.A.F.
PA 8 Sqn. R.N.Z.A.F.
PB 10 Sqn.
PB 10 Sqn. R.C.A.F.
PD 87 Sqn.
PD 450 Sqn.
PD 303 Sqn.
PF 43 O.T.U.
PF 227 O.C.U.
PG 619 Sqn.
PG 608 Sqn.
PH 12 Sqn.
PI Silverstone
PJ 59 Sqn.
PJ 130 Sqn.
PK 316 Sqn.
PK 315 Sqn.
PL 144 Sqn.
PM 103 Sqn.
PN 1552 R.A.T. Flt.
PN 41 Sqn.
PN 252 Sqn.
PO 463 Sqn.
PO 467 Sqn.
PO 46 Sqn.
PO 104 Sqn.
PP 203 Sqn.
PP 311 Sqn.
PQ 206 Sqn.

PR 609 Sqn.

PS 264 Sqn.

PT 402 Sqn.

PU 53 Sqn.

PU 187 Sqn.

PV 275 Sqn.

PW 224 Sqn.

PW 57 O.T.U.

PX 295 Sqn.

PY 1527 R.A.T. Flt.

PZ 53 Sqn.

PZ 59 Sqn.

PZ 456 Sqn.

Q1 Q Flt. 1 A.A.C.U.

Q3 613 Sqn.

Q6 1384 C.U.

Q7 29 M.U.

Q8 B.A.F.O. Com. Wing

Q 3 F.T.S.

Q 6 F.T.S.

QA 224 Sqn.

QB 424 Sqn.

QC 168 Sqn.

QD 304 Sqn.

QD 42 Sqn.

QD 654 Sqn.

QE 12 Sqn.

QE C.F.E.

QF 98 Sqn.

QF 1323 Flt.

QG 63 O.T.U.

QI Swanton Morley

QJ B.A.F.O. Com. Wing

QJ 92 Sqn.

QJ 616 Sqn.

QK A.P.S. Hawkinge

QL 422 Sqn.

QL 413 Sqn.

QM 42 Sqn.

QM 254 Sqn.

QN 28 O.T.U.

QN 214 Sqn.

QO 432 Sqn.

QO 304 Sqn.

QO 3 Sqn.

QP Kirmington

QQ 83 Sqn.

QQ 1651 H.C.U.

QR 61 Sqn.

QR 223 Sqn.

QS 620 Sqn.

QT 57 Sqn.

QT 142 Sqn.

QU N. Ireland Com. Flt.

QV 154 Sqn.

QV 19 Sqn.

QW 1516 Flt.

QX 50 Sqn.

QX 233 Sqn.

QX Coastal Comd. Com. Flt.

QY 235 Sqn.

QZ 4 O.T.U.

R1 R Flt. 1 A.A.C.U.

R2 P.A.U.

R4 A.P.S. Fairwood Common

R7 A.E.U.

R8 274 Sqn.

RA 100 Sqn.

RA 410 Sqn.

RAA 500 Sqn.

RAB 501 Sqn.

RAC 502 Sqn.

RAD 504 Sqn.

RAG 600 Sqn.

RAH 601 Sqn.

RAI 602 Sqn.

RAJ 603 Sqn.

RAK 604 Sqn.

RAL 605 Sqn.

RAN 607 Sqn.

RAO 608 Sqn.

RAP 609 Sqn.

RAQ 610 Sqn.

RAR 611 Sqn.

RAS 612 Sqn.

RAT 613 Sqn.

RAU 614 Sqn.

RAV 615 Sqn.

RAW 616 Sqn.

RB 10 Sqn. R.A.A.F.

RB 66 Sqn.

RB 35 Sqn. S.A.A.F.

RC 5 L.F.S.

RCA Reserve Comd. Com. Flt.

RCB 12 R.F.S.

RCD 12 R.F.S.

RCD 15 R.F.S.

RCE 61 Gp. Com. Flt.

RCF 62 Gp. Com. Flt.

RCG 63 Gp. Com. Flt.

RCH 64 Gp. Com. Flt.

RCI 66 Gp. Com. Flt.

RCJ 17 R.F.S.

RCK 3 R.F.S.

RCL 14 R.F.S.

RCM 1 R.F.S.

RCO 6 R.F.S.

RCP 7 R.F.S.

RCR 11 R.F.S.

RCS 16 R.F.S.

RCT 18 R.F.S.

RCU 22 R.F.S.

RCV 24 R.F.S.

RCW 25 R.F.S.

RCX 2 R.F.S.

RCY 5 R.F.S.

RCZ 9 R.F.S.

RD 67 Sqn.

RE 29 Sqn.

RE C.F.E.

RF 1510 Flt.

RF 303 Sqn.

RF 204 Sqn.

RG 208 Sqn.

RG Earls Colne

RH 88 Sqn.

RJ 46 Sqn.

RJ Thornaby
RK 10 O.T.U.
RL 603 Sqn.
RL 38 Sqn.
RM 26 Sqn.
RN 72 Sqn.
RO 29 Sqn.
ROA 661 Sqn.
ROB 662 Sqn.
ROC 663 Sqn.
ROD 664 Sqn.
ROG 666 Sqn.
RP 288 Sqn.
RQ Colerne
RR Filton
RR 407 Sqn.
RR 615 Sqn.
RS 30 Sqn.
RS 157 Sqn.
RS 229 O.C.U.
RSA 23 R.F.S.
RSB 10 R.F.S.
RT 114 Sqn.
RT 8 Sqn.
RU 414 Sqn.
RU Hendon
RUA Aberdeen U.A.S.
RUB Birmingham
          U.A.S.
RUC Cambridge
          U.A.S.
RUD Durham U.A.S.
RUE Edinburgh U.A.S.
RUG Glasgow U.A.S.
RUL London U.A.S.
RUM Manchester
          U.A.S.
RUN Nottingham
          U.A.S.
RUO Oxford U.A.S.
RUQ Queens U.A.S.
RUS St. Andrews
          U.A.S.
RUY Leeds U.A.S.

RUZ Southampton
          U.A.S.
RV 1659 H.C.U.
RW 36 Sqn.
RX 25 Sqn.
RX 456 Sqn.
RY 313 Sqn.
RZ 241 Sqn.
S1 S Flt. 1 A.A.C.U.
S6 Maintce. Comd.
     Com. Flt.
S7 500 Sqn.
S8 328 Sqn.
S9 16 Gp. Com. Flt.
S 3 F.T.S.
S Valetta Trspt. Comd.
SA 445 Sqn.
SA 486 Sqn.
SB 464 Sqn.
SC Prestwick
SD 501 Sqn.
SD 139 Sqn.
SD 72 Sqn.
SE 431 Sqn.
SE 95 Sqn.
SE 428 Sqn.
SF 137 Sqn.
SG 9 O.T.U.
SG Stn. Flt. Lincs
     Sec.
SH 240 Sqn.
SH 216 Sqn.
SH 64 Sqn.
SJ 1 Sqn. R.N.Z.A.F.
SJ 21 O.T.U.
SK 165 Sqn.
SL 13 O.T.U.
SM 305 Sqn.
SM 315 Sqn.
SN 152 Sqn.
SN 230 O.C.U.
SO 145 Sqn.
SO Stn. Flt. S/E Sec.
SP 400 Sqn.

SP 110 Sqn. R.C.A.F.
SP Doncaster
SQ 500 Sqn.
SR 101 Sqn.
SS 1552 R.A.T. Flt.
ST 54 O.T.U.
ST 228 O.C.U.
SU Turnhouse
SV 1663 C.U.
SV 218 Sqn.
SV 8 Sqn. R.A.A.F.
SW 111 Sqn.
SW 253 Sqn.
SW 435 Sqn.
SW 1678 Flt.
SX Stn. Flt. Methwold
SY 139 Sqn.
SY 487 Sqn.
SY 613 Sqn.
SZ 315 Sqn.
T1 T Flt. 1 A.A.C.U.
T2 46 M.U.
T5 Abingdon
T6 Melbourne
T7 1 A.A.C.U.
T 79 Sqn.
T 36 Sqn.
TA 4 O.T.U.
TA 235 O.C.U.
TAL Aldermaston
          Com. Flt.
TB 77 Sqn.
TBR Staff College Flt.
TC 170 Sqn.
TCA 1 Radio Scl.
TCE Stn. Flt. Carew
     Cheriton
TCN Stn. Flt. Cran-
     well
TCO Stn. Flt. Cosford
TCR 1 Radio Scl.
TCW Stn. Flt. Carew
     Cheriton
TD 320 Sqn.

TD 126 Sqn.
TE 1401 Flt.
TE 53 Sqn.
TE Desborough
TF 127 Sqn. R.C.A.F.
TF 29 O.T.U.
TFA 1 Scl. of Photy.
Farnborough
TH 418 Sqn.
TH 20 Sqn.
THE Para. Test. Flt.
THI A. & A.E.E.
THL 24 Gp. Com. Flt.
THO Stn. Flt. Horn-
church
TIH 1 Film Prod. Unit
TJ 52 O.T.U.
TJ 206 Sqn.
TK 149 Sqn.
TL 35 Sqn.
TLO Stn. Flt. Locking
TM 504 Sqn.
TMA 4 Radio Scl.
Madley
TMD 4 Radio Scl.
Madley
TME 4 Radio Scl.
Madley
TML 4 Radio Scl.
Madley
TN 1 O.T.U.
TN 33 Sqn.
TN 30 Sqn.
TN 30 O.T.U.
TO 61 O.T.U.
TO 228 Sqn.
TO 226 O.C.U.
TOC 2 I.T.S.
TP 73 Sqn.
TP 198 Sqn.
TQ Bramcote
TQ 202 Sqn.
TQ 102 Sqn.
TR 59 Sqn.

TR 265 Sqn.
TS 657 Sqn.
TSA Stn. Flt. St. Athan
TSI R.A.F. Belgian
Trg. Scl.
TSM 4 Radio Scl.
Swanton Morley
TSN R.A.F. Belgian
Trg. Scl.
TSO 27 Gp. Com. Flt.
TT 1658 C.U.
TTE 22 Gp. Com. Flt.
TU 1 T.T.U.
TU Dyce
TV 4 Sqn.
TV 1660 H.C.U.
TW 90 Sqn.
TW 141 Sqn.
TWM 1 Scl. of Photy.
Wellesbourne
Mountford
TWY Tech. Trg.
Comd. Com. Flt.
TX 11 O.T.U.
TY 24 O.T.U.
U2 Talbenny
U4 667 Sqn.
U5 51 M.U.
U6 436 Sqn.
U7 A.D.L.S.
U7 1697 Flt.
UA 269 Sqn.
UB 455 Sqn.
UB 63 Sqn.
UB 164 Sqn.
UD 452 Sqn.
UF 601 Sqn.
UF 24 O.T.U.
UG 16 Sqn.
UG 1654 H.C.U.
UH 2 Sqn. R.N.Z.A.F.
UH 202 C.T.U.
UJ 27 O.T.U.
UK C.F.E.

UL 576 Sqn.
UL 608 Sqn.
UM 152 Sqn.
UM 626 Sqn.
UN Faldingworth
UO 84 Sqn.
UO 19 O.T.U.
UP 4 Sqn.
UP 605 Sqn.
UQ 211 Sqn.
UQ 1508 Acctn. Flt.
UR 84 Sqn.
US 28 Sqn.
US 56 Sqn.
UT 17 Sqn.
UT 51 Sqn.
UT 461 Sqn.
UU 202 Sqn.
UU 203 A.F.S.
UU 61 O.T.U.
UU 226 O.C.U.
UV 6 O.T.U.
UV 17 Sqn.
UV 460 Sqn.
UW 55 O.T.U.
UX 214 Sqn.
UX C.F.E.
UY 10 O.T.U.
UZ 306 Sqn.
V4 6 M.U.
V6 615 Sqn.
V7 R.W.E.
V8 570 Sqn.
V9 502 Sqn.
V 1435 Flt.
VA 264 Sqn.
VA 113 Sqn.
VA 125 Sqn.
VB 334 Sqn.
VC 655 Sqn.
VD C.G.S.
VE 110 Sqn.
VE Kirton-in-Lindsey
VF 99 Sqn.

VF Stn. Flt. Lindholme
VG 210 Sqn.
VG 285 Sqn.
VI 169 Sqn.
VK 85 Gp. Com. Flt.
VL 12 Sqn. S.A.A.F.
VL 167 Sqn.
VM 1561 Met. Flt.
VN 50 Sqn.
VO 180 Sqn.
VO 98 Sqn.
VP Stn. Flt. Exeter
VQ 201 Sqn.
VQ 28 O.T.U.
VR 419 Sqn.
VS 31 Sqn.
VS Met. Com. Sqn.
VT 84 Sqn.
VT 216 Sqn.
VT 1556 R.A.T. Flt.
VT 51 Sqn.
VU 36 Sqn.
VU 246 Sqn.
VV Sumburgh
VW 118 Sqn. R.C.A.F.
VW Chedburgh
VX 206 Sqn.
VY 85 Sqn.
VZ 412 Sqn.
W1 12 Sqn. S.A.A.F.
W2 80 Sqn.
W3 Hemswell
W4 G.P.U.T. Flt.
W5 Castle Camps
W6 18 M.U.
W9 24 M.U.
W 234 Sqn.
WA Manorbier
WA 5 O.T.U.
WA Stn. Flt. Yorks Sec.
WB 72 Sqn.
WB B.C.I.S.
WC 309 Sqn.
WD 206 Sqn.

WD Leeming
WE 59 Sqn.
WF 525 Sqn.
WF 238 Sqn.
WG 128 Sqn.
WG 26 O.T.U.
WH A.P.S. Acklington
WH 330 Sqn.
WH 228 Sqn.
WJ 17 O.T.U.
WK 1316 Flt.
WL 434 Sqn.
WL 612 Sqn.
WL 431 Sqn.
WM 68 Sqn.
WN 172 Sqn.
WN 527 Sqn.
WN 22 O.T.U.
WO 130 O.T.U.
WP 90 Sqn.
WP 269 Sqn.
WQ 12 Gp. Com. Flt.
WQ 604 Sqn.
WQ 209 Sqn.
WR Moreton-in-Marsh
WR 235 Sqn.
WR 248 Sqn.
WR 40 Sqn. S.A.A.F.
WS 9 Sqn.
WT 35 Sqn.
WT Stornoway
WV 18 Sqn.
WV 142 Sqn.
WX 302 Sqn.
WY 28 O.T.U.
WY 541 Sqn.
WZ 19 Sqn.
WZ Graveley
X2 Stoney Cross
X3 111 O.T.U.
X6 290 Sqn.
X9 517 Sqn.
XA 489 Sqn.
XA Stn. Flt. Essex Sec.

XB 224 Sqn.
XC 26 Sqn.
XC 41 Sqn.
XD 13 O.T.U.
XD 139 Sqn.
XD 16 Sqn.
          R.N.Z.A.F.
XE 123 Sqn.
XE C.B.E.
XG 16 O.T.U.
XG 299 Sqn.
XH 296 Sqn.
XJ 261 Sqn.
XJ 13 O.T.U.
XK 46 Sqn.
XL 1335 T.C.U.
XL 226 O.C.U.
XM 182 Sqn.
XM 652 Sqn.
XN 22 O.T.U.
XO 112 Sqn.
XO 57 O.T.U.
XP 174 Sqn.
XQ 64 Sqn.
XQ 86 Sqn.
XR 71 Sqn.
XR 2 Gp. Com. Flt.
XS 106 Sqn.
XT 603 Sqn.
XT 1657 C.U.
XU 7 Sqn.
XV 49 Sqn.
XV 2 Sqn.
XX 6 Sqn. R.N.Z.A.F.
XY 186 Sqn.
XY 90 Sqn.
XZ 48 Sqn.
Y2 442 Sqn.
Y3 518 Sqn.
Y3 202 Sqn.
Y5 Dallachy
YA 14 Sqn. R.C.A.F.
YA Netheravon
YB Bentwaters

YB 29 Sqn.

YB 17 Sqn.

YD 255 Sqn.

YE 289 Sqn.

YE 1353 Flt.

YF 280 Sqn.

YF Stn. Flt. Scampton

YG 502 Sqn.

YH 21 Sqn.

YI 423 Sqn.

YJ Metheringham

YK 274 Sqn.

YM 601 Sqn.

YM 1528 R.A.T. Flt.

YN 604 Sqn.

YO Downampney

YO 401 Sqn.

YP 23 Sqn.

YQ 217 Sqn.

YQ 616 Sqn.

YS 77 Sqn.

YS 271 Sqn.

YS 518 Sqn.

YT 65 Sqn.

YU Lossiemouth

YV 48 Gp. Com. Flt.

YW 1660 O.C.U.

YW 230 O.C.U.

YX 614 Sqn.

YX 54 O.T.U.

YY 78 Sqn.

YY 1332 C.U.

YY 241 O.C.U.

YZ 617 Sqn.

YZ 4 Sqn. R.N.Z.A.F.

YZ 1651 C.U.

Z2 437 Sqn.

Z4 10 M.U.

Z5 462 Sqn.

Z8 45 M.U.

Z9 519 Sqn.

ZA 10 Sqn.

ZA Met. Com. Sqn.

ZB 1658 C.U.

ZD 222 Sqn.

ZD 6 Sqn.

ZE 52 Sqn.

ZE C.F.E.

ZE 293 Sqn.

ZF 308 Sqn.

ZG 94 Sqn.

ZG 10 O.T.U.

ZH 501 Sqn.

ZH 266 Sqn.

ZJ 96 Sqn.

ZK 25 Sqn.

ZK 24 Sqn.

ZK 1668 H.C.U.

ZL 77 Sqn.

ZL 427 Sqn.

ZM 185 Sqn.

ZN 106 Sqn.

ZO 196 Sqn.

ZP 109 Sqn.

ZP 74 Sqn.

ZP 15 Sqn. S.A.A.F.

ZQ A.F.D.U.

ZQ B.C.I.S.

ZR 613 Sqn.

ZR 1333 C.U.

ZS 6 Sqn.

ZS 48 Sqn.

ZS 1336 C.U.

ZT 602 Sqn.

ZT 258 Sqn.

ZU 1664 C.U.

ZW 48 Sqn.

ZW 1359 V.I.P. Flt.

ZX 145 Sqn.

ZX 55 O.T.U.

ZY 247 Sqn.

ZZ 220 Sqn.

1B 43 Gp. Com. Flt.

2 220 Sqn.

2A Stn. Flt. St. Eval

2B 272 M.U.

2H Brawdy

2J 443 Sqn.

2K 1668 C.U.

2L 9 M.U.

2M 520 Sqn.

2N Foulsham

2O 84 Gp. Com. Flt.

2P 644 Sqn.

2Q 88 Gp. Com. Flt.

2V 206 Sqn.

2V 547 Sqn.

2V 18 Gp. Com. Flt.

2W 3 G.R.S.

2Y 345 Sqn.

2B 23 M.U.

3D 48 M.U.

3E 100 Gp. Com. Flt.

3F B.A.F.O. Com.
Wing

3G 111 O.T.U.

3H 80 O.T.U.

3J 13 M.U.

3L C.R.S.

3M 48 Gp. Com. Flt.

3O Wratting Common

3R 3 R.S.U.T. Flt.

3S 3 Gp. Com. Flt.

3T Acaster Malbis

3V 1 Gp. Com. Flt.

3W 322 Sqn.

3X 38 M.U.

3Y 577 Sqn.

4A 2 Gp. Com. Flt.

4B 5 Gp. Com. Flt.

4D 74 Sqn.

4E 1687 Flt.

4H 142 Sqn.

4J 5 M.U.

4K Stn. Flt. West
Malling

4L Melton Mowbray

4M 34 Sqn.

4M 695 Sqn.

4Q C.C.F.A.T.U.

4Q 59 O.T.U.

4S R.W.E.

4T Portreath
4U 30 M.U.
4V 1846 Flt.
4X 230 Sqn.
4Z B'r Com. Com. Flt.
5A 329 Sqn.
5D Gibraltar
5F 147 Sqn.
5G 299 Sqn.
5H Chivenor
5I Stn. Flt. Benson
5J 126 Sqn.
5K 39 M.U.
5L 187 Sqn.
5N 38 Gp. Com. Flt.
5O 521 Sqn.
5R 33 Sqn.
5S 691 Sqn.
5S 17 Sqn.
5T 233 Sqn.
5V 439 Sqn.
5W Snaith
6B Tempsford
6C P.R.D.U.
6D 631 Sqn.
6F 1669 H.C.U.
6G 223 Sqn.
6H 96 Sqn.
6H 1688 Flt.
6J 34 Sqn.
6O 582 Sqn.
6Q Pembroke Dock
6R 41 O.T.U.

6T 608 Sqn.
6U 415 Sqn.
6V Cottesmore
6Y 171 Sqn.
6Z 19 M.U.
7A 614 Sqn.
7B 5 Sqn.
7B 595 Sqn.
7C 296 Sqn.
7D 57 M.U.
7G Northolt
7H 84 Gp. Com. Flt.
7I Acklington
7K S.R.T.U.
7L 59 O.T.U.
7M 1 P.T.S.
7N S.F.U.
7T 196 Sqn.
7U Bardney
7X Aldergrove
7Z 1381 C.U.
7Z 105 O.T.U.
8A 298 Sqn.
8B Acctn. Flt.
8C 12 M.U.
8D 220 Sqn.
8E 295 Sqn.
8F 1381 C.U.
8F 105 O.T.U.
8H 8 Gp. Com. Flt.
8I A.P.S. Spilsby
8I A.P.S. Acklington
8J 435 Sqn.

8K 571 Sqn.
8L 91 Sqn.
8O B.A.F.O. Com.
   Wing
8P 525 Sqn.
8Q 695 Sqn.
8Q 34 Sqn.
8T 298 Sqn.
8U Ballykelly
8V 6 O.T.U.
8W 612 Sqn.
8Y 15 M.U.
8Z 295 Sqn.
9E B.A.F.O. Com.
   Wing
9F Stn. Flt. Stradishall
9G 441 Sqn.
9J 326 Sqn.
9J 227 Sqn.
9K 1 T.T.U.
9M 1690 Flt.
9N 127 Sqn.
9O 44 M.U.
9P 85 O.T.U.
9R 603 Sqn.
9R 229 Sqn.
9S M.A.E.E.
9T S.F.U.
9U 644 Sqn.
9W 296 Sqn.
9X 20 M.U.
9X 1689 Flt.

APPENDIX VIII

Abbreviations

A.A.C.U. Anti - Aircraft Co-operation Unit

A.A.E.E. Aircraft and Armament Experimental Establishment

A.A.F. Auxiliary Air Force

A.A.S.F. Advanced Air Striking Force

A/C Aircraft

A.C. Army Co-operation

A.D.G.B. Air Defence of Great Britain

A.D.L.S. Air Delivery Letter Service

A.E.A.F. Allied Expeditionary Air Force

A.F.D.U. Air Fighting Development Unit

A.F.S. Advanced Flying School

A.H.Q. Air Headquarters

A.I. Airborne Interception

A.N.S. Air Navigation School

A.O.P. Air Observation Post

A.P.S. Armament Practice Station

A/S Anti-Submarine

A.S.R. Air/Sea Rescue

A.S.V. Air-to-Surface Vessel

A.T.C. Air Training Corps

B.A.F.O. British Air Forces of Occupation

B.E.A. British European Airways

B.O.A.C. British Overseas Airways Corporation

B.S.A.A.C. British South African Airways Corporation

C.B.E. Central Bomber Establishment

C.C.F.A.T.U. Coastal Command Fighter Affiliation Training Unit

C.C.F.I.S. Coastal Command Flying Instructors' School

C.F.E. Central Fighter Establishment

C.F.S. Central Flying School

C.G.S. Central Gunnery School

C.O. Commanding Officer

C.O.W. Coventry Ordnance Works

C.U. Conversion Unit

D/N Day and Night

E/A Enemy Aircraft

214

E.F.T.S. Elementary Flying Training School

E.T.P.S. Empire Test Pilots' School

F.A.A. Fleet Air Arm

FAW. Fighter All-Weather

F.B. Fighter Bomber

F/Bt. Flying-boat

F.L.S. Fighter Leader School

Flt. Flight

F.R. Fighter Reconnaissance

F.T.S. Flying Training School

G.C.I. Ground-Controlled Interception

G.H. Radar Blind Bombing Equipment

Gp. Group

G.R. General Reconnaissance

G.R.S. General Reconnaissance School

G.T.S. Gunnery Training School

H.C.U. Heavy Conversion Unit

H/S High Speed

H2S Airborne Radar Navigational and Target Locating Aid

I.A.F. Independent Air Force or Indian Air Force

I.F.F. Identification—Friend or Foe

I.T.S. Initial Training School

L/R Long-Range

M.E.A.F. Middle East Air Forces

M.C.S. Metropolitan Communication Squadron

Met. Meteorological

M/R Medium-Range

M.R. Maritime Reconnaissance

M.U. Maintenance Unit

N.F. Night Fighter

O.C.U. Operational Conversion Unit

O.T.U. Operational Training Unit

P.A.U. Pilotless Aircraft Unit

P.R.U. Photographic Reconnaissance Unit

P.T.S. Parachute Training School

R.A.A.F. Royal Australian Air Force

R.Aux.A.F. Royal Auxiliary Air Force

R.A.T.F. Radio Aids Training Flight

R/C Radio Control

R.C.A.F. Royal Canadian Air Force

R.D.F. Radio Direction Finding

R.F.C. Royal Flying Corps

R.N.A.S. Royal Naval Air Service

R.N.Z.A.F. Royal New Zealand Air Force
R/T Radio Telephony
R.W.E. Radio Warfare Establishment
S.A.A.F. South African Air Force
S.D. Special Duties
S.E.A.C. South-East Asia Command
Sec. Sector
Sqn. Squadron
S/S Single-seater
Stn. Station
T.A.F. Tactical Air Force
T/B Torpedo Bomber
T.C.U. Transport Conversion Unit

T.E.U. Tropical Experimental Unit
T.S.R. Torpedo Spotter Reconnaissance
T.T. Target-Tower
V.I.P. Very Important Person
U.S.A.A.F. United States Army Air Force
U.S.A.F. United States Air Force
U.S.N. United States Navy
V.H.F. Very High Frequency
V.L.R. Very Long Range
W/T Wireless Telegraphy

Numbers of Squadrons formed in the Royal Air Force

R.A.F., 1–187, 189–299

Polish, 300–309

Czecho-Slovak, 310–313

Polish, 315–318, 663

Dutch, 320–322

French, 326–329

Norwegian, 330–334

Greek, 335–336

French, 340–347

Belgian, 349–350

Yugo-Slav, 351–352

R.A.F., 353–358

R.C.A.F., 400–445, 664–666

R.A.A.F., 450–464, 466–467

R.N.Z.A.F., 485–490

R.A.F., 500–504, 510–521, 524–544, 547–550, 567, 569–571, 575–578, 582, 587, 595, 597–598, 600–605, 607–628, 630–631, 635, 639–640, 644, 650–662, 667–673, 679–684, 691–692, 695

APPENDIX X

Chiefs of Air Staff

18 Jan. 1918. Maj.-Gen. Sir Hugh M. Trenchard, K.C.B., D.S.O.

15 April, 1918. Maj.-Gen. Sir F. H. Sykes, K.C.B., C.M.G.

31 March, 1919. M.R.A.F. Sir Hugh M. Trenchard, Bt., G.C.B., D.S.O., D.C.L., LL.D.

1 Jan. 1930. M.R.A.F. Sir John M. Salmond, G.C.B., C.M.G., C.V.O., D.S.O., LL.D.

1 April, 1933. A.C.M. Sir W. G. H. Salmond, K.C.B., K.C.M.G., D.S.O.

23 April, 1933. M.R.A.F. Sir John M. Salmond, G.C.B., C.M.G.,
Temporary only. C.V.O., D.S.O., LL.D.

22 May, 1933. M.R.A.F. Sir Edward L. Ellington, G.C.B., C.M.G., C.B.E.

1 Sept. 1937. A.C.M. Sir Cyril L. N. Newall, G.C.B., C.M.G., C.B.E., A.M.

25 Oct. 1940. M.R.A.F. Lord Portal of Hungerford, G.C.B., D.S.O., M.C.

1 Jan. 1946. M.R.A.F. Lord Tedder, G.C.B.

1 Jan. 1950. M.R.A.F. Sir John Slessor, G.C.B., D.S.O., M.C.

1 Jan. 1953. M.R.A F. Sir William F. Dickson, G.C.B., K.B.E., D.S.O., A.F.C.

1 Jan. 1956. A.C.M. Sir Dermot M. Boyle, K.C.V.O., K.B.E., C.B., A.F.C.

1 Jan. 1960. A.C.M. Sir Thomas G. Pike, G.C.B., C.B.E., D.F.C. and Bar.

1 Sept. 1963. A.C.M. Sir Charles Elworthy, G.C.B., C.B.E., D.S.O., M.V.O., D.F.C., A.F.C., M.A.

1 April, 1967. A.C.M. Sir John Grandy, K.C.B., K.B.E., D.S.O.

APPENDIX XI

Secretaries of State for Air

3 Jan. 1918. Rt. Hon. Lord Rothermere, P.C.

27 April, 1918. Rt. Hon. Lord Weir of Eastwood, P.C.

14 Jan. 1919. Rt. Hon. Winston S. Churchill, M.P.

5 April, 1921. Capt. the Rt. Hon. F. E. Guest, C.B.E., D.S.O., M.P.

2 Nov. 1922. Rt. Hon. Sir Samuel J. G. Hoare, Bt., C.M.G., M.P.

23 Jan. 1924. Brig. Gen. the Rt. Hon. Lord Thomson, P.C., G.B.E., D.S.O.

7 Nov. 1924. Rt. Hon. Sir Samuel J. G. Hoare, Bt., G.B.E., C.M.G., M.P.

8 June, 1929. Brig. Gen. the Rt. Hon. Lord Thomson, P.C., G.B.E., D.S.O.

18 Oct. 1930. Rt. Hon. Lord Amulree, P.C., G.B.E., K.C.

9 Nov. 1931. Most Hon. Marquess of Londonderry, K.G., M.V.O.

7 June, 1935. Rt. Hon. Viscount Swinton, G.B.E., M.C.

16 May, 1938. Rt. Hon. Sir Kingsley Wood, M.P.

5 April, 1940. Rt. Hon. Sir Samuel J. G. Hoare, Bt., G.C.S.I., G.B.E., C.M.G., M.P.

11 May, 1940. Rt. Hon. Sir Archibald Sinclair, Bt., K.T., C.M.G., M.P.

28 May, 1945. Rt. Hon. Harold Macmillan, M.P.

3 Aug. 1945. Rt. Hon. Viscount Stansgate, D.S.O., D.F.C.

5 Oct. 1946. Rt. Hon. P. J. Noel-Baker, M.P.

7 Oct. 1947. Rt. Hon. A. Henderson, K.C., M.P.

31 Oct. 1951. Lord de L'Isle and Dudley, V.C.

23 Dec. 1955. Rt. Hon. Nigel Birch, O.B.E., M.P.

19 Jan. 1957. Rt. Hon. George R. Ward, M.P.

31 Oct. 1960. Rt. Hon. J. Amery, M.P.

17 July, 1962. Rt. Hon. H. C. P. J. Fraser, M.B.E., M.P.

Minister of Defence for Royal Air Force

1 April, 1964. Rt. Hon. H. C. P. J. Fraser, M.B.E., M.P.
19 Oct. 1964. Rt. Hon. Lord Shackleton, O.B.E., M.P.
5 April, 1966. Rt. Hon. M. Rees, M.P.

Parliamentary Under-Secretary of State for Defence for Royal Air Force

7 Jan. 1967. Rt. Hon. M. Rees, M.P.

Comparative Ranks

R.A.F.	R.N.A.S.	NAVY	ARMY
Marshal of the R.A.F.	—	Admiral of the Fleet	Field Marshal
Air Chief Marshal	—	Admiral	General
Air Marshal	—	Vice-Admiral	Lieutenant-General
Air Vice-Marshal	—	Rear-Admiral	Major-General
Air Commodore	—	Commodore	Brigadier
Group Captain	Wing Captain	Captain	Colonel
Wing Commander	Wing Commander	Commander	Lieutenant-Colonel
Squadron Leader	Squadron Commander	Lieutenant-Commander	Major
Flight Lieutenant	Flight Commander	Lieutenant	Captain
Flying Officer	Flight Lieutenant	Sub-Lieutenant	Lieutenant
Pilot Officer	Flight Sub-Lieutenant	Midshipman	Second Lieutenant
—	Warrant Officer, 1st Grade	—	—
—	Warrant Officer, 2nd Grade	—	—

APPENDIX XIII

Awards of the Victoria Cross

26 April, 1915. Lt. W. B. Rhodes-Moorhouse.
  No. 2 Squadron, R.F.C.
7 June, 1915. Flt. Sub-Lt. R. A. J. Warneford.
  No. 1 Squadron, R.N.A.S.
25 July, 1915. Maj. L. G. Hawker. No. 6 Squadron, R.F.C.
31 July, 1915. Capt. J. A. Lidell. No. 7 Squadron, R.F.C.
7 Nov. 1915. 2nd Lt. G. S. M. Insall.
  No. 11 Squadron, R.F.C.
19 Nov. 1915. Sqn. Cdr. R. B. Davies.
  No. 3 Squadron, R.N.A.S.
1 July, 1916. Maj. L. W. B. Rees. No. 32 Squadron, R.F.C.
2 Sept. 1916. Lt. W. Leefe-Robinson.
  No. 39 Squadron, R.F.C.
7 Jan. 1917. Sgt. T. Mottershead. No. 20 Squadron, R.F.C.
20 March, 1917. Lt. F. H. McNamara. No. 67 Squadron, R.F.C.
2 June, 1917. Capt. W. A. Bishop. No. 60 Squadron, R.F.C.
8 June, 1917. Capt. A. Ball. No. 56 Squadron, R.F.C.
27 March, 1918. Lt. A. A. McLeod. No. 2 Squadron, R.F.C.
30 March, 1918. Lt. A. Jerrard. No. 66 Squadron, R.F.C.
2 April, 1918. Maj. J. T. B. McCudden.
  No. 56 Squadron, R.F.C.
10 Aug. 1918. Capt. F. M. F. West. No. 8 Squadron, R.A.F.
27 Oct. 1918. Maj. W. G. Barker. No. 201 Squadron, R.A.F.
30 Nov. 1918. Capt. A. W. Beauchamp-Proctor.
  No. 84 Squadron, R.A.F.
18 July, 1919. Maj. E. Mannock. No. 85 Squadron, R.A.F.
12 May, 1940. Flg. Off. D. E. Garland.
  No. 12 Squadron, R.A.F.
12 May, 1940. Sgt. T. Gray. No. 12 Squadron, R.A.F.
12 Aug. 1940. Flt. Lt. R. A. B. Learoyd.
  No. 49 Squadron, R.A.F.
16 Aug. 1940. Flt. Lt. J. B. Nicolson.
  No. 249 Squadron, R.A.F.

15 Sept. 1940. Sgt. J. Hannah.   No. 83 Squadron, R.A.F.
6 April, 1941. Flg. Off. K. Campbell.
                                        No. 22 Squadron, R.A.F.
4 July, 1941. Grp. Capt. H. I. Edwards.
                                        No. 105 Squadron, R.A.F.
7 July, 1941. Sgt. J. A. Ward.   No. 75 Squadron, R.N.Z.A.F.
9 Dec. 1941. Flt. Lt. A. S. K. Scarf.
                                        No. 62 Squadron, R.A.F.
12 Feb. 1942. Lt.-Cdr. (A) E. Esmonde.
                                        No. 825 Squadron, F.A.A.
17 April, 1942. Sqn. Ldr. J. D. Nettleton.
                                        No. 44 Squadron, R.A.F.
30 May, 1942. Flg. Off. L. T. Manser.
                                        No. 50 Squadron, R.A.F.
28 Nov. 1942. Flt. Sgt. R. H. Middleton.
                                        No. 149 Squadron, R.A.F.
4 Dec. 1942. Wg. Cdr. H. G. Malcolm.
                                        No. 18 Squadron, R.A.F.
17 March, 1943. Flt. Lt. W. E. Newton.
                                        No. 22 Squadron, R.A.A.F.
3 May, 1943. Sqn. Ldr. L. H. Trent.
                                        No. 487 Squadron, R.N.Z.A.F.
17 May, 1943. Wg. Cdr. G. P. Gibson.
                                        No. 617 Squadron, R.A.F.
11 Aug. 1943. Flg. Off. L. A. Trigg.
                                        No. 200 Squadron, R.A.F.
12 Aug. 1943. Flt. Sgt. A. L. Aaron.
                                        No. 218 Squadron, R.A.F.
3 Nov. 1943. Plt. Off. C. J. Barton. No. 578 Squadron, R.A.F.
3 Nov. 1943. Flt. Lt. W. Reid.   No. 61 Squadron, R.A.F.
26 April, 1944. Wrt. Off. N. C. Jackson.
                                        No. 106 Squadron, R.A.F.
12 June, 1944. Plt. Off. A. C. Mynarski.
                                        No. 419 Squadron, R.C.A.F.
24 June, 1944. Flt. Lt. D. H. Hornell.
                                        No. 162 Squadron, R.C.A.F.
17 July, 1944. Flt. Lt. J. A. Cruikshank.
                                        No. 210 Squadron, R.A.F.
4 Aug. 1944. Sqn. Ldr. I. W. Bazalgette.
                                        No. 635 Squadron, R.A.F.

8 Sept. 1944. Grp. Capt. G. L. Cheshire.
No. 617 Squadron, R.A.F.

19 Sept. 1944. Flt. Lt. D. S. A. Lord.
No. 271 Squadron, R.A.F.

23 Dec. 1944. Sqn. Ldr. R. A. M. Palmer.
No. 109 Squadron, R.A.F.

1 Jan. 1945. Flt. Sgt. G. Thompson.
No. 9 Squadron, R.A.F.

23 Feb. 1945. Capt. E. Swales. No. 582 Squadron, R.A.F.

9 Aug. 1945. Lt. R. H. Gray. No. 1841 Squadron, F.A.A.